Cigarette Nation

Intoxicating Histories

Series Editors: Virginia Berridge (London School of Hygiene and Tropical Medicine) and Erika Dyck (University of Saskatchewan)

Whether on the street, off the shelf, or over the pharmacy counter, interactions with drugs and alcohol are shaped by contested ideas about addiction, healing, pleasure, and vice and their social dimensions. Books in this series explore how people around the world have consumed, created, traded, and regulated psychoactive substances throughout history. The series connects research on legal and illegal drugs and alcohol with diverse areas of historical inquiry, including the histories of medicine, pharmacy, consumption, trade, law, social policy, and popular culture. Its reach is global and includes scholarship on all periods. Intoxicating Histories aims to link these different pasts as well as to inform the present by providing a firmer grasp on contemporary debates and policy issues. We welcome books, whether scholarly monographs or shorter texts for a broad audience focusing on a particular phenomenon or substance, that alter the state of knowledge.

1 Taming Cannabis
   Drugs and Empire in Nineteenth-Century France
   David A. Guba, Jr

2 Cigarette Nation
   Business, Health, and Canadian Smokers, 1930–1975
   Daniel J. Robinson

Cigarette Nation

Business, Health, and Canadian Smokers, 1930–1975

DANIEL J. ROBINSON

McGill-Queen's University Press
Montreal & Kingston · London · Chicago

© McGill-Queen's University Press 2021

ISBN 978-0-2280-0531-5 (cloth)
ISBN 978-0-2280-0532-2 (paper)
ISBN 978-0-2280-0597-1 (ePDF)

Legal deposit first quarter 2021
Bibliothèque nationale du Québec

Printed in Canada on acid-free paper that is 100% ancient forest free (100% post-consumer recycled), processed chlorine free

This book has been published with the help of a grant from the Canadian Federation for the Humanities and Social Sciences, through the Awards to Scholarly Publications Program, using funds provided by the Social Sciences and Humanities Research Council of Canada.

We acknowledge the support of the Canada Council for the Arts.

Nous remercions le Conseil des arts du Canada de son soutien.

Library and Archives Canada Cataloguing in Publication

Title: Cigarette nation : business, health, and Canadian smokers, 1930-1975 / Daniel J. Robinson.
Names: Robinson, Daniel J., author.
Description: Series statement: Intoxicating histories ; 2 | Includes bibliographical references and index.
Identifiers: Canadiana (print) 20200325582 | Canadiana (ebook) 20200326082 | ISBN 9780228005315 (cloth) | ISBN 9780228005322 (paper) | ISBN 9780228005971 (ePDF)
Subjects: LCSH: Smoking—Canada—History—20th century. | LCSH: Smoking—Social aspects—Canada—History—20th century. | LCSH: Cigarette industry—Canada—History—20th century. | LCSH: Advertising—Cigarettes—Canada—History—20th century.
Classification: LCC HV5770.C2 R63 2021 | DDC 394.1/4—dc23

Contents

Figures | vii
Acknowledgments | xi

Introduction | 3

1 Depression-Era Cigarette Marketing and Smoking Culture | 15

2 The Gift of Wartime Cigarettes | 45

3 The Incomparable Cigarette | 80

4 Taxes, Public Smoking, and Lung Cancer | 117

5 Hope and Doubt | 145

6 Marketing Bonanza | 182

7 The View from Ottawa | 217

Conclusion | 242

Notes | 253
Index | 333

Figures

1.1 Imperial Tobacco institutional advertisement, *Toronto Daily Star*, 26 August 1936, 9. | 28
1.2 Imperial Tobacco institutional advertisement, *Toronto Daily Star*, 24 March 1937, 5. | 29
1.3 Imperial Tobacco Canada, "Poker Hands" Premiums Catalogue, September 1935. Collection of the author. | 38
1.4 du Maurier advertisement, *Globe and Mail*, 21 December 1936, 7. | 43
2.1 Cigarette Fundraiser, St Marys, Ontario, 1944. Western University, The Ley and Lois Smith War, Memory, and Popular Culture Research Collection. | 56
2.2 Imperial Tobacco acknowledgment postcard, n.d. Western University, The Ley and Lois Smith War, Memory, and Popular Culture Research Collection. | 61–2
2.3 Macdonald Tobacco acknowledgment postcard, July 1942. Western University, The Ley and Lois Smith War, Memory, and Popular Culture Research Collection. | 63
2.4 A cartoon depicting a Canadian soldier dropping a cigarette in the Netherlands in 1945. Nederlands Instituut voor Oorlogsdocumentatie. DocII 249, Humor, inv. no. 0335A-35. | 71
2.5 Macdonald advertisement, ca 1943. Lake St Louis Historical society, Macdonald Tobacco Collection, box 15, file 31. | 73
3.1 Sweet Caporals advertisement, *Toronto Daily Star*, 10 January 1949, 14. | 85

3.2 Black Cat advertisement, *Telegraph-Journal*, 14 November 1957, 8. | 88
3.3 Members of the Lovat Scouts smoking during combat training in the Canadian Rockies in 1944. Library and Archives Canada, e010980242. | 89
3.4 Smoking patrons in a Canadian Pacific Railway club car, circa 1950. Library and Archives Canada, e003641860. | 89
3.5 Military veterans enjoy beers and cigarettes in Edmonton, circa 1953. Provincial Archives of Alberta, A6766. | 90
3.6 A worker holds a cigarette while operating machinery at the John Inglis Co. Bren Gun plant in Toronto, 10 May 1941. National Film Board of Canada. Library and Archives Canada, e000760464. | 91
3.7 A labourer takes a solitary smoke break during construction of the Polymer Corporation in Sarnia, Ontario, in June 1943. Photo: Page Toles, National Film Board of Canada. Library and Archives Canada, e000761454. | 92
3.8 Pall Mall advertisement, *Toronto Daily Star*, 14 November 1950, 14. | 94
3.9 Toronto lifeguards smoking, ca 1950. Photo: Ronny Jacques. Library and Archives Canada, e010980242. | 97
3.10 Men and women smoke cigarettes on the lawn outside the National Film Board building in Montreal in June 1956. Library and Archives Canada, e010975697. | 101
3.11 Terry's Drug Store, Victoria, BC, 1950. Photo: Duncan Macphail. British Columbia Archives, 198110-006. | 103
3.12 Sweet Caporal illuminated sign at the corner of Sainte-Catherine and St Mathieu streets in Montreal, ca 1945. Hayward Studios / Library and Archives Canada, PA-068979. | 107
3.13 "Sports Timer" in the Vancouver Forum. *Canadian Cigar and Tobacco Journal*, May 1948, 28. | 109
3.14 Secretary of State for External Affairs Lester B. Pearson smokes while talking to reporters in Ottawa in December 1956. Photo: Duncan Cameron. Library and Archives Canada, e007150538. | 115
4.1 Cartoon on public smoking, *Canadian Cigar and Tobacco Journal*, June 1949, 16. | 125

FIGURES

4.2 du Maurier advertisement, *Toronto Daily Star*, 28 March 1950, 10. | 136
4.3 Dorothy Brooks of the Canadian Red Cross distributes cigarettes to Able Seaman I.M. Barnes in a Canadian military hospital in Taplow, England, 14 December 1944. Jack H. Smith / Canada Department of National Defence. Library and Archives Canada, PA-133610. | 137
4.4 Cartoon, *Canadian Cigar and Tobacco Journal*, December 1954, 10. | 139
4.5 Matinée advertisement, *Toronto Daily Star*, 8 March 1958, 2. | 139
5.1 du Maurier advertisement, *Telegraph-Journal*, 12 February 1957, 8. | 159
5.2 Craven "A" advertisement, *Telegraph-Journal*, 22 January 1962, 9. | 167
5.3 Judy LaMarsh, n.d. Library and Archives Canada, e011048364. | 172
6.1 du Maurier King-Size advertisement, *Telegraph-Journal*, 17 September 1964, 10. | 187
7.1 John Munro (second from left), 1968. Photo: J. Galt. Library and Archives Canada, e011196787. | 228
7.2 Paul Paré, 1965. Photo Gaby (Gabriel Desmarais). | 229

Acknowledgments

So many people helped me write this book. I benefited greatly from the writings, advice, and criticism of tobacco scholars like Joanna Cohen, Sharon Cook, Tim Dewhirst, Anne Lavack, André Michael, Rick Pollay, Robert Proctor, Jarrett Rudy, and Cheryl Krasnick Warsh. Cynthia Callard, from Physicians for a Smoke-Free Canada, was indispensable in locating countless industry documents made public via litigation. The manuscript's two anonymous reviewers submitted detailed and insightful critiques which greatly improved this book. Jack Granatstein provided feedback on the chapter dealing with smoking in the armed forces, while Jonathan Vance helped me find cigarette-related materials in a military archives at Western University. Over many lunches, Paul Rutherford served up invaluable commentary on advertising history and smoking culture. Astrid Van den Bossche kindly translated Dutch-language sources. I have great colleagues in Western's Faculty of Information and Media Studies, many of whom shared talk of historical smoking: thanks to Becky Blue, Grant Campbell, Norma Coates, Lilianne Dang, Nick Dyer-Witheford, Alison Hearn, Lisa Henderson, Kathie Hess, Sara Irons, Keir Keightley, Susan Knabe, Karen Kueneman, Shelley Long, Charlotte McClellan, Pam McKenzie, Cindy Morrison, Anabel Quan-Haase, Sharon Sliwinski, Romayne Smith-Fullerton, Sandra Smeltzer, Daniela Sneppova, Tom Streeter, Sam Trosow, Liwen Vaughan, Matt Ward, Sharon Waters, and Ella Young.

I have had the good fortune to work with many bright graduate students and research assistants over the years, who likely got more than their fill of cigarette history. Kind thanks to Kyle Asquith, Andrea Benoit, Lindsay Bolan, Amy Eisner-Levine, Estée Fresco, Jennifer Haynes, Alison

Jacques, Lee McGuigan, Jessica McEwen, Jessica Michel, and Stephanie Ritter. Davin Helkenberg was especially skilled and resourceful in locating and organizing online tobacco company records. Lisa Henderson, my faculty's dean, provided institutional support and funding to help me complete this book. Previous deans Catherine Ross, Gloria Leckie, and Tom Carmichael were similarly encouraging and supportive of this project. Archivists make the historian's world go around, and that's especially the case for Jeroen Kemperman (Nederlands Instituut voor Oorlogsdocumentatie), Eliot Perrin and Geneviève Clavet (Macdonald Stewart Foundation), and the exemplary staff at Library and Archives Canada. Funding for this book came from the Social Sciences and Humanities Research Council of Canada, the Awards to Scholarly Publications Programme (Federation for the Humanities and Social Sciences), the Ontario Tobacco Research Unit, and the Scholarly Project Completion Grant (FIMS-Western University).

Jonathan Crago, my proficient editor at McGill-Queen's University Press, backed this project at the fuzzy idea stage and then graciously put up with my missed deadlines along the way. The staff at McGill-Queen's are a superb group and I am grateful to Lisa Aitken, Kathleen Fraser, James Leahy, Mia Renaud, and Elli Stylianou for their professionalism and dedication to scholarly publishing. Alison Jacques did a standout job producing the book's index.

Over the years, good friends like Jordan Berger, Katia Gianneschi, Randy Heasman, David Himel, and Marit Stiles made scholarship a less lonely pursuit. So too did supportive family members like Rachelle Brisebois, Anne Lockwood, Beth Patterson, Laura Patterson, Carman Robinson, Randy Robinson, Louise Stonehouse, and John Thompson. My wonderful children, Jacob and Cailan, grew up hearing about this project and are probably more glad than I to see it put to rest. Thanks for listening to my shop talk and for sharing insights on contemporary youth smoking and vaping. Poppy Lockwood, my partner extraordinaire, along with her children (Alexandra, Kate, and Geoff), contributed in more ways than they can imagine to the rich pleasures and rewards fostered by caring for one another.

ACKNOWLEDGMENTS

Finally, two people merit special mention. My mother, Patricia Robinson, spoke often with me about her past experiences and struggles as a smoker. She died unexpectedly in 2017 and sadly won't get to see how her story fits within the tapestry of *Cigarette Nation*. Jarrett Rudy, a friend and tobacco historian at McGill University, had for years shared conversations with me about cigarette research and so much else. His book, *The Freedom to Smoke*, was instrumental in moving me into this line of research. In April 2020, soon after this book cleared editorial review, Jarrett died suddenly of heart failure at age forty-nine. So my finish line is bittersweet, coming as it does without celebratory beers with Jarrett in a Montreal pub or seeing my mom's face beam when handed this book.

Cigarette Nation

Introduction

In the mid-1970s, around the time this book ends, I would hop on my bike and ride to a nearby store to buy my mom's cigarettes. I was around ten then. My mom knew the store owner and had made this standing arrangement for when she couldn't make it over. I also ran errands for things like bread and milk, but I barely remember those trips. Cigarettes were different. I still remember my mom's brand – Large King-Size du Maurier – and the deep red look of those packs. I recall too the sense of responsibility I felt ferrying those cigarettes home, likely because most of the adults in my extended working-class family smoked, including both parents and a dozen or so aunts and uncles. On family occasions, those red du Maurier packs shared table space with green (Export "A") and blue (Player's) ones, the tricolour backdrop of holiday celebrations and summer vacations. In our family, cigarette cartons served as Christmas gifts, cigarette packs lay beside cribbage boards during play, uncles blew smoke rings to the delight of nieces and nephews, and moms puffed away while watching *Happy Days* with their kids. In shop class, I made a metal ashtray for Mother's Day. My pre-teen self regarded a government budget as the day you stocked up on cigarettes to beat the next-day tax hike. My high school in London, Ontario, had a designated "smoking pit" where the cool teens hung out, even the non-smoking ones. In Grade 11, our French class visited a high school in Acton Vale, Quebec, where students and teachers smoked *together* during breaks, even sharing cigarettes. Around that time, some friends and I attended a midnight showing of *The Last Waltz* at a repertory cinema. By the end of the film, the air was hazy with cigarette and pot smoke even though the theatre banned smoking.

This book aims to explain how such a vibrant and pervasive smoking culture came to be, some two decades after medical science had causally linked cigarettes to lung cancer and other serious diseases. What few likely realize is that the best years for the Canadian cigarette industry came *after* smoking-and-cancer news surfaced in the early 1950s. In 1950, adult per-capita cigarette consumption stood at 4.9 cigarettes; in 1960 it reached 7.9, rising steadily thereafter until peaking at 9.6 in 1980.[1] Canadians on average, even when controlling for population growth, smoked nearly twice as many cigarettes in the mid-1970s as they did in 1950. Making sense of this paradox requires longitudinal and multi-factorial approaches. It means tracking back to the 1930s, when cigarette smoking first became a staple of social routines and cultural life. During that decade, cigarettes started to seriously displace pipe and cigar consumption, in part due to an influx of female smokers. Smoking accelerated during the war, when cigarette packs became vital appendages for military personnel, lauded for enhancing social solidarity and psychological well-being. By 1949, 72 per cent of men and 42 per cent of women smoked cigarettes,[2] by which point the practice had spanned social class, region, and age group. Cigarettes and socializing went hand in hand; smoking fostered identify formation and self-expression while abetting social interaction and solitary coping.

To understand how Canadian smokers responded to the "cancer scare" during the 1950s and after, it is necessary to fully document and dissect this pre-existing smoking culture. Doing so also requires moving beyond socio-cultural aspects of smoking to engage with developments in business, politics, and medical science. The persistence of Cigarette Nation into the 1970s owes to a series of inter-related factors involving product development, marketing and retailing innovation, public relations, science denialism, and federal government (in)action. For decades after the early 1950s, Canadian tobacco firms and their international parent companies devised and implemented an elaborate strategy to furnish Canadian smokers with hope and doubt: hope in the form of health-reassurance marketing, as seen initially with the advent of filters and later low-tar ("low yield") and "Light/Mild" cigarette brands; doubt in the form of disinformation campaigns denigrating medical research that causally linked cigarette smoking to serious illness. This mounting body of tobacco-and-health science, cigarette executives maintained perennially, remained faulty and "controversial," notably for its neglect of industry-promoted causes of lung cancer like air pollution or viruses. More research and time were needed to produce definitive scientific knowledge about smoking and health. In the meantime, people were urged to stop worrying and carry on smoking.

The historical reconstruction of Cigarette Nation faces challenges due to the "lost world" nature of smoking-enamoured social life. Today, 15 per cent of Canadians smoke cigarettes,[3] about one-quarter the rate seen during the 1940s and 1950s. Cigarette smoking in the postwar years bridged economic classes and social groups, in contrast to today's smokers who are disproportionately drawn from lower socio-economic ranks, a trend that has contributed to the social stigmatization of tobacco smoking. Since the 1980s, governments have progressively restricted or banned indoor smoking, tobacco advertising, and the retail display of cigarettes. Universities, like my own, have enacted campus-wide bans on tobacco sales and smoking, even while outdoors. Many non-smokers today lead lives that seldom cross paths with smokers or cigarettes – an unimaginable state of affairs during the mid-1900s. This trend has been good for public health, but it presents challenges for the historical study of a behaviour and product seen by many social and cultural elites as alien, vulgar, or even pathological. One measure of this is the frequent omission of cigarettes and smoking from historical works in such areas as business, taxation, public health, the 1960s, and wartime consumption, topics in which cigarette smoking often figured prominently.[4] For example, while some two-thirds of men smoked cigarettes in the mid-1900s, historical accounts of masculinity largely neglect cigarette smoking,[5] in stark contrast to treatments of alcohol and manhood.[6] In some of these historical accounts, smoking reveals itself in oblique ways. While absent from chapters and indexes, cigarettes sometimes appear in the photographs of these books, seen wedged between the fingers of bar patrons, politicians, or striking workers.[7] Cigarettes, in this sense, highlight "the humility of things," Daniel Miller's term for how certain objects, like blue jeans, evade direct notice or commentary while still remaining part of "the material background or canvass to everyday life."[8] Cigarettes permeated the quotidian canvasses of mid-twentieth-century social life, very much in plain view if seldom discerned or analyzed by researchers dealing with intersecting topics. One hope for this book is that it helps to correct this historiographical blind spot by encouraging historians of society, culture, business, and politics to recognize and cultivate those instances that converge with cigarette smoking.

Cigarette use during the mid-1900s was a national phenomenon, both geographically and demographically. While certain historical studies of consumption and mass marketing in Canada stress factors like region, class, and ethnicity as determinative,[9] cigarette smoking was pan-Canadian in nature. Leading cigarette brands were marketed and consumed throughout the country, and smoking rates and brand market share varied relatively little by region. The bulk of cigarettes sold were distinctly "Canadian" brands, as popular American ones like Winston or Chesterfield penetrated minimally north of the border. While top-selling Canadian brands like Player's and du Maurier had English origins, their marketing and promotion in Canada were homegrown and did not mirror British practice. The vast majority of the country's cigarettes were manufactured in Canada, using domestically grown tobacco. Consumer surveys underscore the broad-based, "democratic" composition of the smoking populace. By the early 1950s, about six in ten adults regularly smoked cigarettes, representing a wide cross-section of lower-, middle-, and upper-income Canadians. Male smokers outnumbered women, but rising rates of female smoking would close this gender gap by the late 1970s. During these years, Canada constituted a "Cigarette Nation" in terms of social participation, geographic reach, and shared cultural norms.

For these reasons, this book reflects historical accounts of consumerism and mass marketing that emphasize national trends and broadly shared consumer identities.[10] In this vein, Bettina Liverant, in her account of changing ideas and values involving the rise of consumerism in twentieth-century Canada, highlights national developments, noting that "through discussion, measurement, policymaking, storytelling, and academic study, consumer identities became central to social life, and consumer values were woven deeply into the Canadian social imagination."[11] Donica Belisle's study of department stores and mass merchandising similarly documents the roles played by retail workers and shoppers, "from a range of racial, ethnic, and class backgrounds all over the country," in ushering in the "modern Canadian consumer society" by 1940.[12] It bears noting that this book's depiction of cigarette smoking as part of a far-ranging national and modern experience should not preclude others from examining this topic in local, regional, or demographic-specific contexts in order to see if these produced differentiated forms of cigarette use and cultural practices. Given the paucity of historical research on cigarette smoking in Canada, *any and all* scholarship on this subject would be greatly welcomed.

The mundane, taken-for-granted quality of cigarettes, especially before the "cancer scare," complicates historical understanding of smoking. The ancillary nature of cigarette use – one typically smoked cigarettes while doing others things – contributed to the rapid uptake of cigarettes in an urbanizing, modernizing society. People smoked cigarettes while performing other, often more meaningful, activities, like working a shift, going on a date, or fighting on the beaches of Normandy, events that engendered more personal reflection and documentation than the prosaic practice of lighting up. The ordinary, however, need not be inconsequential. Steve Penfold, in his business and cultural history of the donut trade after 1945, underscores how the donut "reminds us that banal things can have considerable analytic power. In this small product – in the technologies that produced it, the places that sold it, and the consumers who ate it – several economic, social, cultural, and political narratives converge."[13] Matthew Hilton similarly refers to the twentieth-century English cigarette as "at once an ordinary and an extraordinary visible communicator of social relations."[14]

The same was true for Canada. Economically, the cigarette industry remapped Ontario's agricultural landscape, furnished the advertising that kept newspapers, magazines, and broadcasters profitable, and sent billions of tax dollars to government coffers. Its social and cultural impact was even greater. "Can I get a light (or smoke)?" became the conversation starter that prefaced countless friendships and marriages. Smoking's mannerisms infused the communication of sexual desire, both on the screen and in the flesh. Being "social" – and feeling socially validated – often meant being a smoker, whether bantering with friends, entertaining at home, or sweet-talking a date. For decades, cigarette smoking was a condition of everyday social life. This reflexive behaviour shaped notions of selfhood and emotional well-being, calming anxious minds and rejuvenating tired bodies and depleted spirits. On the job, smoking buttressed the logic of capitalistic productivity, an agent of efficiency and instrumental purpose, boosting worker concentration and the mental stamina needed for performing repetitive tasks or enduring loathsome conditions. Smoking's animating role in this trinity of sociability, selfhood, and productive labouring rendered the "ordinary" cigarette socially powerful and culturally iconic. The modern cigarette was no doubt "extraordinary" as the disease vector that would kill hundreds of thousands of Canadians by the 1980s. But its extraordinariness lay too in its constitutive role in the social relations and psychological makeup of modern Canada.

Historical sources documenting the social experience of smoking are not plentiful. As previously mentioned, people are more inclined to remember and record events and activities deemed personally significant and meaningful. Letters, diaries, and memoirs generally tell us more about working first jobs, graduating high school, or getting married than they do about the social routines of coffee drinking or cigarette smoking. A perishable packaged good, cigarettes were consumed quickly, literally going "up in smoke" within days of purchase. People did not maintain or pass down cigarettes to loved ones, unlike cars, furniture, or clothing, consumer goods that are well represented in social and cultural histories of consumption.[15] Cigarettes attracted only modest media attention and social commentary for their intentional, manifest features – their tactile and taste pleasures or social attributes – topics that are germane to this study. More often they became newsworthy for other reasons: house fires, high taxes, annoying non-smokers in cinemas, and, of course, endangering the lives of users. Countless newspaper and magazine articles discuss these topics, which this book incorporates, along with other historical sources like opinion surveys and government records, in order to analyze smoking's various social controversies.

To ascertain the mundane experiences of male and female smokers, however, this book draws on an eclectic mix of primary sources engendered by digital-age technology and old-fashioned litigation. For example, parts of this study rely heavily on the Canadian Letters and Images Project, an online archive containing hundreds of digitized letters and diary entries from Canadian soldiers during the Second World War. Without this free-text searchable database, it would not have been possible to assemble and describe the manifold social norms and attitudes of military smokers stationed abroad during the war.[16] This book similarly makes extensive use of consumer market research to illuminate the behaviours, values, attitudes, and demographics of ordinary Canadian smokers. Starting in the early 1950s, tobacco firms commissioned hundreds of these studies, which document in rich detail the social parameters and cultural mores of cigarette use. Of course, one should not conflate these consumer studies with "bottom-up," unmediated accounts of smoking from actual smokers; the purpose and design of these marketing studies reflected in the first order the commercial interests and needs of tobacco manufacturers and advertisers.[17] But this broad assembly of representative sample surveys, focus group studies, and motivational research reports elucidated everyday, "beyond the headlines" features of cigarette smoking in unparalleled ways.

This market research forms part of a massive haul of Canadian tobacco industry documents made public during a Quebec class-action court case which ended in 2015, and which are now available online.[18] A testament to the rigour and breadth of the document discovery process by plaintiffs and defendants, this two-year trial produced thousands of exhibits, encompassing countless tobacco company documents, federal government records, news stories, and cigarette ads. Before this trial relatively few internal documents of Canadian tobacco firms were publicly available; in a stunning reversal, arguably no other economic sector in Canada today counts more of its historical corporate records in full public view than do the country's cigarette makers. These documents form the basis of much of the second half of this book, chronicling in detail how Canadian and foreign cigarette executives worked to market, largely successfully, a product cited widely for producing lung cancer and other diseases.

This book has benefited greatly from the work of many historians of the tobacco trade and cigarette smoking involving the United States,[19] Great Britain,[20] and Canada.[21] Diverse in nature, some of these books tackle specific subjects like cigarette marketing to post-secondary students or smoking by people with mental illnesses. Others, like those by Allan M. Brandt, Robert N. Proctor, and Matthew Hilton, provide far-ranging, general accounts of cigarette promotion, disease, and smoking behaviour which span decades. For Canada, Jarrett Rudy's study of cigar, pipe, and cigarette smoking from the 1880s until the 1930s offers a compelling blend of socio-cultural analysis with an analytical framework that employs liberalism to explain changes in the social rituals of male-centric smoking over the years. Sharon Anne Cook similarly offers an insightful and nuanced account of Canadian women smokers during the twentieth century. She deftly explores how cigarette smoking embodied forms of social empowerment and self-expression for women navigating the pathways of modernity, in occupational and interpersonal contexts.

Similar to Rudy and Cook, this book aims to understand smoking from the perspective of smokers, and not just that of social reformers, medical authorities, or public officials seeking to curb or eliminate the practice. It probes the personal pleasures, social benefits, and forms of meaning making associated with cigarette use. Notably, it explores how Canadians understood and evaluated the health risks of smoking in light of the protracted efforts of industry marketers and public relations experts to placate smokers' concerns about the harms of cigarettes. This book then combines these lines of inquiry with analyses of business and government actors in order to flesh out this composite portrait of Cigarette Nation and provide explanations for its decades-long dominance. This multi-dimensional approach reflects Kenneth Lipartito's call to reimagine the practice of business history by moving beyond the confines of corporate function and marketplace competitive advantage, instead paying greater "attention to the material features of daily routines and everyday practices that take place with objects, technologies, money, labor, and nature." Here the perspectives and behaviours of consumers merit serious consideration alongside those of corporate actors. Researchers should cast widely when devising analytical frameworks, incorporating, if need be, social and cultural theories that provide explanatory power to empirical investigation. The historian's task, Lipartito notes, is to locate, assemble, and interrogate those "gradually coalescing elements" which combine to produce historical outcomes that typically defy mono-causal explanation or do not adhere to ready-made theories of the market or organizational behavior.[22] In this vein, researchers should be open to what Daniel Miller describes as the "glorious mess of contradiction and ambivalence" spawned by the study of consumer goods situated within the "fray of everyday life," and often at the crossroads of commerce, culture, and politics.[23]

Introduction

This book consists of two parts. The first focuses primarily on sociocultural features of smoking and cigarette marketing from 1930 until the mid-1950s. The second half, encompassing chapters 4 through 7, largely examines the views and actions of tobacco executives, government officials, and Canadian smokers in response to mounting reports that linked cigarette use to lung cancer and other illnesses, beginning in the early 1950s. Chapter 1 explores cigarette smoking and promotion during the 1930s, a crucial period in the history of the modern cigarette. (Starting in 1932, per-capita cigarette sales rose every year, with one exception, until the early 1980s.) During this decade, cigarettes increasingly became part of the daily routines and cultural norms of a growing cross-section of people, including women. The decade also saw complaints about low-grade health concerns associated with smoking – coughing, scratchy throats, and "tongue bite." To address these, tobacco firms introduced menthol brands and filter cigarettes, the latter promising to remove "harmful" irritants in cigarette smoke. Canada's largest cigarette maker, Imperial Tobacco Canada (ITC), was heavily criticized during this period for being a "practical monopoly," an agent of price fixing and restraint-of-trade practices. To restore its corporate reputation, ITC commissioned a long-running public relations ad campaign touting the company's virtues to consumers, retailers, and tobacco farmers. Well before the cigarette industry embraced public relations tactics in the wake of the cancer scare, ITC was well versed in the art and method of institutional advertising and the shaping of public opinion.

Chapter 2 examines the role of cigarettes in the lives of Canadian military personnel stationed overseas between 1939 and 1945. The bulk of these cigarettes were not purchased or issued in military rations, but instead sent as gifts by Canadians back home, typically family members, friends, business associates, and charities. These cigarettes, the product of gift-exchange networks, engendered different forms of social relations and meanings than existed for cigarettes procured in the market economy. Gift cigarettes connoted appreciation and gratitude, solidifying a soldier's ties to loved ones, home community, and even the Canadian nation. They were highly prized by military personnel and shared widely, fostering social cohesion and esprit de corps in the barracks and on the battlefield. However, when placed in different contexts like prisoner-of-war camps or the black markets of war-ravaged Europe, gift cigarettes at times functioned very differently. In such places, they became synonymous with social conflict, price gouging, and inhumane exploitation. The book's third chapter discusses the apogee of Cigarette Nation, the decade after 1945 when a solid majority of adults consumed cigarettes and smoking permeated most forms of social life and cultural endeavour. The popularity of cigarettes sprang in part from how they were thought to serve the social and psychological needs of a populace piloting the tumult and vagaries of modern life. Cigarettes fostered sociability and fellowship, while also enhancing psychic equanimity by reducing stress and promoting relaxation. They were touted for increasing the concentration and drive of employees, boosting workplace productivity and occupational achievement. Coupled with these social and psychological factors were extensive marketing and advertising campaigns that made household names of leading cigarette brands. In towns and cities, large and small, cigarette makers sponsored countless sporting and cultural events, inserting company and brand names into the cultural life of local communities across the country.

Chapter 4 examines challenges to the dominion of smoking, two minor and one major. In 1951, the federal government increased cigarette excise taxes, sparking widespread complaints from smokers and tobacco growers and giving rise to a thriving contraband market in American cigarettes sold in Canada. Ottawa soon after reversed course, eventually cutting this tax by 30 per cent in order to stamp out the cigarette black market, thus rendering this problem short-lived. Similarly, tobacco manufacturers were minimally impacted by sporadic efforts to enforce bans on smoking in indoor public spaces like street cars or cinemas. Smokers often ignored such prohibitions, reflecting the view that smoking was an established social right, to be exercised wherever people socialized or congregated. In contrast, medical reports connecting cigarettes to lung cancer, which appeared in the early 1950s, posed a fundamental challenge to the tobacco industry. Cigarette executives responded with a coordinated strategy of denial, dismissing these epidemiological medical studies as third-rate, unproven "statistics." Newspaper and magazines ran stories promoting this message, along with ones touting the benefits of smoking for stress relief, relaxation, and social interaction. All of this contributed to Canadians' deep-seated ambivalence on whether smoking caused cancer.

Introduction

Chapter 5 details the marketing response of Canadian tobacco firms to the cancer scare of the 1950s and early 1960s. The head of Rothmans in Canada, Patrick O'Neil-Dunne, highlighted the cigarette–cancer association in company advertising, arguing that low-tar, filtered brands like Rothmans were safer alternatives for smokers. In 1954, Imperial Tobacco launched filter brands like Matinée, reflecting its research findings that smokers viewed filter cigarettes as inherently safer and healthier than plain-end brands. Cigarette makers later introduced other low-tar brands like Belvedere and Craven "A" to attract smokers beset by health fears. Lung cancer, which emerged as an existential threat to the industry, was soon recast by cigarette makers into a marketing opportunity, resulting in new cigarette types and branding strategies to cater to health-anxious smokers. Coupled with this marketing transformation was the industry's public relations campaign to undermine smoking-and-health science, a strategy shaped in part by Philip Morris and public relations executives from the United States.

Chapter 6 extends this analysis of industry marketing and public relations manipulation into the 1960s and early 1970s, a period of accelerating market segmentation in the cigarette trade. Dozens of new brands were launched and marketing innovations like premium and contest promotions and sport sponsorships featured prominently in the sector. Health-reassurance marketing gained traction with the successful launch of many "Light" and "Mild" brands, most notably Player's Light. These brands contained only marginally lower levels of tar and nicotine, but were nonetheless promoted as safer options for smokers. Teenagers emerged in this period as a sought-after market segment, as evidenced by industry market research targeting people as young as fifteen and by advertising campaigns aimed at youths. The industry stepped up its PR attacks on health research that linked smoking to cancer, even while company scientists accepted this causal association in internal correspondence. Well into the 1960s, surveys showed that Canadians remained uncertain about the cancer risks of smoking, even though the issue was largely settled within the scientific community: smoking caused lung cancer, but many Canadians, especially smokers, remained unsure of this.

The book's final chapter explores the federal government's handling of the smoking-and-health file during the 1960s and early 1970s. While throughout the 1960s many parliamentarians called for health warnings on tobacco products and greater curbs on cigarette marketing, the federal cabinet was slow to engage seriously with this issue, only doing so when National Health and Welfare Minister John Munro introduced a bill (c-248) in 1971 which included a ban on all forms of cigarette advertising. The bill soon stalled in parliament and was ultimately defeated by the industry's successful efforts to recruit and mobilize cigarette retailers, tobacco farmers, newspaper and magazine publishers, and advertisers in opposition to the legislation. Influential cabinet members also opposed Bill c-248, seeing it as a breach of liberal rights and freedoms. The federal government had recently legalized homosexuality and therapeutic abortion, in keeping with Prime Minister Trudeau's "Just Society" reforms holding that individuals, and not the state, should determine actions involving various private matters. If the state should steer clear of the nation's bedrooms, the reasoning went, so too should decisions about cigarette smoking be left to individuals and not government officials.

CHAPTER ONE

Depression-Era Cigarette Marketing and Smoking Culture

INTRODUCTION

In October 1936, mining magnate William Henry Wright bought *The Globe*, an influential Toronto daily. Soon after, he announced that the paper would repeal its twin publishing bans on horse-race betting odds and cigarette advertisements. "I smoke cigarettes myself," he stated, and saw no compelling reason to continue the ad ban.[1] A month later Wright purchased *The Mail*, which he soon merged with his prior acquisition to create *The Globe and Mail*. Soon after, the newspaper ran ads for British tobacco maker Peter Jackson's Canadian launch of "du Maurier Filter" cigarettes. These ads promoted the technological advances and health benefits of filtered cigarettes, a novelty in the 1930s. The du Maurier filter trapped "all irritants before they reach your lips," ensuring a "purer" cigarette, steeped in "mildness" and "pleasing flavour."[2] The repeal of a cigarette ad ban and health-themed cigarette promotion highlight two of the many cultural changes and marketing practices during the 1930s that saw cigarette smoking become a popular, socially normative practice for both men and women.

This was a far cry from the early days of the modern cigarette. Introduced in the 1880s, machine-made cigarettes (and their smokers) were soon after excoriated by social reformers, politicians, and clerics. Fifteen US states passed laws banning the manufacture, sale, or possession of cigarettes before 1922.[3] Canada's House of Commons passed a motion in 1903 calling for a ban on the sale, production, and importation of cigarettes. Five years later, parliament voted to prohibit tobacco use by those under sixteen.[4] For decades, the Woman's Christian Temperance Union campaigned against cigarettes, bemoaning their use as immoral and uncouth, a gateway vice leading to truancy, gambling, drinking, and venereal disease.[5] Before the 1910s, cigarette smokers were characterized as social outcasts: bohemian poets, licentious women, southern European immigrants. Popular attitudes changed during the Great War, when Ottawa furnished soldiers' ration kits with cigarettes and countless volunteer drives sent millions more to the troops overseas. Whether as stress relief, appetite suppressant, mental stimulant, or talisman of fellowship, cigarettes helped soldiers cope with the deprivations of trench life and the horrors experienced when "over the top." Returning soldiers continued to smoke them, transferring their vaunted status as vanquishers of the Kaiser to the former "little white slavers."[6] By the late 1920s, cigarettes had shed their sordid, demimonde reputation, at least when smoked by men. Increasingly, cigarettes carried favourable associations of male sociability, up-tempo modernity, and middle-class respectability. The "modern man" smoked cigarettes, less so cigars, and seldom a pipe.[7]

While the Great War first "legitimized the cigarette,"[8] a process that continued into the 1920s, I argue here that crucial developments occurred during the 1930s that elevated and solidified the domestic tobacco industry while establishing cigarette smoking as a cultural norm. Per-capita cigarette sales rose every year from 1932 until the late 1940s, with sales between 1932 and 1938 jumping an astounding 78 per cent.[9] (In contrast, per-capita cigarette sales declined by 20 per cent from 1920 to 1922 and again by 30 per cent from 1929 to 1932.)[10] Farm production of bright-leaf, flue-cured tobacco, the type used for cigarettes, increased exponentially in Canada, rising from 7,570 acres in 1927 to 69,840 in 1939.[11] By the late 1930s, Canadian farmers produced nearly all the tobacco needed for cigarette manufacturing in Canada, unlike a decade earlier when foreign imports prevailed. Cigarette marketing and advertising were ubiquitous in the 1930s, as evidenced by the many premium and gift rebate campaigns, sports contests, point-of-sale promotions, and athlete and celebrity testimonial advertising. Women, beginning in the late 1920s, became targets of cigarette advertising, and their entry into the ranks of socially legitimate smokers proved a milestone for cigarette makers. Alongside the burgeoning images of women in cigarette ads were the many female stars in Hollywood films lighting up, both on and off the screen. By the late 1930s, cigarette smoking permeated, at times transfigured, forms of social engagement, mass media entertainment, and vernacular expression.

While some of the above-cited factors flowed from changes first set in motion during the Great War, two new developments in the 1930s proved seminal to the long-standing viability of the cigarette industry in midcentury Canada. The country's largest tobacco firm, Imperial Tobacco Company of Canada (ITC), was pilloried by politicians, citizens, and journalists for restraint-of-trade and price-fixing practices. The landmark report of the Price Spreads and Mass Buying Royal Commission, released in 1935, excoriated ITC for its predatory business practices; if fully implemented, the report's recommendations would have decreased ITC's dominant share of the cigarette market. The company faced a serious political challenge: how should a large, quasi-monopolistic corporation overcome negative public opinion and convince voters and policy makers that it was in fact socially legitimate, economically productive, and publicly accountable? The firm turned to public relations in the form of a long-running institutional advertising campaign highlighting the firm's beneficence to its workers, Canadian consumers, and the broader public good. This ad campaign began in 1935 and continued until the early 1940s, long after the crisis precipitating it had subsided. When, two decades later, Imperial Tobacco again embraced public relations professionals and strategies in order to discredit scientific studies aligning cigarettes with lung cancer, it did so with extensive prior experience in this domain.

The second key development during the 1930s concerned the arrival of menthol and filtered cigarette brands. Ads for these appealed to the health anxieties of regular smokers; menthol and filter cigarettes promised to prevent or alleviate coughing, throat irritation, and "tongue bite." They carried physician endorsements and other forms of medical reassurance. Filters, the ads proclaimed, removed "harmful" irritants and impurities in cigarettes, rendering them "purer" and safer for smokers. While sales of menthol and filtered brands waned during the 1940s, their historical significance in the 1930s concerns the type of marketing discourse they initiated and made familiar to Canadians: "health marketing" calmed the fears of symptom-worried smokers, promising technological solutions for bodily ailments and discomforts associated with regular cigarette smoking. During the 1930s, this involved mostly coughing and soreness in throats and mouths. After 1952, when health marketing resurfaced in response to medical reports linking cigarettes to lung cancer, the health stakes proved much higher, as too would be the sales of filtered brands as smokers again pursued the promise of a "healthier" cigarette.[12]

CHALLENGING MONOPOLY POWER

The alarmist front-page headline in the *Toronto Daily Star* ("Canada in Danger of a Dictatorship") in April 1934 did not reference political events in Europe. It concerned a House of Commons report critical of the Imperial Tobacco Company of Canada (ITC) for its buying practices among Ontario tobacco growers. The company had engaged in "under cover buying" by serving as proxy for its parent company, the Imperial Tobacco Company of Great Britain and Ireland. This dampened prices for tobacco farmers, who were placed at a great "disadvantage in dealing with a company of such bargaining strength."[13] The story caught the eye of H.H. Stevens, the minister of Trade and Commerce, who chaired the Committee on Price Spreads and Mass Buying, then investigating restraint-of-trade practices among Canada's largest firms. Stevens vowed to bring tobacco executives before the committee.[14] In early May, Imperial Tobacco president Gray Miller found himself for five hours answering questions before the committee. Committee counsel Norman Sommerville made little pretence of impartiality: "The evidence showed that while the Canadian tobacco growers were toiling in the fields from dawn until dark to eke out a miserable existence, the Imperial Tobacco Company in the last five years piled up profits of $30,000,000." ITC's buying tactics had created "panic among the Ontario growers," while "their wives wept in the fields"; the end result for farmers was a "trail of debts and unpaid loans." Committee members criticized ITC for its monopolistic structure, highlighting its many subsidiary manufacturing firms (B. Houde, Tuckett, National Snuff Company, Punch Cigar, General Cigar) and retailing operations (United Cigar Stores).[15] Taken aback by and seemingly ill-prepared for this questioning, Miller returned to the committee four days later to better present his case, this time with "bulging brief cases, piles of papers and two trunks filled with records." This effort, however, did little to alter the views of committee members that ITC had acted underhandedly to lower prices paid to tobacco growers.[16]

Soon after, Imperial Tobacco confronted more bad publicity. Newspaper reports revealed the "lavish" salaries of ITC executives. Gray earned $86,000, while his predecessor in 1930 had pocketed $142,000 in salary and bonuses, this at a time when "Ontario's panic-stricken tobacco growers were sending out Macedonian cries" of help.[17] Tobacco growers received less than two cents of the 25-cent cost of a cigarette pack. By its own admission, ITC controlled 75 per cent of the Canadian cigarette market.[18] Walter M. Stewart, head of Macdonald Tobacco, soon after testified before the price-spreads committee, claiming that ITC executives had received "advance information" about cigarette excise taxes in the recent federal budget. He provided no supporting evidence, though.[19] H.C. Fortier, a tobacco wholesaler affiliated with Macdonald Tobacco, recounted ITC's "reign-of-terror" sales practices. The ITC sales force regularly monitored the advertising and promotional displays of tobacco retailers. If a competitor's brands were prominent, ITC salesmen threatened to revoke buy-direct privileges for the retailer, which offered higher margins than when buying from wholesalers.[20] The testimony of these witnesses, the committee underscored, was substantiated by the "sheaf of letters from tobacconists all over Canada complaining about threats made to them by the Imperial Company." A Winnipeg retailer described how ITC required him to devote 80 per cent of his display space to Imperial brands or lose buy-direct privileges, adding that "80 per cent means 100 per cent."[21] While testifying before the committee, Earle Spafford, ITC vice-president in charge of sales, did little to refute these charges, claiming that Imperial's sales force sought to "get 90 per cent of the [windowed] advertising, an amount comparable with our sales." H.H. Stevens publicly lambasted ITC for its "dictatorial attitude" and cut-throat actions in the marketplace.[22]

Charges involving restraint-of-trade practices and monopoly power date back to the origins of ITC. In 1895, the American Tobacco Company, which dominated the US market, sought to establish a manufacturing facility in Canada in order to circumvent the high tariffs placed on tobacco products entering British markets. It purchased D. Ritchie and Company and the American Cigarette Company, merging them to become the American Tobacco Company of Canada (ATCC).[23] Soon after, ATCC acquired additional tobacco firms like B. Houde and Empire Tobacco. In 1902, American Tobacco struck a partnership agreement with the Imperial

Tobacco Company of Great Britain, with the goal of reducing competition in international markets. This new entity, the British-American Tobacco Company Limited (BAT), was jointly owned by its American and British parent firms. In 1908, BAT purchased ATCC and changed its name to the Imperial Tobacco Company of Canada.[24] With an initial capitalized value of $11 million, this large enterprise "dominated the Canadian tobacco industry" during the 1910s and for decades after. (While a subsidiary of BAT, ITC operated with relatively little interference from its parent company.)[25] ITC's commercial success owed in part to its consignment system for distributing cigarettes, which effectively penalized retailers for selling or promoting competitors' brands. It also worked to minimize price cutting of ITC brands by retailers. ITC spent generously on advertising, driving customers to stores in search of its brands, which in turn predominated in point-of-sale promotions and shelf space.[26] While dealing with nominally independent retailers, ITC achieved a de facto form of vertical integration in the areas of distribution and merchandising, which weakened competitors and strengthened price maintenance.[27] It tightened its hold on distribution channels in the early 1920s after it acquired United Cigar Stores and its 175 retail outlets across Canada. One historian described its overall marketing strategy as "both skilful and ruthless."[28] When ITC bought Tuckett Tobacco in 1930, *Marketing* characterized the firm as having a "practical monopoly" of the Canadian tobacco market.[29]

Weak anti-trust laws and lax enforcement facilitated ITC's dominance of the tobacco marketplace. Between 1900 and 1911 the total capitalization of federally chartered corporations rose from $13 million to $490 million. In 1902, a Royal Commission was struck to investigate complaints that the tobacco industry had "become the victim of monopolistic control." In the end, the federal government took no punitive actions against any firms.[30] From 1909 to 1913, some 220 firms with assets exceeding $200 million consolidated.[31] Ottawa responded with limited anti-trust actions. Indeed, from 1900 to 1910, only five cases were tried under existing anti-combines laws. Responding to adverse publicity surrounding the post-1909 merger wave, the Laurier government brought in new anti-trust legislation, the Combines Investigation Act of 1910. But here again the law proved ineffectual. The complaints process was cumbersome, lengthy, and often costly. Further reducing the law's authority was the provision that prior violations would not be punished, but only those which persisted *after* an anti-combines judicial ruling was handed down. Hence, it is not surprising that such toothless legislation, relying more on moral exhortation than legal compulsion, was invoked only once during its nine-year tenure, despite numerous examples of restraint-of-trade practices.[32] As Michael Bliss notes, businessmen proved all too willing to forgo the uncertainties of the market for the assurances of guaranteed profits. This "flight from competition," extending to "every nook and cranny of the Canadian business world,"[33] adopted many forms: formal and informal price-fixing agreements; mergers; supplier boycotts; foreign dumping; performance bonds; and even fines levied against violators. While during an earlier, less complicated age, unfettered competition may have abetted individual entrepreneurship and provided the most efficient allocation of economic resources, businessmen by the 1920s argued that the "invisible hand" threatened to choke them of their economic livelihood.[34]

THE PRICE-SPREADS ROYAL COMMISSION

To H.H. Stevens, firms like Imperial Tobacco – large monopolies able to dictate terms and prices to farmers and retailers – were the antithesis of the proper role of business in a free-enterprise economy. Before elected to the Commons in 1911, Stevens had worked as a grocer and realtor; as a Conservative MP he cast himself as defender of the small businessman and entrepreneur, both threatened by the avarice and predations of Big Business. In 1930, R.B. Bennett's Tories came to office and Stevens was made minister of Trade and Commerce. By 1934, he had become a regular, outspoken critic of corporate concentration, which he labelled a "canker" on the Canadian economy.[35] These views earned him many accolades and heaps of fan mail from ordinary Canadians, and Bennett thought it wise to channel his ambitions into a parliamentary special committee to investigate the price spreads between what producers received for their commodities and the final prices paid by consumers. Stevens was named its chairman, and the committee met more than sixty times in 1934, hauling before it executives from firms like Canada Packers and Eaton's.[36] Similar to what ITC executives experienced, committee members often lashed out at these officials, which both the press and ordinary voters eagerly lapped up. Stevens became the "people's hero," a rising star among the Tory backbench and rank-and-file party members. His attacks, though, were made against the traditional financial bedrock of the Conservative Party, a concern for many of his cabinet colleagues.[37] The work of this committee proved so politically popular, however, that Bennett opted in July 1934 to elevate its status to that of a royal commission, with Stevens again serving as chair. This emboldened Stevens, whose attacks on Big Business accelerated in the summer months, creating more friction with his cabinet colleagues and later with Bennett himself. This came to a head in October when Stevens, now lacking Bennett's full support, resigned from cabinet. While still a member of the royal commission, he was no longer its chairman.[38]

In March 1935, Stevens leaked the royal commission's draft report to the press, in a bid to ensure that its draft recommendations were not watered down. When the final report was tabled in the Commons on 12 April, it offered some hard-line assessments and prescriptions. The report noted that large firms had "blocked" competition in many industries; these firms had effective "freedom from legal liability," while also evading "moral responsibility for inequitable and uneconomic practices." This situation "need[ed] cleansing,"[39] with only the federal government having the administrative capability and constitutional authority to restore competitive balance to the marketplace. The first economic sector discussed in the report was tobacco. Since ITC controlled at least 70 per cent of the tobacco market, this industry was characterized as "obviously monopolistic." Canadian firms faced little competition from foreign competitors owing to high duties on tobacco imports. ITC had acted to "manipulate raw materials costs and to sell its product in a sheltered market."[40] While ITC enjoyed high profits, "growers, dealers, a majority of manufacturers, the Wholesaler and the retailer have been faced with meagre profits or in some cases, absolute losses."[41] Retailers were forced to comply with ITC's "unfair competitive practices" or face the business-crippling prospect of seeing three-quarters of their product inventory withdrawn.[42] The company had engaged in "oppressive tactics and unethical methods to promote the sales of its products in every part of the country."[43]

Among the report's many recommendations were calls for greater financial disclosure by corporations, including executive salaries and bonuses. Its boldest recommendation was for the creation of a Federal Trade and Industry Commission to deal with the "growth of concentration," whose mandate would be the "prevention and regulation of monopoly and monopolistic practices," while providing greater protection for consumers and primary producers.[44] The commission would pursue "rigorous" enforcement of the Combines Investigations Act, which would also be amended to include a "more comprehensive definition of monopolies and monopolistic practices."[45] The proposed commission would work to restore healthy competition to the marketplace, with primary focus on the needs of small business, farmers, and labourers.[46] The government bill introduced soon after to deal with the commission's recommendations, however, proved tepid. There would be no powerful new commission; any new regulatory actions would fall to the already overburdened Dominion Tariff Board. Bennett cited constitutional concerns for this half-measure, but his simmering feud with Stevens was also a key factor.[47] W.W. Kennedy, chair of the commission, described the proposed legislation as "practically useless," and Stevens similarly dismissed it.[48] There would be no powerful, New Deal–type agency to regulate big business in Canada.[49] Any lingering hopes for this ended with the Liberals' electoral win in October 1935. Incoming Prime Minister Mackenzie King saw no need to revisit the commission's recommendations.

PUBLIC RELATIONS ADVERTISING

For ITC, the events of 1934 and early 1935 were no doubt troubling. For decades, the company's market dominance and international affiliation had helped to shield it from commercial uncertainty and political challenge. But here was a Conservative government, the traditional ally of corporate Canada, attacking business practices that were at the core of ITC operations and profitability. Other warning signs were on the political horizon. The newly formed Co-operative Commonwealth Federation sought to implement a democratic socialist agenda and reduce the power of big business. The Social Credit Party, which later in 1935 would capture the Alberta legislature, advocated the use of monetary policy to redistribute wealth to ordinary citizens. ITC's conundrum was qualitatively different from business problems like expanding market share or reducing production costs. At issue here was the social legitimacy and political viability of a large corporation with a monopolistic grasp of its marketplace. In the past, Ottawa had largely turned a blind eye to corporate concentration and restraint-of-trade practices. But that now seemed likely to change.[50]

Large US corporations facing similar situations had responded with institutional advertising to elevate their social standing and cultural authority. In the early 1900s AT&T and US Steel confronted anti-trust forces with advertising designed to articulate a "corporate personality," indeed a "corporate soul," in pursuit of public approval. Firms like Metropolitan Life, General Electric, and General Motors followed suit with advertising that highlighted company endeavours such as funding for the arts or workplace welfare programs. The broader aim was to have large corporations assume a place alongside "society's basic institutions of family, church, community, and state."[51] These efforts accelerated during the Depression, when public confidence in the business system eroded. Business leaders saw themselves in a struggle to preserve free enterprise, threatened, it was thought, by the New Deal state and big labour. Business needed to "tell its story" to society as a whole, in order to educate the public about its economic and social importance. In 1933, John Hill and Don Knowlton established the public relations firm Hill and Knowlton, which counselled clients like the American Iron and Steel Institute on how to generate corporate goodwill among the public.[52] For increasing numbers of corporations during the 1930s, Inger L. Stole notes, "selling business itself and its contributions to the entire economic system was just as important as selling its products."[53] Advertising, what James Webb Young called the "torch of business," would be used to sell the very idea of business to voters.[54] In this vein, public relations functioned as an ongoing, "fundamental system of business hygiene," rather than as ad hoc actions to handle periodic crises.[55]

In January 1935, ITC launched an institutional advertising campaign, a long-running series of bi-weekly ads promoting the social and economic merits of the firm. Notably, the campaign ran well into the 1940s, long after the immediate crisis precipitating it had ended. On 28 January, an ad introduced ITC as a "faithful servant of the people of Canada," which in the coming months would tell the fascinating story of tobacco's journey from fields to lungs.[56] The campaign's significance was discussed early on in the advertising trade press.[57] Given the focus of the Stevens Committee, it should not surprise that tobacco retailing was treated first. The ad, "Always ... Everywhere," described how ITC brands could be found in 17,500 retail venues across Canada, making them "quickly and easily available to Canadian users of tobacco, at all seasons of the year, at all hours of the day." Widespread distribution formed part of ITC's broader mission "to serve the Canadian public."[58] The doctrine of public service appeared in ads describing the roles of scientific crop selection and advanced manufacturing in maintaining "purity and freshness" in all ITC brands.[59] The company worked tirelessly to "satisfy, precisely and effectively, every known taste of sizable extent."[60] These ads then turned to working conditions at ITC. Its Montreal factory had a "well-equipped hospital" with resident nurses and doctors providing medical advice and care to employees. Milk rations were freely provided to "underweight cases."[61] ITC offered long-term illness and disability coverage, group and life insurance, and a joint-contributory pension fund for male employees.[62] There were sanitary washrooms, inviting lunchrooms, and manicured gardens, all of which made the "daily round of the worker unusually pleasant and care-free."[63]

None of these rosy depictions dealt with wages, however. Workers in ITC's Montreal factory, 70 per cent of whom were female, earned an average weekly wage of $12.22 in 1933, 20 per cent less than in 1929. This was low even for female-dominated sectors. For example, in the women's clothing garment trade, which was 74 per cent female, average weekly earnings were $15.84. These facts, along with others that reflected poorly on ITC, became public in April 1935 with the release of the Royal Commission Report on Price Spreads.[64] ITC, in advertising its employee welfare schemes, mirrored the actions of firms like US Steel and International Harvester. Facing anti-trust opposition, they had advertised their employee housing programs and on-site child care services in order to generate goodwill among the wider public.[65]

By summer 1935, ITC ads were promoting broader social contributions and scientific accomplishments. Consumers would always find their favourite cigarettes while on vacation since ITC brands were sold nearly everywhere in Canada,[66] and the company's "fair pricing" policy meant that they would not pay more in remote locations.[67] ITC discouraged "price cutting," which meant that wholesalers earned more to support their families.[68] Workers in the cardboard, aluminum foil, and cellophane sectors similarly benefited from company purchase orders.[69] ITC assisted tobacco growers by providing "cultivation experts" and "necessary plants for experimentation," which in turn produced higher-grade tobacco.[70] The firm's scientists laboured constantly to create "newer, better things," while being "always receptive to new ideas from whatever source they may come."[71] In the factory, advanced machinery rolled cigarettes at the "modern magic" rate of 23 per second.[72] Months of "research and experimentation" had produced the cellophane outer wrapper for cigarette packages.[73] Women employees, "carefully selected for their keen eyesight," provided first-rate quality control.[74] In the August 1936 ad, "Toward One Goal ... Perfection!" (figure 1.1), readers learned how Imperial's "continuous research" program ensured the "purity" of its cigarettes, a production standard "maintained with the meticulous care of a royal infant's diet." It added: "This Company spends many thousands of dollars every year upon research work alone, conducted in a spirit of 'critical investigation.' We consider this money well invested, since it enables us to bring to you finer, more nearly perfect Imperial Tobacco products."[75] Claims like this were not unusual during the interwar years, when companies greatly expanded research and development operations. In the United States, the number of scientists in industry research labs increased tenfold from 1920 to 1940, rising from 2,775 to 27,777.[76] As Jeffrey Meikle noted for the 1930s, corporations touted scientific breakthrough and technological innovation as markers of "unending material progress" in the machine age.[77] While success in the cigarette industry arguably turned more on marketing know-how than on cutting-edge production techniques, ITC frequently appealed to and appropriated the cultural authority of science and industrial technology.

It also invoked medical authority, as seen in the ad "These Are the Facts," which appeared in March 1937 (figure 1.2).[78] The ad's text is rather banal:

people smoked cigarettes for their manifold pleasures, made possible by high-quality tobacco and rigorous production methods. Cigarettes provided "pleasure, satisfaction and comfort," but were "not in any sense a cure-all." A curative for what goes unsaid, only that the smoker's enjoyment came from the "clean, gratifying smoke" of top-grade tobacco and manufacture. The ad's centrepiece is a white-coated man wearing a head mirror, a common signifier for medical doctor in the early 1900s. The physician-with-head mirror (or stethoscope) was a familiar visual motif in American cigarette advertising from the 1930s until the 1950s, seen especially with R.J. Reynolds's Camels, which had fictional and actual doctors endorse the "throat-easy" mildness of that brand.[79] Canadians routinely read American magazines during the interwar years, making this visual icon part of the lexicon of familiar cultural symbols.[80] The ad's text does not mention throat irritation, coughing, or sinus troubles, complaints made by cigarette smokers in the 1930s. The industry's response to this feedback was to introduce filtered and menthol brands, promoted for their "cooler," milder attributes (see below). The ad's iconography references this health context; the physician, staring intently at the reader while holding up a cigarette, symbolically yokes medical expertise to advance meanings of consumer safety and health reassurance. This is done both for cigarettes in general and for ITC brands in particular, since these brand names are listed in the ad, one of the first to do so in this campaign.[81]

Since the late 1800s, moral and social reformers had derided cigarettes as unhealthy; they stunted growth, weakened lungs, and caused other mental and physical "degeneracies."[82] While such critics were largely discredited by the 1930s, unease over the healthiness of cigarettes continued in the vernacular vein of "coffin nail" and "cancer stick" quips. Interwar clinicians used the term "Tobacco Heart" to describe smoking-related angina, arrhythmia, and cardiac arrest.[83] In 1928, the *New England Journal of Medicine* published an article showing a causal link between tobacco smoking and cancer.[84] In 1931, the insurance industry researcher Frederick Hoffman released a study that causally pegged booming cigarette consumption to rising rates of lung cancer.[85] Similar research was done and published in South America and Europe during the 1930s, most notably in Nazi Germany.[86] These findings were generally not taken up by the press, and medical doctors, arguably a majority, remained skeptical that

1.1 To combat negative publicity, Imperial Tobacco launched a multi-year public relations ad campaign in 1935. Imperial Tobacco institutional ad in the *Toronto Daily Star*, 26 August 1936.

1.2 An early example of health-reassurance advertising from Imperial Tobacco. Imperial Tobacco institutional ad in the *Toronto Daily Star*, 24 March 1937.

tobacco caused disease.[87] But tobacco companies, in at least one instance, were aware of these nascent findings. In 1939, the research director at American Tobacco, Hiram R. Hanmer, responded to a query about Angel H. Roffo, the Argentine researcher whose work with lab animals and cancer patients had shown causal relationships between tobacco tar exposure and cancer. Though Roffo's work was published mostly in German and Spanish, Hanmer was not caught off guard: "We have been following Roffo's work for some time, and I feel that it is unfortunate that a statement such as his is widely disseminated."[88] By the late 1930s, Allan M. Brandt argues, tobacco smoking's role in causing cancer had become a subject of "unresolved debate."[89]

Public relations advertising functioned to influence "unresolved debates," aiming to align public interest with corporate interest. In 1939, Earle Spafford, ITC vice-president, reflected on the firm's institutional advertising campaign, now four years old: "We have tried to imagine ourselves chatting to our customers face to face," presenting the "human side of the industry—what it means to the people who depend upon it for their livelihood or look to it for a form of enjoyment."[90] Well before the tobacco industry's massive public relations response to the "cancer-scare" crisis of the 1950s,[91] Imperial Tobacco had become versed in the art and mechanics of institutional advertising, articulating and promulgating its "corporate soul" to the Canadian public.

THE POLITICAL ECONOMY OF TOBACCO

One of ITC's institutional ads spotlighted Canada's tobacco farming sector.[92] "Canada" is perhaps a misnomer, given the crop's geographic specificity. In 1938, Ontario produced 97 per cent of the country's raw leaf tobacco,[93] most of which was grown in the "new" tobacco belt of Norfolk, Elgin, and Oxford counties in southwestern Ontario. As late as the mid-1920s, very little tobacco was grown in these counties; only then was the area's sandy soil shown to be suitable for bright leaf, flue-cured tobacco used in cigarettes.[94] Tobacco farming and the flue-curing of bright leaf began soon after and spread quickly. By 1937, the value of Ontario's tobacco crops reached nearly $15 million, with farmers fetching much higher prices than those in the early 1930s that had caught the attention of H.H. Stevens and others. In 1937, they received 27 cents a pound, up from 16 cents in 1932.[95] By 1939, Ontario's tobacco fields supplied nearly all of the domestic market for cigarette production, while also exporting 27 million pounds of flue-cured tobacco.[96]

The late 1930s were heady times for tobacco growers and their communities, as a *Maclean's* reporter discovered.[97] Tobacco-growing counties had "scorned the depression,"[98] as seen by the building boom in hotels, theatres, and stores. Towns like Simcoe, Delhi, and Tillsonburg had lowered municipal taxes, paid off debentures, and reduced relief rolls. Simcoe had built a new public pool, tennis courts, and floodlit baseball diamonds. It had three cinemas, up from one in 1935. The ITC-owned processing plant in Delhi hired up to 1,500 workers each fall to sort, grade, and process flue-cured tobacco leaf. Tillsonburg's housing shortage was matched by a sea of parked cars on its main street on Saturday afternoons. Garnet Murphy, who had recently moved to the area to drive a taxi, had no regrets: "Am I glad I came to Simcoe? Mister, glad's not the world for it. I'm singing!"[99]

While most tobacco was grown and cured in southwestern Ontario, the bulk of manufacturing occurred hundreds of miles away. In 1939, 87 per cent of the nearly $70 million tobacco manufacturing industry was located in Quebec, mostly in Montreal, where firms like ITC and Macdonald Tobacco were based.[100] That year, tobacco manufacturing employed nearly 11,000 people, whose $9.7 million in wages and salaries would have circulated mostly in and around Montreal.[101] As noted earlier, the industry was also highly concentrated, with the handful of firms producing over $1 million in goods comprising 91 per cent of the total sector.[102] Tobacco farming and manufacturing played relatively small roles in the Canadian economy. In 1939, tobacco farming comprised less than 3 per cent of total crop values,[103] while manufacturing operations formed less than 2 per cent of the country's gross value of production.[104] But the inverse was true for taxation. In 1938, the federal government collected nearly $36 million in tobacco excise taxes (and, to a much lesser degree, custom duties on tobacco), accounting for 8 per cent of Ottawa's total tax revenues ($436.2 million) that year.[105] ITC alone provided roughly 7 per cent of federal tax revenues, a fact it advertised as "serving the national treasury."[106] Prior to the Second World War (when personal and corporate income taxes rose precipitously, reducing the relative weight of excise taxes),[107] almost one in ten federal tax dollars came from a handful of Montreal manufacturers and, by extension, tobacco farmers in three Ontario counties. Never again would the Canadian tobacco industry wield as much fiscal clout is it did in the 1930s.[108]

The political implications of this are noteworthy. In 1935, the federal Liberals won office in an electoral landslide, taking 171 of 245 seats. The Liberal Party remained in power until 1957, later dubbed the "government party" for its long-standing political acumen and administrative competence.[109] In 1935, the federal Conservatives elected four members in Montreal, one less than its haul for the entire province. In the 1940 federal election, the Tories were shut out of Montreal, a losing streak that continued until 1953.[110] The federal Liberals reigned supreme in Quebec for more than twenty years after 1935, winning more than 80 per cent of its seats and nearly all of those in Montreal. In Ontario, seven federal ridings (Brant, Brantford, Elgin, Haldimand, Middlesex-East, Norfolk, Oxford) were located in or abutted tobacco-growing areas. Here again the Liberals proved dominant, winning all but one of these ridings in 1935 and 1940.[111] The federal government held jurisdiction over excise taxes, so tobacco-related revenues flowed to Ottawa and not the provinces. Provincial sales taxes at this time were negligible, totalling just $2 million of the $245 million in provincial government revenues in 1937.[112] Unlike in recent decades, the provinces factored little in the regulation and taxation of tobacco. The tobacco industry – a non-competitive, highly concentrated sector – looked out onto a political landscape strikingly similar to itself. Its political dealings were mainly with only one level of government that was controlled by the same party for a generation. The bulk of its factories and workforces were in the Liberal fortress of Montreal, ensuring continual representation by government MPs. A near monopoly industry had for its political bedfellow a quasi one-party state.

WOMEN SMOKERS

The political-economic might of the tobacco industry was paralleled by the expanding cultural reach of cigarettes in the 1930s. In 1920, tailor-made cigarettes comprised 42 per cent of the manufactured tobacco product market in Canada, rising to 63 per cent by 1939.[113] Per-capita sales of cigarettes rose 78 per cent from 1932 to 1939, while cigar consumption in that time declined by 7 per cent.[114] Some of this growth came from pipe and cigar smokers, mostly men, switching to cigarettes. But another factor is significant: women enthusiastically took up cigarette smoking in the 1930s. Cigarette companies did not market directly to women until the late 1920s.[115] The first such campaign occurred in 1927 with advertising for ITC's Player's Navy Cut, whose tagline read: "Men may come and men may go, but Player's Navy Cut are a constant ever."[116] The campaign was deemed risky, not for its sexual innuendo but for concerns that appealing to women would embolden the "puritanical fanatics" who opposed cigarettes outright.[117] Later ads in this campaign featured bobbed, stylish women smoking cigarettes. A year later, a writer in the advertising trade press commented on the many "tea table matronly" women in cigarette ads, a hopeful sign that female smoking was moving beyond the "flapper" set.[118] Jarrett Rudy similarly notes that cigarette advertising in Montreal dailies did not target women directly until the late 1920s.[119] But by the early 1930s much had changed, as seen with the many cigarette ads aligning female smoking with ideals of the modern, middle-class woman who was recreationally active, sexually confident, and upwardly mobile.[120] A reporter surveyed Toronto tobacconists in 1930 and learned that female cigarette buyers were no longer "steal[ing] out furtively ... with their packages in paper bags."[121] Mackenzie King, at the wedding of a friend's daughter in 1933, remarked (disapprovingly) in his diary about the ordinary manner in which the bride smoked cigarettes alongside the groom, even while toasting with champagne.[122] In 1934, Queen's University established a smoking room in its women's residence, ostensibly with a "view to having cigarette smoking by girl students confined in close quarters."[123]

Women featured prominently in cigarette ads in newspapers, magazines, and on billboards, which in turn served to normalize female smoking while communicating symbolically in other ways. Images of women as steeple-chase racers or convocating students broadened the range of recreational pastimes and professional endeavours that were socially permissible for women.[124] These ads offered revised notions of womanhood, in which pleasure-seeking behaviour coexisted with social respectability. Ads depicting women smoking in social settings or out in public reinforced the then-radical idea that women receive equal opportunity and treatment in all areas of public life.[125] "This summer especially," commented one tobacconist in 1937, "I've noticed a good many women smoking on the street, exercising their equal rights with men."[126] Cigarettes functioned as erotic signifiers, providing "otherwise respectable women," Sharon Anne Cook argues, a "licence to develop and exercise a sexually charged and independent persona in ways that probably would not have been possible for them, given the restrictive societal norms that governed women's behaviour."[127] The 1930s "modern girl" projected her "independent woman"[128] status via cigarette smoking, a notion playfully rendered in a 1938 ad for Sweet Caporals. In the ad a hopeful man leans toward a young woman standing under some mistletoe and asks: "Have you seen the mistletoe?" Her response: "Yes – but where are my Sweet Caps?"[129]

CINEMATIC SMOKING

Hollywood offered up more female smoking role models. Lacking a domestic feature-film industry, Canadians avidly watched American movies during the 1930s.[130] One study of Hollywood cinema of the 1930s found that 30 per cent of heroines smoked, compared with 3 per cent of female villains.[131] In *Morocco* (1930), Marlene Dietrich orders her male companion to "cigarette me, big boy," a form of sexual bravado matched by Jean Harlow in *Hell's Angels* (1930) when she asks a soldier "to come up for a cigarette and a drink?"[132] Women smokers in film "telegraphed sexual desire without there needing to be any further demonstration of her interest."[133] The sex symbol Mae West smoked cigarettes throughout *I'm No Angel* (1933) and *She Done Him Wrong* (1933) and her publicity photos often pictured her with cigarette and extended holder. The Hays Production Code, adopted in 1934, required filmmakers to curtail sexualized behaviour and discourse, which in turn resulted in greater use of on-screen smoking to convey sexual messaging. Bette Davis, in *It's Love I'm After* (1937), blows smoke in a lover's face as a form of sexual invitation.[134] Male sexual desire took the form of lighting two cigarettes and placing one in a woman's mouth. Cinematic smoking conveyed more than sexual meanings. A character's shyness or awkwardness was shown by fumbling with matches or cigarettes. Anxiety manifested itself as staccato puffing or chain smoking. Male dexterity and ingenuity were displayed by lighting a cigarette one-handed. Cinematic smoking constituted "an implicit language of gestures and acts" that facilitated character definition and plot development.[135]

Many people, especially youths and young adults, were attracted to the glamorized portrayal of smoking on the big screen. A Mass Observation study in Britain attributed the upswing in smoking's perceived sophistication to its positive portrayal in Hollywood movies of the 1930s.[136] Smoking film stars were sexy and savvy, dynamic and discriminating. For young women, the visual, performative nature of cinematic smoking – its ability to project personality types and character traits – proved especially captivating.[137] Many on-screen smokers also endorsed cigarettes in advertisements. A Gold Flake ad in 1935 promoted the Alfred Hitchcock film *The 39 Steps* by featuring its two stars, Madeline Carroll and Robert Donat. The ad reminded readers to see the upcoming movie and highlighted Donat's "magnetic charm" and "hint of sophistication" that captured women's hearts. "His cigarette, of course, is a Gold Flake."[138] In 1937, American Tobacco contracted with more than forty stars and their Hollywood studios to advertise cigarettes in conjunction with film release dates. In one instance Gary Cooper, in a testimonial ad for Lucky Strikes, plugs his upcoming film, *Souls at Sea*.[139] This form of synergistic cross promotion enhanced the studios' bottom line, broadened the star's public exposure, and boosted the cultural standing and popular appeal of cigarettes, both for particular brands and the entire product category.

ORDINARY HABITS

Cigarettes proved ideally suited to a modern, urbanizing society. (In 1931, for the first time, the census counted more urban than rural Canadians.)[140] Cigarettes could be smoked quickly in an increasingly time-pressed society.[141] They could be smoked while doing other activities: preparing dinner, working a switchboard, processing insurance claims. Cigarette smoke was more palatable than that of cigars or pipes, an important consideration as people spent more time in enclosed spaces like office buildings, streetcars, and stores. The anonymity and alienation of city life were eased by conversation breakers like "Got a light?" or "Mind if I smoke?" Asked by a young woman about a suitable gift for her nineteen-year-old boyfriend, etiquette columnist Kathrine de Peyster suggested "a carton of the young man's favorite cigarettes, or a book."[142] Their ubiquity spawned a sea of accessories: smoker cabinets, ashtrays, car lighters, cigarette cases, and even waterproof belt buckles for holding cigarettes while swimming. Eaton's sold a "Smo-kee" handbag, with an in-built cigarette case, and a vanity bag equipped with a pop-up cigarette case.[143] Life Savers chewing gum advertised itself as a "cigarette's best buddy" for freshening the mouth, and Wrigley's Juicy Fruit promised to make "the next smoke taste better."[144] Elizabeth Arden toothpaste was a "boon to cigarette smokers who like to keep fastidious always." The patent medicine "Kellogg's Asthma Relief" even came in cigarette form.[145]

Cigarette smoking infused visual description and linguistic expression. Wool suits in an Eaton's ad came in "Swagger Blue" or "Nicotine Brown,"[146] while dresses were sold in "Sky Mauve" or "Cigarette Brown."[147] A Chrysler roadster came "finished in beautiful cigarette cream shade."[148] An Eaton's ad for Orchid Eye Shadow promised to make your eyes as "soft and purplish-blue as the smoke from your favourite cigarette."[149] Advice on waist-thinning exercises came in this form: "since you are probably counting on a cigarette silhouette by next Tuesday, you will want the best."[150] To demonstrate the heat-resistant quality of the surface of Frigidaire refrigerators, salesmen placed lit cigarettes on them.[151] How fast could Uptown Tire change your tires? They'd "put them on while you enjoy a cigarette."[152] How affordable was the food supplement Knox Gelatine? It "cost less than a pack of cigarettes per day."[153] Aqua Velva was even cheaper, costing "less than one cigarette a day"[154] Cigarettes – as metaphor, point of reference, or adjective – permeated the popular vernacular of Canadians by the late 1930s.

PREMIUM HABITS

Premium promotions further ingrained cigarettes into the daily lives of Canadians.[155] The most popular of these was ITC's "Poker Hands" promotion, launched in 1925 by its Turret brand. Poker hands were included in cigarette packages, to be collected and later redeemed for prizes like umbrellas or bridge sets.[156] This promotion grew increasingly popular, and by the mid-1930s most of Imperial's cigarette brands (Turret, Sweet Caporals, Winchester, Guinea Gold, Millbank) offered Poker Hand rebates. By 1935, more than two hundred gift items were available. At the low end, there were items like playing cards, toilet soap, and toothpaste. At mid-level, consumers chose from gloves, socks, or teapots. Those with many poker hands could select from silver cutlery sets or tea settings. There were gifts for men (shaving cream, suspenders), women (stockings, face powder), and even children (doll, harmonica, toy dog). Brand-name goods like Gillette razors and Eastman film were available. Practical items like scissors and kettles could be had, as well as refined display goods like cut-glass tumblers and silver-plated comports. All of these were presented in illustrated catalogues, disseminated widely across the country (figure 1.3).[157] Smokers could redeem poker-hand coupons for gifts at any of the more than twenty "Poker Hand Premium Stores" in seventeen cities across Canada, including four in Montreal. In 1935, rumours circulated that ITC planned to cancel the promotion, spawning long, bank-run-style lines at stores, as one journalist noted: "At the height of the 'run,' long queues formed and scores of people patiently waited for their premiums while the staff worked at high pressure counting coupons with machine-like rapidity." ITC took out newspaper ads denying the rumour.[158]

Other cigarette makers followed suit. Macdonald Tobacco offered one hundred or so premium gifts in exchange for cigarette-package panel fronts. Grothe's Grads cigarettes, marketed as a high-end brand, had a "Save the Bridge Hands" premium promotion. My Fortune cigarettes advertised $1,500 in monthly cash prizes.[159] For ITC and other cigarette makers, premium marketing promoted volume selling and brand loyalty. At a broader level, it allowed people to acquire goods that might not otherwise have been possible in a Depression-era economy. By making cigarettes the conduit to a cornucopia of material goods, premium marketing reinforced the centrality of cigarettes in the emerging consumer society. Cigarettes not only provided corporeal pleasure and social engagement, they functioned as a de facto currency in an exchange system featuring a wide array of consumer goods. Through their alignment with "badge goods" like cut-glass tumblers, cigarettes also absorbed symbolic meanings like cultural refinement and social respectability, what semioticians refer to as "associative transfer."[160]

Contest promotions were also common, many involving sports. In 1932, Turret awarded $15,000 in cash prizes to those correctly guessing total goals scored in the current NHL season. Winning entries on Turret packages earned double the prize amounts.[161] Some three million entries were received, and Turret held a similar contest for the following NHL season.[162] Draegerman cigarettes offered NHL tickets for those guessing the time of the first goal at an upcoming Toronto Maple Leafs game.[163] British Consols paid out $100 in weekly prizes in 1933 for correct estimates of weekly goal

1.3 During the 1930s, cigarette makers used gift-coupon schemes and contest promotions to boost sales. Imperial Tobacco Canada's "Poker Hands" Premiums catalogue, September 1935.

tallies in the NHL.[164] Sports-related advertising was similarly widespread. Turret promoted Australian billiards pro Walter Lindrum and his upcoming match in Canada with British counterpart Tom Newman, with the winner receiving the "Turret Cigarette Trophy."[165] Gold Flake cigarettes sponsored an American bridge team in 1933, which toured Canadian cities, playing matches against local teams. In larger halls, "each play [was] flashed upon a large board" so spectators could follow the action.[166] Philip Morris launched a campaign in 1936 featuring NHL stars such as Lionel Conacher, Syl Apps, and Turk Broda, all touting the "mild, smooth, satisfying" merits of its Navy Cut cigarettes.[167] Buckingham advertising featured many testimonials from sports figures, among them tennis pro Bill Tilden, Toronto Argonauts coach Lew Hayman, and golf pro Jules Huot.[168] After five hours in a steel barrel coursing through the Niagara rapids, daredevil William Hill's "first thought on coming out" was for a Buckingham cigarette.[169] Goody Rosen, the "Toronto boy who made good" by signing with the Brooklyn Dodgers, talked up Buckinghams for steadying his nerves and concentration during baseball play. Toe Blake, the NHL's leading scorer in the 1938–39 season, promoted the "throat easy" mildness of Buckinghams in 1939.[170]

HEALTH MARKETING

This "Throat Easy" theme became a fixture of Buckingham advertising, especially after 1930 when ITC bought the Tuckett Tobacco Co. which marketed the brand. Testimonial ads featured actors, singers, and radio hosts, people whose professional livelihoods depended on vocal performance. Radio announcer Herb May explained that "if a cigarette irritated my throat, I'd have to give them up." But Buckinghams were "easy on my throat." Louise King, who "sang every night," championed the brand's "throat-easy" attributes. Buckinghams were the "only Cigarette treated by Ultra Violet ray in Canada," making them milder for mouth and throat.[171] Similar appeals were issued by other brands. Benson & Hedges promoted Oxford cigarettes as "mellow mildness for delicate throats."[172] Advertising for Grothe's Roxy brand read: "Give your throat a permanent VACATION" from "harshness, bitterness and bite in your cigarette smoking." Smoke

Roxy and "rule out throat irritation and morning after effects." Grothe also took out an ad in the form of an "unsolicited testimonial" letter from a physician who found Roxy "less irritating to the throat than any cigarette I have ever smoked."[173] This theme was picked up by ancillary products. Allenburys Pastilles promised relief from throat irritation caused by "one cigarette too many." Smith Brothers Cough Drops were there "when your palette is as dry as dust from smoking." Ads for Zubes Lozenges hailed "Chain Smokers – with gravel throats."[174] The Denicotea cigarette holder allowed people to "smoke the healthy way" because the holder's cartridge "remove[d] the harshness, prevent[ed] throat irritation and g[ave] your favorite cigarette a new mildness."[175]

The most significant marketing response to smoking-related health concerns in the 1930s came in the form of menthol and filtered cigarettes. Introduced in Canada in the early 1930s, menthol cigarettes provided an anaesthetizing, cooling effect in the mouth when smoked, reducing the harshness of the cigarette smoke. Menthol had long been used as a medicinal cough suppressant, and tobacco makers sought to draw on its "therapeutic association with cough and cold remedies" to appeal to health-concerned smokers.[176] In the United States in the late 1920s, Axton-Fisher introduced Spuds, the first "menthol-cooled" brand, encouraging smokers to try them when they had colds or sore throats.[177] Spuds arrived in Canada in the early 1930s, with ads touting its mentholated "cool smoke" for "leav[ing] most of its irritants in the butt of the cigarette."[178] Later Spuds ads described how "tongue-bite" in cigarettes was caused by the "heat in the smoke," which could be avoided by using "menthol-cooled Spuds."[179] Another ad carried the header "Nagged by Nicotine?" and asked readers: "Do you smoke a lot, and worry about what cigarettes are doing to you? You can ease your mind by making better use of the *filter* effect of the butt of your cigarette. Here's how: pull lightly when you light up. Smoke slowly, and not too far down. But to get real smoking enjoyment, try Spuds ... whose menthol-process naturally condenses more of the tars and acids."[180] The "filter effect" did not involve an actual filter (though Spuds also came in a cork-tipped version), but was rather a preventative technique performed by the smoker to minimize the intake of "tar and acids." Other Spuds ads described how menthol produced a "16% cooler smoke," prevented "tongue-bite and husky-voice," and kept the smoker's "tongue and throat in moist-cool comfort."[181] Cameos were "air-conditioned by menthol" and when inhaled as "cool as a fresh breeze." A 1938 seasonal ad for Cameos featured Santa Claus saying: "Say CAMEO When you want a *Menthol* Cigarette."[182] Advertising for Macdonald's Menthol (with "cool as a Cucumber" written on the package) featured a woman smoking a cigarette with the caption: "Doctors Recommend Them." She adds: "When I changed to Macdonald's Menthol my throat said 'O.K.' ... so did my doctor."[183]

Filtered cigarettes appeared in Canada in the mid-1930s and were widely advertised for their health benefits. The niche brand De Reszke promoted its filtered cigarettes for "not only prevent[ing] particles of tobacco from entering the mouth, but also filter[ing] any harmful nicotine out of the smoke."[184] In May 1936, Brown & Williamson launched Viceroy, the first major filtered cigarette brand in the United States; it did well in the market, selling some 20 million packages in the first six months.[185] Afterwards major filter-brand launches occurred in Canada. British maker Carreras launched Craven "A" in Canada in 1937. These cork tipped cigarettes, a man proclaims in one ad, were a healthy choice: "I know from medical experience that a cigarette made *specially* to *prevent sore throats* is the right cigarette to smoke."[186] In another Craven "A" ad, a caption reads: "as a doctor I cannot recommend any brand but personally I smoke Craven 'A.'"[187] In 1937 Macdonald Tobacco introduced a filtered version of its flagship Export brand, promising consumers "new smoking enjoyment" since the filter worked to "eliminate nicotine."[188] (The belief that nicotine, and not tar, was potentially harmful was likely reinforced by insecticides advertising nicotine as the active ingredient.)[189]

The most heavily advertised filter brand was Peter Jackson's du Maurier, launched in fall 1936. Its filters constituted the "first vital improvement ever made in cigarettes," a technological feat on par with "wireless, air-conditioning, [and] streamlining." The filters removed "smoke impurities" and delivered "real cigarette pleasure" (figure 1.4). In countless ads running many years, men and women lauded the merits of filtered smoke,[190] calling on consumers to "discover for yourself why all that could harm is trapped in the tip, all that delights comes through."[191] The du Maurier filters "refine[d] the smoke while the cigarette burn[ed]" and "trap[ped] only irritants."[192] The ads did not disclose the composition of the filters, but most cigarette filters in the 1930s were made from fibrous materials like wool, cotton, or paper.[193] Most of these ads carried added medical conviction in the form of an endorsement from *The Lancet*, a leading British medical journal, which read: "We have tested these cigarettes and find them to be cooler and less irritating than ordinary cigarettes of good quality without the Filter Tip."[194] Later, in 1954, Imperial Tobacco acquired the rights to du Maurier and the brand would later become its top seller, largely due to its appeal to women. In its official corporate history, ITC attributed du Maurier's success in the 1930s to marketing efforts that were "aimed specifically at women."[195] But, as shown here, du Maurier advertising in the 1930s was largely unisex, appealing generically to men and women with a core message: du Maurier filters offered a modern, technological solution for people's health concerns about cigarettes. They made cigarette smoking safer, less worrisome, by removing harmful ingredients in tobacco smoke that could irritate and damage mouths and airways.

CONCLUSION

The political, economic, and cultural standing of smoking had strengthened considerably by the start of the Second World War. As wartime exigencies escalated, fewer people spoke of ITC in terms of "oppressive tactics and unethical methods," as had the Price Spreads Royal Commission just a few years earlier. Public concerns over corporate concentration and price fixing in the tobacco trade had largely dissipated. Geographically concentrated in Montreal, tobacco manufacturers confronted few competitive pressures, since two companies controlled more than 90 per cent of the cigarette trade. Bright leaf tobacco farming was now similarly concentrated in a belt of sandy soil in southwestern Ontario. By 1940, women had become bone fide cigarette smokers. Whether seen with etiquette columnist advice that cigarettes at dinner parties be "passed after the salad course"[196] or with press accounts of women smoking outdoors and "exercising their equal rights with men,"[197] cigarette smoke had acquired decidedly feminine hues by decade's end. Women appeared regularly in cigarette advertising, and female leads in Hollywood films frequently lit up, both on and off the screen. This served to align cigarettes with desirable

1.4 Introduced in the 1930s, filtered cigarettes promised to reduce "smoke impurities" and throat irritation among smokers. du Maurier ad in the *Globe and Mail*, 21 December 1936.

personality types and character traits, a powerful and emulative message for women experiencing new social settings involving workplace, post-secondary institution, dance hall, or streetcar. Cigarette advertising, coupled with smoking in public, functioned symbolically to strengthen notions of political and personal empowerment for women. Cigarettes meshed well with urban living, integrating seamlessly into modern routines of leisure, work, romance, and family life. The cigarette-as-metaphor shaped vernacular understandings of fashion, body type, time, and personal finance, to name a few. In advertising and smoking behaviour, cigarettes ingratiated themselves with popular pastimes like bridge, poker, and bingo. In gift rebate catalogues, they shared space with desirable consumer goods like Gillette razors and ceramic tea pots. Here, as Kenneth Lipartito and others have argued, the work of business and cultural history effectively co-penetrate, as cigarette marketers laboured to discursively conflate particular brands with particular forms of popular culture, seen with devotees of both the NHL and Louise King.[198]

A recurring vein of marketing discourse involved descriptors such as "mild," "mellow," and "throat easy," which appeared often in advertising and on cigarette packages. A regular smoker might consume fifty or more cigarettes per day, producing side effects like coughing and throat irritation. Some in the trade drew from the alcohol industry's playbook and counselled "moderation" in cigarette smoking.[199] But the pharmacology of nicotine addiction (even if little understood then) propelled many to smoke more cigarettes than they may have wanted. Nicotine dependence and chain smoking – what made cigarette smokers such profitable repeat-business customers – produced unwanted side effects that clashed with the urbane, fashionable image of cigarettes framed by advertising and cinema. The tobacco industry's "remedy" for this came in the form of menthol and filtered cigarettes, both introduced in the 1930s. Menthol's prior therapeutic association with cold remedies, coupled with the cooler taste sensation of mentholated tobacco, was meant to appeal to those who worried about cold-like symptoms arising from smoking. Similarly, high-tech, modern filters promised to trap harmful particulates in cigarette smoke that diminished flavour and inflamed tissue. As a 1937 du Maurier ad proclaimed: when "you filter the smoke it's bound to be cleaner."[200] While sales of filtered brands declined in the 1940s, this ultimately proved short-lived. After news stories in the early 1950s linked cigarettes to lung cancer, the industry reintroduced filtered cigarettes to stunning effect: filtered brands in Canada would vault from 2 per cent of the market in 1952 to 55 per cent in 1962, buttressed again by forms of "health marketing" designed to reassure existing and prospective smokers.[201] As we shall see, the industry's later response to the postwar "cancer scare" was not novel, but one that drew upon the cultural lexicon of cigarette promotion dating back to the 1930s.

CHAPTER TWO

The Gift of Wartime Cigarettes

> The food was very acceptable but please, if you send anything, concentrate on cigarettes.
> — William Martyn, 8 February 1941[1]

> I was just thinking the other day and it was on what you could send me from Canada (1) Cigarettes (2) Noxzema (3) A can of peanut butter (4) Blue letter forms (5) Gum (6) and I could stand a turtle neck sweater for I really need them. (7) And more cigarettes.
> — Gordon Dennison, 20 March 1944[2]

INTRODUCTION

In 1940, Private James Baker of the Princess Patricia's Canadian Light Infantry arrived in England, where he would spend most of the next four years. A non-smoker, by late 1941 he was writing family members for cigarettes. It was his practice to "always carry a full packet of cigarettes," since "nothing helps break up the ice among people more than the offer of a cigarette." Among his peers, "nine out of ten" smoked cigarettes, "especially at night."[3] He later wrote to thank his grandfather for sending cigarettes: "my crew is extremely grateful to you because when they came we were completely out of smokes." A man in his unit, Baker noted, smoked "over 60 a day" and "going without [was] a bit hard on him."[4] Throughout the war, Baker's family and friends sent him many cigarette parcels and Baker regularly wrote back to thank them, sometimes effusively. While the professed abstainer derived no corporeal pleasure from these cigarettes (unlike the chocolates sent him), Baker understood their socio-cultural attributes. He offered smokes to acquaintances new and old, enabling him to navigate socially in a country with different customs and beset by rationing and goods shortages. He shared his cigarettes with fellow soldiers, often regular smokers contending with irregular supplies. In doing so, Baker fostered gratitude, camaraderie, and social cohesion among the men in his unit. His letters of thanks for Canadian cigarettes strengthened ties to family and friends back home. For Baker, donated cigarettes prompted acts of sharing, caring, and communication that strengthened social ties and group solidarity.

Cigarettes took on different meanings in the memoir of Stanley H. Winfield, a twenty-one-year-old in the Royal Canadian Air Force serving in occupied Germany in 1945. He was stationed in Gross Hehlen, a village 20 kilometres from Bergen Belsen – an irony not lost on Winfield, who was Jewish. Soon after his arrival, he recalled a visit to the town cinema, accompanied by Canadian and British soldiers. On the street were "dozens of displaced persons, mostly Jews evacuated from Belsen," who would wait for a soldier to "throw away a cigarette butt and then dash after it." Winfield was shocked to see fellow soldiers "purposely toss a butt into a dirty gutter or down a shallow drain so that the poor displaced persons must fish for it." Winfield later grew inured to "having about three men or children scramble after my cigarette butt." The cigarette black market flourished in Gross Hehlen, in which "our boys [were] acquiring articles worth hundreds and hundreds of dollars for practically nothing."[5] A Zeiss camera cost as little as five hundred Canadian cigarettes, or about two dollars when bought in Canada. Desperate Germans sold heirloom jewellery and precious stones for as little as one hundred cigarettes. For Winfield and other soldiers, the power of cigarettes lay in arbitrage trading: what cost pennies in Canada could sell for many multiples of that in wartorn Europe. Cigarettes were prized not only by desperate habituated smokers, but also for their role as de facto currency amid collapsed monetary systems and bankrupt treasuries. Soldiers traded cigarettes for food, clothing, medicine, sex – almost anything. Here the cigarette-laden soldier stood at the apex of an economic system at times rife with profiteering and social exploitation.[6]

These contrasting accounts by Baker and Winfield highlight the broad expanse of Canadian soldiers' experiences with cigarettes during the war. Cigarettes engendered acts of social benevolence and moral depravity. Cigarettes originating as a gift from a loved one might end up as scavenged butts in the hands of a Holocaust survivor. They travelled a course from monetized commodity to cherished token and sometimes back again. Wartime cigarettes inhabited multiple sites of power – social, psychological, economic – depending on the context of procurement, transmission, and consumption. Historians have documented the popularity of cigarettes during the Second World War. Cheryl Krasnick Warsh describes this period as the "apex of tobacco's positive image."[7] Matthew Hilton writes that cigarettes "helped to win the war for the nation," in the process establishing Britain as a "nation of smokers," as evidenced by the 80 per cent male smoking rate of the late 1940s.[8] Smoking rates similarly increased in Canada during the war, as seen by the doubling of per-capita cigarette sales between 1939 and 1945.[9] This chapter, however, deals less with domestic consumption than with cigarette use by Canadian soldiers abroad. Some 1.1 million Canadians donned uniforms during the war, more than half of whom served overseas.[10] Cigarettes were a ubiquitous feature of military life, integral to social and psychological aspects of training for and fighting war, as well as surviving in POW camps.

Unlike in the US Army, Canadian servicemen received most of their cigarettes outside of military-ration channels.[11] The bulk of cigarettes consumed by Canadian soldiers overseas were sent to them as gifts from family, friends, and various organizations. The tax-free status of gifted Canadian cigarettes made this form of giving affordable, and cigarettes soon became the most requested gift item among soldiers. Canadian soldiers responded to cigarette gifts with letters and postcards expressing gratitude, producing cycles of gift exchange and reciprocal obligation that benefited both donors and recipients. Gift exchange theory helps to explain this phenomenon. This theory originated with the work of Marcel Mauss, whose 1925 book *The Gift* examined widely shared reciprocal gift-giving practices and their role in strengthening the social fabric, mostly in pre-industrial societies. Gift sharing and forms of reciprocal obligation promoted communal values over individualist ones like utilitarianism. They enhanced social integration, shared norms, and common rituals. More recently, anthropologists and sociologists have built upon Mauss's ideas to explain how gift giving functions to integrate individuals into communities and social networks. David Cheal argues that gift giving in Western societies links "people together in small social worlds," countering the "pressures of large social systems that tend to pull people apart."[12] Jacques Godbout and Maurice Godelier adopt Maussian ideas to show how gifts and corresponding social protocols create and affirm social bonds and forms of cultural reproduction.[13] Most notably, Aafke E. Komter examines political studies on social solidarity and anthropological works on gift exchange in order to show how gift-generated gratitude functions as both moral virtue and as an integral "part of the chain of reciprocity" that strengthens social bonds. For Komter, "things-as-gifts, social relationships, community, and solidarity are inextricably tied to one another."[14] While anthropological and theoretical works on gift exchange are common, the same cannot be said for historical treatments of the topic, especially for the twentieth century.[15]

For Canadian soldiers abroad, gift cigarettes produced meanings and socio-cultural outcomes that differed from those of cigarettes acquired by purchase or military ration. Cigarettes-as-gifts generated letters of gratitude to friends and family, cementing transatlantic social ties. Cigarette fundraising and corresponding donations by community groups, businesses, service clubs, and schools in Canada strengthened the attachment of overseas soldiers to home towns or former workplaces. The strong preference of soldiers for Canadian cigarette brands articulated forms of national identity and patriotism. The common practice of sharing gift cigarettes among fellow soldiers fostered camaraderie and social cohesion in military units, enhancing, arguably, their fighting effectiveness.[16] Gift cigarettes, at times, entered the market economy, reflecting how gift-exchange practices and market systems sometimes co-penetrated. The meanings and social functions of cigarettes were not fixed; they sometimes changed markedly, even during the lifespan of a single carton. As Komter underscores, the changing contexts of human relationships serve as a starting point for determining the meaning of gifts: "It cannot be known in advance whether things are gifts or commodities. It depends on the nature of the social relationship within which things are exchanged."[17] This point, as we shall see, is especially germane for cigarettes in war-decimated Europe and in POW camps, where gift-exchange protocols and marketplace relations sometimes overlapped.

CIGARETTES AND THE HOME FRONT

In the Second World War, Canadian consumers experienced a vastly different regulatory landscape than seen during the Great War. Between 1914 and 1918, Ottawa adopted a largely laissez-faire approach to domestic consumption, avoiding most measures to control prices and constrain spending. As a consequence, wartime inflation was high, vaulting 43 per cent from 1914 to 1918.[18] The country mobilized relatively few resources for military production, which in 1918 comprised only 15 per cent of Canada's gross national product. During the Second World War, the federal government adopted a more interventionist course of action. In 1941, it imposed wage and price controls. Soon after, production bans were placed on consumer durables like automobiles, radios, and electric refrigerators. To ensure equitable distribution of staple goods, coupon rationing was launched in 1942 for items like sugar, coffee, tea, butter, and gasoline. Meat joined the list soon after. Beer, liquor, and wine sales were rationed, and curbs were placed on liquor advertising and tavern operating hours. Canadians planted victory gardens, dined in meatless restaurants, organized salvage drives, and bought war bonds, measures that helped dampen consumer spending and divert resources to military production.[19] These policies produced a remarkable national achievement: by 1945 military production accounted for one-half of Canada's gross national product. Inflation remained in check, rising only 19 per cent between 1939 and 1945. While, as Graham Broad argues, consumer spending after 1939 outpaced that of the Depression years, the many restrictions on home front consumption meant that Canadians "were forced to choose from a narrower range of sometimes inferior goods."[20] Given the full-employment economy, the promise of postwar bond redemptions, and the strong purchasing power enabled by low inflation, it was, arguably, a trade-off that most Canadians accepted willingly.

Notably, cigarettes and other forms of tobacco evaded most forms of state control on consumer spending. Ottawa did not regulate tobacco manufacturing or sales during the war, and tobacco was not rationed, unlike many other consumer goods.[21] Cigarettes, unlike spirits or cosmetics, were thought to enhance workplace performance and the psycho-social lives of soldiers overseas. The bright-leaf tobacco used in cigarettes was grown mainly in Canada and nearly all cigarettes were manufactured domestically. Thus the industry did not harm the country's trade balance or foreign exchange accounts. Taxation, however, was a different matter. Alongside hikes in personal and business income taxes, excise taxes on tobacco rose sharply during the war. The first wartime federal budget in June of 1940 imposed a new 10-cent-per-pound tax on raw leaf tobacco. The tax on cigarette papers jumped from two to five cents per 100 papers. Ottawa also doubled the excise tax on cigarettes, lifting it from $3 to $6 per 1,000 cigarettes.[22] Cigarette consumption, however, kept rising, which prompted Finance Minister James Ilsley to hike the excise tax to $10.50 per 1,000 cigarettes in 1943.[23] By 1944, Ottawa's take from a 35-cent cigarette package was about 20 cents.[24]

High tobacco taxes boosted the cigarette black market in Canada. In 1945, there were 3,226 police seizures of bootleg cigarettes, the highest tally since 1934.[25] Cheaper American cigarettes were smuggled into Canada and sold clandestinely, sometimes by organized crime elements. Navy personnel and other sailors acquired low-cost cigarettes in Newfoundland and US ports and sold them for profits when back in Canada. Canadian troops could buy tax-reduced cigarettes on military bases in Canada; on occasion, they sold these to civilians, though regimental orders forbade the practice.[26] Illicit cigarettes, however, formed only a small part of the domestic cigarette market during the war, as seen by the number of legal cigarettes sold in Canada for domestic use doubling between 1939 and 1945, rising from 7.1 billion to 14.2 billion.[27] With many good-paying jobs available, most smokers could afford the higher prices. Buying fully taxed cigarettes also resonated patriotically, as seen in this 1944 account of a "Mr. Smoker" lighting a fully taxed cigarette. By doing so he had "just contributed another cent to buy the implements of war." After a week of smoking he had financed "a steel helmet for a fighting Canadian," and after two weeks he had "smoked enough to buy an anti-tank mine." If he kept at it for a year he would bankroll a "2² trench mortar and twenty-five trench mortar bombs." At this point, "Mr. Smoker" could sit back and "watch the Nazis smoke."[28]

TOBACCO FOR THE TROOPS

When, in 1940, Tory MP Douglas Ross spoke of cigarettes in the House of Commons as "hardly in the category of luxuries" but "almost a necessity in the army," he affirmed a long-standing view of tobacco's role in military conflict.[29] For decades, tobacco had been sent to Canadian soldiers on the front lines. In 1885, tobacco companies provided cigars to Canadian soldiers fighting in the Northwest Rebellion. Macdonald Tobacco sent pipe and chewing tobacco to Canadians engaged in the Boer War in South Africa. During the Great War, Imperial Tobacco donated millions of cigarettes to organizations raising money to provision the Canadian Expeditionary Force with tobacco.[30] Tobacco's crucial importance to fighting troops was a common refrain in news stories and industry advertising during the war. One 1915 ad for Stag chewing tobacco featured men in an explosion-marred trench, along with a corporal's first-hand account: "What hurt us most was the poisonous gas, which made the air green and yellow, choking and poisoning men where they stood. Tobacco saved many lives in that battle ... Now whenever we notice the gas, we chew tobacco, which greatly helps."[31] A 1915 newspaper account described how an army doctor treated wounded men without morphine or other analgesics: "Every wounded man who came to our dressing station was given a cigaret, and then he didn't care how we hurt him dressing his wounds." He described a leg amputation in which the patient "asked first for a cigaret, and while we cut it off he didn't miss a puff, and never said a word."[32] A letter-to-the-editor writer declared that if a "man has given up his home and friends to fight among bombs, shrapnel, shells, and poisonous gases" he is entitled to "any bit of comfort" available from cigarettes.[33] Julia Henshaw, in a 1917 address to the Daughters of the

Empire, implored her audience to view cigarettes not as "a luxury or even a comfort," but as an "absolute necessity" for the troops overseas, especially wounded men who had "nothing to ease the pain and shock but a cigaret."[34] A military chaplain addressing the Presbyterian General Assembly described Canadian soldiers as "living in sodden trenches filled waist deep with mud and water," for whom cigarettes were their "only comfort."[35] Whether as psychological "comfort" amid the rats, shelling, and mud of the trenches or as medical aid in ramshackle operating theatres, tobacco was an "entitlement good," owed to soldiers for their profound and harrowing sacrifices.

Canadian troops in France and England were issued small sums of tobacco in their weekly rations. They could also buy discounted cigarettes at YMCA and Knights of Columbus canteens, with the most popular brands being Woodbine, Ruby Queen, and Gold Flake. To augment these supplies, newspapers organized fund-raising campaigns. Between 1915 and 1918, the Montreal *Gazette* raised nearly $200,000 to purchase some 25 million cigarettes and hundreds of thousands of packages of fine-cut and chewing tobacco for Canadian troops abroad.[36] After soldiers complained about the poor quality of the British cigarettes initially given to them, the *Gazette* contracted directly with Imperial Tobacco to have brands like Sweet Caporals and Old Chum sent directly to soldiers. Tobacco smoking, especially cigarettes, was a common sight in training camps and front-line trenches. Desmond Morton writes that "many soldiers routinely smoked fifty cigarettes a day."[37] Tim Cook similarly depicts tobacco use as pervasive, noting too how cigarette smoke masked the stench of "lingering poisonous gases, decomposing bodies, and the rankness of unwashed bodies" that permeated the trenches.[38] Jarrett Rudy's claim that the Great War conferred on the cigarette a "new legitimacy as a 'manly smoke'"[39] is reflected in one 1918 ad for Army Club cigarettes depicting a soldier set to go over the top of his trench, accompanied by this poem:

> When you're waiting for the minut[e]
>   To charge the blooming Hun,
> While the bullets singing over
>   Make you finger with your gun
> And you know that Fritz is waiting –

> Of course it will be a rub –
> But you'll feel a whole lot better
> If you've got an ARMY CLUB[40]

In addition to Army Club, military themes infused the advertising and package designs of cigarette brands like Rock City's "King George's Navy" and ITC's "Player's Navy Cut," the latter heavily promoted during the war.[41] In this vein, Macdonald Tobacco would later launch its "Canadian Legion" brand of cigarettes in 1937. The brand's packaging and advertising featured the name and crest of the Royal Canadian Legion, which received a share of the proceeds.[42]

Military themes in cigarette promotion were common after 1939 as well. Imperial Tobacco ran a "Salute to the Navy!" ad campaign for its Player's Navy Cut brand, which lauded the work of naval convoys in providing Britain with "supplies vital to the bastion of freedom."[43] The company commissioned artist Gordon Grant to make Turner-inspired paintings of military vessels, reproductions of which ran in ads for Player's.[44] Ads for "Wings" cigarettes depicted bombers and men in uniform.[45] Macdonald Tobacco's "Lassie" saluted proudly in ads, posters, and on packages.[46] Shown in full Scottish regalia, at times sword in hand, she was, as Warsh notes, a powerful female icon, portrayed as "muscular rather than fashionably thin." Lassie was one of the very few female personas shown in combat-like poses in ads or propaganda images.[47]

CIGARETTE FUNDRAISING

Given the experience of the Great War, it should not surprise that supplying soldiers abroad with cigarettes became a high priority for many during the Second World War. Ottawa's contribution here was largely fiscal: it waived federal taxes on cigarettes shipped abroad to Canadian servicemen and women. Thus a carton of three hundred cigarettes could be purchased and mailed overseas for just one dollar, less than half the fully taxed cost in 1943. Prepaid orders were sent to tobacco manufacturers, which then processed and shipped the cigarettes to designated soldiers abroad. Each shipment included a company-issued postcard with the address of the donor, enabling recipients to conveniently send thank-you messages. As early as February 1940, cigarette makers were advertising this tax-free option.[48] In one Imperial Tobacco ad, a soldier proclaimed "We Want Sweet Caps!" alongside a description of how one dollar could furnish a fighting man with three hundred Sweet Caporals or Winchesters.[49] Macdonald advertised similar terms for its British Consols, Export, and Legion brands.[50] While tax-free pipe and fine-cut tobacco were also available, cigarettes predominated in these ads. If during the Great War cigarettes were one of various types of tobacco used by soldiers, by 1939 they had become the default mode of smoking for Canadian troops.

Once again the provisioning of combat troops with cigarettes became a national duty, a profound obligation to provide "pleasure and comfort to those to whom we are now so indebted."[51] Moral obligation, patriotism, and heartfelt desire to support kin and kith combined to exalt cigarette giving as both virtuous and victory advancing.[52] This was evidenced by the many "cigarette funds" that operated during the war. The two leading national organizations were the Buckshee Fund and the Overseas Cigarette Fund, with the latter having sent over 73 million cigarettes by March 1944.[53] Other national bodies like the Imperial Order Daughters of the Empire and the Canadian Red Cross were similarly active.[54] The Women's Association of the Governor-General's Horse Guards was sending 40,000 cigarettes monthly in 1942.[55] Groups like the RCAF League of Canada and the Canadian Patriotic Club raised money for cigarette shipments by running events like bingos, bake sales, and cricket matches.[56]

Local communities and workplaces similarly took up this cause. Residents of Temagami, Ontario, raised $120 in 1941 for the Red Cross and the Soldier Cigarette Fund.[57] By April 1942, the Sons of England in Brampton had sent 830,000 cigarettes to local-area men stationed abroad.[58] The Shelburne Rotary Club held regular dances in order to send three hundred cigarettes monthly to local soldiers stationed in England.[59] The Ontario townships of Beverly and Ayr held "monster bingo games" and a carnival in 1943 to supply area men with cigarettes.[60] Similar bingo fundraisers were held in St Marys, Ontario (figure 2.1). The Mount Pleasant Lions Club in Vancouver held regular raffles to send three hundred cigarettes monthly to three hundred local-area residents serving overseas.[61] Major Rev. Mike Dalton, a Windsor-area clergyman stationed in Britain, drew upon his "Windsor friends" to raise money for cigarettes for the men in his regiment. By March 1942, Dalton had distributed about 50,000 cigarettes, which were in great demand since one cigarette "costs more in the Canteen than 2 cups of tea."[62] Employees in workplaces similarly contributed. Over the course of a year, workers at National Steel Car in Hamilton sent over 500,000 cigarettes "to our old employees" serving abroad.[63] A Vancouver company mailed 60,000 cigarettes as a Christmas present to members of the First Battalion Seaforth Highlanders fighting in Italy in 1943.[64] Maple Leaf employees in Edmonton sent cigarettes to former workers now in uniform. One of these, Steve Dwernichuk, wrote to express his gratitude by saying "I just lit a Sweet Cap now and is it ever good ... keep up the good work, as we are all trying to do our bit out here."[65] The Bloor District Business Men's Association in Toronto placed "cigarette bank" donation boxes in area stores to ensure that "every soldier, sailor or air force man who has enlisted from the district is supplied with cigarettes regularly."[66] Schoolchildren joined in. Students at Oakville High School put on theatrical performances in order to "buy cigarettes and chocolate bars" for seamen on the school's adopted ship, HMCS *Niagara*.[67] In 1944, Toronto's Forest Hill Public School held a medieval-themed "war tyme fayre," which raised $4,000 for cigarettes and "comfort parcels" for Canadian troops in Europe.[68] Since much of this cigarette largesse benefited area residents serving abroad, these actions affirmed local identity, communal solidarity, and strengthening ties between distant soldier and home community. For soldier recipients, these gift cigarettes symbolized the backing of entire communities and carried meanings and sentiments not found in canteen-bought cigarettes.

The role of cigarette fundraising in enhancing civic pride and local identity is exemplified by the case of Verdun, Quebec. In December 1940, city officials established the Mayor's Cigarette Fund (MCF) in support of Verdun soldiers who were serving overseas. Within a year, the MCF had surpassed the Red Cross as the city's most popular war charity, drawing widespread backing from community groups, churches, unions, and business organizations. MCF donation boxes were placed in cinemas, churches, and workplaces. Children ran lemonade stands and sold hand-made brooches for the MCF. Twice yearly, the fund sent cigarettes to some 6,300 service men and women.[69] This charity, more than any other in Verdun,

> **SOLDIERS' CIGARETTE BINGO**
>
> Proceeds to supply Cigarettes to
> Service Men Overseas
>
> **TOWN HALL, FRIDAY, JAN. 14th, '44**
> 8.30 SHARP
> First Game Free $3.00
>
> **20 Games for 25 cents - Prize $2.00**
> 4 Feature Games $5.   1 Feature Game $10.
> 3 Door Prizes $2.00 each.
>
> SPONSORED BY THE TOWN OF ST. MARYS
>
> Nº 38   Nº 38

2.1 During the Second World War, workplace and community fundraisers to send cigarettes to overseas Canadian soldiers were commonplace. Cigarette Fundraiser ticket from St Marys, Ontario, in 1944.

"expressed the community's commitment to the war and particularly to Verdunites' role in it."[70] Notably, the MCF drew support from the Société Saint-Jean Baptiste, the French Canadian nationalist group that rarely backed war-related causes.[71] The MCF, Serge Durflinger argues, promoted feelings of "wartime cooperation among French and English speakers and united them in a shared view of local and national patriotism. At the local, grassroots level, so clearly represented by the MCF, Verdun's war was based in community cooperation, not competition. Moreover, the MCF cemented ties between Verdunites on the home front and those on the battle front."[72] Cigarette donations serving as a transatlantic bond between Canada and the war front (where cigarettes were "scarce as hens' teeth") were also represented visually in cigarette fund advertising.[73]

CIGARETTES AND SOLDIERS OVERSEAS

RCAF flyer Francis Scandiffio, like tens of thousands of Canadian servicemen, spent years in Britain during the war. He passed the time in training, flying missions, socializing, writing friends and family, and lamenting the scarcity of Canadian cigarettes. Many of his wartime letters survive, shedding light on his many fixations with cigarettes. Drawing from one year of this correspondence (1942), we find Scandiffio telling his sister Esther in January 1942 that cigarettes were as "scarce as snowballs in heaven," and a constant source of frustration for him and fellow soldiers. He implored another sister, Millie, soon after to send him a few hundred cigarettes every week, for which, he joked, he would "buy you a Coca Cola" and "wash your parlor floor."[74] In June, he graciously thanked Millie for sending 1,000 cigarettes: "boy, am I ever glad, because I haven't had a cigarette from Canada for nearly a month or more." In October, he praised Esther and Millie for sending cigarettes, adding that he hoped the other men in his unit "would hurry up and get their parcels from home because they're so damn hard to satisfy." Despite his erratic supply, Scandiffio managed to send three hundred cigarettes to a Canadian cousin stationed in Ireland, who was "not having as much luck with the mail as I am."[75] Just before Christmas while on leave in London, Scandiffio, nearly out of cigarettes, dropped "in to see what the R.C.A.F. Overseas headquarters would do about it." They gave him three hundred cigarettes "to carry me over Xmas and New Years."[76]

Scandiffio's experiences with cigarettes would have been familiar to many Canadian soldiers in Britain. After each gift of cigarettes, he responded with a written expression of gratitude, typically to a family member or friend in Canada. He relied on people and organizations back home to supply many of his cigarettes, especially the sought-after Canadian brands. (English cigarettes, as discussed below, were derided as costly and foul tasting.) When received, Canadian cigarettes were routinely shared with friends and military colleagues, even if sometimes grudgingly. Canadian cigarettes were often scarce, but when "luck with the mail" ran strong there were periods of windfall, tempered in part by the social norms of sharing. Soldiers acquired Canadian cigarettes from a patchwork of sources: family, friends, Canadian-based cigarette funds, and organizations in Britain like Ontario House or the RCAF Overseas Headquarters. This ensemble of donors supplied soldiers with cigarettes well beyond that allowed by meagre ration allotments or costly canteen purchases. Donated Canadian cigarettes strengthened family networks, camaraderie in the ranks, and national patriotism, while also boosting individual morale.

More than chocolate, beer, or candy, cigarettes (especially Canadian ones) were integral to the sensual, psychological, and social experiences of preparing for and waging war.

GIFTS, GRATITUDE, AND SHARING

Canadian soldiers often expressed gratitude for their gifts of cigarettes, sometimes in superlative or melodramatic ways. "God bless you," wrote Karl Butler to his mother in early 1940 upon receipt of her cigarette parcel. Prior its arrival, Butler had been lying on his bunk "trying to figure out where the next cigarette was coming from when out of a clear sky the problem was solved."[77] Royal Canadian Navy member William Martyn thanked his father for cigarettes by saying: "boy! are they appreciated," and later described another cigarette shipment as "exceedingly generous."[78] After getting cigarettes from his aunt, Henry Davis wrote her to say that he "certainly live[d] to get parcels from home," especially since it was hard to get any "chocolate or cigarettes over here." On 7 June 1944, Davis wrote his mother from England, amid the "turmoil" of D-Day, to thank her for cigarettes: "I never appreciated anything so much in all my life. It's a relief to have a good Canadian cigarette & plenty of them. I want to thank you from the bottom of my heart."[79] That same month Geoffrey Turpin profusely thanked his family for a cigarette parcel, "which I had been praying for, and Winchesters too, which I haven't seen for a long time."[80] From a Canadian Army hospital in England, Private Kinnart wrote to thank the Ontario government for cigarettes, noting that "the boys in the hospital here hope you keep up the good work."[81]

Canadian troops in combat zones were especially grateful for cigarettes. Letters and stories in the *Canadian Cigar and Tobacco Journal* describe tobacco-related survival episodes, like that of a soldier bending over to light a cigarette and missing incoming shrapnel or gunfire.[82] One Canadian officer, blinded in North Africa, recounted how "cigarettes made life more bearable" while he was unable to read.[83] Betty Gentles gave her RCAF beau, Bill Maitland, a silver cigarette case, which later "saved his life" when it stopped a piece of anti-aircraft flak.[84] RCAF gunner Stuart Vallieres lay bleeding heavily on the night ground in Germany, having parachuted from a crashing plane. Realizing that he would "probably bleed to death" if not found soon, Vallieres lit cigarettes in the dark to attract the searching Germans, who later saved his life with a blood transfusion and surgery.[85] Francis Scandiffio wrote his sister in May 1942 about a recent close call: "There I was – on my back, 10,000 feet up and no instruments, three Huns on my tail and only four rounds left so what did I do? You're right, Esther, I nonchalantly lit a cigarette and escaped in the smokescreen. Whew! ... Thanks for the cigs. You're too kind."[86] Arthur Haley, an Army stretcher bearer in northern France in 1944, recounted that "the very first thing" he did when reaching a wounded soldier was to place a lit cigarette in his mouth in order to alleviate panic attacks.[87] RCAF pilot James Goodson, who later in the war joined the US Army Air Force, was shot down over Germany in 1944 and captured by the Gestapo. Told he would soon be executed, he asked for something to smoke and was given a cigar. He blew smoke rings, which intrigued his German interrogator. "I started teaching him how to blow smoke rings. And that started a bond between us." The interrogator then opted to send Goodson to a POW camp instead of a firing squad.[88] Privates W.J. Brooks and R. Graham wrote jointly to thank "the People of Ontario" for donated cigarettes. Fighting in France in 1944, they relayed that "when things get tough a cigarette is the first thing we reach for and we can do without eats so long as we have our smokes."[89] Similarly, Major-General R.F.L. Keller wrote to thank the Ontario government for a shipment of 20,000 cigarettes, received in Normandy in July 1944: "they reached me during a very savage battle and thus I was able to put them in my scout-car and take them right out to where they were needed most – and at a time like that, a smoke is the only relaxation a soldier can have."[90]

Imperial Tobacco understood the emotional appeal and marketing potential of gratitude. Advertising its cigarettes for overseas soldiers in 1944, it proclaimed: "If you could glance through our file of grateful letters from servicemen overseas, you would appreciate more fully your opportunity to enjoy – *at any time* – the cigarettes which are Canada's favourites over here, over there, everywhere."[91] The *Canadian Cigar and Tobacco Journal* confirmed this when noting that thousands of thank-you messages were sent daily to "individuals, organizations and clubs that have generously sent cigarettes to Canadian fighting men stationed in every corner of the globe." While often taken for granted in Canada, cigarettes meant "much more than that to Canada's fighting forces on foreign soils. They are one of the great morale builders and comforts that the men receive. Letters from service men and surveys made in overseas camps show that cigarettes rank second in their choice of things they want from home. Letters, of course, hold first spot on their lists."[92] By sending cigarettes, Canadians offered material support for family members, friends, and local residents serving abroad. They also demonstrated their moral worth by giving to those who had given the higher gift of enlistment for overseas service. This cycle of giving, gratitude, and reciprocal obligation in turn produced heartfelt notes of thanks and recognition, highly valued by both resident Canadians and soldiers abroad (figure 2.2, figure 2.3).

Once received, cigarettes were commonly shared with fellow soldiers. Jack Andrews, in his account of RCAF service, noted that "cigarettes were usually shared around."[93] When James Baker received a cigarette parcel in 1942 from the "The Overseas Birthday Club," he doled them out to army mates who "were most welcome."[94] Infantryman David Simpson joined a new Army regiment fighting in Normandy in 1944 and asked about buying cigarettes. A fellow soldier then "threw me three hundred," saying only that Simpson try to return the favour when his next batch of cigarettes arrived. For Simpson, this incident carried profound significance: "I never had been involved with this type of friendship, because I was just new, you know. And so that really struck me. And it was always that way. The regiment came first and the people in the regiment. And it was really strong."[95] Karl Butler recounted comically what transpired after getting a parcel of candy and Canadian cigarettes: "The gang over here almost mobbed me. I salvaged half a nut bar and one [cigarette] package of Spuds and the rest went among the crowd." Soon after, however, "one of the boys from Picton received a package and I did better on his than I did on my own. A few minutes before he had no smokes, so I gave him a package of mine."[96] On another occasion, RCAF member Arthur Morlidge asked his family to "keep the cigarettes coming," since he received only thirty cigarettes weekly in his rations: "That is 4 2/7 cigarettes a day. Subtract that half cigarette for butts, three for a man's three bumming friends & you only have one cigarette a day."[97] Cigarette sharing, by fostering sociability, facilitated greater co-operation among these men.[98]

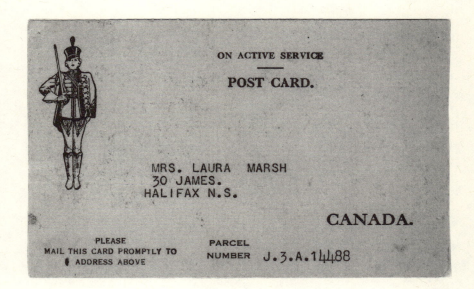

2.2 *Above and following page* Gift cartons of cigarettes came with return address–filled postcards from the sender, allowing soldiers to conveniently express their gratitude. Imperial Tobacco acknowledgment postcard, n.d.

no cigs from C.B. yet — Jan 7th —

Dear Laura: thanks a
the cigs I had none before
they came how are you dear
ad lonesome for you be g[?]
when I come ba[ck]
not before lov[e] my l[ove]
you and the children
Always Yours (Honey Jo)

R.C.A.F. Overseas Records 12-1-42

Dear Mother & Dad.
          Received your parcel of cigarettes
today and thanks very much as they are certainly
appreciated and hard to get here. Going up to
Dorncaster on Saturday so will write you from
there. Still waiting for letters from you and
Dorothy. Best of luck for 1942 Love to all
                                    Ray.

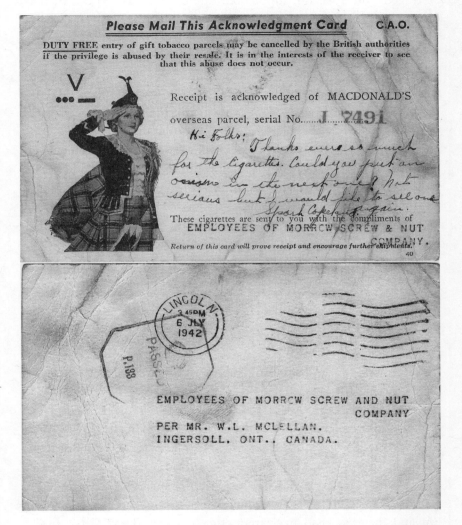

2.3 Cigarettes as gifts cemented bonds between giver and recipient, fostering "feelings of connectedness" between soldiers and family and friends back home. Macdonald Tobacco acknowledgment postcard, July 1942.

Tragedy, on occasion, supplanted humour in this respect. In 1943, Harold Hall was fighting in Sicily when he was concussed by a shell: "all I could remember [wa]s the chap who got hit the worst; he wanted a cigarette." Hall give him one and tried to comfort him by saying, "You're going to be alright," to which the man replied, "No, I've had it."[99] Richard S. Malone, a brigade major in the First Division, had a similar experience in Sicily. He encountered a group of Canadian soldiers injured by shrapnel, one of whom lay dying: "blood was oozing out of the ragged holes in his chest wall. He was conscious, but I knew there was nothing I could do except pull the shirt back over the fatal wounds." The dying soldier asked Malone to care for the others, "but could he have a cigarette first?" Malone gave him one and tended to another wounded man. "I glanced back at the young officer. He had taken only a couple puffs on the cigarette and then slipped away … without a whimper."[100] Cigarette sharing assumed both waggish and sombre forms, boosting esprit de corps in the barracks and serving as last rite for dying men in battle.

"NOTHING LIKE A CANADIAN CIGARETTE"

Among soldiers' various complaints about cigarettes, two stood out: Canadian cigarettes were too often scarce and English cigarettes afforded very poor substitutes.[101] It was, as Edward Loney wrote in 1944, "either a feast or a famine with [Canadian] cigarettes," if too often the latter.[102] William Martyn, on HMS *Indomitable*, remarked that "scarcity is felt" when he attempted to get Canadian cigarettes while in port.[103] Wilson Orval lamented in February 1944 that he had had no cigarettes since Christmas. Another soldier complained to his mother about not having enough cigarettes in England; the few Canadian cigarettes that had arrived provided "a big lift & that's about all we live for over here."[104] William Watson was "not short of anything except cigarettes," imploring his correspondent to "please send some as soon as possible."[105] The shortage of Canadian cigarettes became more galling after the arrival of American soldiers in England in 1942, who, as one observer noted, "had far more cigarettes and pay than the other forces."[106] In 1944 there were calls to replace Canada's "gift cigarette" procurement system with one in which tax-free cigarettes were distributed

The Gift of Wartime Cigarettes

through military ration channels, similar to the method used by the Americans.[107] Complaints about cigarette shortages prompted Canada's postmaster general and the minister of National Defence to pledge in June 1944 to speed up the delivery of Canadian cigarettes to troops overseas.[108]

In the absence of Canadian cigarettes, Canadian soldiers turned despairingly to English cigarettes, often made from inferior tobacco and filler ingredients owing to wartime shortages.[109] Canadians often complained about their high cost,[110] unfamiliar texture, and awful taste. Edward Bryer described English cigarettes as "drier and not like ours at all."[111] Gordon Dennison maintained that "you can hardly smoke them for they are so hard on the throat";[112] William Watson dismissed them as "really lousy."[113] In addition to "cost[ing] a fortune," Albert Gould held that "English fags [were] horrible" and "terrible."[114] For Harry Hansell, they were "just coffin nails," so "lousy" that he went "back to [his] pipe."[115] Franklin Hamil of the 48th Highlanders later recalled how much he despised English "Victory" cigarettes while fighting in Italy; to demonstrate how bad they were, he later said, he need only "hand a Victory cigarette to someone, tell them that's the cigarette we Canadians in Italy were given and I ask him to smoke it."[116] Fighting in France in 1944, Bill Turpin could get only "Limey" cigarettes, which kept him going, but, for him, there was "nothing like a Canadian cigarette."[117]

The many positive portrayals of Canadian cigarettes by soldiers constituted low-key affirmations of national pride, a form of consumer nationalism compatible with civic nationalist values like collective sacrifice and patriotic duty.[118] A similar phenomenon exists more recently with Tim Hortons and the Canadian Armed Forces, seen especially during the recent war in Afghanistan. When Tim Hortons opened an outlet on the Canadian military base in Kandahar in 2006, it was heralded as bringing a familiar, reassuring slice of Canadiana to an inhospitable war zone. Tim Hortons campaigns like "Buy a Cup for a Soldier" championed the gift of quintessential Canadian coffee as providing both creature comforts and "taste-of-home" equanimity for the men and women serving abroad. For these troops, Tim Hortons coffee and baked goods constituted reminders of and connections to Canada, articulating forms of national identity and patriotism via the embrace and consumption of an iconic brand.[119] During the Second World War, this type of consumer nationalism involved the product category of "Canadian cigarettes," rather than particular brands or companies.

Periods of cigarette "famine" were on occasion displaced by times of "feast." By 1942, more soldiers reported receiving 1,000-cigarette parcels rather than the 300-cigarette ones more commonly sent earlier in the war.[120] In August 1942, Peter Scandiffio received 1,300 cigarettes in the span of a few days, and another soldier wrote of getting "1,200 cigarettes the other day, all at once."[121] Scandiffio wrote that he was "almost swamped with parcels ... with yours and Donny's coming in together with 1,000 cigarettes from Ann and Mike. In no time at all I'll be able to corner the cigarette market."[122] Scandiffio was joking, but Canadian soldiers on occasion sold surplus cigarettes while in Britain. Alfred Nelson asked his mother for cigarettes in December 1942 so that he could "cash in on them, as I'm not a strong smoker and they bring a fair price."[123] William Bell, in the RCAF's 404th Squadron stationed in Scotland, wrote his parents: "I sold the cigarettes I had, except what I gave away, but could sell another thousand quite easily, so you can take $2.50 out of my allowance and I'll make $7.50 on it." Bell simultaneously gave away and sold cigarettes, highlighting his dual involvement in gift-exchange and marketplace practices. On this matter, Bell wrote his mother again in July 1942: "Can also sell any amount of cigarettes you'll take the trouble to send, so take some of my money and send me a few thousand. I have guys from the R.A.F. [Royal Air Force] asking for them. They give 1'6 or about 35 cents for 25 of them so I can do O.K. on them. If you send me a box later on put in a small can of condensed milk, a can of coffee, a carton of gum. However, if you send the cigs I can buy those things with the profits."[124] For the arbitrageur Bell, tax-free cigarettes that cost one dollar in Canada sold for about $4.20 to his British buyers. While lucrative, these margins paled in comparison to those seen later across the English Channel.

CANADIANS IN THE NETHERLANDS

For many Canadian servicemen, much of their time spent in active conflict took place in the Netherlands. After helping to liberate northeastern France and much of Belgium in September and October of 1944, the First

Canadian Army crossed into the southern Netherlands. The Battle of the Scheldt, in the southwest of the Netherlands, ended in November after entrenched German defences were painstakingly uprooted, enabling the Belgian port of Antwerp to supply the Allied war effort. Following a winter layover in the south of the country, Canadian forces moved east to invade Germany in February 1945. In April, the First and Second Canadian Corps launched operations to liberate the western and northeastern parts of the Netherlands still under German occupation. After overcoming stiff German resistance, a truce was reached on 28 April to allow food shipments to reach the many starving residents of Rotterdam and Amsterdam. More than 7,600 Canadians died fighting to liberate the Netherlands between October 1944 and May 1945, a degree of national sacrifice which animates the special relationship that has existed between the Netherlands and Canada since the war.[125]

Cigarettes form part of this story, both before and after the country's liberation, as do the social customs of sharing and gratitude. Steven Mulder, a Dutchman from Groningen liberated by Canadian forces in mid-April 1945, wrote in his diary of the many types of Canadian cigarettes ("Winchester, Goldflake, Navy Cut") that were handed out by Canadian soldiers to the exuberant, appreciative Dutch. Mulder then described the following encounter:

> Tonight I spoke to a Canadian captain (3 stars on his epaulets). He said that the Canadians were 100% volunteers, the only country in the world without conscription. He enjoyed fighting in occupied countries and to see people cheer them on. But he thought it troubling that the Canadians always had to fight, while the English served as occupation troops. After having liberated France, Belgium, and the Netherlands, he hoped to go to Denmark, after which he hoped to go home in 3 months. He receives 2000 cigarettes per month: 1000 from his wife, and 1000 from the "firm." He smokes 20 cigarettes per day and gives away the rest. The best tobacco is for the army. The Canadian people get a lesser quality. Now, on Saturday, he's reading the papers that were printed in London on Thursday. The soldiers and officers are almost impossible to distinguish, except for the textile stars on the epaulets.[126]

This account is noteworthy. Mulder spoke English well and he socialized with many Canadians. In the midst of his laudatory description of the captain and of Canadian soldiers in general (volunteer status, fighting prowess, close affinity between officers and rank and file), he singles out the captain's cigarette habits, how he gave away most of his supply, some 1,400 cigarettes shared monthly. Magnanimous cigarette sharing became one of the virtues of Canada's fighting forces.

Similar accounts were recorded during the heady days of Dutch liberation in spring 1945. Jeanne Teding van Berkhout-Tutein Nolthenius visited Harskamp, a Canadian military camp near Apeldoorn, soon after the area was liberated in April. She reported that "all those Canadians were giving cigarettes away."[127] Historian Michiel Horn's early childhood memory of the First Canadian Corps entering Baarn in early May 1945 is of soldiers distributing cigarettes among cheering crowds and of Horn collecting the empty cigarette packages, for which he would "never forget the image on it: a bearded sailor," referring to Player's Navy Cut.[128] Photos of these celebratory days depict "extraordinarily generous" Canadian servicemen doling out cigarettes to jubilant civilians and Canadians and Dutch smoking happily together.[129] In one photo, a Canadian soldier shakes hands with a smiling Dutchman on a bike, each with a cigarette in his mouth.[130] During the initial post-liberation period, "friendly relations between soldiers and civilians were encouraged," with "one of the best methods" for achieving this goal being the "offering [of] cigarettes."[131] Fittingly, the cigarette packages bearing these offerings to the Dutch people carried notices, in bold red letters, stating: "GIFT: To Canadian Troops on Active Service. Not for Re-Sale."[132] What originated as gifts from friends and family in Canada were in turn shared with Dutch civilians, not unlike what had happened previously among Canadian soldiers in troop barracks or on battlefields. Such forms of sharing highlight what Avner Offer calls "indirect reciprocity," whereby the original donor is not the immediate beneficiary of reciprocal exchange associated with gift giving.[133]

Cigarette sharing celebrated and symbolized the victory over Nazism, with the "V for Victory" index and middle fingers now clamped around a cigarette. The practice served as secular acts of communion, bringing together two peoples – Canadian servicemen and Dutch civilians – who had experienced extreme hardship and collective sacrifice for a common cause. In 1945, the Dutch government partially repaid this debt of gratitude with a gift of 100,000 tulip bulbs for Canada, with tens of thousands more bulbs also sent in later years. These donations initiated the Canadian Tulip Festival in 1953, since held annually each spring in Ottawa. While today tulips are the "flower that symbolizes an historic friendship between peoples,"[134] in the Netherlands during the spring of 1945 the symbolic markers of bi-national friendship were most often cigarettes.

By the summer of 1945, however, Canadian soldiers had begun to sell their cigarettes for profit. This occurred in part because of delays in repatriating Canadians due to the shortage of transport vessels. In May 1945 about 170,000 Canadian soldiers were in the Netherlands. By August, only 59,000 had shipped out to Canada. As late as December, some 10,000 Canadian soldiers remained in the Netherlands, many embittered by the prolonged stay. The Canadian presence was also boosted by Canadian soldiers serving in occupied Germany who took their leaves in the Netherlands, typically in Amsterdam.[135] Horn argues that while Canadian soldiers had been "initially generous with their cigarettes," they gradually came to "ask for more than gratitude" for their cigarettes, especially after they realized their commercial value. High inflation coupled with weak public confidence in paper currency meant that by mid-1945 cigarettes routinely functioned as a "reserve currency in the black market," used to purchase other goods.[136] Canadian cigarettes were at the centre of this black market, in large part because few other types were available before Dutch tobacco factories were again operational.[137] According to Horn, 1,000 cigarettes, which cost three dollars back in Canada, could net as much as $400 worth of Dutch guilders or comparable goods on the black market. The head of the Canadian Army in the Netherlands, Lieutenant-General Guy Simonds, wrote in a 1946 report that the "great majority" of Canadians troops in Holland "habitually sold cigarettes to the civilian population."[138]

With the proceeds from cigarette sales, Canadian soldiers bought expensive valuables which they shipped back home. They also lived well in the taverns and dance halls of Amsterdam. When RCAF member Stanley Winfield went to Amsterdam for leave in 1945 he brought along lots of cigarettes. In a dance hall his first night there, he and a friend "surveyed the assortment of Dutch girls who had volunteered to act as hostesses that night." They met two women who "became our companions for the entire three days," which were filled with "movies, swimming, dancing and even horseback riding." The cost to Winfield for this two-person, three-day sojourn? About four dollars, or one thousand Canadian cigarettes "sold on arrival at two [Dutch] guilders per cigarette."[139] The Dutch women who dated Canadian soldiers were well supplied with cigarettes, which they often resold or shared with friends and family.

The social economy of cigarettes was even mentioned in the visitor's guide, *All About Amsterdam*, published in 1945 for Canadian and British soldiers on leave in Amsterdam. Along with descriptions of Dutch history, art, and "doing a pub-crawl," the guide explained the country's cigarette situation for military visitors:

> If during the first few days you have been besieged for cigarettes – please forgive us. If the people have tried to exchange their watches and camaras [sic] for tobacco, please forget it. Before the war, due to the excellent tobacco crop, imported from our overseas empire, Holland was a smoker's paradise. Cigarettes and cigars of all qualities were manufactured here and sold and exported at very reasonable prices. Before you came we were hungry and oppressed, but the tobacco-loving people were also starving for cigarettes.[140]

A cartoon in the guide, titled "The Amsterdam Kid Who Didn't Want a Cigarette," dryly lampooned the perceived Dutch desperation for tobacco. In it a visiting soldier responds incredulously to a Dutch youngster who does not pester him for cigarettes.[141] The Dutch obsession with cigarettes was also depicted in other cartoons of the time. In one ("When I Drop a Cigarette in Holland!") Dutch men are shown fighting each other over a cigarette dropped by a Canadian soldier (figure 2.4).

Tobacco black markets and scenes of scavenging for cigarette butts were not unique to the Netherlands. US Army historian Forrest Pogue witnessed a thriving cigarette black market in France during the winter of 1944–45. Members of a US Army railway supply company had bribed officials to siphon off military-issued cigarettes for sale in the French black market. For a time they were so successful that GI cigarette rations were temporarily suspended.[142] American soldiers could buy a carton of cigarettes for one dollar in military canteens and resell them for ten dollars.

The Gift of Wartime Cigarettes

2.4 A cartoon depicting a Canadian soldier dropping a cigarette in the Netherlands in 1945. Canadian troops stationed there after the war were well supplied with cigarettes, unlike most Dutch citizens.

The soldier's musette bag, Pogue wrote, was "used so often to transport black market items that it was universally known as 'the black market bag.'" In parts of Paris, he observed, "ragged old men and women" jumped on, and sometimes fought over, cigarette butts discarded by soldiers. The salvaged tobacco was then dried, rolled into cigarettes, and sold on the black market.[143] Charles Lynch, reporting for the *Toronto Daily Star* in October 1945, described how a cigarette in Berlin could fetch the equivalent of 40 cents. "Cigarettes," he wrote, were "regarded as the currency in nearly all black market transactions."[144] A historical account of postwar displaced persons in Europe describes how "armies of children searched the streets for cigarette butts; waiters collected their patrons' still-smoking discards; and everyone seemed prepared to pounce on the soldier's tossed 'cig.'"[145] The unbridled economic power of cigarettes in places like postwar Berlin, Amsterdam, and Paris produced crime syndicate profiteering and regular displays of human degradation.

"CIGARETTES WERE BETTER THAN MONEY"

Cigarettes factored prominently in the social and economic organization of prisoner-of-war (POW) camps during the war. Canadians often sent cigarettes to Canadian POWs, actions supported by international agreement and federal government policy. After the capture of a Canadian serviceman, Ottawa notified his family that "the official next of kin only may forward a personal parcel and this once every three months. However, cigarettes, books, games, etc. are not considered personal parcels and may be sent at any time by anyone through the duly licensed dealers."[146] These items were sent to the Red Cross, which coordinated their delivery to individual POWs. Cigarettes sent to POWs cost less than those shipped to non-detained soldiers, since both postage fees and federal taxes were waived. Only 76 cents was needed to send three hundred cigarettes to a POW in Europe; better still, $1.90 provided 1,000 cigarettes (figure 2.5).[147] German officials, Jeffrey A. Keshen argues, "generally respected the Geneva Convention,"[148] meaning it was likely that most of the cigarettes sent to the nearly 8,000 Canadian POWs held by Germany during the war were in fact received. (This was not the case for Canadian POWs under Japanese rule.)

The newsletters of organizations advocating for POWs, which were sent to the families of POWs, carried cigarette ads. "Just like a breath of Canadian air," read one by Imperial Tobacco in October 1943, "Sweet Caps will cheer our boys in Axis prison camps with thoughts of home – of Canada – *of you!*"[149] Canadian POWs wrote letters to family and friends asking for cigarettes and thanking them for prior offerings. Some of these letters, in anonymous form, were later reprinted in POW newsletters. In one from early 1944 a POW describes how "parcels of sunlight" had lifted his spirits. In "the first few months everything looked black and the future held no hope. Then food, clothing, books, games and cigarettes began to come in from the Red Cross and the world became full of sunshine again."[150] Another POW letter writer underscored the uplifting effect of cigarettes on morale: "Just as my cigarettes were all gone, three cig. parcels came through for me this week – who says luck is against me?"[151] Jack LeRoy, captured in Sicily in 1943, was more blunt in his assessment while writing to his sis-

2.5 For Canadian prisoners of war, donated cigarettes raised morale and served as a de facto currency in the camps, often traded for food, clothing, and other necessities. Macdonald ad, ca 1943.

ter: "Don't bother sending over anything but smokes, if possible. Anything else is just a waste of money."[152]

Canadian POWs in Germany were at times awash in cigarettes. John Colwell spent years in Stalag Luft III, a POW camp in Sagan, Germany (where he also played a planning role in "The Great Escape"). As detailed in his diary, Colwell received a total of 4,500 cigarettes between February and May 1944, an average of 45 cigarettes per day. His cigarette donors included the Toronto Overseas League, BC House, Vancouver's Castle Hotel, Toronto Hamper Fund, Victoria Overseas League, POWRA Montreal, and various friends and family. Colwell also received soap, chocolate, biscuits, and canned sardines, but, by far, the most common gift item was cigarettes.[153] Captured in the Dieppe Raid in 1942, Lance-Corporal Thomas Denek spent nearly three years in a German POW camp. When liberated in March 1945, he described cigarettes and camp life to a journalist: "We didn't need to buy cigarettes, we were cigarette millionaires, thanks to the swell way the home front behaved. Cigarettes were tax free and folks poured them in. Each of us averaged from 600 to 2,000 butts monthly."[154] Canadian merchant seaman Gordon Omstead, interned in a POW camp near Bremen, Germany, later described how cigarettes "were worth a fortune – you could buy anything with them; I gathered that they could even buy sex." Omstead managed well, having enough cigarettes to trade for a contraband radio to listen to war news on the BBC.[155]

Canadian POWs routinely shared their cigarettes. Norah Foster recalled how her husband, a Royal Air Force gunner in a POW camp in Italy, depended a "great deal" on cigarettes and food parcels from his Canadian and American counterparts. When an "airman received a parcel it was the custom for him to go round the hut (about 48 men to a hut) and deposit a cigarette on each bed."[156] For Canadian and Allied POWs under the harsh rule of the Japanese military, single cigarettes were often "shared by several men, despite urgent warnings from the medical officers against this mouth-to-mouth sharing because of the likelihood of spreading dysentery and diphtheria." While such "sharing may have been unhygienic," Charles Roland argues that it had "survival and morale value," which, for many POWs, trumped health concerns.[157] Cigarettes boosted morale in other ways. RCAF member Paul Ramage, in Stalag Luft III, helped organize a carnival for fellow POWs and guards, the centrepiece being a "Swami" who walked on hot coals and nails. (The "Swami" was in fact a double amputee with partial wooden legs, which, rather comically, ignited briefly during the performance.) Admission was paid in cigarettes or chocolate bars. The event likely raised morale more so than it did smokes or sweets. "After all expenses," Ramage wrote, "we had 200 cigarettes and four chocolate bars," which were then used to "buy eggs to keep the Swami happy" and to "return the sheets to the kitchen with appropriate bribes."[158] Cigarettes here operated as currency, but one that served the collective goal of boosting esprit de corps rather than accumulating private capital.

Cigarettes in POW camps typically served as a functional currency, enabling forms of economic exchange. The value of camp items was set in cigarettes. Labour tasks – even chores done for others – were measured in cigarettes. Cigarettes provided a mechanism for deferred payment, allowing credit to be issued and later repaid when the next cigarette parcel arrived. Even gambling losses were tallied in cigarette form.[159] Such an economic system provided tangible benefits to Canadian POWs. They used cigarettes to strike deals with German guards for larger rations and sought-after items like potatoes and bread.[160] Paul Ramage described how many German guards "were bribable with goodies such as cigs and chocolates." Thomas Denek told a reporter how in his POW camp, "money couldn't buy anything, but cigarettes were better than money," noting that "guards often would offer to do special favors for one of our cigarettes."[161] The cigarette economy could also produce feelings of bitterness and resentment. A non-smoking "Canadian officer from Kitchener" in a German POW camp sold his cigarettes for the price-gouging sum of "$60 a package of 20." The buyers thought it better "to pay the heavy price demanded than to part with any of our meagre food rations." The Canadian officer, according to a fellow POW, then "failed to add to his popularity by dreaming out loud of the trip he was going to make after the war on the money he had received for cigarettes which hadn't cost him a cent."[162]

The most unsettling accounts of cigarettes as currency involved POW camps run by the Japanese. There, as Roland notes, cigarettes soon transitioned from being a "normal commodity to that of currency."[163] Lt Col. W.J. Home, commanding officer of the Royal Rifles of Canada imprisoned in Hong Kong, described a package of Canadian cigarettes as being "worth their weight in gold," which, in practice, meant about twenty duck eggs.[164] One Hong Kong detainee traded a gold tooth for two packages of cigarettes. Half a cigarette bought a little "sweet sauce or an issue of black China tea." A whole cigarette bought a bun and two or three cigarettes some stew. Incredibly, emaciated POWs traded their food for cigarettes.[165] Ray Squires, a Canadian medical sergeant in a Japanese camp, estimated that 40 per cent of POWs exchanged bread and rice for cigarettes, valued, ironically, for their ability to reduce hunger pangs.[166] Squires also witnessed desperate Canadian POWs "bumming cigarettes and scrambling for butts discarded – often as deliberate enticements to humiliation – by the Japanese guards." Even after their liberation, former POWs continued to use cigarettes as currency. When a group of recuperating ex-POWs in Niigata, Japan, "ran out of 'money' they sent someone back to camp for more American cigarettes." These men never left their hotel rooms, as one later recalled: "The Japanese girls bathed us, and fed us, and what have you ... We initially paid with yen but we ended up paying with blankets and cigarettes."[167]

The far-reaching power of cigarettes is perhaps best illustrated by the case of RCAF flyer John McGuire Taylor, imprisoned in Stalag Luft III in Sagan, Germany. When the advancing Soviet Army forced the evacuation of the camp in January 1945, Taylor, along with some 11,000 POWs and their German guards, began marching west in the bitter cold and snow. Their meagre rations had to be eaten frozen. A few days later Taylor's group arrived in the town of Freibaldau. There, the "the guards lost control" and "in no time we had corrupted the town with cigarettes," easily so since "the German civilian only get 2 a day!" Taylor and other POWs traded "plenty of cigarettes" with a German family for a meal of soup, bread, and apples. The German civilians and POWs also exchanged home addresses, suggesting the melding of gift giving and market-exchange practices. Taylor and fellow POWs continued marching west, sleeping in fields at night and carrying little besides cigarettes, which proved priceless: "Cigarettes are the most valuable thing here. Only yesterday I heard that someone had paid $20 for 200. After the first three weeks the majority had run out. I have luckily brought about 1000 cigarettes & 2 lbs of Tobacco & so have managed very well. It's incredible being short after the thousands that we had in Sagan." By this point, the German guards had "given up any attempt to feed us," and, for the duration of the march, Taylor and others lived on food acquired from local farmers, for which "we bartered cigarettes."[168] That cigarettes played no small part in Taylor surviving this harrowing ordeal may register ironically with present-day observers, cognizant of the product's dire health record. But, as we have seen, Taylor's gruelling trek was but one of countless instances in which donated cigarettes enabled Canadian soldiers to endure, even survive, the physical trials and psychic traumas of war.

CONCLUSION

Writing to his family from the Netherlands in October 1944, Elmer Bell reflected on his experience with smoking while in the army: "We seem to smoke an awful lot more here than in civil life. I don't know why that is but it is so."[169] (The author Paul Fussell, an infantryman in the US Army during the war, was more blunt about smoking's appeal: "Let it suffice to note that anyone in the services who did not smoke cigarettes was looked on as a freak.")[170] Certain factors explain the ubiquity of cigarette smoking among Canadian troops. Bell and his fellow smokers were part of a long tradition, dating back to at least the 1880s, of supplying tobacco to Canadian troops at war, whether via military rations, tobacco companies, benevolent organizations, or friends and families. Press accounts portrayed cigarettes as essential items for overseas servicemen, both instrumentally for winning the war and morally as recognition of self-sacrifice and service to nation. Lightweight, compact, and portable, cigarettes aligned well with the logistical imperatives of waging highly mobile military campaigns. On a psychological level, many believed that smoking eased the sometimes crippling anxieties produced by war, whether as panic attack while under enemy fire or as existential crisis during a sleepless night. The federal government opted not to regulate the production and sale of tobacco, as it did for many discretionary items like beer, coffee, or sugar. Cigarettes, in effect, became a non-discretionary good during the war, notably so for those sent to uniformed combatants. Tobacco and cigarettes were widely available in Canada during the war, if progressively costlier due to tax increases. Ottawa, however, waived all taxes on cigarettes purchased for overseas troops and POWs, creating a strong financial incentive for people and organizations to give the gift of cigarettes. Curiously, in contrast to Ottawa's interventionist handling of domestic consumption and labour-force mobilization during the war, the bulk of responsibility for provisioning soldiers with cigarettes fell to private parties: loved ones, friends, colleagues, charities, and businesses.

Soldiers' complaints about cigarette scarcity and "famine" indicate that this procurement method was at times inconsistent. But this system of private donations proved constant and far-reaching in one key sense: gift cigarettes sent to soldiers produced meanings, symbolic associations, and social practices that differed from those of cigarettes acquired by purchase or military issue. A carton of cigarettes received from a service club in a soldier's home town affirmed notions of local identity or civic pride. Soldiers' zealous pursuit and prideful embrace of "Canadian cigarettes," especially when juxtaposed against foul-tasting English ones, constituted a form of consumer nationalism, for which quotidian goods like cigarettes became signifiers of Canadian identity and values, even a Canadian way of life. Cigarettes sent by parents, siblings, and grandparents became tangible markers of familial love and attachment, a taste of hearth and home in a far-flung, often hostile, setting. Return letters expressing gratitude coupled with the reciprocal obligations of gift giving enhanced "feelings of connectedness" between soldiers and family and friends back home.[171] The cultural norms of sharing among fellow soldiers meant that Canadian cigarettes reinforced group membership and social cohesion among one's "band of brothers," whether in military units or POW camps.

Cigarettes, of course, were material objects, delivering nicotine, aroma, and flavourful tar to habituated smokers. But when their procurement and usage were entwined with the protocols of gift giving, sharing, and gratitude, they served to establish and deepen social relationships between people. Cigarettes as gifts cemented bonds between givers and recipients, affirming what Komter describes as the moral basis of "community and a shared culture," in this case involving Canadian troops abroad.[172] In POW camps, cigarettes coexisted in gift-exchange and economic contexts, whether seen with cigarette sharing among prisoners or the trading of cigarettes with guards for food and amenities. The communitarian properties of gift cigarettes, however, quickly evaporated when these goods entered the black markets of war-ravaged Europe. There, gift cigarettes traded among strangers as high-value commodities in contraband markets where price gouging, social mistreatment, and corruption were common, as were monetary windfalls for some smokes-laden soldiers. Importantly, cigarettes in both gift-exchange and economic contexts exhibited considerable cultural power and exalted social status, an understanding of which soldiers carried with them into their postwar lives.[173]

Ralph Allen, a war correspondent for the *Globe and Mail*, witnessed first hand the Normandy invasion of June 1944. He later wrote that his "most vivid memory" of D-Day was that of a lone Canadian soldier entangled in barbed wire on the beach. "I knelt beside him and discovered he'd bled to death. Beside him was a pack of Canadian cigarettes – open, with one cigarette out and beside it a lighter. I tried the lighter. It was clogged. The poor man had been trying to have one last smoke and the lighter hadn't worked. Nothing had worked for him that day."[174] One could interpret this incident as an unfortunate, ironic instance of mechanical malfunction: a simple lighter failing to work during the largest sea-to-land invasion in history, itself a grand feat of logistics and technological prowess. We might instead consider this "most vivid" of deaths (on a day when mangled bodies littered the beaches) with renewed focus on the soldier's readied but unlit Canadian cigarette. Most probably a gift, it likely harboured personal meanings and memories, whether of a caring mother, home-town sweetheart, or boisterous bunkmate. The pathos of this unrequited cigarette resides with the unsettling prospect that this soldier died alone in every possible sense.

CHAPTER THREE

The Incomparable Cigarette

INTRODUCTION

In January 1949, a sub-committee of Toronto City Council recommended amending the Lord's Day Act to permit the sale of cigarettes on Sundays. In backing this measure, Councillor David Balfour maintained that buying cigarettes on a Sunday should be no different than playing golf or watching a ball game on that day: "It makes us the laughing stock of cities all over the U.S. and Canada. The sooner we get away from these picayune things the better."[1] A few months later Canada's Gallup poll published its first national survey on cigarette use, confirming Balfour's view that smoking was now a cultural norm in Canada. Fifty-eight per cent of adults, the survey found, smoked cigarettes regularly, including 72 per cent of men and 42 per cent of women. Moreover, the number of smokers would likely rise, as cigarette consumption predominated among younger Canadians, with 64 per cent of those under thirty lighting up, compared with 44 per cent for those over fifty. Cigarette smoking was also more common in faster-growing urban areas; 66 per cent of adults in cities larger than 100,000 smoked cigarettes, compared with 48 per cent in rural Canada, prompting the Gallup organization to title its poll release, "City Life Conducive to Cigarette Smoking."[2]

In the decade after 1945, smoking and cigarette promotion were ubiquitous in Canada. Smoking a "butt" for any occasion was a taken-for-granted "right" of most adults, inflecting the social routines and cultural practices of men, women, and, increasingly, teens. Cigarette ads infused newspapers and magazines, while tobacco companies sponsored dozens of radio shows, including the highly popular *La Famille Plouffe*. Cigarette promotion was common in recreation halls, curling rinks, bowling alleys, and hockey arenas across the country. Cigarettes were now widely available, sold in grocery stores, restaurants, variety stores, and drug stores – no longer primarily in tobacco shops and newsstands as was the case a generation earlier. Nearly half of Canadian women smoked, a social fact that served to disqualify lingering moral attacks on women lighting up. Cigarette smoking was the quintessential modern habit, conferring cosmopolitanism, verve, and urbanity on its practitioners. Soaring cigarette sales, the enhanced visibility of smoking in public venues and the mass media, and liberalizing attitudes towards tobacco combined to elevate cigarette smoking to a hegemonic cultural practice. The post-1945 years were the zenith of Cigarette Nation; never again would as high a proportion of Canadians smoke cigarettes in a social climate largely devoid of contestation and recrimination.

This state of affairs owed to the myriad ways in which cigarette smoking was thought to promote the social and psychological needs of Canadians. Smoking abetted social outreach, a mode of smoking described by Jason Hughes as an "expression of sociability," one that affirmed group affiliation and even social solidarity.[3] Similar to that seen during the Second World War and discussed in chapter 2, smoking promoted camaraderie and social belonging. It combatted social isolation, connecting people to one another, as seen with the social rituals of sharing cigarettes with friends or providing a smoke to a stranger if asked. People also maintained that smoking promoted psychological well-being and good mental habits. Cigarettes reduced stress and anxiety, promoted relaxation, aided concentration, and enhanced workplace productivity. Smoking was entwined with the reflexive project of self-identity formation, part of the "lifestyle" that people adopted to pilot changing social situations and complex institutions in modern Canada.[4] The perceived benefits of cigarette smoking were far-reaching and commonly understood. Smoking promoted social engagement, while serving as a coping mechanism for harried psyches. It functioned as stimulant in the workplace and relaxant in the tavern or coffee shop. It operated along these different axes – social and psychological, recreational and occupational – in ways that proved highly complementary and pliable.

THE CIGARETTE MARKETPLACE

Cigarette production ballooned during the Second World War, rising from 7.1 billion cigarettes in 1939 to 17.6 billion in 1945, while average daily consumption of cigarettes nearly doubled, climbing from 2.4 cigarettes per adult in 1939 to 4.5 in 1945.[5] By war's end, fully 99 per cent of the tobacco used for cigarette production was grown in Canada, putting an end to past reliance on US tobacco imports to furnish manufacturers.[6] Cigarettes comprised 35 per cent of the dollar value of all tobacco sold in Canada in 1935, rising to 52 per cent in 1945.[7] This growth accelerated after the war, as the manufacturing value of cigarettes rose from $207 million in 1945 to $332 million in 1955.[8] One year later, tobacco firms produced 27.3 billion cigarettes, which now accounted for two-thirds of the dollar value of tobacco manufacturing in Canada.[9] While cigarette output soared, the opposite was occurring with production facilities and employment: 56 tobacco manufacturing plants operated in Canada in 1955, down from 86 in 1945.[10] During this same period, the number of tobacco manufacturing employees declined from 12,164 to 9,529.[11] The remaining workers, however, earned high wages (unlike their counterparts of the 1930s), as evidenced by the sector's average wage gains of 193 per cent between 1949 and 1959, second only to those of brewery workers.[12] Industry concentration and mass production methods characterized cigarette manufacturing in the decade after 1945, in which declining numbers of workers earning higher salaries laboured in larger factories churning out ever-higher tallies of cigarettes.

Market research and public opinion surveys of the late 1940s document the broad appeal of cigarette smoking. A 1947 marketing survey of people in sixty Canadian cities found that 68 per cent of men and 39 per cent of women smoked cigarettes. Some two-thirds of women smokers were regular users, with the other third smoking occasionally. Twenty-three per cent of men smoked cigars and 34 per cent smoked pipes.[13] The results reveal that many men smoked cigarettes along with other forms of tobacco, such that more than three-quarters of men smoked at least one type of tobacco. A 1949 Gallup poll confirmed these high rates of cigarette smoking: 72 per cent of men smoked cigarettes, with some three-quarters of these smokers doing so regularly. Forty-two per cent of women identified as cigarette smokers, about half of whom were regular smokers. Cigarette smoking was common in most demographic groups, while especially popular among younger adults, city dwellers, and Quebeckers. One-quarter of cigarette users said they became regular smokers before the age of sixteen.[14] A 1951 Gallup survey confirmed smoking's continuing appeal, with 69 per cent of men and 42 per cent of women identifying as cigarette smokers; slightly more smokers now identified as regular users as compared with 1949.[15]

In 1950, the market research firm Elliott-Haynes conducted a large survey of cigarette smokers covering brand preferences and buying habits, interviewing some 6,500 smokers across Canada.[16] Researchers identified smokers and then asked about current and former cigarette brands. The survey's results offer a valuable snapshot of the mid-century cigarette market in Canada, the first of its kind to do so. Four companies dominated the cigarette trade, controlling 98 per cent of the market: Imperial Tobacco Canada (50 per cent); Macdonald Tobacco (31 per cent); Rock City (11 per cent), and Tuckett (6 per cent). The top two cigarette brands controlled 63 per cent of the market, with ITC's Player's capturing 36 per cent and Macdonald's Export 27 per cent. Rounding out the top four brands were ITC's Sweet Caporals (9 per cent) and Rock City's Black Cat (7 per cent). While all leading brands were marketed nationally, sales at times varied by region. For example, the brand share of Player's ranged from a low of 33 per cent in Quebec to a high of 46 per cent in the Maritimes. Export controlled 22 per cent of the market in British Columbia, compared with a high of 31 per cent in Ontario.[17]

Gender and age factored minimally in the composition of brand share. Men and women chose Player's and Export, the two leading brands, in near-identical numbers; 37 per cent of male smokers chose Player's, as did 38 per cent of women smokers. For Export, the comparable figures were 27 per cent (men) and 25 per cent (women).[18] Among the top four brands, only Black Cat had a gender-delineated clientele, with women preferring it at nearly twice the rate as men. Only two brands skewed heavily male – Buckingham and Winchester, both of which sold poorly. Given the small market share of brands with gender-based appeals, most likely 80 per cent or more of cigarettes sold in Canada in 1950 involved brands appealing more or less equally to men and women, when taking into account the lower overall smoking rate of women. This consumption pattern reflected conventional marketing wisdom that women would use brands with masculine appeals (like Player's), while men would not do likewise with feminine brands.[19] Indeed, *La Presse*, in the same issue in June 1953, ran two Player's ads, one targeting women and the other promoting the brand as a Father's Day gift.[20] The age of smokers generally did not impact brand identity or consumer preference. Smokers in their twenties, thirties, and forties chose leading brands like Player's and Export in roughly similar numbers. The only exception was Sweet Caporals, which drew disproportionately from smokers over fifty.

The Canadian cigarette market in 1950 was largely homogeneous and staid: two companies dominated the industry, in which two brands – Player's and Export – controlled nearly two-thirds of the market. The cigarette sector was a duopoly with limited competition. The products on the market were largely uniform, as most leading cigarette brands came in standard lengths (72 millimetres), featured plain-end (unfiltered) formats, and consisted of bright-leaf tobacco grown in Canada. Promotional expenditures were relatively low: ad spending in Canada averaged 6 cents per 1,000 cigarettes sold, compared with 30 cents per 1,000 cigarettes in the United States.[21] A mass-marketing orientation prevailed, not one defined by market segmentation and product differentiation, which would not occur until the 1960s. This "mass over class" marketing strategy conflated the consumer market with a broad cross-section of the population.[22] The cigarette industry embodied a "petty consumption" ethos, Steve Penfold's term for the Canadian donut trade after 1960. Low prices, standardized products, and broad-based consumption proved a formula for commercial success, while also giving rise to new social rituals and cultural meanings inflected by donuts and donut shops.[23] In the decade after 1945, cigarettes were similarly democratic and universal, owing to ecumenical marketing and to the way smoking reconfigured social behaviour and personal routines, becoming in the process culturally iconic. Cigarette advertising promoted this democratic message. A 1948 ad for Philip Morris cigarettes featured a column of male and female faces with the caption: "Jack and Joan, Don and Doris – They All Call for Philip Morris."[24] A 1949 Sweet Caporals ad featured head shots of different men

3.1 Cigarette marketing in the 1940s and early 1950s employed a "mass over class" approach, targeting a broad cross-section of the population rather than market segments. Sweet Caporals ad in the *Toronto Daily Star*, 10 January 1949.

and women against a backdrop of dozens of listed occupations (e.g., bricklayer, manicurist) with the caption, "they all smoke and enjoy SWEET CAPS" (figure 3.1).[25]

A consumer survey by Canadian Facts for Imperial Tobacco in 1955 sheds additional light on the cigarette market. A prominent market research firm, Canadian Facts conducted in-depth consumer studies for ITC throughout the 1950s and 1960s.[26] For the 1955 survey, the firm interviewed

3,600 people in thirty cities.[27] Fifty-eight per cent of Canadian adults smoked cigarettes, which included 68 per cent of men and 47 per cent of women. Notably, the female smoking rate was 5 per cent higher than that recorded by Gallup in 1951, while the male smoking rate was largely unchanged. Similarly, when asked if people in general were smoking more, less, or about the same today as they were five years ago, 63 per cent of respondents said "more," compared with 10 per cent who said "less." Among the "more" respondents, the top-cited explanation was smoking's stress relief and relaxation attributes. The most popular brands in 1955 were Player's, with 32 per cent of market share, and Export with 27 per cent. Black Cat (8 per cent) and Sweet Caporals (6 per cent) rounded out the top four brands. With the exception of a small decline in Player's brand share, the cigarette market largely matched what the Elliott-Haynes study had found in 1950. Such continuity reflected a key finding of the Canadian Facts survey: brand switching among smokers was uncommon, with only 7 per cent of smokers having done so in the past year.[28]

The Canadian Facts study revealed nascent signs of gender segmentation in the cigarette market. While the male–female makeup of Player's smokers approximated that seen in the Elliott-Haynes's survey of 1950, Export smokers now skewed more male; 32 per cent of male smokers chose Export, compared with just 23 per cent of female users. This was the start of a widening gender gap among Export consumers, as the brand would skew increasingly male and, later, working-class.[29] This trend paralleled the restoration of traditional gender roles starting in the 1950s, which historians depict as a conservative reaction to the fluid gender norms and wider occupational possibilities that were available to women during the war and shortly after.[30] The growth in white-collar jobs during the 1950s also meant that more employers increasingly valued cognitive skills and social aptitude over brawn and tenacity. All of this contributed to "a general unease over traditional gender roles that expressed itself in a growing concern over the 'decline' of the male."[31] During the 1950s, Canadians also endowed male veterans with a sense of "special entitlement," which, as Christopher Dummitt notes, saw Ottawa promoting "a certain kind of masculinity after the war," one that shored up the "rights of this manly entitlement."[32]

SOCIABILITY, PRODUCTIVITY, AND THE SELF

When Canadian Facts asked people in 1956 why they smoked, many of the replies stressed smoking's social attributes. Twenty-nine per cent of smokers chose the option, "finishing touches to good things like food, drink, friendship," while 19 per cent said that cigarettes "put them at ease with other people." Another 19 per cent believed that smoking provided them with "something in common with other people."[33] These views situate cigarette use in the tradition of a "smoking Gemeinschaft," Jason Hughes's term for a smoking culture premised on social interaction and communal values. This mode of smoking reflected the centuries-long history of tobacco sharing in communal settings like taverns and coffee houses[34] (figure 3.2). As seen in chapter 2, cigarette smoking among soldiers enhanced male camaraderie and social cohesion in the ranks, aspects of which endured after the war. For example, governments and tobacco firms continued to send free cigarettes to Canadian soldiers stationed abroad and to military veterans in hospitals until the mid-1950s.[35] A 1951 Ontario school textbook outlined the role of smoking in promoting "social health" and living in "harmony with other people of other kinds." Cigarette smoking strengthened the "socially satisfactory personality." Group smoking shored up "important male friendships" and combatted social isolation. This textbook portrayed smoking as a "fairly universal" social custom that promoted "friendliness and comradeship," while representing a "normative and sanctioned masculine activity."[36] This mode of "social smoking" is similarly revealed by one eighteen-year-old woman's query to an advice columnist in 1947, asking if she were in fact a bone fide smoker since she did not smoke alone and only smoked cigarettes given to her by friends.[37]

Ads and photographs during this period highlight smoking's role as social lubricant. When people got together, they smoked – in pubs, parks, legion halls, bingo parlours, on dates, and during family gatherings. Smoking fostered camaraderie, social belonging, and good cheer (figures 3.3, 3.4, and 3.5). It affirmed group identity and communal values, lessening social isolation and individual alienation. This mode of smoking constituted more collective social practice than instances of individual behaviour.[38] It reflected the long-standing view of cultural anthropologists and other

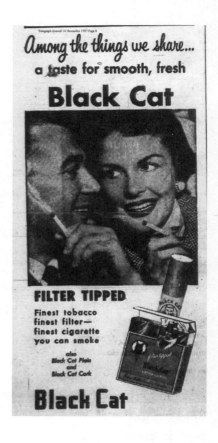

3.2 Sociability and smoking went hand in hand, both at home and in public. Black Cat ad in the *Telegraph-Journal*, 14 November 1957.

3.3 *Opposite top* Members of the Lovat Scouts, a Scottish regiment, enjoy a smoke break during combat training in the Canadian Rockies in 1944.

3.4 *Opposite bottom* Smoking patrons in a Canadian Pacific Railway club car, circa 1950.

social scientists that characterized consumption as a "very social act wherein symbolic meanings, social codes, relationships" are produced and reproduced.[39] In line with the expansive view of culture advanced by Raymond Williams, incorporating social circumstances and the habits and routines of ordinary people,[40] cigarette smoking was arguably a key pillar of mid-twentieth-century popular culture, owing to its prominence in quotidian life and the social rituals of most adults. This was especially so in cities and industrial areas where cigarette smoking was most common.

A marketing study in 1956 found that seven in ten Canadian smokers reported being able to smoke cigarettes while on the job.[41] During the war, the right to smoke cigarettes in US defence industries had been a feature of labour militancy and working-class solidarity. "Worker-smokers" engaged in wildcat strikes and other forms of labour unrest to secure the

3.5 Military veterans enjoy beers and cigarettes in Edmonton, circa 1953.

right to smoke on the factory floor. The end of workplace smoking bans, according to Gregory Wood, contributed to the "widened acceptability of smoking" both during and after the war[42] (figures 3.6 and 3.7). When, in 1954, Gallup asked former pipe smokers in Canada why they had quit, often taking up cigarettes instead, the most common reply concerned the pipe's out-of-step modernity, especially related to work, as one respondent observed: "I couldn't work and smoke [a pipe] at the same time."[43] Cigarette smoking was a supplementary activity that could be done while performing other tasks, unlike pipe smoking which typically required dedicated time. Cigarettes boosted productivity, improved mental concentration on assembly lines, and helped workers perform boring and repetitive tasks or deal with stressful conditions.[44] The latter point was curiously driven home in 1945 when Hamilton Fire Chief William Murdoch, alarmed by near-fires during recent break-ins, appealed to burglars

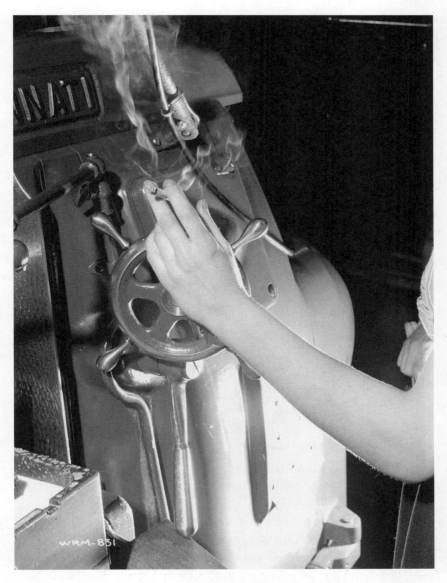

3.6 A worker holds a cigarette while operating machinery at the John Inglis Co. Bren Gun plant in Toronto, 10 May 1941. On the job, cigarettes were touted for enhancing productivity and mental acuity.

3.7 A labourer takes a solitary smoke break during construction of the Polymer Corporation in Sarnia, Ontario, in June 1943.

not to smoke while "on the job." Murdoch emphasized that "because of the hazardous nature of their work – the haste and nervous tension – burglars and shop breakers were more likely to drop butts in dangerous places than others."[45]

Coupled with this enhanced productivity discourse was another that framed cigarettes as dietary substitutes for time-pressed workers, especially women. In 1946 Ontario's health minister, Russel T. Kelley, cautioned that a "doughnut, soft drink and cigarette" was not proper lunch fare for the "business girl, or anyone else."[46] Two years later a home economist addressing a women's business club lamented that "the standard luncheon diet of many business women is 'dangerously close' to the cup-of-coffee and a cigarette combination." Busy women required vegetables, fruits, and meat in their diets.[47] Nutrition expert Dr W.M. McCormack similarly bemoaned the "growing number of adults" who skipped breakfast and instead took "quick satisfaction from a cigarette and a cup of coffee."[48] Cigarettes, in this vein, were "fuel," an energy source for on-the-go workers, fortifying them for the day's labour. This mirrored earlier advertising claims for patent medicines and chewing gum, promising vigour and mental acuity for tackling hectic work schedules.[49] Cigarettes could be smoked quickly, highlighting "speed and immediacy in modernity, a quick and joyful jolt to the senses and then on with the day."[50] In this sense, Brandt notes, they were the "ideal substance for an industrial age of consumption."[51]

Canadian Facts reported in 1956 that half of all smokers used cigarettes because they "relaxe[d] them."[52] During the postwar years, tobacco advertisers and smokers often praised cigarettes for delivering stress relief and relaxation.[53] In 1946, a British war bride in Canada argued that she and other war brides had only started smoking cigarettes because the war had been "awfully hard on the girls' nerves."[54] British women during the war had in fact "extolled the personal and social benefits – indeed the necessity – of cigarettes" for their ability to calm nerves.[55] Others in Canada lauded cigarettes for reducing stress and irritability.[56] A Sweet Caporals ad in 1948 featured a young maid relaxing with her feet up and smoking a cigarette while on a break from work.[57] In 1950, ads for Pall Mall maintained that the "secret" of financially successful men lay in their ability to relax, with Pall Mall cigarettes offering up a "merveilleuse détente."[58] Another ad proclaimed that "active people know it's smart to relax," promising that you "get more enjoyment and relaxation when you smoke Pall Mall"[59] (figure 3.8). At this time, the cultural authority of professional psychology was on the rise in North America.[60] During the war, psychologists had worked closely with Ottawa to administer aptitude and intelligence tests for recruit selection and to mobilize public opinion in support of the war effort.[61] After 1945, as Mona Gleason notes, psychological advice was "plentiful" in Canadian newspapers and magazines, constituting "an important feature

3.8 Cigarettes were promoted for stress relief and relaxation, a coping mechanism for daily hardships and "jangled nerves." Pall Mall ad in the *Toronto Daily Star*, 14 November 1950.

of the postwar cultural landscape."[62] People were increasingly cognizant of psychological well-being and mental health, which were more likely framed in the vernacular of "the blues," "jangled nerves," and "the jitters."[63] Cigarettes, in this vein, were helpful tools to manage the stresses of modern life, restoring equanimity to frazzled minds. Smoking helped people compensate, consciously or not, for what was missing in their lives, helping them cope with daily hardships. A "very strong fundamental reason for smoking," Canadian Facts reported in 1956, "appears to be in the realm of giving the individual self confidence and boosting his morale."[64]

Psychological understandings of smoking, however, did not extend to nicotine addiction or chronic dependence. During the 1940s and 1950s, medical authorities and laypeople regarded cigarette smoking as a "social" habit and not as bio-chemical addiction to nicotine. Cigarette smoking was a customary practice, not unlike regular coffee drinking, and smoking was even thought to help people overcome real addictions to alcohol or opiates. Medical and popular accounts of addiction generally did not include tobacco use until the 1970s.[65]

Cigarette smoking featured as well in the articulation of self-identity in the postwar era. Anthony Giddens argues that the concept of self-identity changed during the latter 1900s, when a priori factors like family, religion, or locality proved less influential in fashioning one's sense of self. Instead, self-identity was constructed in a process that was ongoing and reflexive, requiring individual effort and calculation. Commodity goods featured in this process, part of the various "lifestyles" that people adopted while assembling and projecting self-identity. For Giddens, a lifestyle constituted an "integrated set of practices which an individual embraces, not only because such practices fulfil utilitarian needs, but because they give material form to a particular narrative of self-identity." These lifestyles consisted of routinized practices involving "habits of dress, eating, [and] modes of acting."[66] The common practice of cigarette smoking featured in such lifestyles, as noted by Ernest Dichter, the renowned motivation researcher, whose 1947 book, *The Psychology of Everyday Living*, had an entire chapter on smoking. In it, Dichter argued that "the way we smoke is characteristic of our whole personality," and that the "mannerisms of smokers [were] innumerable."[67]

In 1956, the Canadian sociologist Erving Goffman published his seminal book *The Presentation of Self in Everyday Life*, which employed theatrical metaphors like "front-stage" and "back-stage" to depict how the modern self interacted with others in public and semi-private contexts. Goffman discussed smoking as part of "back-stage" relaxation and rejuvenation; in one example, he described how flight attendants on non-busy flights would, after performing their initial duties, "settle down in the rearmost seat, change from regulation pumps into loafers, light up a cigarette, and there create a muted circle of non-service relaxation."[68] A similar example concerned stay-at-home mothers who viewed the area between home and playground as mostly "back-stage." Accordingly, these mothers wore "jeans, loafers and a minimum of make-up," and walked with a "cigarette dangling from their lips as they push[ed] their baby carriages and openly talk[ed] shop with their colleagues."[69] This example is illustrative: it was not the presence of the cigarette but its location in the mouth that challenged public decorum. As countless cigarette ads and contemporary photographs demonstrate, social convention held that the proper way for a woman to hold a cigarette was between index and middle finger, pointed upwards at roughly a 45-degree angle, positioned at the side of the face; never should a cigarette be "dangling" in the mouth. To maintain feminine respectability while smoking in "front-stage" contexts, women needed to ensure that lipstick was not left on cigarettes ends or tobacco threads on lips, and that fingers, nails, and teeth were free of tobacco stains.[70] Smoking in "front-stage" areas, such as beaches, conveyed notions of independence and personal empowerment for women in public spaces where female bodies were subjected to the critical gaze and aesthetic judgment of others (figure 3.9).

To sum up, the popularity of cigarette smoking in the decade after 1945 owed to the many ways in which it aligned with the social customs, workplace demands, and psychological needs of Canadians. Smoking strengthened the social fabric, whether one shared a pack with friends or offered a smoke to a stranger when asked. Smoking connected people with one another, strengthening group identity and elevating what today would be called "social capital." These same cigarettes, when brought on the factory floor, enhanced self-regulation, industriousness, and mental focus for the job at hand. Cigarettes provided social licence for authorized respites ("smoke breaks") from the assembly line or the typing pool, providing workers with short bouts of rest and rejuvenation to better manage their workdays. When brought home, these same cigarettes might energize tired bodies or serve as an emotional resource for coping and relaxation, relieving, if temporarily, the stresses and anxieties underpinning fraught lives. Cigarette smoking helped people construct the self-identity needed to navigate complex and changing social situations. Smoking signalled and confirmed social membership ("a means of identity proclamation, a marker of oneself to others") while also functioning personally as a "marker to oneself and *of* oneself."[71] For many, the very notion of selfhood was intertwined with modes of cigarette smoking.[72]

3.9 By the mid-1950s, more than half of women between eighteen and twenty-five smoked cigarettes, which functioned as symbolic markers of self-identity and femininity. Toronto lifeguards smoking, ca 1950.

WOMEN SMOKERS

As noted above, female smoking rates climbed after 1945. A small and diminishing share of Canadians, especially older ones, disapproved of this trend. When the septuagenarian Prime Minister Mackenzie King wrote in 1946 that he "dislike[d] very much seeing lipstick on the lips of girls and seeing them smoke cigarettes," he expressed views not uncommon to his generation.[73] The president of the Kitchener-Waterloo Overseas Wives'

Club, a war-bride support group, underscored this generational divide: "much of the ill-will between war brides and their in-laws was caused by the fact that virtually all of the brides smoke," while "many mothers-in-law do not approve of them smoking in the home."[74] By 1955, 51 per cent of women between eighteen and twenty-five smoked cigarettes, compared with 38 per cent of those over forty.[75] For younger women, cigarette smoking was a symbolic marker of personal autonomy and independent thinking. When, in 1949, a teenage girl wrote to ask newspaper advice columnist Mary Starr if she should continue to accept the undesired cigarettes offered by dates or instead smoke her own brand, the response was illuminating:

> I am sure that [question] was never presented to writers on etiquette of a previous generation. Years ago the odd girl may have written asking would it be proper to accept a cigarette when offered one, and where and when should it be smoked, but even this would have been considered very daring. Nowadays, of course, it is the accepted thing for girls to smoke or not to smoke according to their own personal preference. Many girls, like yourself, have favorite brands of cigarettes. Under the circumstances, the best plan is to be quite frank with your escort and say, "Do you mind? I prefer my own brand."[76]

This spirit of female independence was also seen in a newspaper account about former prospector "Klondike Kate," who, at sixty-nine, was attending a Klondike reunion in Vancouver. The accompanying photo showed her rolling a cigarette with the caption: "she loves to roll her cigarettes *herself*."[77] When women who had previously been barred from a Montreal meeting of pipe-smoking enthusiasts finally gained entry in 1950, the headline in *La Presse* declared: "Les fumeuses ont gagné leur point."[78] Women's embrace of smoking was part of a broader shift in the redefinition of socially acceptable behaviour, derived less from formal institutions and traditional beliefs and more from the consumer marketplace. The presentation of self, especially for women, increasingly overlapped with the consumption of commodity goods. In this context, cigarette smoking for women helped to fashion forms of self-identity, while also signalling affiliation with desired social groups.[79]

Sharon Anne Cook covers similar terrain in her analysis of mid-twentieth-century Canadian women smokers. There was increasing social acceptance of women smoking, both in public and at work, especially in pink-collar jobs in the growing service economy after 1950. Women worked from desks affixed with ashtrays. Cigarette smoking bolstered their social and working lives, providing them with necessary "social capital in new circumstances," helping to "construct a new type of waged woman on the Canadian landscape." These women smokers, Cook argues, "negotiated the spaces between modernity's workplace culture, with its concomitant values of independence, suppressed negative emotions, and cool sophistication, and an older prescription of the respectable woman based on Christian duty, selflessness, and purity. The advantages of smoking for the waged woman were many, with the decision to smoke a rational response to the rigours of workplace culture."[80] Favourable depictions of female smoking and middle-class respectability went beyond the workplace. Advertisements showed women smokers in sophisticated poses and settings. When the Canadian Pacific Railway added women's smoking sections to its lounges and trains, it affirmed the place of women in the "modern smoking society."[81] Women who entered the traditional male domain of universities in the 1940s and 1950s took up smoking in large numbers. This was part of a broader strategy, dating back to the 1930s, in which cigarette smoking served to lay claim to (traditionally male) public spaces, while also providing a "prop to aid discussion and focus attention on the speaker."[82] These advances did not go unchallenged, as seen by one letter writer to the *Toronto Daily Star* in 1947: "Women, generally, are worse cigarette smokers than men. It is as though they have never properly learned how to handle a cigarette without being objectionable. They light cigarettes only to forget them. Instead of tasting the enjoyment themselves, they foist the smoke on everyone else in the room."[83] But comments like these, defending smoking as a male purview and depicting women smokers as unskilled dilettantes, were, by the mid-1950s, few and far between.

Smoking cemented academic peer networks and was also integral to heterosexual dating rituals on campuses in the 1950s. "The potential for serious young women to show off their hands to good effect or contrive to gently frame the face in softening smoke, like the iconic Bette Davis," Cook writes, "telegraphed important social messages, often saturated with sexual content."[84] In this sense, smoking functioned as both social practice and bodily communication, enabling different modes of self-presentation: expressive, stylized, or corporeal. For female university students, cigarette smoking conveyed long-standing attributes like femininity and sophistication while also symbolizing autonomous thinking and coming-of-age intellect.[85] Cigarette smoking was conflated with ideas about women's emancipation, and notions of social and political freedom more generally, while simultaneously providing tangible forms of self-control, such as stress management and weight monitoring[86] (figure 3.10).

TEEN SMOKERS

Canadian youths increasingly took up cigarette smoking in the postwar years. Since the late 1800s, moral reformers had dissuaded boys and girls from smoking by claiming that cigarettes stunted growth, fostered moral turpitude, and served as a gateway to vices like drinking or gambling. For youths, tobacco had long been a source of illicit pleasure as a transgression of social norms. The milder form of tobacco in cigarettes, as compared with cigars or pipes, meant that cigarettes were much easier for youths to inhale. Canadian teens, young and old, smoked cigarettes but at levels difficult to gauge accurately before the mid-1950s.[87] In 1950, a Quebec reader asked an advice columnist in *Le Devoir* if ten years of age was too young for a boy to start smoking. That the question needed to be asked suggests that scenes of children smoking cigarettes in Quebec were not uncommon. Notably, the reply from "Dr. Remy" stated only that ten was "a little young" to start smoking.[88] Complaints about teen smoking in the form of letters to the editor suggest the practice was on public display. In 1948, Dan Boland lamented that "thousands" of underage boys were "inveterate cigarette smokers" in Toronto.[89] Toronto school board trustee Albert Cane, alarmed by the sight of elementary school boys smoking in the street, adopted a motion at a board meeting to require "proper authorities" to enforce laws against smoking by minors.[90] One Toronto letter writer in 1952 claimed there was "nothing pretty about seeing a young girl of 14 or 15 with a cigarette hanging out of her mouth," adding that it was "unfortunate that this disgusting habit is so widespread among our people."[91] A

The Incomparable Cigarette

3.10 Men and women smoke cigarettes on the lawn outside the National Film Board building in Montreal in June 1956.

news account described a "reported increase" in the number of cigarette smokers at a Brockville public school, concluding that the prime responsibility for this lay with parents and not teachers.[92]

A marketing survey done in 1955 offers an early empirical measure of teen smoking. Researchers conducted a telephone survey of 600 teens (aged twelve to nineteen) in Toronto, Montreal, and Edmonton. The cigarette smoking rate for the entire twelve-to-nineteen group was 16 per cent, though it was much higher for one cohort: 39 per cent of boys aged sixteen to nineteen smoked cigarettes, compared with just 12 per cent of same-age girls. (These smoking rates were likely underreported, since the survey's methodology required teens to answer smoking-related questions on the phone while in the family home.) Nine per cent of boys aged twelve to fifteen smoked. The most popular brand among teens was Player's, chosen by 28 per cent of smokers (35 per cent of boys), followed by Matinée Cork with 18 per cent (25 per cent of girls). According to this survey, gender-based brand selection was more prevalent among teens than among adult smokers at this time.

The results of this smoking survey appeared in *Marketing*, the trade magazine of the Canadian advertising industry, as part of a series on the consumption habits of high school students. Conducted by Canadian High News, a little-known marketing firm, the survey also asked about soft drink and candy bar consumption. The accompanying article alerted cigarette makers to the bottom-line promise of targeting teens. The 1951 census counted 340,000 students in Canada, a number slated to rise as the Baby Boom demographic aged into their teen years. When non-smokers were asked what brand they would pick if they started smoking, only one-quarter could offer a choice. This meant that non-smoking teens had "an open mind that can be influenced by the right kind of advertising specifically directed at the smokers of tomorrow." Cigarette manufacturers, thus, had a "wide open potential market among high school students," who should be targeted soon.[93]

CIGARETTE RETAILING

Changes in the cigarette retailing landscape after 1945 likely contributed to youth smoking. During the interwar years, cigarettes were sold mostly by tobacconists, who specialized in tobacco and related accessories and sold few other product lines. Beginning in the late 1930s, and accelerating after the war, cigarettes were increasingly sold in more accessible retail venues: variety and general stores, chain stores, restaurants, and grocery stores (figure 3.11). Teens were far more familiar with these retailing venues than with tobacco shops, as were mothers with young children.[94] The *CCTJ*, the trade magazine for the tobacco trade, wrote about this issue extensively, advising cigarette merchants on how best to compete in this changing retail environment. Much of the advice centred on developing

3.11 By the 1950s, most cigarettes were no longer sold in tobacco shops but in venues like variety and drug stores, places where children and teens often visited. Terry's Drug Store, Victoria, BC, 1950.

sales appeals that went beyond traditional male clienteles and connected with homemakers, as well as children and teenagers.[95]

In the late 1940s, CCTJ articles carried headlines like "Back-to-School Promotions ... Plan Them Now!" and "Toys Mean Extra Profits for the Alert Tobacconist," promoting the merits of stocking diverse product lines and crafting retail displays that appealed to mothers. A tobacco retailer in 1949 made up identity cards for his adult customers, which authorized children to purchase cigarettes on their parent's behalf.[96] A CCTJ article in 1954 discussed selling toys in tobacco shops.[97] Another article counselled tobacconists to stock Halloween supplies and to be generous with trick-or-treaters ("kids don't forget, and they tell their elders to shop at 'That nice Mr. Jones'").[98] The magazine advised tobacco retailers to collect the names, addresses, and birthdays of children who came in the store in order to send them birthday cards. That would cost a little, but "the value in goodwill, both from these youthful customers and their parents, is great."[99]

Other articles promoted doll sales in tobacco shops and stocking toys and children's games for Christmas.[100]

A 1955 piece asked tobacconists if they were "on the Davy Crockett 'Bandwagon,'" carrying toy guns and coonskin hats made popular by the TV show.[101] That same year, the *CCTJ* began carrying ads for Kool-Aid.[102] A profile of Dave Gordon and his Toronto tobacco shop highlighted how he made children feel welcome in his store by giving them free candy and gum "before setting off for school." According to Gordon, the "10, 12 and 14-year-old kids are your customers of tomorrow," and if you "treat them well now, they will remember and return as their buying power increases."[103] Not surprisingly, rising rates of teen smoking were sometimes blamed on unscrupulous retailers selling cigarettes to minors while maintaining that "they don't know how old the boys are."[104] Provincial enforcement of laws prohibiting cigarette sales to under-sixteen teens was sporadic and largely ineffective during the 1950s.[105]

Tobacconists faced mounting competition from other retail sectors for the cigarette trade. In 1950, *Marketing* magazine reported that American grocery stores were now the leading retailer of cigarettes, with some 40 per cent of sales.[106] Sales in tobacco stores remained flat between 1952 and 1954, rising from $86 million to $87 million, at a time when overall cigarette sales grew robustly.[107] As homemakers bought more cartons of cigarettes at supermarkets, the *CCTJ* advised tobacco vendors to push the "carton habit" with their own customers. (Ironically, this article ran adjacent to another titled, ""What about ... Cigarettes and Cancer?")[108] During the 1950s, articles appeared touting stock diversification for tobacconists, encouraging them to add lines like cosmetics, beauty products, cameras, watches, and even electrical appliances.[109] The changing nature of cigarette retailing affected the *CCTJ* itself. In February 1956, the magazine adopted a new name, the *Canadian Cigar, Tobacco and Variety Journal*; six months later it again changed its name to the more succinct *Tobacco and Variety Journal*. The magazine's editors underscored that the "modern" cigarette trade had in recent years "turned increasingly to the variety trade."[110] To illustrate, the magazine ran a feature in 1956 on Carter's Smoke and Candy Shop in Streetsville, Ontario. The store featured "smoker's supplies, confectionary of all kinds, candies, magazines, comic books, cigarettes as well as films and toys."[111] These "smoke and candy shops" no doubt served as welcoming spaces for children and young teens, acculturating them to cigarette brands and their customers, and to the act of smoking itself.

NATIONAL ADVERTISING AND PROGRAM SPONSORSHIP

In October 1948, *Marketing* magazine surveyed the state of cigarette advertising in Canada. It judged this ad category to be bland and unadventurous, unlike its American counterpart, which it depicted as "dominant, persistent and irrepressible." Tepid cigarette advertising in Canada most certainly did not stretch "copywriters' imaginations ... to the breaking point."[112] To illustrate, advertising for Canada's top-selling cigarette brand, Player's, continued to use its war-era "Navy" theme for years after 1945.[113] Ads for Macdonald's Export consisted mainly of rotating shots of its trademark Scottish "Lassie." As one observer noted in 1951, Macdonald's Lassie had long been "reminding smokers from coast to coast of Macdonald's cigarettes and tobacco, looking out pleasantly from store cut-out or hanger, posters, and the pages of newspaper, magazine and farm paper, observing that basic rule of successful advertising – 'Keeping everlastingly at it.'"[114] Advertising slogans were often mundane, such as this one for Buckingham in 1949: "Not one, not two, but three ... three fine tobaccos in one cigarette means mild, cool taste in a Buckingham."[115] Play-it-safe slogans for Player's included "Player's Pleases More Canadians Every Day" and "Mildest, Best Tasting."[116] Export sported the banal tagline, "Canada's finest cigarette." A Player's ad campaign in the early 1950s described its tobacco quality and sound production methods in plodding fashion.[117]

This nondescript advertising was on occasion offset by promotional spectacle (figure 3.12). In 1950, ITC erected a first-of-a-kind outdoor advertising sign in Montreal, complete with fluorescent colour and black lighting. The appeal of this large sign, visible to drivers crossing the Jacques Cartier bridge, lay in technical wizardry: "regular reflectors, giving ordinary light, flash on and off, remaining on for four seconds and off for eight. While the regular reflectors are off, the background disappears and only the words above remain, giving off an iridescent glow." A similar sign was erected on Davenport Road in Toronto.[118] In 1954, Macdonald installed a massive Export-themed scoreboard in Vancouver's Empire Stadium. Standing 40 feet wide by 20 feet high, the illuminated sign was described as Canada's "largest and most modern football scoreboard."[119]

Imperial Tobacco was also a prominent sponsor of radio and television programs after 1945. In 1948, the Guy Lombardo radio show featured regular plugs for Player's.[120] In 1951, Player's sponsored *Bold Venture*, a radio show featuring Humphrey Bogart and Lauren Bacall.[121] The brand also backed *The Denny Vaughan Show*, a year-long series running five nights weekly on twenty-seven radio stations. Most notably, Player's sponsored *La Famille Plouffe*, a 1952 radio program adapted from Roger Lemelin's celebrated 1948 novel *Les Plouffe*, which depicted working-class family life in Quebec.[122] Player's extended this sponsorship to the televised version of the show, starting in November 1953, which became immensely popular in French-speaking Canada. In 1955, Player's advertising supported the hit TV comedy show *Father Knows Best* featuring Robert Young.[123] ITC's Sweet Caporals sponsored *Smoke Rings of Memory*, a ten-minute music program broadcast on weekdays.[124] Ogden's, another ITC brand, advertised on *Saddle Rockin' Rhythm*, a fifteen-minute radio program, and the *Smiley Burnett* show, which aired in 1951 and 1952.[125] Notable non-ITC sponsorships included Tuckett's Buckingham, which underwrote the eponymous *Buckingham Theatre*, a radio drama, along with *Signs of the Times*, a series of five-minute movies on topical events which ran in Canadian cinemas.[126] Certain sponsorships proved more successful than others. An ITC survey in 1955 found that 92 per cent of French-speaking smokers could identify Player's as the sponsor of *La Famille Plouffe*, while only 17 per cent knew that Export supported the *Vic Obeck* TV show. Only 6 per cent of smokers could identify Buckingham as the sponsor of the TV show *Sports Club*.[127]

While the sector's national advertising and program sponsorship may not have garnered industry plaudits or marketing awards, they made certain cigarette brands highly familiar to Canadians. Top-selling brands like Player's were advertised and marketed extensively. As cigarette-related health concerns developed during the 1950s, cigarette advertising performed an important latent function: by populating the mass media and everyday visual culture with favourable depictions of smoking, this advertising served to normalize cigarette use in Canadian society, allowing ordinary people to believe that "moderate" smoking remained safe

3.12 Outdoor cigarette ads, like this Sweet Caporal illuminated sign at the corner of Sainte-Catherine and St Mathieu streets in Montreal (ca 1945), were ubiquitous in urban centres.

and socially beneficial; for how could something so omnipresent and auspiciously portrayed in national print and broadcast media be lethal to its users?

MACDONALD TOBACCO AND LOCAL PROMOTION

Scholars of advertising history typically examine this topic at the national or international levels.[128] As a consequence, less is known about local and community-based marketing and advertising practices. Along with national advertising and program sponsorship, cigarette promotion was common in local communities across Canada, as evidenced by the marketing of Macdonald Tobacco, the nation's second-largest tobacco maker.[129] Macdonald employed various promotional tools to conflate brand names with local traditions, events, and pastimes. By advertising extensively in hockey arenas, curling clubs, baseball grounds, and bowling alleys, the company wove brand identity into the fabric of community life across Canada.

In 1945, Macdonald supplied the Nelson Civic Centre in Manitoba with five curling score boards, each emblazoned with brand advertising.[130] Two years later, the firm distributed 150 of these scoreboards to curling clubs throughout western Canada.[131] In 1948, Macdonald furnished a hockey arena in Temiskaming, Ontario, with a "Sportimer" clock, mounted above the ice, with one side brandishing an Export ad and the other side a promotion for British Consols.[132] In 1949, Macdonald paid $350 to install an electric scoreboard clock in Memorial Arena in Walkerton, Ontario, which advertised Export.[133] Some of these arena clocks carried high price tags. A single-sided Sportimer for an arena in Newcastle, New Brunswick, cost $850; a four-sided Sportimer clock in a St Catharine's arena totalled $3,000 (figure 3.13).[134] Cigarette advertising at baseball parks was comparatively cheaper. An ad sign in the outfield of the Montreal Baseball Park cost $600 per season, while a similar one in Trois-Rivières was only $200 per year.[135] In 1947, Macdonald erected a 6-feet-by-45-feet ad sign in the outfield of the Vancouver Baseball Stadium; similar advertising at the Wanderers' Baseball Club Grounds in Halifax was said to have "stimulated a lot of favourable comment" from fans and club representatives.[136]

Alongside signage at sports venues, Macdonald advertised regularly in game programs and team yearbooks. Some of these were for well-known entities like the program of Maple Leaf Gardens, which cost the firm $1,100 per season to advertise Export.[137] Export ads also ran in the program of the Montreal Forum for Canadiens hockey games.[138] In 1950, Macdonald paid $26,000 to print 65,000 colour calendars for Maple Leaf Gardens, which also featured brand advertising.[139] But this type of ad promotion was not limited to big cities or professional teams. Macdonald advertised in the programs of the Quebec Senior Hockey League and the Glace Bay Community Hockey Club, two among the dozens of hockey programs that regularly carried Export or British Consols ads.[140] The firm did likewise for curling associations, advertising in the roster books of the Winnipeg Curling Club, the yearbook of the Ontario Curling Association, and the Quebec Curler's Annual.[141] Countless other sport organizations benefited from Macdonald advertising in programs and yearbooks, in-

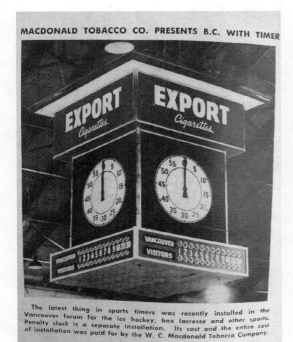

3.13 Imperial Tobacco and Macdonald Tobacco installed game clocks in countless sporting venues across Canada, including this "Sports Timer" in the Vancouver Forum.

cluding the Quebec Badminton Association, the Alberta Lawn Bowling Association, the Summerside Ladies Major Softball League, the Lachine Rowing Club, the Cartierville Boating Club, the Hamilton Redwing Baseball Club, the Alberta Provincial Rifle Association, and the BC Highland Dancing Association.[142]

Macdonald also advertised in bowling alleys, places like Fingard's Bowlodrome in Saskatoon. In 1946, the company arranged with a local agent to set up twenty-five ad signs in the venue, for a cost of $75. Macdonald also paid $550 to print 100,000 bowling score sheets, which featured cigarette advertising.[143] The owners of Fingard's were likely pleased to receive a year's worth of score sheets for free; Macdonald too benefited from this arrangement. Throughout the bowling alley, the firm's ads were highly visible to patrons; but bowlers also interacted intimately with Macdonald advertising while performing the cognitive work of bowling – calculating and recording scores after each round of play. In the 1940s and

1950s, bowling embodied social interaction and communal values, since people typically bowled in groups, often playing on teams and in leagues.[144] Bowling alleys were unique sites of Canadian popular culture.[145] Popular with both men and women, they combined individual performance with spells of spectatorship and conversation; individual and group competition commingled with camaraderie and mutual support. This blend of social engagement and individual performance (and corresponding performance anxiety) ensured that bowling alleys were popular sites for cigarette smoking, especially so since they predominated in cities where cigarette consumption was highest. As such, they were ideal sites to market cigarettes, whether with at-a-distance signage or the up-close utility of score sheets. And since many patrons smoked while engaging in something deemed enjoyable and socially rewarding, smoker-bowlers became part of the "marketing mix" in places like Fingard's Bowlodrome.

Macdonald did not use consumer research or marketing strategy to determine its ad spending in small-town venues or team programs. The firm's advertising was handled by Harold F. Stanfield Limited, a small Montreal ad agency whose main client was Macdonald. Stanfield fielded requests from groups across Canada seeking Macdonald advertising dollars for their publications, recreational venues, or in-kind contributions in the form of time clocks and scoreboards. Stanfield passed along these requests to Macdonald executives, who most often approved them. Stanfield then handled the subsequent arrangements. (Such community-based marketing was also in keeping with Macdonald's long history of philanthropic spending.)[146] Macdonald was by no means a model business in the late 1940s and 1950s, when it was better known for poor management and lacklustre marketing. When, in 1956, Peter Gage came from England to take up a head-office position at Macdonald, he encountered a troubling situation: "we had no marketing department and no Research Development department." There were few qualified managers. Manufacturing facilities were fifty years out of date and unable to produce the 35 million cigarettes per day needed to fulfill existing sales orders. Macdonald's response to this situation, he later said, was to have the company president and his wife open "the mail in the morning which comprised orders for the cigarettes. They had an adding machine and when the total came to the amount of cigarettes you could produce in the factory he didn't open any more mail."[147]

Since Macdonald did no cost–benefit analyses of its community-based marketing, its effect on the company's balance sheet is not known. But this marketing-cum-public relations spending arguably produced benefits that went beyond the corporate bottom line. By inserting company and brand names into recreational spaces where people socialized and played, this type of marketing aligned corporate presence with grassroots activities and local traditions. It married brand promotion with positive social values like sportsmanship, co-operation, and fair play. Export cigarettes were associated with local rituals like watching a baseball game, curling, and other cultural activities shaping community life. Programs and yearbooks bearing cigarette ads were typically not jettisoned like newspapers, but preserved as keepsakes or as chronicles of family and local history.

Roland Marchand, in a related context, analyzed institutional advertising by large US companies seeking to align corporate identity with community values and local institutions. Firms like AT&T sought to define themselves as "agent[s] of public service" or "social servant[s]," and not mere competitors in the marketplace. They did this to legitimize and humanize the abstract, profit-seeking corporation by appropriating small-town beliefs and community norms.[148] These corporations, over time, understood that the "image of neighborliness seemed a very desirable one to promote on both the local and the national level."[149] Macdonald's advertising was not explicitly institutional or driven by public relations goals; it did not have a proper marketing department, much less a public relations operation. But such marketing, transpiring at the heart of local cultural enterprise, arguably fostered trust and goodwill with local populaces. By interweaving company name and branded product into the myriad spaces of community life, Macdonald, however unwittingly, presented itself as an agent of "social benevolence," and not just as a for-profit company.[150] The corporate goodwill earned in this respect would arguably later prove important, as Macdonald, along with other tobacco firms, sought to convince people that the health risks of cigarettes were unfounded.

THE TRIUMPHANT CIGARETTE

The Canadian press frequently lauded the tobacco growing and cigarette manufacturing sectors after 1945. A *Canadian Business* article in September 1946 touted the cigarette industry as a major success story.[151] The tobacco-growing belt of southwestern Ontario produced 16,000 year-round farming jobs, with another 40,000 field jobs created during harvest periods. Three thousand more people worked in processing facilities to sort, dry, and pack tobacco. Tobacco manufacturing created an additional 11,000 jobs. In 1945, Canada imported almost no tobacco, while exporting 16 million pounds, mostly to the United Kingdom. The distribution and marketing sides of the industry, the article noted, contributed indirectly to the creation of tens of thousands of other jobs, including commercial artists, ad copy writers, radio programmers, newspaper writers, and retail workers. In 1945, the industry contributed $310 million to the federal government in the form of excise and import duties and sales taxes.[152] A CBC radio broadcast about the tobacco-belt Ontario town of Delhi described it as a "miniature Klondike," whose population increased three-fold during the summer and fall harvest months.[153] *Saturday Night* served up more accolades in 1954.[154] Manufactured cigarettes were valued at $290 million; the tobacco industry provided an estimated 300,000 full and part-time jobs in Canada, which included growing, manufacturing, distribution, marketing, and retailing, along with secondary employment in sectors like paper, cardboard, tinfoil, and matches. Cigarettes were the "tax-collector's special pride and joy," providing Ottawa with hundreds of millions annually, making industry leader Imperial Tobacco "Canada's biggest individual taxpayer."[155]

Media reports also extolled the social and cultural merits of cigarette smoking. A 1946 editorial in the *CCTJ* proclaimed smoking as "one of the greatest blessings in this world." It was so socially beneficial that "everybody should be able to smoke everywhere, so long as there is no danger involved. Lawyers should smoke in court, and so should the magistrate and so should the character in the dock. The policeman should be able to chew on a pipe as he makes his rounds, and the bank clerk blow smoke through his nostrils as he flicks his fingers over that wonderful green stuff." The federal government, the magazine stated, should pass legislation to promote such a smoke-at-will society.[156] The sense of popular entitlement concerning cigarette smoking was seen during V-E Day celebrations in Halifax in May 1945. When celebrants morphed into looters, smashing store windows in search of alcohol and cigarettes, the owner of Norman's Restaurant handed out cigarettes to placate the rioters. "Despite the flying bottles and other missiles," one account noted, his actions "cut down considerably on what would have been his total loss."[157] The courts also affirmed the *sine qua non* nature of cigarette smoking. In 1951, a Saskatchewan judge presided over a case involving a store owner suing a man for past debts, which entailed determining allowable household expenses for the defendant. Judge George W. McPhee ruled that the cost of cigarettes "for a man's wife and grown-up daughter" were "legitimate items in the family budget." When objections were raised, the judge replied: "It would be a bold individual who would say cigarettes are not a necessity to modern women."[158]

Other incidents highlight the social prominence of cigarettes in postwar Canada. When the plane of a Royal Canadian Air Force flyer crashed in an isolated area of northern Ontario in 1946, the pilot managed to survive alone for twenty-nine days. When rescued, according to one account, the "first thing he asked for was a cigarette."[159] In 1950, Canadian newspapers reported that Princess Margaret had ended speculation about her smoking status when she was seen smoking a cigarette at an official function.[160] Four years later, the Duchess of Kent visited Quebec City and the press dutifully reported on her smoking habits. At a reception, she declined offers of sherry and orange juice, opting instead for a "cigaret which she puffs with a long black holder, barely inhaling." Her black Japanese fan matched her cigarette holder and hat, demonstrating a fashionable eye for smoking accessories.[161] A 1953 article in *La Presse* described tobacco as "une herbe magique," owing to its world-wide usage.[162] The CCTJ regularly showcased elderly people who had smoked since childhood, including Thomas Suggs, who at his 109th birthday celebration in St John's proclaimed proudly: "I've been smoking 100 years ... since I was in petticoats."[163] Fellow Newfoundlander Premier Joey Smallwood boosted smoking's social stature at a Dominion-Provincial conference in Ottawa in 1950. Smallwood lit a cigarette during the meeting, described by observers as an act that "made history," since it was the "first time that anyone at this conference or any public sessions of previous conferences, had smoked." Soon after Smallwood started puffing, "pipes, cigars and other cigarettes were lighted up both at the conference table and among the advisors seated in the chamber around the conference table" (figure 3.14).[164]

CONCLUSION

The postwar cigarette industry was a paradox of sorts. By no means a powerhouse within the Canadian economy, tobacco manufacturers employed only about 9,500 people in 1955, a tiny sliver of the workforce in a country of 15 million people. The manufacturing value of tobacco was about $330 million that year, again small potatoes in a nation with a gross national product of $28 billion.[165] Cigarette production methods had changed little since the 1930s and technological innovation did not feature in the industry. While economically peripheral, the cigarette trade, nonetheless, proved paramount in social and cultural terms. Six in ten Canadians smoked cigarettes regularly in the early 1950s, with users drawn from both sexes, all age and socio-economic groups, and all regions of the country. It was in the social and cultural aspects of consumption, and not the realms of production or economic output, that cigarettes made their true and enduring mark on the nation. A mass-produced commodity, cigarettes were consumed by a broad cross-section of Canadians.

Cigarettes were consumed broadly in demographic terms, but also frequently; smokers typically puffed away on twenty or more cigarettes a day, in a variety of settings and contexts. Steve Penfold notes how common commodities like donuts became part of the "mundane matters of everyday life" and later woven "into the daily business of commuting, flirting, playing, and hanging out."[166] Cigarettes in mid-twentieth-century Canada functioned similarly, subtly embedding and shaping daily rituals, while also populating the foreground of social interaction and cultural activity. Advertising abetted these smoking-related cultural changes, not just in the mass media but in the nation's baseball fields, hockey arenas, and bowling alleys. Seen here was the synergistic promise of promoting cigarettes (and smoking as sociability) in community-making recreational spaces in towns and cities across Canada. These places, as Roland Marchand

3.14 Secretary of State for External Affairs Lester B. Pearson smokes while talking to reporters in Ottawa in December 1956.

notes, offered the "ambience of that social formation most redolent of comfortable, friendly and agreeable relationships among individuals and groups – the local community."[167] For cigarette marketers, inhabiting these spaces conferred authenticity and cultural legitimacy.

For many, cigarette smoking was a sensible course of action, helping people traverse social worlds and manage inner-life challenges. Cigarettes infused face-to-face relations with friends, family, and colleagues; they helped individuals fashion and project a sense of self-identity in modern society, which, as Giddens notes, could be "inherently unsettling," a place where people were racked by feelings of "restlessness, foreboding and desperation." Smoking was both compass and anchor for those navigating the "shifting experiences of day-to-day life" amid the "fragmenting tendencies of modern institutions."[168] As such, cigarettes became a "device for expressing the irreducible particularity of [one's] innermost self."[169]

While, as we have seen, cigarettes were a measure of modern industrial time ("smoke breaks"), they also worked to suspend "the passage of ordinary time," by enabling smokers to indulge in solitary reflection or introspective stock-taking.[170] Smoking contributed to the making of "we time" and "me time." We might reflect on the above when noting the rough doubling of the female smoking rate since the 1930s, a pace of growth outstripping that of men. Like men, women faced the challenge of negotiating unfamiliar social terrain while maintaining a coherent sense of self and personal equanimity. But they also faced the added difficulty of doing all this in social, economic, and familial settings whose power structures often privileged men and discriminated against women. Theirs was the harder row to hoe, arguably creating more incentive for women to adopt smoking as a coping mechanism.

By the early 1950s, cigarette smoking had achieved a high degree of social legitimacy. Given the soaring popularity of smoking, tobacco executives might well have thought that this state of affairs would continue unchallenged for years. But legitimacy – whether political, social, or cultural – is never a permanent or fixed condition. It is always contested and, as Keith Walden notes, subject to ongoing debate by "different groups and individuals, each attempting to assert its own understandings, derived from its own assessments of interests."[171] No sooner had cigarette smoking reached this zenith of consumer uptake and social acceptance – a time when politicians lit up freely at conferences and people turned a blind eye to teen smoking – than an extraordinary new challenge threatened this state of affairs: news stories on medical studies linking cigarettes to lung cancer began to appear in the early 1950s. Preserving the social legitimacy of smoking in this new era would see cigarette firms deploy an arsenal of measures, among them disinformation campaigns to malign medical science and downplay the health risks of smoking.

CHAPTER FOUR

Taxes, Public Smoking, and Lung Cancer

INTRODUCTION

Death and taxes, the saying goes, are the only sure things in life. For postwar smokers, this adage took on added meaning as Ottawa raised already-steep cigarette taxes at a time when news stories about medical studies linking cigarettes to the deadly disease of lung cancer began to appear. Tobacco and taxes had long been bedfellows, but not until the 1930s, when cigarette sales began to climb sharply, did tobacco taxes form a sizeable share of federal revenues. In 1938, Ottawa took in $36 million from tobacco excise taxes and custom duties, about 8 per cent of federal tax revenues that year.[1] Burgeoning cigarette use coupled with tobacco tax hikes during the Second World War saw Ottawa's take from tobacco sales rise to $103 million in 1942 and then to $170 million in 1946. In less than a decade, federal revenues from cigarettes had grown more than four-fold.[2] After the war, Ottawa axed wartime taxes on "luxury" goods like chocolate and jewellery, but not cigarettes. In 1951, however, the Liberal government hiked cigarette taxes, a move strongly opposed by tobacco growers, manufacturers, and retailers. Canadian smokers, in large numbers, challenged this tax increase by opting for cheaper American cigarettes smuggled into Canada and then sold on the black market. One year after the tax hike, Ottawa reversed course and began cutting cigarette taxes, soon dropping them below their 1951 level. The government's decision was a response to effective industry lobbying and a drop in federal revenues caused by contraband sales. This tax revolt proved both popular and successful, reflecting the unwillingness of Canadian smokers to endure high "wartime" taxes on something that had become a staple feature of family life, social interaction, and workplace habits.

In March 1949, the *Toronto Daily Star* reported on a US medical study making "a possible connection" between "too heavy cigarette smoking and lung cancer." Ninety-six per cent of the study's two hundred lung cancer patients had smoked at least one pack of cigarettes daily, researchers revealed.[3] In the following years, other newspaper stories would report on medically documented ties between cigarettes and lung cancer. While, for tobacco executives, high taxes were a manageable, even surmountable, problem, scientific reports linking cigarettes to lung cancer posed an existential threat to the industry. For the six in ten Canadians who smoked regularly, cigarettes permeated socializing, job sites, and self-identity. How would they respond to news that the common cigarette was a purported silent killer? Skeptically, it would seem. When, in 1954, the first national survey asked Canadians if they thought cigarette smoking caused lung cancer, only one in four answered in the affirmative, despite widespread press coverage and topical awareness of the issue.[4]

Explanations for this skepticism are many. While, in the early 1950s, news organizations reported on medical research involving smoking and cancer, some of these accounts carried emphatic denials of this association by cigarette executives and other scientists. Conflicting and contradictory accounts of the health harms of smoking characterized some news coverage of this issue, while other news reports and opinion pieces promoted the social and psychological benefits of smoking. As well, prolific cigarette advertising in newspapers and magazines reinforced the social acceptability of both product and practice. Canadians, since at least the 1930s, regarded cigarettes as mildly unhealthy, a product that triggered coughs, throat irritation, and colds. These garden-variety health complaints carried into the postwar years, arguably impeding the uptake of a new health paradigm centred on serious disease and fatal outcomes. This, in part, was because Canadians viewed cancer with equal measures of fear and despair in the 1940s. Limited treatment options meant that cancer diagnoses were typically followed by unbearable pain and agonizing death. Veils of secrecy and shame surrounded the disease, with people hiding the fact that loved ones had cancer or had died from it. Thus Canadians were culturally and cognitively biased against believing that a causal association existed between the ubiquitous social practice of smoking and cancer, society's most feared disease. Since the 1950s, studies have shown that smokers, as compared with non-smokers, are more likely to discredit evidence connecting smoking to cancer. This is emblematic of "motivated reasoning," a psychological theory describing how people engaged in dangerous behaviours adopt justifications and arguments to minimize the perception of these risks, in ways that seem logical and credible to them. Motivated reasoning constitutes the intellectual work of continued smoking, enabling smokers to manage the cognitive dissonance linked to behaviour deemed harmful, even lethal, by medical experts.

While cigarette smoking was a socially normative practice by the late 1940s, areas of opposition remained with respect to smoking in public. In buses, cinemas, and restaurants, smokers and abstainers clashed over the socially acceptable limits of smoking around others. Sometimes these complaints involved fire safety or litter from cigarette butts; more often they concerned non-smoker objections to indoor air that was thick with cigarette smoke. This opposition contrasted with pre-war complaints about public smoking, which typically involved the moral censure of female smokers on streets or other public places. Complaints after 1945 were far less likely to be gendered or concern outdoor smoking; instead they mostly dealt with instances of indoor smoking occurring near others, entailing competing notions about the appropriate boundaries of personal space for people in close proximity. Non-smokers held that individual space should encompass one's surrounding air space, while smokers dismissed this view as out of date and priggish, one that ignored the centrality of smoking in modern urban life, which included public transit and gathering places like restaurants. In larger cities, where most adults smoked, proponents of unrestricted public smoking routinely maligned their critics as social backsliders or fastidious killjoys.

CIGARETTE TAXES AND SMUGGLING

During the Second World War, the federal government repeatedly raised excise taxes on cigarettes, such that by 1944 Ottawa's take from a 35-cent pack of cigarettes was about 20 cents.[5] When these cigarette taxes remained in place after the war, smokers and tobacco retailers complained bitterly.[6] In 1947, a magazine writer charged that a 20-cents-per-pack federal tax was far too high and threatened to put cigarettes out of reach of working people.[7] A letter writer in the *Toronto Daily Star*, identified as "a 1914 Veteran," vented about high tobacco taxes: "I do not think that any government has ever imposed a more vicious tax on the worker."[8] In 1949, Ottawa cut excise taxes on a host of products (e.g., soft drinks, candy bars, jewellery, cosmetics) that had been initially taxed during the war, but did not do the same for tobacco and liquor.[9] The Liberal government soon after raised cigarette taxes to fund postwar social programs and Canada's participation in the Korean War. The 1951 federal budget hiked excise taxes by 15 per cent, boosting it from 20 to 23 cents per pack.[10] In provinces like Quebec, which levied a sales tax on cigarettes, a pack could cost as much as 43 cents. In provinces without provincial cigarette taxes, like Ontario and Alberta, cigarette packs sold for about 40 cents.

Not surprisingly, opposition to costly cigarettes was strongest in Quebec, which also had the highest smoking rate in Canada. Quebeckers complained about high cigarette prices, often drawing comparisons to US cigarettes, which sold for about half the price of Canadian smokes. In December 1951, Le Conseil Fédéré des Métiers et du Travail de Québec et Lévis called on Prime Minister Louis St Laurent and Finance Minister Douglas Abbott to cut tobacco taxes, deemed responsible for the growing black market in cigarettes that threatened tobacco manufacturing jobs in Canada.[11] Imperial Tobacco (ITC) president Edward Wood agreed, blaming high cigarette taxes for the contraband market.[12] There were calls to avoid these taxes by buying cigarette-rolling machines and fine-cut tobacco and making one's own cigarettes.[13] Another observer called for a cigarette boycott, claiming that with "a minimum of nail-biting" a smoker could "easily reduce his cigarette consumption to half," which in turn would lower cigarettes prices to "a more reasonable level."[14] The Flue-Cured Tobacco Marketing Association lobbied Ottawa to axe tobacco taxes and lower the cost of a cigarette pack to 30 cents.[15] In February 1952, Ontario tobacco growers met with Abbott to press for a 12-cent cut to the excise tax.[16]

These lobbying efforts paid off. The federal budget of April 1952 lowered cigarette excise taxes from 23 to 20 cents per pack.[17] The move, however, did not appease ITC's Wood, who called the drop "insufficient" and "disappointing."[18] He and others called for deeper cuts to cigarette taxes.[19] In

December 1952, 1,500 tobacco growers attended a rally in Tillsonburg, Ontario, calling for more tax rollbacks. Growers complained that high taxes had reduced cigarette sales, resulting in less tobacco crop acreage. Attendees adopted a nine-point resolution in support of lower taxes, later delivered to Abbott. Tobacco grower John D. Bowerman maligned cigarette taxes as "grossly unfair," underscoring that Ottawa "should be reminded that tobacco is no longer a luxury," but a "real necessity." Fellow grower J. Fred Thomas attacked high taxes by referencing cross-border cigarette shopping: "Almost every smoker in Windsor makes at least one trip a week to Detroit for a week's supply of cheaper U.S. cigarettes." With what they saved in doing this, he claimed, "each smuggler can afford to take his wife to a show and dinner."[20] Tobacco growers and retailers argued that cigarette sales in Canada had risen after the excise tax cut of 1952 and that more tax cuts would further boost cigarette sales and federal tax revenues.[21] Soon after, Ottawa gave in to this lobbying: the 1953 federal budget reduced excise taxes on cigarette packs by another four cents, now 16 cents per pack, a 30 per cent reduction from two years earlier.[22]

Ottawa's decision to cut this tax was also a response to burgeoning cigarette smuggling during the early 1950s. In the United States, the excise tax was 8 cents per pack, allowing cigarettes there to be sold for about 20 cents, roughly half the price of Canadian cigarettes.[23] There was a strong economic incentive for "entrepreneurs" to buy American cigarettes in bulk and smuggle them into Canada to sell on the black market. Much of the organized cigarette smuggling occurred in Quebec, due to its porous land border with the United States. In the months following the excise tax hike of 1951, a stream of news stories reported on cigarette smuggling and arrests. Between April and November 1951, Canadian authorities apprehended eight million contraband US cigarettes in Canada, mostly in Quebec.[24] Two seizures in the Eastern Townships in November 1951 netted the RCMP an astounding 1.3 million contraband cigarettes.[25] Most of these US cigarettes were destined for large centres like Montreal, the hub of illicit tobacco selling in Canada. There, contraband cigarette dealers worked brazenly, even selling in the city's office towers.[26] In Toronto, dealers peddled bootleg American cigarettes on street corners and in barber shops and hardware stores, selling them for 10 to 15 cents less than Canadian cigarette packs.[27] In December 1951, there were reports of "hundreds of truckloads" of smuggled American cigarettes regularly making their way into Canada. The "desperado drivers" of these trucks were undeterred by police patrols or roadblocks, owing to potential profits of $3,000 per delivery.[28] Two-thirds of Montreal smokers in 1951 were said to have recently smoked contraband cigarettes.[29] The Ontario Flue-Cured Tobacco Marketing Association estimated that roughly one billion cigarettes were smuggled into Canada in 1951. As Ottawa lowered cigarette excise taxes, the estimated volume of smuggled American cigarettes also declined, from some 800 million in 1952 to 350 million in 1953.[30] Similarly, the federal government reported that authorities had seized 164,000 contraband cigarettes in the first four months of 1954, down from 2.5 million in the same period in 1953.[31]

In their readiness to consume illicit American cigarettes, often furnished by crime syndicates, otherwise lawful Canadians readily and repeatedly broke the law in their entitled quest to secure affordable smokes. In light of how cigarettes had become mainstays of social interaction and personal well-being, Canadians most likely viewed these black-market purchases as legitimate acts of resistance against unfair levels of taxation on a product seen as non-discretionary and indispensable.[32] If this meant smoking American cigarettes instead of Canadian ones, then many in the country's burgeoning ranks of smokers would relinquish their own domestic brands to do so.

PUBLIC SMOKING

While smoking was commonplace by the late 1940s, pockets of opposition remained concerning smoking in public. People often complained about smoking in public spaces where the practice was restricted or prohibited (e.g., buses, cinemas, restaurants), with letters to the editor about this subject appearing regularly in newspapers like the *Toronto Daily Star*. In 1949, one letter writer criticized out-of-control smoking on Toronto buses, referring to the signs restricting smoking to the rear of the bus as a "waste of paint," given the frequency of violation. Smokers "annoy[ed] non-smokers by smoking any place in the bus," including in crowded aisles. This occurred routinely, he wrote, because authorities did not enforce existing rules on smoking and did not recognize the fire hazards posed by lit cigarettes in crowded, confined spaces.[33] Others similarly bemoaned the non-enforcement of smoking restrictions on Toronto buses.[34] Widespread smoking on Gray Coach bus lines had made one man "deathly sick."[35] Commuters vented about cigarette burns on overcoats and asthma sufferers being forced to "endure intense agony from the stifling atmosphere of the buses," calling on transit authorities to stop these "inconsiderate addicts" from disturbing other passengers "in order to gratify their own selfish habits."[36]

In 1948, Toronto Mayor Robert Saunders called on the provincial government to allow cities to ban smoking in "crowded department stores" and other large retailers, citing safety reasons.[37] Restaurant patrons complained about smokers who blew "smoke into other people's faces," resulting in "their urge to eat [being] snuffed out by smoke drifting under their noses and ashes being blown about by air-cooling systems."[38] A former Toronto resident who had returned to the city was shocked by smokers' "lack of consideration for others" in shops, restaurants, and on the street: "one cannot enjoy a meal without smoke puffed in one's face, and cigarette butts and boxes strewn about till you feel you are eating them along with your meal." Complain about this, she said, and "you are immediately dubbed [a] crank."[39] Another person was disgusted by the sight of a butcher smoking while carving meat and by a barber smoking while cutting hair.[40] A cinema-goer in 1948 called for enforcement of smoking restrictions in theatres, describing how he had seen two burning cigarettes tossed from a balcony onto a woman who "could have had her hair set on fire."[41] Others complained about the "annoying habits of smokers in buses, trains, and eating places" and the pervasive litter from cigarette packs, butts, and matches. One individual had "holes burned in his hat and clothing by carelessly thrown burning butts," and called for signs being posted in public spaces highlighting the dangers of careless cigarettes.[42] Smokers even criticized fellow smokers: "Some of us smokers are a rude lot, wholly unmindful of the wishes of others." The problem lay with the "rude few who smoke where it says no smoking, and where others object," and who really needed to "be put in their proper place."[43]

The long litany of complaints suggest it was more than just the "rude few" who breached bylaws, establishment rules, and etiquette norms by improperly smoking in public. As discussed in chapter 3, cigarette smoking in indoor workplaces – offices, factories, even hospitals – accelerated during and after the war, reflecting the growing popularity of smoking and the view that cigarettes improved the concentration and productivity of workers. By the early 1950s, cigarettes were an accepted feature of job sites for blue-, white-, and pink-collar workers. Smokers in turn sought to extend this prerogative to other public spaces – educational, recreational, mass transit – where restrictions existed for safety or the consideration of non-smokers. In major cities, where about two-thirds of adults smoked cigarettes, it was relatively easy to impugn critics of smoking in public as "cranks" or killjoys. In 1946, a man wrote a letter to the editor attacking the "continually crabby" women who complained about smoking on Hamilton streetcars. A Second World War veteran, he spoke "for a lot of returned men" who thought that smoking restrictions on transit cars made Hamilton "way behind the times." If these whining women would just "stay off street cars during rush hours, when hard-working men are trying to get home for supper," he wrote, then the problem would be solved (figure 4.1).[44]

A generation before, complaints about public smoking typically centred on women, for whom smoking on a street was portrayed as a moral offence. Proximity to the cigarette smoker (and side-stream smoke) mattered little in characterizing such behaviour as a breach of etiquette and social norms. The mere presence of a woman smoking in public violated social propriety and feminine respectability. By 1950, this type of moral critique had largely dissipated, at least in urban Canada. Instead, complaints about public smoking rarely dealt with open-air occurrences, focusing on indoor spaces and proximity to the offending smoker, all of which engendered conflict involving competing understandings of personal space. As urbanization and industrialization brought more people into more confined spaces, the milder aroma of cigarettes was preferred to the coarser hues and smells of pipe and cigar smoke, whether in factories, office buildings, streetcars, or apartment blocks. But, while more palatable, cigarette smoke proved far more pervasive in indoor areas than had been the case for pipe and cigar smoke. The air in buses, streetcars, and restaurants was often blue with cigarette smoke. For smokers, this was an accepted by-product of exercising an individual's "right" to smoke

4.1 Opponents of public smoking were often derided as busybodies and killjoys, attacking a pastime which smokers viewed as a quasi-public right after 1945. Cartoon on public smoking in the *Canadian Cigar and Tobacco Journal*, June 1949.

cigarettes anywhere, reflecting smoking's crucial place in adult socialization and personal identity.[45] Those offended by cigarette smoke, one Hamilton veteran proclaimed, should "go and take a cave some place in the Rockies." He, "along with a good many other boys," had gone to war to "keep this country a place where a man could exercise his normal rights as a free citizen."[46]

For such smokers, personal space encompassed the surrounding air in which their tobacco smoke dissipated. Non-smokers (and sometimes the odd smoker) who felt violated by indoor cigarette smoke countered that personal space should include one's immediate airspace and the corresponding right to breathe unsullied air.[47] Critics of public smoking also framed it as a violation of the social contract governing respectful interaction between strangers in public: by smoking carelessly and intemperately, and littering indoor areas with cigarette butts, these smokers were disdainful of others.[48] But critics of public smoking were waging a rearguard campaign; the prevailing trend saw cigarette smoking colonize ever more indoor public spaces. The director of a boarding school in Ontario described how he had allowed older teen boys to smoke cigarettes only in their bedrooms during daytime. Soon after he learned how offering limited smoking privileges for the few could devolve into "smoking everywhere," day or night, for the many.[49] In 1953, the president of Ottawa's Carleton College appealed to students to stop smoking in class, citing a petition by 50 students requesting this ban. But a counter petition signed by 143 students successfully opposed this initiative, arguing that decisions on in-class smoking be left to individual professors.[50]

CANCER NEWS

By far, the most serious challenge to smoking's hegemonic standing came from medical studies linking cigarette use to lung cancer. In the late 1940s, the thoracic surgeon Alton Ochsner published clinical-observation studies revealing that lung cancer patients were very likely to have smoked, leading him to conclude that cigarette smoke irritated lung tissue, producing tumours in some cases.[51] In 1950, Ernest L. Wynder and Evarts A. Graham published a paper based on data from six hundred lung cancer patients. They concluded that cigarette smoking was a primary etiologic factor for lung cancer, then a rare disease among non-smokers. Researchers accounted for the higher rate of lung cancer among men by noting the higher historical rates of male smoking and the long latency period from smoking initiation to the onset of lung cancer. Mounting rates of lung cancer in the past two decades mirrored rising levels of cigarette consumption in the United States.[52] Soon after, British researchers Richard A. Doll and A. Bradford Hill published a retrospective study that paired lung cancer patients with a control group of healthy subjects. Incredibly, every one of the study's 647 lung cancer patients had smoked cigarettes. Doll and Hill also demonstrated that lower levels of female lung cancer were explained by contrasting rates of historical smoking for men and women. Their research showcased the explanatory power of epidemiology to determine causality for diseases like smoking-induced cancer, for which laboratory experiments with humans were not ethically possible. As Brandt argues, Doll and Hill "brilliantly and explicitly" laid out the "basis for a systematic epidemiological approach to determining causality in noninfectious chronic disease," underscoring that "modern epidemiology was constructed around the problem of determining the harms of smoking."[53]

Subsequent studies validated the conclusions of Wynder and Graham and Doll and Hill. E. Cuyler Hammond and Daniel Horn published findings in 1953 and 1954 from a sample of 200,000 men between fifty and sixty who were followed for four years.[54] Among the 12,000 deaths occurring in this period, lung cancer mortality was twenty-four times higher among smokers than non-smokers. Smokers were more likely to die from coronary heart disease. The link between smoking and disease did not vary significantly between city and country, countering claims that urban air pollution was a significant cause of lung cancer. Hammond and Horn's data revealed that nearly 40 per cent of deaths among smokers were attributable to cigarette use.[55]

Tobacco executives and some scientists criticized these epidemiological studies, dismissing them as "statistical" and lacking the scientific rigour of clinical observation or laboratory experimentation. One key study refuted these critics. Graham, Wynder, and Adele Croninger published an article in 1953 based on a study in which tobacco tar was painted on mice. During the year of observation, 44 per cent of tar-painted mice developed cancerous tumours, results that attracted widespread interest in medical circles and the general public.[56] Because lab experiments exposing humans to tar painting or cigarette smoke were not ethically possible, the bulk of smoking-and-health research during the 1950s employed epidemiological methods, whose results proved consistent and compelling. By the mid-1950s, most public health authorities and cancer scientists believed that cigarette smoking was very harmful to the health of smokers.[57]

Canadian newspapers reported on these medical studies, especially the *Toronto Daily Star*. As early as March 1949 the *Star* ran a story on research at a conference of the American Cancer Society, reporting "a possible connection between too heavy cigarette smoking and lung cancer." The study of two hundred patients with lung cancer had found that 96 per cent of subjects had smoked at least one pack of cigarettes daily during the past twenty years. "Researchers stressed that from these studies it cannot be concluded that heavy smoking causes lung cancer. But they felt excessive smoking might be a factor where susceptibility to cancer of the lung already exists."[58] In October, the *Star* reported on Evarts A. Graham's study of four hundred lung cancer cases, for which he concluded that it was "very rare" for a patient not to be a past or present "excessive cigarette smoker."[59] In July 1950, the *Star* recounted the findings of Ochsner and Wynder linking cigarette smoking to lung cancer, presented at the International Cancer Research Congress.[60] The newspaper similarly wrote about Doll and Hill's 1950 report for the British Medical Research Council, which argued that cigarettes were "an important factor in cancer of the lungs." A typical forty-five-year-old man smoking twenty-five or more cigarettes daily, the article noted, was "50 times more likely to contract cancer than a non-smoker."[61] The *Star* reported on other research by Wynder and Ochsner, quoting Wynder as saying that only 15 of the 1,000 lung cancer male patients studied were non-smokers, and that "prolonged and heavy use of cigarettes increases up to 20 times the risk of developing lung cancer." The newspaper later quoted Ochsner that there was a "definite parallelism between the sale of cigarettes in the U.S. and the increasing incidence of cancer of the lung."[62]

The *Toronto Daily Star* also published editorials on the health risks of cigarette smoking. The first of these, in November 1952, cited recent medical studies reporting that cigarette use increased one's risk of acquiring lung cancer and heart and bronchial diseases. The editorial presciently noted that it was the "tars in tobacco smoke" that were "feared as possible cancer-producing agents"; people continuing to smoke, the paper warned, should do so moderately and consult their physician.[63] A 1953 *Star* editorial referenced a study of US hospital patients, noting that "excessive and prolonged use of tobacco, especially cigarettes" was an "important factor" in contracting lung cancer.[64] Two months later, another editorial recounted how an official from the American Cancer Society had advised a Canadian audience that lung cancer rates among cigarette smokers were at least ten times higher than those of non-smokers. Cancer experts, the editorial stated, were "increasingly concerned about the rising incidence of lung cancer and its possible relationship to excessive smoking."[65] In November 1953, the *Star*'s editorial writers reiterated that cigarette smoking was "one of the suspected causes of lung cancer" according to recent findings by British and American scientists.[66] Soon after, the *Star* called on researchers to develop methods to "remove the cancer-producing element in tobacco" in response to the quadrupling of lung cancer deaths among men in the past two decades.[67]

The Canadian version of *Reader's Digest*, English- and French-language versions, also covered the health dangers of smoking. In April 1950, Roger Williams Riis wrote an in-depth feature on the health charges levied against cigarettes, research for which, he claimed, involved reading some one hundred books and articles.[68] Riis covered a broad array of smoking-related health topics, starting with research on cigarette use and throat irritation, coughing, and impaired breathing. He covered the presence of benzo-pyrene in cigarette tar, a chemical later found to be carcinogenic.[69] He examined research on smoking's effects on digestion, gastrointestinal disorders, ulcers, and cardiovascular conditions like Buerger's disease. His most extended discussion concerned research linking smoking to cancer. Here he presented the early work of Graham and Wynder, describing how Graham's research had found that 95 per cent of two thousand lung cancer patients had in fact smoked at least one pack of cigarettes daily. He discussed Ochsner's position that a causal relationship linked cigarette smoking to lung cancer. Riis then went through scientific findings on smoking and cancers of the tongue, mouth, and lip. Near the end of the article, he quoted an insurance executive, Dr Robert A. Goodell, who said that "Il semble bien que la mortalité soit légèrement plus élevée à cause du tabac."[70] The health case against smoking was so compelling, Riis believed, that he cut his own rate of use from forty to ten cigarettes per day while researching and writing the article. Riis's piece generated so much reader interest that *Reader's Digest* followed it up with an article offering tips for quitting smoking.[71]

Most Canadian magazines and newspapers, however, did not report on the health harms of smoking to the same extent as the *Toronto Daily Star* or *Reader's Digest*. Indeed, many news stories and opinion pieces during the 1940s and 1950s routinely denied or downplayed the health risks of cigarette use. Robert H. Felt, a physician writing in *Maclean's* in 1943, highlighted the benefits of cigarette smoking while minimizing the health concerns. The state of medical research to date, he wrote, did not connect smoking to heart disease, elevated blood pressure, or adverse outcomes during pregnancy. The known health risks of smoking were manageable, mostly involving conditions like coughing and nasal irritation. Cigarette tar did not cause cancer since it was not "applied continuously to the body tissues." Only pipe smokers risked cancer, but only in the area of the lip where the pipe was regularly placed. Cigarette smoking, Felt argued, caused only two conditions, both rare: amblyopia, or dimness of vision; and Buerger's disease, which impaired blood circulation. The health risks of smoking were in fact so inconsequential that "most insurance companies no longer enquire into the smoking habits of an applicant for life insurance. If they regarded the use of tobacco *per se* as an important factor in high death rates they would not abandon this question." Only smokers with pre-existing health problems like angina or ulcers should be concerned and consult their doctor about continued smoking. For all others, one "needn't worry much about your smoking," provided it was done in moderation. Cigarette smoking provided psychological benefits due to its ability to "quiet the nerves." The "satisfaction that millions of confirmed smokers derive" from smoking, he wrote, "must not be overlooked."[72] Similarly a 1946 article in the CCTJ praised smoking for promoting psychological and spiritual well-being. The typical smoker

> starts his day with a measure of quiet thoughtfulness, good for his glands and easy on the heart. His taste for sweets is well under control, and if he reaches for a cigarette or his tobacco pouch instead of a cocktail glass, he may even do less drinking. Being a little short of breath, especially as the years wear on, he tends to preserve a wholesome tempo. If he sprints less he does instead have more than time for meditation and the inner life, and correspondingly more energy to apply to his mental problems.[73]

E.L. Chicanot, writing in *Saturday Night* in 1948, proclaimed that "you may puff peacefully while doctors disagree" about the health of smoking. While readers may have heard old wives' tales about smoking stunting the growth of children or shortening life expectancy, they need not worry. Such "vague fears" may have "taken the edge off enjoyment" of smoking, but Chicanot advised his readers to jettison these for the "pure pleasure from smoking."[74] Medical doctor Irvin S. Koll, writing in the CCTJ in 1949, stated that moderate smoking was "literally harmless."[75] A 1951 article in *Le Soleil* discussed scientific findings about cigarette tobacco containing four types of Vitamin B.[76] In a 1952 medical advice column, Dr T.R. Van Dellen discounted the causal connection between cigarette smoking and lung cancer. A definitive answer to that question, he wrote, would only occur when scientists could "produce cancer experimentally from some or all of the products contained in cigarette smoke." Van Dellen cited other possible explanations for rising lung cancer rates, including gasoline fumes, industrial dust from chromates, asbestos, tar, nickel, and how the influenza pandemic of 1918–19 weakened the lungs of survivors, rendering them more susceptible to bronchitis and lung cancer.[77] In a 1954 article, *Maclean's* writer Sydney Katz posed the question: "Can cigarettes kill you?" He answered with a qualified "No," citing other possible explanations for rising lung cancer rates such as air pollution, aging populations, and better cancer diagnostic technology.[78] Another journalist contended that while mounting health charges were levied against cigarettes, this did "not prove that smoking is guilty." Unforeseen factors, he said, may yet solve this health puzzle, not unlike the plot of a murder mystery: "It may well be that we have read only enough of a life-and-death detective story to be convinced that a disinterested son murdered old Lord Plushbottom though it was really the butler who did him in. The trail is confused by baffling clues and a rogues' gallery of shady characters who act like accomplices."[79]

Similar views persisted well into the 1950s. In 1954, a writer in *Saturday Night* contended that the link between smoking and lung cancer was "still regarded in most quarters as unproven."[80] In the article "Smokers of the World Unite," P.G. Wodehouse wrote in tongue-in-cheek fashion about smoking and health concerns: "First it was James the Second, then Tolstoy, then all these doctors and now – of all people – Miss Gloria Swanson," had taken up the anti-smoking cause. In mocking health concerns about smoking, Wodehouse adopted the common rhetorical stance of conflating contemporary tobacco-health science with earlier moral critics of cigarette smoking who linked the habit to juvenile delinquency or female impropriety. To those maintaining that quitting smoking would improve one's sense of smell, Wodehouse quipped that since he lived in New York he often found himself "wishing that I didn't smell the place as well as I do."[81] The *Toronto Daily Star* passed along the advice of physician William F. Rienhoff to "go ahead and smoke – moderately"; Rienhoff did not believe that smoking had "anything whatever to do with causing lung cancer," believing that the "whole thing" had been started by a "couple of my medical friends, whose names I won't mention, who happen to be fanatics on the subject of non-smoking."[82] The *Telegraph-Journal* in St John, New Brunswick, reported in 1954 that the British physician who had performed lung-cancer surgery on the chain-smoking King George VI believed that "smoking does not cause cancer of the lung." The more likely culprit, he maintained, was air pollution in cities.[83] The *Telegraph-Journal* also reported on a Toronto meeting of heart specialists, who "stressed that there is no conclusive evidence that smoking induces heart disease." Cigarette smoking was only a concern for people with pre-existing heart conditions.[84] In 1954, University of Western Ontario scientist R.W. Begg claimed that polluted air was as likely a cause of lung cancer as smoking, adding: "No one has shown that by getting a mouse to inhale cigaret smoke you will produce lung cancer."[85] During the mid-1950s, Montreal's *La Presse* carried headlines like "Le tabac ne causerait aucun cancer au poumon" and "La cigarette est inoffensive pour les gens en santé"[86]

Health textbooks taught in Canadian schools were also non-committal on this issue. One popular text, *Good Health* (1951), co-authored by the physician and former Ontario deputy minister of health J.T. Phair, claimed that not all people were susceptible to the harmful effects of tobacco and that smoking was a universal "social custom that makes for friendliness and comradeship." Other health textbooks and teaching guides in the 1950s, Sharon Anne Cook notes, similarly depicted smoking as "one of the harmless social activities in which young men engage," essentially upholding the "commonplace nature of smoking among adolescents."[87] A 1955 Canadian booklet entitled *You're Growing Up* described cigarette smoking as harmful for growing teens but less so for adults: "Some doctors and research workers think that smoking is fairly harmless to most *healthy adults* who smoke *moderately*."[88] A *Toronto Daily Star* editorial later criticized the state of classroom instruction on this subject: "It is typical of the behind-the-times attitude of Ontario education that no provision to teach our children the new knowledge of cancer dangers from smoking is being planned for Ontario schools."[89]

This state of indifference was seen as well in the bimonthly publication *Health*, Canada's leading health magazine for laypeople. Published by the Health League of Canada, the magazine was read by tens of thousands of subscribers, as well as by visitors to hundreds of doctor and hospital waiting rooms.[90] Throughout the 1950s and early 1960s, as Sara Wilmshurst argues, *Health* was "nonchalant about the risks of smoking and largely ignored early epidemiological studies of lung cancer." Indeed, the magazine accepted cigarette advertising until 1960. An article in 1953 portrayed tobacco as a "pure means of enjoyment"; later offerings were "skeptical of chronic disease epidemiology and regarded smoking as a private matter between clinician and patient, not a public health concern." As late as 1963, a *Health* writer characterized smoking-and-health science as contested rather than consensual, claiming that not for decades "may [we] know for certain whether prolonged cigarette smoking causes lung cancer." Only in the mid-1960s did *Health*'s editorial content begin to reflect the prevailing scientific consensus on smoking and portray it as a serious public health problem.[91]

Canadians seeking accurate information and sound guidance about smoking and health confronted a hit-or-miss mediascape in the 1950s. While some outlets like the *Toronto Daily Star* and *Reader's Digest* reported regularly and carefully on medical studies linking smoking to lung cancer and other diseases, others dismissed such studies as premature or flawed, at times even extolling the psychological benefits of lighting up. Matthew Hilton found similar results for media coverage of smoking and cancer in the United Kingdom during this same time period, concluding that "smokers' understanding of the official anti-smoking message was highly dependent on the newspaper they read."[92] British tabloids largely avoided the issue for fear of depressing their blue-collar readers about something that was a "central pillar of working-class life." Reputable broadsheets often treated the topic in a "jocular light-hearted" fashion or exhibited "aggressive scepticism triggered from a belief that preventive medicine offered a threat to British 'freedom.'"[93]

Some historians, working as expert witnesses for tobacco firms, have argued that media coverage of smoking-and-health science during the 1950s and 1960s was pervasive and broadly received, creating a "common knowledge" understanding of the serious health risks of smoking among the general public.[94] This claim, however, rests on the near-impossible task of knowing which specific newspapers or magazines – and which specific articles – Canadians read and which of these were thought credible enough to influence belief or behaviour. Readers of *Maclean's* and *Saturday Night*, two leading consumer magazines in the 1950s, rarely encountered accurate accounts of the medical case tying smoking to morbidity and mortality. And publications with laudable records in this respect like the *Toronto Daily Star* also carried cigarette ads exalting the social desirability of smoking, whose volume far exceeded that of editorial copy on smoking and health.

The "common knowledge" thesis does not adhere to a research tradition in media or communication studies. While it might seem analogous to the "effects" school of media studies (sometimes called the "Columbia School"), begun in the 1940s by Paul F. Lazarsfeld, Robert Merton, and Elihu Katz, this in fact is a misreading. As Lazarsfeld and Merton proclaimed in a landmark 1948 essay on media effects research, "to know the number of hours people keep the radio turned on gives no indication of the effect upon them of what they hear."[95] To assess empirically the impact of media content on people meant studying not just transmission but also reception and audience response. When this multi-stage research was conducted it generally showed that mass-mediated messages were most influential when supplemented by other modes of communication (e.g., face-to-face contact) and when they channelled pre-existing values and attitudes. Owing to these mitigating factors, this approach was more commonly called the "limited effects" school of media studies.[96] In sum, the mere presence of historical media messages or content (articles, editorials, programs, ads, etc.) does not constitute prima facie evidence of corresponding awareness, belief, or behaviour on the part of the broader populace.

HEALTH, PUBLIC OPINION, AND SMOKING

Canadians had associated cigarette smoking with mild health complaints like coughing and throat irritation since at least the 1930s, when filter and menthol cigarettes were introduced to address these concerns. These minor health irritants long predated the health paradigm framed by lung cancer, which began to gain popular awareness in 1952–53. While not life threatening, these mild health concerns were familiar to most smokers. When the Gallup poll first asked Canadians about their smoking habits in 1949, it reported that 49 per cent of smokers had in the past tried to quit, most unsuccessfully, with health improvement cited as the number one reason for doing so.[97] Similarly, in late December 1951, when Gallup next polled on smoking, its press release noted that health considerations in the lead-up to the New Year meant that "one hears many a pledge to give up cigarettes."[98] The survey asked the one in seven Canadians who had quit smoking why they had done so: better health again came out on top, followed by saving money.[99]

Evidence of these health concerns can be seen in the cigarette marketplace. A 1945 ad for the Zeus Cigarette Holder touted how the product would remove "most of the harmful nicotine and tar, making your cigarette more enjoyable."[100] Ads for du Maurier cigarettes stressed the health benefits of the brand's filter, which "guards physical fitness" and was the "common-sense method of preventing smoker's throat because it effectively retains irritants."[101] The "guards physical fitness" claim appeared routinely in du Maurier advertising until at least 1953. Other du Maurier ads in the late 1940s and early 1950s touted its advanced filter technology, seen with statements like, "No smoker's throat for me!," "banishes smokers' throat," and "constant protection for your throat."[102] A Craven "A" ad in 1950 proclaimed that the brand "will not affect the throat."[103] In May 1951, ITC launched Viceroy cigarettes in Canada, advertising for which touted the "hygienic" filter containing "7,200 square millimeters of filter, scientifically channelled for extra absorbance" (figure 4.2).[104] The market for filter cigarettes was relatively small, forming 2 per cent of sales in the early 1950s. Most smokers were aware of these low-grade health concerns but not sufficiently moved by them, choosing instead to continue to smoke plain-end cigarettes, which often had high tar and nicotine levels. But the persistence of the filter market segment since the 1930s, coupled with Gallup surveys showing top-of-mind awareness of garden-variety health concerns, meant that smokers could well believe, as we shall see, that cigarettes were "unhealthy" but not necessarily a cause of lung cancer.

The common association of cigarettes with medical settings likely further clouded Canadians' understanding of smoking and health. A recurring visual motif during and after the war was that of a nurse or hospital

4.2 Even before cigarettes were linked to lung cancer, filter brands like du Maurier touted their benefits for lesser ailments like throat irritation and coughing. du Maurier ad in the *Toronto Daily Star*, 28 March 1950.

4.3 *Opposite* Dorothy Brooks of the Canadian Red Cross distributes cigarettes to Able Seaman I.M. Barnes in a Canadian military hospital in Taplow, England, 14 December 1944.

worker giving cigarettes to patients-soldiers, exchanges symbolizing heart-felt care and profound gratitude (figure 4.3).[105] Rather than destroying confiscated contraband cigarettes, authorities sometimes gave them to patients in military and veterans hospitals.[106] Macdonald Tobacco donated often to health organizations in the Montreal area. In 1946, it supplied free cigarettes to patients at Ste Anne de Bellevue Veterans' Hospital, while also advertising in its publication the *Bulletin*.[107] The company ran ads in *Canadian First Aid*, a quarterly publication of the St John Ambulance Association, while providing cigarettes for that organization's Christmas party held for hospitalized veterans.[108] It bought full-page ads in the *Nurses' Review* and *Student Nurses Annual*, published by the Royal Victoria

Hospital in Montreal.[109] In 1952, Macdonald advertised Export cigarettes in *The Canadian Nurse* and in the yearbook of the Faculty of Medicine at the University of Ottawa.[110] The company's philanthropy supported the Royal Victoria Hospital, including its cancer research operations, prompting the hospital president to thank the company in 1952 for its "great and bountiful interest in the Hospital."[111]

What effect did news reports about cigarettes and lung cancer have on smoking behaviour? A Gallup poll in March 1954 showed a decline in the rate of male cigarette smoking, down from 74 per cent in 1949 to 64 per cent in 1954.[112] In 1955, a Canadian Facts survey uncovered similar results; 68 per cent of men smoked cigarettes in 1955, down from 74 per cent in 1952.[113] A similar decline, however, did not occur with women; Canadian Facts found that 47 per cent of women self-identified as cigarette smokers in 1955, barely changed from the 49 per cent who did in 1952. Younger women were most likely to smoke; 51 per cent of those between eighteen and twenty-five did so, compared to 38 per cent of those over forty.[114] This contrasted with the pattern for men; 70 per cent of eighteen-to-twenty-five-year-olds smoked, similar to the overall male smoking rate of 68 per cent. The decline in the male smoking rate resulted mainly from older men quitting the habit. Eleven per cent of men over forty said they had quit smoking, the highest percentage of any age group in the Canadian Facts survey. While the overall adult smoking rate (male and female combined) fell from 62 per cent in 1952 to 58 per cent in 1955, researchers found that remaining smokers were not "smoking any fewer cigarettes per day than they were a year ago."[115] Indeed, industry statistics reveal that they were smoking more; per-capita sales of cigarettes among adults rose from 4.9 in 1952 to 6.4 in 1955, a 31 per cent increase.[116]

Reports linking cigarettes to cancer produced a sudden upswing in the sale of filter cigarettes after 1953. Filter cigarette brands comprised 2 per cent of sales in 1952. The "cancer scare," which began gaining traction in 1953, prompted smokers to seek out options perceived as safer, with filters initially fulfilling this need. By 1955, filter brands captured 8 per cent of the market, rising steadily after so that by 1962 they accounted for 55 per cent of sales (figure 4.4).[117] In 1955, women opted for filter brands at three times the rate of men, with 13 per cent of female smokers choosing them, compared with 4 per cent of male smokers.[118] Matinée, an ITC filter brand launched in 1954, grew swiftly to capture 4 per cent of the market one year later, driven mainly by female adopters. Filter brands, Canadian Facts reported in 1955, had exerted the "most important influence on the brand share picture during the past year."[119] While filter brands and other forms of "health reassurance" marketing are discussed in greater detail in chapter 5, it bears noting here that filter cigarettes were the first major product innovation to upend the duopolistic stasis of the cigarette industry of the early 1950s; these brands, notably Matinée, were also pioneers in successfully targeting women in large numbers as consumer segments. Market segmentation and product differentiation, which transformed the cigarette industry in the 1960s, developed initially as a marketing response to the health concerns of smokers, largely women (figure 4.5).

To what extent did Canadians believe that smoking caused lung cancer? The first national survey in Canada to ask this question was a Gallup poll released in July 1954. The pollster asked: "Have you heard or read anything recently that cigarette smoking may be a cause of cancer of the lung?" Incredibly, 89 per cent said they had, an exceptionally high level of awareness

4.4 *Top* When lung cancer fears emerged in 1953, Canadian smokers turned to filtered brands, which were perceived as healthier. A decade later more than half of cigarettes sold in Canada had filters. Cartoon from the *Canadian Cigar and Tobacco Journal*, December 1954.

4.5 *Bottom* Imperial Tobacco introduced the filter brand Matinée in 1954, as part of its health-reassurance marketing strategy. Matinée ad in the *Toronto Daily Star*, 8 March 1958.

of a public issue. Gallup then asked: "Do you think cigarette smoking is one of the causes of lung cancer or not?" Only 25 per cent of adults said "Yes," while 34 per cent said "No." Sixteen per cent offered qualified responses. The remaining 25 per cent were undecided. These results are striking. After more than two years of ongoing press coverage about studies linking tobacco to lung cancer, only one-quarter of Canadians believed that cigarette smoking was one of the causes (not the primary cause) of lung cancer. Indeed, a smoking–cancer skeptic could support the "one-of-the-causes" position while also believing that air pollution or viruses were more consequential causes of lung cancer. The qualified responses in the survey typically concerned the amount smoked, that heavier smokers as opposed to moderate ones were more at risk for lung cancer. While at this time people typically understood a "heavy" smoker to be someone smoking more than one pack per day, "moderate" smoking could encompass up to fifteen cigarettes daily, a rate of consumption which still put people at risk for lung cancer.[120] These survey results warn against conflating awareness, knowledge, and belief when assessing historical public opinion: while nine in ten Canadians were aware of smoking–cancer reports, fewer than three in ten believed them to be true.

The reluctance of Canadians to link cigarettes causally to cancer owed in part to prevailing attitudes about the disease, one that "horrified and paralyzed" people.[121] North Americans regarded cancer as capricious, agonizing, enigmatic, and nearly always fatal. Poor diagnostic methods before the 1940s meant the disease was often discovered in later stages, resulting in the friends and loved ones of cancer patients witnessing protruding tumours, festering wounds, and excruciating pain. People ignored their own cancer symptoms in fear of a positive diagnosis and a subsequent painful death. People spoke about cancer in hushed tones, since a sense of shame and taboo surrounded the disease, with some even believing it was contagious. Cancer sufferers sometimes concealed their condition for fear of losing friends or employment. Physicians, on occasion, did not disclose cancer diagnoses to patients, believing the news would only worsen their suffering and remaining quality of life.[122]

This "conspiracy of silence" extended to death certificates and newspaper obituaries, which often omitted cancer as cause of death.[123] In 1954, the Toronto police reported that a forty-year-old physician had "stabbed himself to death with a paring knife" because he feared he had lung cancer caused by smoking. His suicide occurred one day before his scheduled lung X-ray.[124] Cancer, Barbara Clow notes, "eclipsed most other ailments in the popular culture of North America because [it] inflicted an especially grievous form of suffering," a belief that "remained as keen in the 1940s as it had been in the 1920s."[125] These fears were not irrational or imaginary, but often based on first-hand experience of the disease, as James T. Patterson states: "what they knew about cancer they learned from watching friends or loved ones turn sick and die from it, sometimes slowly, expensively, and agonizingly."[126] Given this prevailing view of cancer based in existential fear and loathing, it is understandable that survey respondents might reject outright, viscerally and unreflectively, smoking–cancer causation, especially if they also smoked.

The 1954 Gallup poll on smoking and lung cancer produced another noteworthy finding. The survey's press release reported "that 'heavy' smokers – those smoking a pack or more per day – were most likely to refute a connection between cigarette smoking and lung cancer."[127] Other researchers uncovered similar results. In 1954, Evarts Graham observed that doctors who smoked were less inclined to believe in the causal relationship between smoking and cancer, writing that it was "their own addiction to this drug habit which blinds them. They have eyes to see but they see not because of their unwillingness or inability to give up smoking." He added that he had "never encountered any non-smoker who makes light of the evidence or is skeptical of the association between excessive smoking and lung cancer."[128] A year later, the American Cancer Society surveyed lung specialists, pathologists, and oncologists and found similar results: among those smoking a pack or more daily, 31 per cent agreed that heavy smoking could cause lung cancer; among non-smokers the respective figure was 65 per cent.[129]

This divergence of opinion between smokers and non-smokers is emblematic of motivated reasoning, a psychological theory developed in the 1980s and which remains influential among psychologists and political scientists.[130] According to the theory's founder, Ziva Kunda, when people are motivated to reach a particular conclusion they develop justifications, search out supporting evidence, and draw selectively on prior beliefs to arrive at such a position.[131] People regard this decision-making process as objective and rational, unaware they are accessing "only a subset of their relevant knowledge" and that "they would probably access differential beliefs and rules in the presence of different directional goals, and that they might even be capable of justifying opposite conclusions on different occasions."[132] Notably, Kunda examined how directional goals impacted people's evaluation of scientific evidence. Participants in one study, divided into four groups of low and high caffeine-consuming men and women, were presented with scientific evidence that high rates of caffeine consumption posed health risks for women, but not for men. The high-caffeine women viewed the evidence as less persuasive than the low-caffeine women. The high-caffeine men, however, did not discount the study like their high-caffeine female counterparts, indicating that "only subjects who stood to suffer serious personal implications if the article were true doubted its truth."[133]

In developing the theory of motivated reasoning, Kunda drew on prior studies of cognitive dissonance, including one evaluating reactions to the 1964 US Surgeon General's report highlighting the cancer risks of smoking. The study, published in 1965, found that smokers viewed the Surgeon General's findings as less credible than did non-smokers, underscoring that "people threatened by scientific evidence are motivated to disbelieve it."[134] More recently, Kraft et al. have argued that people's "beliefs and deliberations about science can be fundamentally biased by prior attitudes and initial affective responses," and that forms of "science denial" resulting from motivated reasoning may well be "fundamental to our basic cognitive architecture."[135] In the 1950s, smokers confronting medical news linking cigarettes to lung cancer, which was most often fatal, were no doubt highly motivated to devalue or discount entirely this evidence.

CONCLUSION

The rise and fall of cigarette excise taxes and resulting contraband cigarette markets, while short-lived, remain noteworthy for a couple of reasons. In 1950, 17.1 billion cigarettes were sold in Canada, compared with 15.6 billion in 1951, a drop of 9 per cent. To put this in perspective, this was the only decline in year-over-year sales of manufactured cigarettes between 1932 and 1968.[136] Contraband cigarettes filled some of this 1.5 billion decrease in legal cigarette sales, and we should not discount the possibility that some cost-sensitive smokers bought fewer cigarettes or quit entirely due to higher prices. Second, at the exact historical moment when Canadians first confronted news of smoking's association with lung cancer, cigarette prices were declining for the first time since the 1930s. Cuts to federal excise taxes made cigarettes about 20 per cent cheaper in 1953 than two years earlier. That Ottawa would bend to lobbying by tobacco growers, manufacturers, and retailers in a country where a majority of adults smoked cigarettes is not surprising. Widespread cigarette smuggling also impacted federal revenues and undermined respect for lawful authority and public order. It remains, nonetheless, a tragic irony of public health that declining cigarette prices coincided with Canadians' first encounters with news reports on the serious health harms of smoking, given what later became known about the relationship between low tobacco prices and higher rates of smoking.[137] Similarly, the harmful health effects of exposure to second-hand cigarette smoke would not be known for decades, when it would overturn notions of public smoking as mere social nuisance or personal irritant. When, in the 1980s, public smoking was recast as a public health issue, opponents of second-hand tobacco smoke gained the moral high ground and political backing to ban smoking in many indoor public places.[138]

Media coverage of the smoking-and-health issue proved uneven during the 1950s. While publications like the *Toronto Daily Star* provided comprehensive and accurate reporting on medical research linking smoking to lung cancer, other news reports rejected these findings as premature or alarmist. News stories and op-ed pieces continued to highlight the psychological rewards of regular puffing. Similar forms of ambiguity appeared in school health textbooks and *Health*, the country's leading magazine on healthy living and medical advice, which did not alert readers to the serious health harms of smoking until well into the 1960s. News reports on smoking and cancer moved some older men to quit smoking. But younger men and women of all ages generally did not follow suit, continuing to smoke at similar or higher rates than before the "cancer scare," with increasing numbers opting for filtered brands. This was the start of a paradoxical trend that persisted until the late 1960s; a gradual decline in smoking prevalence was coupled with a steady increase in per-capita cigarette consumption. Smokers, whether as recent entrants or remaining stalwarts, comprised a slowly declining share of the adult population but smoked increasing numbers of cigarettes per day.[139] This consumption pattern rendered these smokers more susceptible to lung cancer and other smoking-related diseases.

In the mid-1950s, an overwhelming majority of Canadians were aware of smoking-and-cancer news, but only one-quarter believed this to be true. Given the patchy state of news coverage, their skepticism about cigarettes causing lung cancer was understandable. Cancer instilled terror and despair in Canadians, who already possessed a more benign health framework for cigarettes comprising coughs, sore throats, and out-of-breath stair climbing. Surveys found that smokers were more likely to dispute smoking–cancer causation than non-smokers, findings consistent with the psychological theory of motivated reasoning. Smokers were cognitively predisposed and highly motivated to dispute the smoking–cancer thesis and formulate alternative explanations for the sharp rise in lung cancer cases. As we shall see, tobacco executives eagerly helped them in this respect, promoting dubious counter-explanations for the growth of lung cancer while unceasingly reassuring smokers about the safety of cigarettes.

CHAPTER FIVE

Hope and Doubt

INTRODUCTION

In 1953, North American cigarette firms faced an acute crisis: a trickle of news stories linking smoking to lung cancer, starting around 1950, had become a steady flow. In December, the shares of tobacco firms experienced a major sell-off, slashing company valuations to annual lows. According to market analysts, the cause of this was "new charges by doctors linking cigarette smoking with cancer of the lung."[1] Some smokers vowed to cut back on the habit or quit entirely. In the United States, cigarette sales declined by 2 per cent in 1953 and another 4 per cent in 1954, the first year-over-year declines seen since 1932.[2] In Canada, the situation was only slightly better. Cigarette sales remained flat in 1954, but this was in marked contrast to the 17 per cent sales increase seen the year prior.[3] The industry's "cancer scare," however, had only a short-term effect on company bottom lines. In 1955, cigarette consumption began climbing again; between 1953 and 1963 per-capita sales of manufactured cigarettes in Canada rose 53 per cent, compared with the 27 per cent increase seen in the 1945–53 period.[4] The cigarette market of the early 1960s consisted of some seventy brands, nearly half of which had been launched since the late 1950s.[5] Multinational tobacco companies like Tabacofina, Rothmans, and Philip Morris entered the Canadian market in the late 1950s and early 1960s, buying up domestic tobacco firms and establishing their own production facilities. A decade after the "cancer scare" of 1953–54, Canadian cigarette makers were experiencing higher sales and profits, operating in a market that was more competitive, more capitalized, and more diversified. Paradoxically, as the health risks of smoking gained scientific credence in the 1950s and early

1960s, the cigarette industry became economically stronger and more politically assured.

How did this happen? Cigarette manufacturers reframed the smoking-and-cancer issue from being a potentially ruinous development into a marketing opportunity to exploit and profit by. In 1958, Rothmans, in a series of ads, publicly acknowledged the likelihood of a link between cigarettes and lung cancer. Patrick O'Neil-Dunne, the head of Rothmans' Canadian operations, highlighted this association because the firm's flagship brand, Rothmans King Size Filter, had an advanced filter and contained less tar than its main competitors. The company promoted Rothmans' cigarettes as "safer" options for health-anxious smokers who were unwilling or unable to quit; Rothmans, a recent arrival to the Canadian market, deployed this strategy to "shake up" the cigarette industry and capture brand share from established players like ITC and Macdonald Tobacco. While such flagrant health-appeal marketing proved short-lived, other firms adopted this commercial strategy. ITC conducted extensive market research on the health concerns of Canadian smokers, developing new products to address these needs. The company introduced filter brands – such as Matinée in 1954 – on the heels of consumer research illuminating smokers' health concerns, which proved especially pronounced among women and young people. Smokers viewed filtered cigarettes as markedly safer than plain-end ones, an understanding the industry promoted, if more by calculated inference than direct appeal. "Health marketing," however ironic and disingenuous, secured a strong foothold in the cigarette industry by the early 1960s, as evidenced by the rising popularity of filter brands and low-tar ones like Belvedere and Craven "A". By 1963, firms like ITC and Rothmans had not only weathered the "cancer scare" but had capitalized on it to identify and tap into new markets, creating new products for health-worried consumers. Such health reassurance marketing hindered quit attempts, thus keeping anxious consumers in the smoking ranks.

A two-pronged public relations strategy accompanied the industry's marketing efforts. With the short-lived exception of O'Neil-Dunne, tobacco executives publicly and repeatedly denied that a proven relationship existed between smoking and disease, while also maligning the mounting body of scientific evidence that upheld this view. Industry leaders disparaged epidemiological science as "statistical" and baseless, a cheap pretender compared with bench science and clinical observation. They instead attributed rising rates of lung cancer to factors such as industrial contaminants, air pollution, diesel fumes, road tar, and even viruses. They asserted that longer human lifespans and better diagnostic technology contributed to the upswings in lung cancer and respiratory disease. While denying that smoking caused serious illness, cigarette executives reassured the public that industry scientists were hard at work investigating the chemical properties of tobacco smoke in order to solve the smoking-and-health "controversy" once and for all. Incomplete and inconsistent scientific results to date, industry officials maintained, meant that cigarettes had not yet been proven unsafe. Since smoking provided tangible benefits like stress relief and concentration, smokers should carry on lighting up until all the facts were known.

Alongside this denialist doctrine were moves to consolidate decision making and action on smoking and health into a single, industry-wide body. This approach first appeared in 1962 when the leaders of Canada's largest cigarette firms struck a voluntary agreement to end tar and nicotine references in advertising in order to avoid antagonizing federal officials. Soon after, cigarette manufacturers established an "ad hoc" committee for senior tobacco officials to regularly discuss and plot coordinated action on smoking and health. This co-operative strategy also included US officials. On various occasions, executives from the Tobacco Industry Research Committee and Hill & Knowlton, a New York public relations firm, visited Canada to help their Canadian counterparts. American officials conducted research and wrote briefs, backgrounders, and reports. They advised on media outreach and other public relations activities in Canada. When, in 1963, the federal health minister first took up the smoking-and-health issue, industry executives met with senior Cabinet ministers, including the prime minister, to dampen government actions. The effectiveness of industry organizing and lobbying was seen during the National Conference on Smoking and Health, a federal policy conference held in November 1963. This proved to be an unqualified success for the cigarette industry, as it adeptly outmanoeuvred opponents in government and health organizations.

THE DOCTRINE OF DENIAL

Alarmed by the mounting body of medical studies linking smoking to lung cancer, the CEOs of America's largest tobacco companies met on 14 and 15 December 1953 in the Plaza Hotel in New York. Out of these meetings came a plan of action. The public relations firm Hill & Knowlton was hired to draft and implement a campaign of public reassurance by demonstrating that tobacco firms were doing everything possible to discern the truth about smoking and to remedy any possible harms found in cigarettes. Alongside programs of industry research and public education, Hill & Knowlton would develop a far-ranging public relations program to provide "reassurance" to the public by highlighting "weighty scientific views which hold there is no proof that cigarette smoking is a cause of lung cancer."[6] The first stage of this public relations campaign began in January 1954, when full-page ads ran in hundreds of American newspapers. (These ads were widely reported upon in the press, most often favourably.)[7] These ads, titled "Frank Statement to Cigarette Smokers," affirmed the tobacco industry's high regard for public health and that it would do everything necessary to ensure that cigarettes were safe for smokers.

To that end, the "Frank Statement" announced the formation of an industry-funded scientific body, the Tobacco Industry Research Committee (TIRC), which would support research on "all phases of tobacco use and health."[8] Soon after, TIRC hired Clarence Cook Little as its scientific director. Little was a noted biologist and, not coincidentally, a long-time skeptic of the health harms of smoking. Little soon became the industry's primary spokesman on health and smoking topics, whose views on smoking and disease remained largely unchanged over the years: no credible scientific proof ever linked smoking to lung cancer or other diseases. Little's function, and that of TIRC in general, was, as Brandt notes, to "produce and sustain scientific skepticism and controversy in order to disrupt the emerging consensus on the harms of cigarette smoking."[9] TIRC and Little sought to recast the consolidating scientific paradigm on smoking and disease into an epistemological state mired in uncertainty and controversy, necessitating additional research and continued debate.

Little's promotion of this scientific "controversy" appeared in news stories in Canada. In a 1954 *Toronto Daily Star* story on smoking and cancer, Little is quoted as saying that the "cause is much, much more complicated than that. We must beware of our eyes. We see a guy inhaling smoke, and he has lung cancer ... and we tie the two together. Fumes from auto combustion would seem a much more likely source of tars that could cause cancer."[10] Other stories in Canadian newspapers contain similar denials of smoking–cancer causality.[11] In a *Toronto Daily Star* account in July 1957, Little stated that "non-smokers get lung cancer. The vast majority of heavy smokers never get lung cancer. Obviously, there is no simple cause and effect mechanism resulting from cigaret smoking."[12] When US Surgeon General Leroy E. Burney issued a strong warning against tobacco smoking in 1959, Little responded by saying that the science supporting Burney's position was based on dated "statistical studies that admittedly are not supported by experimental evidence." According to Little, "new evidence" showed that "people described as the world's heaviest cigaret smokers have low lung cancer death rates compared with people who smoke less but have been long exposed to urban air pollution."[13]

Other industry-funded scientists similarly denied the health risks of smoking in Canadian news stories during the 1950s. Dr Joseph Berkson, chief medical statistician of the Mayo Clinic, claimed that epidemiological studies showed only a "meaningless association" between smoking and lung cancer and that cigarette smokers experienced "equal or lower death rates from cancer than the general public."[14] In a *Toronto Daily Star* article in 1955, a TIRC official dismissed a study on smoking and cancer of the larynx as merely a "repetition of points of view previously publicized," underscoring that "the specific cause of lung cancer or any other kind of human cancer has not been discovered and [that] widespread research still is needed."[15] In another news story in 1957, Dr Harvey B. Haag of the Medical College of Virginia discussed his research on the death rates of smokers, saying it was "evident that cigaret smoking *per se* is not necessarily or invariably associated with a higher risk of lung cancer or cardiovascular disease or with diminished longevity."[16]

Canadian tobacco executives similarly denied any association between smoking and serious illness. In February 1954, E.C. Wood, president of

Imperial Tobacco Canada (ITC), dismissed the cigarette–cancer "scare," drawing a parallel with prior "widespread scares that a certain vegetable became poisoned through canning and that use of a certain type of metal pot or pan in cooking foods engendered poisoning." These claims, he said, later proved baseless. In his view, the "reported increase" in lung cancer cases was "statistical rather than clinical," and most likely the result of advances in medical diagnosis. "Science," he said, was "giving closer study to lung cancer in relation to occupational diseases and to the increasing air pollution of our fast-growing industrial areas." In addition to co-operating closely with relevant "medical and scientific organizations" on this matter, ITC's "laboratories [were] continually studying all phases of tobacco itself as well as its growth and preparation." ITC's research to date, Wood affirmed, had "found nothing to substantiate claims that tobacco smoking is a causative agent of lung cancer."[17] In 1957, he told a *Toronto Daily Star* reporter that "everything so far indicates there is nothing to these reports that cigarets cause lung cancer. It's just the work of a lot of bald-headed men. Just statistics."[18] In 1961, Robert J. Leahy, former Philip Morris executive and recently installed president of Benson & Hedges Canada, stated there was "no laboratory proof whatsoever that cigaret smoking causes cancer" and that the "cancer controversy" was "just a matter of statistical guessing."[19]

American tobacco executives issued similar denials that appeared in Canadian newspapers. Paul M. Hahn, president of the American Tobacco Company, stated in January 1954 that "it had not been proved that cigarettes have ever caused a single case of lung cancer."[20] Quoted in the French-language newspaper *Le Devoir*, E.A Darr, president of R.J. Reynolds Tobacco, said: "Je peux déclarer sans crainte de contradiction que les adversaires de la cigarette n'ont pu, jusqu'à aujourd'hui, supporter leur théorie par une seule preuve substantielle. Ils se sont plutôt satisfaits de baser leurs 'prétentions' sur des associations d'idées." He added: "Aucun indice, reperé jusqu'ici au cours d'intensives recherches n'a réussi à établir une relation directe entre le cancer du poumon et la fumée de la cigarette."[21] In 1955, a Canadian magazine quoted Darr as saying that the American Cancer Society, by highlighting the lung cancer risks of smoking, was "attempting to destroy the tobacco industry."[22]

These statements reflected the US and Canadian tobacco industries' strategy of denial used for decades after the early 1950s: epidemiological evidence was merely "statistical" and thus inferior to scientific results produced in the laboratory; better diagnostic technology meant that lung cancers identified today went undetected in the past; dangerous carcinogens dwelt in industrial and white-collar workplaces; air pollution, especially from gas and diesel engines, caused lung cancer; and the tobacco industry was investing heavily in health research, either in-house or by outside scientists, which promised to later solve the smoking–cancer "controversy."[23]

ROTHMANS' TRUTH CAMPAIGN

A number of tobacco multinational companies entered the Canadian cigarette market in the late 1950s and early 1960s. (Prior to this period, only ITC was foreign-owned, its parent company being British American Tobacco [BAT]). In 1957, Tabacofina, a Belgian tobacco company, set up operations in Canada. A year earlier, Tabacofina had bought a controlling interest in the Venezuelan tobacco maker Quintana Company, part of a broader campaign to increase the firm's presence in the bright-leaf cigarette market outside of Europe.[24] Soon after, Rothmans of Pall Mall, the UK multinational, followed suit. They were the first major foreign competitors to enter the Canadian cigarette market in more than a quarter century. Tabacofina launched two brands in 1957: Carousel, a plain-end, and Belvedere, a filter-tip. The company's ten-year goal was to control 10 per cent of market share.[25] Rothmans' ambitions were even greater: its five-year objective was to control 30 per cent of the market. Rothmans spent heavily on advertising, prompting others to compete accordingly. Space devoted to cigarettes in the three main Toronto dailies rose from 24,000 lines in August 1957 to 95,000 lines two months later. Total cigarette ad spending more than doubled from 1957 to 1958.[26] In 1958, Rothmans assumed control of Rock City Tobacco and its Craven "A", Black Cat, and Sportsman brands, which together accounted for 12 per cent of the market. Two years later, Rothmans-owned brands had an estimated 16 to 20 per cent of the cigarette trade.[27] In 1958, a third multinational entered the

Canadian market when Philip Morris bought Benson & Hedges Canada, soon after building a production facility in Brampton, Ontario. Four years later, Benson & Hedges bought Tabacofina's Canadian assets, which included well-known brands like Belvedere and Mark Ten.[28] By 1962, the "Big Four" cigarette marketplace had taken shape, with ITC controlling about half the market. Macdonald Tobacco owned about one-quarter of this market, Rothmans possessing about 15 per cent. Benson & Hedges captured the remaining 5 per cent of sales.[29] All but Macdonald Tobacco were owned by foreign multinationals.

Rothmans employed unorthodox tactics to capture market share in Canada, one that riled other tobacco companies and even its own corporate head office in London. Rothmans operations in Canada were led by Patrick O'Neil-Dunne. Born in Ireland and educated in the United States, O'Neil-Dunne joined Rothmans in the 1930s, gradually moving up within the company while working in varied departments such as tobacco leaf purchasing, finance, and marketing. After serving as a fighter pilot in the Royal Air Force during the Second World War, he rejoined Rothmans, eventually becoming the firm's world technical director when he arrived in Canada in 1957.[30] Rothmans flagship brand, Rothmans King Size Filter, was a filtered, reduced-tar cigarette, which O'Neil-Dunne believed would appeal to smokers worried about the "cancer scare."

In the summer of 1958 Rothmans' Canadian operation issued a series of ads addressing the cancer issue head on. The first of these, titled "An Announcement of Major Importance," was a full-page institutional ad that ran in many Canadian newspapers in late June.[31] The ad advised readers about a recent meeting of the Canadian Medical Association, during which delegates were shown a "graphic display which suggested a link between smoking and lung cancer." Rothmans wanted Canadians to know "that the problem of the relationship between cancer and smoking has for many years engaged the attention" of the company's research division. Rothmans researchers had for some time "accepted the thesis" that "the greater the tars reduction in tobacco smoke, the greater the reduction in the possible risk of lung cancer." The company was duty bound to "find a solution to the problem." By developing low-tar filter brands that also delivered taste and flavour, company researchers were working to "modify combustion to reduce [the] carcinogens found" in cigarettes. The ad concluded by extolling the health advantage of King Size cigarettes: "the extra length of King Size cigarettes enables the smoker to stub out a longer butt, for it is the last one-third of the length of a cigarette which, if smoked, generates more heat – hence more tars."

Rothmans published similar "research announcement" ads in the following weeks, including one in the *Toronto Daily Star* on 13 August.[32] Bearing the header, "The International Cancer Congress and Cigarette Smoking," the ad discussed a recent meeting of the ICC, providing a "brief summary of the facts as they stand today." The first of these facts was a bombshell: "Rothmans Research Division accepts the statistical evidence linking lung cancer with heavy smoking." This was done as "a precautionary measure in the interest of smokers." (It qualified this by noting that the exact biological basis of this connection was not yet known.) The ad confirmed that tobacco tar on animal skins had "produced cancer and therefore indicates that tobacco smoke condensate contains carcinogenic substances which are at least active to those animals." The "majority of the active carcinogenic agents" in tobacco smoke derived from the "fraction which is eluted with carbon tetrachloride from the neutral tar." The news was not all bad, Rothmans stated, since research showed that reducing tar levels in cigarettes could reduce the risk of acquiring lung cancer: an "increasing section of scientific opinion believes that if the tar intake from a single cigarette were reduced to the range of 18 to 20 milligrams (mgs.), there would be a significant reduction in the *possible* risk of lung cancer." Fortunately, Rothmans King Size Filter cigarettes contained up to 39 per cent less tar than leading filter brands. Rothmans pledged to continue "its policy of all-out-research" and to "give smokers of Rothmans cigarettes improvements as soon they are developed." The ad highlighted smoking's links to lung cancer, while offering health reassurance to worried smokers in the form of low-tar Rothmans brands, while the company's researchers worked to fully solve the problem.

O'Neil-Dunne elaborated on this marketing strategy in letters to colleagues. Writing an associate in Australia in July 1958, O'Neil-Dunne recounted his recent visit to the International Cancer Congress in London.[33] He described the strong consensus among public health officials concerning the close association between smoking and lung cancer: "statistically, the link is absolute," O'Neil-Dunne wrote, adding that "chemically and biologically, the link has been proved beyond doubt on animals." For O'Neil-Dunne, the key consideration was that "on the assumption that one cannot stop the human race from smoking, the question now is simply one of what is the medical profession and the tobacco industry going to do about it." On the industry research front this meant developing and promoting filtration, lowering cigarette tar yields to 18 mg or less, and continuing to "search for [a] chemical neutralizer of carcinogens in tobacco."[34]

The health concerns of smokers, O'Neil-Dunne argued, represented an untapped marketing opportunity: "One of the strange features about this problem," he wrote, "is that manufacturers who have established sales will violently oppose admission of the [smoking–cancer] link or any action in that direction, whereas manufacturers who have not got sales … are thankful for the link as the cheapest and easiest way of establishing new sales with a new brand and knocking out old established successful trade-marks." O'Neil-Dunne recalled that when he worked at Rothmans' Australian operations, it was "the British government's lung cancer pronouncement (and our action thereto) which gave Australia its present wonderful filter sales." In the absence of an industry-wide agreement to ban the "health angle in filter advertising," the cigarette trade would be susceptible to having "an O'Neil-Dunne enter[ing] your market and blast[ing] you to blazes." Rothmans' smoking-and-cancer awareness ads had "busted [this] wide open and which is the prime cause of our quick success" in the Canadian market.[35] For O'Neil-Dunne, the "lung cancer scare" was a prime opportunity for recent market entrants like Rothmans to capture brand share from established players like ITC, by promoting Rothmans King Size Filters as a "solution," if temporarily, to health-worried smokers.

The self-assured O'Neil-Dunne presented similar views to the *New York Times* in July 1958. In the story, O'Neil-Dunne is quoted as saying that "a link between smoking and lung cancer had been proven 'beyond all reasonable doubt.'"[36] The *Times* article described how most tobacco firms "are engaged in cancer research, but Rothman's is believed to be the first anywhere to acknowledge that lung cancer is definitely linked to smoking." O'Neil-Dunne maintained that many scientists believed that "the risk of lung cancer would drop sharply" if tar levels were lowered to 18 mg or less per cigarette. Better filters and getting people to smoke only two-thirds of a cigarette would also improve the health of smokers. Not surprisingly, US tobacco executives were appalled by this message. On the heels of the *Times* article, Timothy V. Hartnett, chairman of TIRC, issued a statement that did not mention Rothmans by name, referring only to a "foreign company's statement on smoking," which Hartnett deemed was baseless: "Scientific evidence simply does not support the theory that there is anything in cigarette smoke known to cause human lung cancer."[37]

Soon after, O'Neil-Dunne defended his marketing strategy and related public statements to Sydney Rothman, chairman of the Rothmans board.[38] The "upshot" of Rothmans' press releases and health-awareness ads, O'Neil-Dunne wrote, was front-page attention in newspapers throughout Canada, British, the United States, and Australia. ("You cannot buy this for any money.") The resulting publicity served to "make us overnight leaders in research and the most feared and most sought-after company in North America." Bold actions like these were needed if Rothmans were to avoid "eating the crumbs which fall from the B.A.T.'s table." Rothmans' prior entry into the American market had gone poorly and O'Neil-Dunne was adamant that this not happen in Canada.

By late August 1958, O'Neil-Dunne had backtracked somewhat. In a five-page letter to Rothmans officials, he assured them that "future releases affecting our standing in the world will have prior overseas clearance."[39] These releases would be limited to topics like the history of tobacco or king-size cigarettes and not "the cancer controversy." But O'Neil-Dunne continued to defend his marketing strategy involving smoking and cancer. He claimed that the first series of smoking-and-health ads had boosted the company's Canadian sales from 120 million to 150 million cigarettes per month. The ad campaign referencing the International Cancer Congress and subsequent publicity then "took us overnight to a strong 200 million per month." Rothmans' market research showed that "we have given plain end, high tar cigarettes the cancer image, and the first to show signs of cracking is Macdonald's Export." He added:

> One reason why our sales up to the "cancer releases" lacked zing was because many people have sampled our cigarettes and given it up because it was too mild. We were forced to start with an English image and 50% Rhodesian blend in a market which was largely attuned to

30 to 40 mgs. tar. One of the greatest victories which we have achieved by this release is that our product is no longer accused of mildness and those who know it to be mild from past sampling have come back with the thought "No wonder they are so mild – Rothmans research has made them cancer free!" There is a big difference between having a "cancer" image and having a "cancer-free" image.[40]

O'Neil-Dunne similarly defended his position to Timothy Hartnett, the head of TIRC, writing him on 9 September to take issue with Hartnett's statements which had "belittle[d] our Companies." O'Neil-Dunne noted that Rothmans had conducted health-related research for much longer than had TIRC, noting that it had manufactured filter cigarettes for over fifty years. Rothmans, O'Neil-Dunne wrote, would not "argue against" the "majority view of medical opinion on the statistical evidence" regarding smoking and lung cancer. Rothmans was not in the high-tar end of the market. He argued that "the smoking public must by now be utterly confused by all the hocus pocus, charges and counter-charges on such a simple pleasure as smoking. That is why our customers welcome the publication of what we believe to be the true facts as they become available from time to time." To be deemed credible by the general public, cigarette firms must acknowledge the growing body of medical research that connected tobacco smoking to disease, as Rothmans in Canada had recently done.[41]

O'Neil-Dunne's confidence in Rothmans cornering the market for health-anxious smokers had seemingly waned by December 1958. By then O'Neil-Dunne was postulating that "the educated man reasons as follows: Rothmans would not have admitted the statistical link between smoking and cancer unless they knew the answer. If they know the answer and their products are free from carcinogens, so does the Imperial or any good cigarette manufacturer. Therefore, any good filter product suits me." Thus, according to O'Neil, "contrary to what I expected, the market is placid and we are back to bashing advertising to get our share of the trade – ever so slowly."[42] In other words, ITC's Matinée and du Maurier brands, as we shall see, had become successful at playing Rothmans' own game of health marketing.

By the following year, O'Neil-Dunne's overt health marketing gambit had effectively ended, owing to pressure from its corporate parent. Rothmans ads returned to prosaic themes like "the best tobacco money can buy." Soon after, John Devlin replaced O'Neil-Dunne as head of Rothmans Canadian operations and O'Neil-Dunne would spend the rest of his career at Rothmans in places like Chile, Singapore, and Kenya, eventually retiring in 1972. A colourful character and brash risk taker, he later wrote a popular book on roulette, once playing a roulette game for thirty-one straight days at a Macao casino, winning $35,000.[43] Not until the early 2000s would Canadian tobacco executives again speak frankly and publicly about the recognized cancer risks of cigarette smoking.

IMPERIAL TOBACCO, FILTERS, AND HEALTH

Imperial Tobacco spent heavily on consumer survey research during the 1950s and 1960s. For much of this research, ITC commissioned Canadian Facts, a leading market research firm with many blue-chip corporate clients.[44] These consumer studies measured brand preference and smoking-related behaviour, attitudes, and opinions. These annual surveys, which began in 1952, contained large sample sizes – ranging between 3,600 and 12,000 respondents – which allowed for statistically reliable data collection on smaller subsets of consumers. The methodology used was the scientifically rigorous (and expensive) practice of area-probability sampling and face-to-face interviewing in people's homes. The resulting reports typically ran to more than one hundred pages and featured dozens of tables, brand image indexes, and cross-tabulations. These surveys constituted sophisticated and methodologically rigorous examples of market research and stand as an unparalleled historical resource for analyzing cigarette marketing and smoking-related attitudes and behaviour in mid-century Canada.

These surveys document in rich detail the rapid uptake of filter cigarettes during the 1950s and early 1960s, along with underlying health concerns propelling this behaviour. In 1954, the market for filter cigarettes in Canada was small, comprising about 2 per cent of sales. One year later, however, 8 per cent of smokers now used filter brands, with ITC's Matinée brand possessing half of this market.[45] Two groups predominated among early adopters of filter cigarettes: women and young people. In 1955, 13 per cent of female smokers listed filter offerings as their brands of choice, compared with just 4 per cent for men. Each subsequent year saw a steep increase in the number of women smokers choosing filter brands: 33 per cent reported doing so in 1956, rising to 49 per cent in 1957, a year when just 21 per cent of male smokers did so.[46] By early 1959, 52 per cent of female smokers lit up with filter cigarettes.[47] In just five years, the number of women smoking filters had gone from barely noticeable to majority preference (figure 5.1).[48]

Young people – those between eighteen and twenty-five – similarly embraced filters early on. The Canadian Facts report for 1955 noted that "filter tips are relatively more popular with young smokers of both sexes."[49] Two years later, survey results found that 50 per cent of "New Smokers" (nearly all of whom were under twenty-five) smoked filters, compared with 32 per cent of all smokers. One-third of new smokers used Matinée, the most popular brand among this group.[50] The 1958 report attributed the highest rate of filter use (60 per cent) to women aged eighteen to twenty-five, concluding that "filters remain more popular among young people than among older people."[51]

In 1959, the Canadian Facts survey began asking questions about the perceived health benefits of filter cigarettes. Respondents were asked if "filter tips are safer for your health than plain ends." Among women, 56 per cent agreed, 24 per cent disagreed, and 20 per cent had no opinion. Among men, the respective figures were: 44, 36, and 20. A clear majority of decided opinion among women and men maintained that filtered brands were healthier options.[52] Among filter smokers, the results were even more one-sided. Seventy-two per cent agreed that filters were safer, while 14 per cent disagreed, and 14 per cent were undecided. Fully 84 per cent of decided opinion among filter smokers held that filter cigarettes were safer for health than plain-end ones. (Conversely, just 32 per cent of plain-end smokers viewed filters as healthier.) Filter smokers who viewed filter cigarettes as healthier were then asked if "some filters are safer for your health than other filters?" Forty-four per cent of these people agreed, 23 per cent disagreed, and 33 per cent offered no opinion. Among filter smokers, the report observed, "health is a major motivating factor in brand selection."[53] The "Highlights" section of the report underscored this when noting that "filter smokers are strongly convinced filters are safer than

Hope and Doubt

5.1 Filter brands like du Maurier and Matinée that touted health claims proved initially popular with women and well-educated smokers, starting in the mid-1950s. du Maurier ad in the *Telegraph-Journal*, 12 February 1957

plain ends (non-filter smokers disagree), and a majority of smokers believe some filters are safer for your health than others."[54]

In a section of the report titled "Health," cigarette brands were evaluated in terms of health associations. Survey results showed that Matinée smokers were the "most dedicated to the superior health aspect of their own brand." When asked to pick the safest brand on the market, fully 98 per cent of Matinée smokers picked their own brand; the second-highest result was the 79 per cent of du Maurier smokers who picked du Maurier as safest.[55] The survey constructed "brand personality" indexes for cigarette brands involving attributes like "mildness," "least harmful for health," "full flavoured," and "fashionable/high class." Respondents rated each of these attributes on a seven-point scale for specified cigarette brands. The results showed Matinée and Rothmans to be "both above average on the health concept." Notably, another filter brand, Macdonald's Export "A", was "not considered a healthy brand," but instead one that was "chosen for its stronger, fuller flavour."[56]

A section of the 1959 report, labelled "Health Research," discussed smokers' views on whether "some cigarette companies are really trying to lick the health problem," a question posed in the survey. Among the 71 per cent of smokers who offered an opinion, 63 per cent said "Yes" and 37 per cent said "No." Rothmans and Matinée smokers scored the "highest in crediting their own brand or company" with taking action to "lick the health problem." The upshot of this was that the "smoking public" had given "the tobacco industry credit for taking a constructive attitude towards the health aspect of smoking." Imperial Tobacco and Rothmans stood "about equally well regarded in this matter."[57]

THE VIEW FROM PARLIAMENT

On 16 December 1953, MP Stanley Knowles questioned Paul Martin, minister of National Health and Welfare (NHW), in the House of Commons about news reports connecting smoking to lung cancer. What research, he asked, was the ministry conducting on this matter?[58] Martin identified no specific ministry involvement with this file, a fact that prompted him to ask his deputy minister, G.D.W. Cameron, to examine suitable courses of action. Cameron contacted Neil McKinnon, a professor in the School of Hygiene at the University of Toronto, to inquire as to the extent and nature of medical research on smoking and lung cancer, conveying to him that "needless to say this is a very sensitive point because of the enormous industry dependent on tobacco sales."[59]

Cameron also arranged to confer with Imperial Tobacco officials. On 25 January 1954 Cameron met with ITC vice-president John M. Keith and the company's manager of research and development, Leo Laporte. Prior to this meeting, Cameron wrote in a later memo to Martin, ITC executives had contacted officials at the National Cancer Institute (NCI), the Canadian Medical Association, and the National Research Council. Cameron described Keith and Laporte as "very well informed about current knowledge and take the view that a link between cigarette smoking and lung cancer has not been established. They know that a number of experts agree with them. However, they are also keen to make the right moves and this is why they" had contacted NCI. Cameron asked Keith and Laporte if serious research work had been done on filter tips with respect to the smoking–health issue. Cameron's account of their response is worth quoting at length, in light of the fact that ITC was on the cusp of marketing filter brands to placate smokers' cancer worries:

> They pointed out that they could not devise a filter tip without knowing the specific substances in tobacco smoke which may cause cancer. They also pointed out that if a filter tip is really effective and takes the tar, which is the suspect substance, out of the smoke then the filter tip must be so tight that you can hardly draw air through it and what does come through is so unsatisfactory that you might as well give up smoking. However, if it were known that a specific substance in the tar was the cause of the tumour the chemists might quite well devise some trick for screening it out of the tobacco smoke.

Cameron and the ITC officials agreed that a recommended course of action for ITC would be to donate funds ("without strings attached") directly to NCI in support of lung cancer research. Cameron was advised that ITC president E.C. Wood had instructed Keith and Laporte to determine "the sort of thing which [Minister Paul Martin] might be willing to say, either in the House" or elsewhere, "regarding the concern of the Company and the support which the Company may give to cancer research."[60]

Two points are noteworthy about Cameron's memo, one of the earliest federal government documents to address the smoking–cancer issue. Keith and Laporte were highly doubtful that scientific research on filters could render cigarettes both safe and sufficiently satisfying for smokers; rather, ITC officials emphasized the "magic bullet" approach that scientific inquiry would, one day, identify and extract carcinogenic elements in tobacco tar. Second, ITC executives were keen to ensure that contributions in support of cancer research would be acknowledged publicly by the federal government. Indeed, Laporte's account of this meeting described Keith as asking Cameron that should ITC fund cancer research at NCI then "what was Dr. Cameron's opinion of leaving any publicity or announcement to Mr. Martin who could at some suitable time introduce the matter into House debates?" Cameron, according to Laporte, viewed this as an "excellent method of gaining the necessary publicity without the appearance of advertising or deliberately making it a matter of public relations."[61] Before deciding on this issue, ITC executives sought and secured assurances that a research donation would receive public endorsement from the minister for health and national welfare.

In March 1954, eleven Canadian tobacco companies, including ITC and Macdonald, announced they would collectively donate $100,000 to the NCI "for the support of research work related to lung cancer."[62] The money would be disbursed over five years to support research projects chosen by the NCI.[63] While this NCI-administered program had a greater arm's-length relationship with tobacco firms than did TIRC in the United States, it bears noting that some early recipients of NCI cancer research funds were acknowledged skeptics of smoking's links to cancer and other diseases. In a 1955 article in *Le Devoir*, NCI grant holder and McGill professor C.P. Leblond is quoted as saying: "Jusqu'ici, il a été impossible de provoquer le cancer chez des cobayes à l'aide des goudrons de cigarettes; mais l'expérience n'est pas rendue à un stage ou l'on peut tirer des conclusions assurées." Another grant recipient cited in this article was Hans Selye, an endocrinologist and stress expert at the University of Montreal who, starting in 1954, would receive hundreds of thousands of research dollars from Canadian and US tobacco firms over many years, while also publicizing the stress-relief benefits of smoking.[64]

ROYAL COLLEGE OF PHYSICIANS OF LONDON REPORT

In March 1962, the Royal College of Physicians of London released a lengthy report documenting the serious health risks of cigarette smoking. It concluded that cigarette smoking was the "most likely cause of the recent world-wide increase in deaths from lung cancer," as well as an "important predisposing cause of the development of chronic bronchitis." Moreover, the report stated, smoking "probably increases the risk of dying from coronary heart disease, particularly in early middle age." Patients who smoked and had "productive coughs" were at greater risk for "disabling bronchitis and they may also have an increased risk of lung cancer." Two of the report's recommendations called for doctors to stop smoking in front of patients and for them to counsel patients with bronchitis, peptic ulcers, and arterial disease to quit smoking.[65]

Even before its release, ITC executives had worried about the forthcoming Royal College report. Leo Laporte, vice-president of research and development, and vice-president John Keith met in February with officials from the National Cancer Institute, the Canadian Medical Association, and the Department of National Health and Welfare in a bid to determine what they knew about the upcoming report.[66] When the report was issued soon after, ITC president Ed Wood rebuked its findings in a press release. The Royal College report, Wood said, was "merely another review of old statistical data," which did not "offer any new scientific findings." It relied upon data "still in dispute and under continuing study." It overlooked or dismissed "recent research findings and a growing body of evidence that indicate many factors may be involved in lung cancer and heart disease." These factors included "previous chest infections, viruses, environmental pollutants, heredity and diet." The report, Wood claimed, was filled with "gaps and apparent discrepancies," which in turn underscored the need for additional scientific research. He emphasized how ITC and Macdonald Tobacco had for years funded "independent research in Canada into questions of smoking and health," findings that had shown no "need for any modification of tobacco or to justify broad scale attacks against the use of cigarettes for enjoyment and relaxation." To date, there was no scientific basis to support anti-smoking education campaigns or "unfair" regulatory "restrictions against the industry."[67]

Following the release of the Royal College report, senior health bureaucrats in Canada took preliminary action. In April 1962, the Dominion Council of Health (DCH) – comprising mainly federal and provincial deputy ministers of health – issued a forceful statement on smoking and health.[68] The "overwhelming evidence," the Council stated, pointed to a "direct relationship between cigarette smoking and lung cancer." The risk of lung cancer corresponded with the volume of cigarettes smoked. Describing cigarette smoking as "a form of addiction," the Council stated that the "most practical preventive measure is to encourage young people not to commence the habit of smoking." The Council threw cold water on the view that filter cigarettes were healthier options: "To date attempts by filtering cigarette smoke to remove injurious substances do not appear to be satisfactory – a false sense of security would appear to go along with the use of filters." (Later, in December 1962, the Council established a special committee on smoking and health.)[69] The Council's statement is noteworthy for its early use of the term "addiction," at a time when smoking was typically characterized as a personal or social "habit" that could be stopped with sufficient willpower. The DCH statement was also prescient in noting that filter cigarettes offered no health advantages over plain-end ones.[70]

INVOLVEMENT OF THE AMERICAN TOBACCO INDUSTRY

Troubled by this changing climate, ITC executives turned for help to American tobacco and public relations executives with extensive experience managing smoking and health issues. In August 1962, ITC hosted a meeting at the Royal Montreal Golf Club, which included Timothy Hartnett from the TIRC and W.T. Hoyt and R.W. Darrow from Hill & Knowlton, a public relations firm that worked closely with the US tobacco industry. ITC officials at the meeting included Wood, Keith, and Laporte. The minutes of the meeting highlight Keith's concern that the Canadian Medical Association would decide to discourage smoking "from the education point of view." To counter this, a consensus arose that ITC should act to "maintain our contact with the Canadian medical authorities and observe developments." Wood expressed concern that six thousand copies of the Royal College report had been sold in Canada; Norman Dann, ITC's manager of public relations, was charged with investigating if "any bulk orders were placed for free distribution by any 'anti-'group." In the United States, TIRC had published 550,000 copies of *Tobacco and Health*, an industry booklet refuting smoking–cancer science, with 300,000 copies sent to physicians, medical authorities, and tobacco company employees. ITC officials would consider distributing *Tobacco and Health* to Canadian doctors, after assessing if the publication needed to be "Canadianized."

Participants then discussed TIRC-related activities of Clarence Little, concluding that "Dr. Little's valuable services could be made available for the Canadian scene if the situation seemed to warrant it." The optimal platform for Little's public relations work involved hosting small luncheons for scientists or science journalists. Wood requested five hundred copies of a Congressional report that included statements by Little. Wood and others also discussed the need for more Canadian-based research on viral causes of lung cancer. In this vein, Laporte indicated that "some suggestions might be forthcoming from T.I.R.C. on projects for research in Canada which could be passed through ... the NCI Tobacco Research Fund." Later, Hoyt and Darrow from Hill & Knowlton discussed their tobacco-related public relations work in the United States. The "drill" there was to "ascertain in major centres and communication centres who is writing on Smoking and Health" and then contact them "on a personal basis," sometimes repeatedly. Hill & Knowlton had done this with fifty-five reporters and writers in fifteen American cities. ITC would consider "setting up similar lines of communication in Canada either directly or through an intermediary."[71]

The meeting at the Royal Montreal Golf Club laid the groundwork for ITC's subsequent handling of the smoking and health issue. The action plan adopted by ITC was decisively shaped by the input of American tobacco and public relations executives. ITC would explore the merits of a TIRC-style research program for Canada. It would employ public relations practices, modelled on American experience, to target and liaise with Canadian journalists writing about smoking and health. And ITC would look into disseminating pro-industry sources like *Tobacco and Health* to Canadian physicians and medical officials.

INDUSTRY AGREEMENT TO END "TAR ADVERTISING"

In October 1962, ITC moved to strike an agreement among Canada's major tobacco firms to "drop tar advertising," claiming it was for the "best interests of the industry."[72] Current advertising for Belvedere and Craven "A" cited their cigarettes' low tar levels in an attempt to assuage the health concerns of smokers (figure 5.2). It was now important, an ITC memo argued, to avoid "doing anything which would provide anti cigarette publicity for the Canadian Cancer Society," especially since "they are getting underway with their educational campaign in the schools." Tobacco companies should act collectively to counter the calls of "anti cigarette forces" wanting government regulation of the industry. It was important to not leave any "impression with the public that the tobacco industry considers tar a dangerous element to the health of a smoker." The industry, according to the memo, faced an existential crisis; anti-tobacco "forces" were "everywhere and ... looking for opportunities to further their cause." The memo raised the disturbing spectre of a "Government Tobacco Monopoly" resulting from the "growing strength of the Socialist forces in Canada." Budding French Canadian nationalism constituted a "dangerous trend developing in Quebec," depicted as "basically socialism." The very survival of the cigarette industry operating in a free market hinged on ending "tar advertising" soon.[73]

ITC president Ed Wood wrote his counterparts at major Canadian tobacco firms in pursuit of an agreement to end tar and nicotine references in all cigarette promotion. The ongoing "statistical case" made against the health of cigarettes had resulted in the industry bearing the "brunt of this welter of adverse publicity." Wood elaborated:

> There is no doubt in my mind that we as manufacturers contribute to the public apprehension and confusion by reference to tar and nicotine in our advertising. If our desire is to reassure the smoker, there is the real danger of misleading him into believing that we as manufacturers know that certain levels of tar and nicotine remove the alleged hazard of smoking. In so doing I believe we are performing a disservice to the smoker and to ourselves for we are assisting in the creation of a climate of fear that is contrary to the public interest and, incidentally, damaging to the entire industry.[74]

Wood expressed concerns that continued tar and nicotine appeals in advertising would "compel government authority to take a firm stand on this matter." To avert this, he called for an industry-wide agreement to end

5.2 In 1962, cigarette manufacturers agreed to stop mentioning tar levels in advertising – as seen in this ad for Craven "A" – believing they produced negative health associations among the public. Craven "A" ad in the *Telegraph-Journal*, 22 January 1962.

the practice.[75] Wood's entreaty was received positively. Rothmans president J.H. Devlin supported Wood's proposal, even calling for additional measures to counter the "specific health attacks against our industry" by the press and other groups. Without these measures, Devlin worried the end result would be to shift "health claims" from "the advertising pages to the editorial" pages.[76]

On 29 October 1962, tobacco company presidents met to discuss the matter. All but the head of Benson & Hedges had previously endorsed Wood's proposal to ban tar advertising. While the minutes of the meeting are not available, the industry's heightened fears of government intervention are evident in the "Suggested Opening Paragraphs" notes prepared for Wood. They described an "ominous time in the life of our industry," besieged as it was by "the weight of medical statistics and public concern." The federal government was "taking a keen interest in our activities," and the industry was "already in a real sense on trial."[77] By the end of the meeting, Benson & Hedges had joined with the others to endorse the ITC proposal. This policy statement called for all parties to "refrain from the use, direct or implied, of the words tar, nicotine or other smoke constituents that may have similar connotations, in any and all advertising material or any package, document or other communication that is designed for public use or information." The preamble of the policy statement required signatories to endorse the position that scientific studies on smoking and cancer were "based essentially on statistical data" and that no "cause-and-effect relationship" had been uncovered in "clinical or laboratory studies."[78] Soon after, officials sent a copy of the policy statement to Waldo Monteith, federal minister of national health and welfare.[79]

The policy statement did not spring from industry concerns that smokers might erroneously attribute health benefits to low-tar brands. Rather, ITC and other cigarette firms were motivated by fears of a "socialist" government using the tar advertising issue as a pretext to impose severe regulations on the industry. Indeed, the policy statement contained no monitoring body or terms of enforcement; signatory firms agreed only to "informing individual staff and respective agencies as to the policy and possibly release to the Minister of National Health & Welfare."[80] When Wood advised BAT about the agreement he underscored that signatories had "agreed to give absolutely no publicity to this policy – not even to our advertising agencies."[81] The policy statement's primary audience was the federal government, not Canadian consumers. As well, an advertising ban on phrases like "low tar" and *explicit* health references did not include *implicit* health messaging in promotional communication. Canadian Facts surveys done in the early 1960s, discussed above, showed how Matinée and du Maurier smokers attributed health benefits to their brands irrespective of tar counts. Terms like "mild" and "light," ostensibly referring to smoother inhalation, connoted positive health associations among smokers. In securing industry-wide support for the policy statement, ITC laid the groundwork for the formation of the Ad Hoc Committee of the Canadian Tobacco Industry. This committee, consisting of the presidents of the country's top four tobacco firms, began meeting regularly soon after to discuss smoking-and-health matters and coordinate industry action on this file.

FEDERAL GOVERNMENT RESPONSE

In early 1963, health and medical officials in Canada took preliminary steps to address smoking and public health. In January, the Committee on Cancer of the Canadian Medical Association, which included NHW Deputy Minister G.D.W. Cameron, established an educational program on cigarette smoking and health. The CMA thought this important since the "public so far is apathetic" and not yet in acceptance of the full "implications of the widespread habit of cigarette smoking." The committee's educational programs would "stress the hazards of excessive cigarette smoking."[82] NHW Minister Waldo Monteith also favoured this approach.[83] In April 1963, a report by the NHW's Committee on Smoking and Health argued for the department to go beyond merely evaluating scientific evidence on smoking and disease and become active in educating people that the "cigarette smoking habit is an important contributory cause of lung cancer" and "probably associated with the incidence of other diseases, including particularly, chronic bronchitis and coronary heart disease." Health agencies, the report noted, had a "duty to inform the public about the risk to health connected with cigarette smoking," especially for children. To that end, the department should co-operate with other health organizations to develop anti-smoking educational campaigns.[84]

ITC responded to these developments with a forty-one-page report, presented to the Canadian Medical Association in May 1963 on behalf of the Canadian tobacco industry. The document restated what had become industry dogma on smoking and lung cancer. The proposed CMA anti-smoking campaign was socially irresponsible, since its supporting evidence lacked "experimental and clinical proof," based, as it was, on "statistical association studies" and "selected data and selected opinions." The CMA had ignored the "substantial body of scientific literature" that did not attribute lung cancer to smoking. There were in fact "many factors" related to the etiology of lung cancer, and it was "unwarranted to designate any one of these as the major or primary cause." The CMA's tunnel-vision approach undermined overall public health: if the "public should become convinced that such complex health questions as lung cancer have been resolved, will this not delay and hamper, through lack of funds and lack of interest, the further research that all scientists believe is necessary for the solution of these problems?" The "complex" causes of lung cancer included radiation exposure, pollution, "anxieties and neuroses," viral infections, and various chemicals, explanations supported by "many scientists."

The report reiterated the industry view that the elevated prevalence of lung cancer owed to factors like increased longevity, medical diagnostic advances, and more accurate reporting on death certificates. There was no "ready-made solution" to this problem since smoking was not "the simple answer." The single-cause approach, when later shown to be wrong, threatened to "shake the public's faith in future public health efforts."[85] A better scientific model, the ITC report maintained, was that adopted by the US Surgeon General's Advisory Committee on Smoking and Health, which had been studying the issue since 1962. The far-ranging approach of the Advisory Committee, the report claimed, was a "clear indication of the complexities involved." (Notably, after the Surgeon General's report was released in January 1964, ITC and other Canadian cigarette firms denounced it for concluding that cigarette smoking was a primary cause of lung cancer.) ITC restated its support of scientific research on tobacco and health, citing past funding of cancer research at NCI. The report also reaffirmed that the industry did not "direct our advertising to minors, nor promote smoking by them." The CMA's proposed education campaign, which was "based on fear," would not deter children from smoking.[86]

It is important to situate these industry views within the context of tobacco-and-health science. By 1963, scores of articles had appeared in reputable medical and scientific journals linking smoking to lung cancer. A strong consensus existed among oncology researchers that cigarette smoking was a major cause of lung cancer.[87] The Canadian tobacco industry dismissed this sizeable body of knowledge as "simplistic" science, because it focused only on a single cause (smoking). In contrast, "complex" research investigated multiple causes (e.g., air pollution, viruses). "Simplistic" research was denigrated for its epidemiological method ("statistics") and for not using clinical or lab-based approaches, the purported "gold standard" of scientific inquiry. The industry's threshold of proof was set impossibly high: the smoking–disease association would be deemed causal only when human cells subjected to cigarette smoke turned cancerous in a controlled laboratory setting. Like its American counterpart, the position of the Canadian industry amounted to a coordinated strategy to deny, even subvert, the empirical verities of normative science.[88] Indeed, the secretive Policy Statement signed by the presidents of Canadian tobacco firms in October 1962 codified this denialist position, which in turn was repeated widely to journalists and the broader public. For example, in June 1963 ITC's Leo Laporte told a *Montreal Gazette* reporter that "no substance as found in tobacco smoke is known to be the cause of lung cancer in humans."[89] May Stewart, president of Macdonald Tobacco, was even more dismissive: "It hasn't been proved in any way, shape or form that smoking causes cancer."[90]

The federal Cabinet first discussed the issue of smoking and health on 4 June 1963. This file was handled by national health and welfare minister Judy LaMarsh, a lawyer from Niagara Falls who was first elected to the Commons in a 1960 by-election; she was also the only woman in Prime Minister Pearson's Cabinet (figure 5.3).[91] LaMarsh introduced for discussion a series of measures to reduce cigarette smoking, especially among teens and young adults. She sought approval for NHW to hold a conference on smoking and health, which would include medical researchers and federal and provincial health officials. Cabinet reluctantly agreed, with the proviso that tobacco growers and cigarette executives also be invited to the conference. (At this time, many Cabinet ministers smoked cigarettes, even during meetings, when the "Cabinet room was often blue with smoke.")[92] LaMarsh then presented the statement on smoking and health that she planned to read in the Commons. Her Cabinet colleagues asked for and secured changes to make the statement as "neutral and dispassionate as possible." Cigarette smoking became a "contributory" cause of lung cancer, not an "important contributory" cause. Smoking "may also be" associated with bronchitis and heart disease, rather than "is also probably." The proposed program of scientific research and education, totalling $600,000 over five years, would "deal with" smoking rather than be "for the control of" it.[93] On 17 June, LaMarsh announced in the House the government's initiative on smoking and health, along with the upcoming policy conference.[94]

In response, ITC executives met with senior government officials about LaMarsh's agenda. On 17 June, Keith visited NHW Deputy Minister Cameron and LaMarsh in Ottawa. Keith judged Cameron to be restrained

5.3 National Health and Welfare Minister Judy LaMarsh first raised the smoking-and-health issue in Cabinet in June 1963. Fellow ministers, however, opposed her bid for enhanced health promotion about the harms of smoking.

on this issue, unlike others in the department. In his view, Cameron's position was that there had been "some over-indulgence in cigarette smoking," for which "some moderation of the custom would be desirable." Cameron thought that the conference and departmental education programs would "have as their objective moderation rather than control." LaMarsh's position, however, was more worrisome: "In her view, it would have to be a programme more definite than a campaign on moderation and she seems to be particularly concerned about teenage smoking." Keith held a low opinion of LaMarsh, disparaging her as "a 'light weight' for a Federal Minister, who would quickly respond to public and political pressure. Most of her remarks appeared to be tied around political situations, rather than factual situations."[95]

Keith met soon after with two senior Cabinet members: Charles Drury, minister of Defence Production and the MP for Saint-Antoine-Westmount, the Montreal riding that was home to ITC's headquarters, and Prime Minister Lester Pearson. Drury arranged the meeting with Pearson, held on 21 June, which included Keith, Laporte, Paul Paré, and Drury. Laporte's report of the meeting described a "very friendly" reception by the prime minister. During the meeting ITC officials informed Pearson about the company's past engagement on the smoking and health front, highlighting its support of the Tobacco Industry Research Fund administered by the National Cancer Institute. Laporte described Pearson as sympathetic to the industry, noting how Pearson dismissed LaMarsh's public display of quitting a two-pack-a-day smoking habit as "somewhat of a theatrical gesture." Pearson, Laporte claimed, indicated that support in Cabinet for LaMarsh's House statement of 17 June was not deep and that Cabinet members had "perhaps not too carefully" read the statement. Pearson promised to "have a word with" LaMarsh about related statements in the future.[96]

Pearson was not fully forthcoming with ITC officials. Cabinet had in fact considered LaMarsh's statement carefully, even diluting its more contentious wording. Laporte, however, regarded LaMarsh's statement in the House as an "obvious acceptance of the statistical association as proof of a cause-and-effect relationship of smoking and lung cancer and that it was an indictment of the industry."[97] The meetings with Drury and Pearson, however, likely alleviated some of the concerns by ITC officials about possible "socialist" government action on this file. Pearson had provided specific reassurances to Keith and there was also the confidence gained by ITC executives in realizing they could secure meetings with senior Cabinet ministers on short notice. Keith and colleagues were able to convey their concerns directly to the prime minister, while apprising him of the company's record of corporate social responsibility with respect to funding cancer research at NCI. Having the ear of powerful figures like Drury and Pearson allowed ITC officials to see that future end runs around "light weight" ministers like LaMarsh were entirely possible. And LaMarsh, a newcomer to elected office, was most definitely not among the Cabinet's inner circle, which included men like Paul Martin, Paul Hellyer, Jack Pickersgill, and Walter Gordon.[98]

ITC officials prepared extensively for the National Conference on Smoking and Health, scheduled for late November 1963. On 22 July, Keith contacted Devlin, his Rothmans' counterpart, to discuss the conference. Keith thought it advisable for "all of us in the industry" to "get together" to discuss "the approach that the industry might take" for the conference. It was, Keith maintained, "advisable for the industry to go to Ottawa as a group with a fairly well-developed approach to the problem."[99] One week later, Keith wrote LaMarsh to say that he had contacted the heads of major tobacco companies in Canada and that "all have agreed that the tobacco industry should act as a group and appoint delegates to represent it at your conference" in November.[100] This fit the industry's pattern of the past year, in which it endeavoured to speak with a single voice on smoking and health.

To prepare for the conference on Smoking and Health, ITC officials again called on TIRC and Hill & Knowlton executives. On 14 August 1963, ITC hosted another meeting at the Royal Montreal Golf Club, which included Timothy Hartnett from TIRC and W.T. Hoyt and Carl Thompson from Hill & Knowlton. ITC representatives included Wood, Keith, and Dann. There was agreement at the meeting that the industry's written submissions to the conference would include substantial input from Hill & Knowlton officials, who would "prepare sections on education, advertising, labelling, taxation, moderation, and economics of the industry." Hill & Knowlton would also "develop a release which we would like Judy LaMarsh to send out after the conference is over. This will probably be the 'Ideal' statement from our point of view and would primarily stress that more research is needed."[101] At a meeting of Hill & Knowlton and US tobacco executives in New York one month later, it was made clear that Hill & Knowlton would "have close liaison with [the] Canadian group and will continue to work together on any developments." According to one participant, this was because the "most dangerous area in Canada is what tobacco industry agrees to do (i.e., restrictive advertising, any admission of probable guilt, etc.)."[102] To aid the work of Hill & Knowlton, ITC would commission an opinion survey. To assist Hill & Knowlton with press relations before and during the conference, the respective merits of public relations firms in Canada were discussed, including Public & Industrial Relations, Inc., the one eventually chosen for this assignment.

ITC viewed the LaMarsh conference as less of an opportunity to learn about and debate the positions of various stakeholders related to smoking and health. Rather, the company was concerned more with developing centralized, consistent, and persuasive messaging for the conference, while working to cultivate favourable press coverage. To do this, ITC would rely heavily on American help.[103] (Years later, when a Philip Morris employee requested an internal copy of the Canadian industry's submission to the LaMarsh Conference, she described it as a "handy dandy" report that "was a product of Philip Morris and Imperial [ITC].")[104]

The extent of ITC's preparations for the National Conference on Smoking and Health was impressive. The company consulted with other tobacco firms to ensure that the industry spoke with a unified voice at the conference, to avoid off-script remarks of the O'Neil-Dunne kind. ITC officials lobbied Liberal Cabinet ministers, most notably LaMarsh, Drury, and Pearson, along with NHW mandarins like Cameron.[105] Company executives also cultivated ties with senior bureaucrats in other federal departments, including David Sim, deputy minister of National Revenue, Customs and Excise. In August 1963, Sim wrote E.C. Wood to express his gratitude, noting that the "salmon arrived in first-class condition and what we did not use immediately are being kept for the odd special occasion." Sim added: "I am afraid that you have been laying out quite a bit of money on my behalf and I would like to hear from you in that regard so that we can get squared away." Sim sympathized with Wood for having to endure the many "sensational and almost inflammatory articles" in the press on smoking-related disease.[106]

NATIONAL CONFERENCE ON SMOKING AND HEALTH

When the two-day conference began on 25 November, it did so under a pall. US president John F. Kennedy had been assassinated three days earlier and his funeral took place on 25 November, prompting the cancellation of the conference's evening reception. In the face of massive media coverage of the Kennedy tragedy, the conference received far less press coverage than anticipated.[107] About sixty participants attended the conference, drawn from organizations like the CMA, NCI, Canadian Cancer Society, Canadian Heart Foundation, Association des Médecins de Langue Française du Canada, and the Canadian Public Health Association. All of the provinces were represented, typically by ministers or deputy ministers of health. There were a half-dozen representatives from NHW. Representing the tobacco industry were company presidents Keith (ITC), Devlin (Rothmans), and Leahy (Benson & Hedges). Other ITC attendees included Laporte, Dann, and Dr L.P. Chesney, Medical Director of Health Service.[108] Minister LaMarsh chaired the proceedings.[109] Most of the first day was taken up with statements and presentations of briefs. In her statement that day, LaMarsh noted that the goal of the conference was to assist her and department officials in "delineating areas for action and establishing program priorities," notably education campaigns. These would likely be developed in consultation with provincial counterparts and non-governmental health organizations. She also pledged departmental funding for research on the "behavioural, constitutional and motivation aspects of the smoking habit."[110]

The tobacco industry's submission to the conference was a detailed eighty-nine-page report, complete with 143 bibliographic references and a four-page glossary.[111] (By comparison, the Canadian Public Health Association submitted a six-hundred-word brief, consisting mostly of reprinted motions about smoking and health from past annual meetings.[112] The statement of the National Cancer Institute was only about three hundred words.)[113] One of the few submissions available in English and French, ITC also sent advance copies of its brief to conference attendees, which was not the case with most submissions. The document was grouped into sections on lung cancer prevalence, laboratory experiments, epidemiology of lung cancer, clinical and pathological observations, and cardiovascular disease.[114] The report took issue with the "widespread emotional criticism" of the opponents of smoking, characterized by "exaggeration, disregard of fact, and basic intolerance toward the use of tobacco."[115] Laporte's oral presentation of the report questioned the science that linked smoking to disease, describing it as selective and fuelled by "emotional attitudes stemming from personal prejudices about the use of tobacco." Such moral posturing had blinded critics to the lack of "definitive scientific data concerning the causes of cancer and heart disease." The preoccupation with smoking, to the exclusion of other probable causes of lung cancer and heart disease, would in fact "delay the final solution of the health problems by diverting and delaying essential research."[116] The report, reinforced by Laporte's presentation, argued that redirecting lung-cancer research away from cigarette smoking and towards other "causal" areas like pollution would best serve the long-term health interests of smokers and non-smokers alike.

The tobacco industry also submitted a short brief dealing with proposed smoking education programs in schools. Noting that schools faced increasing pressure to use class time for non-academic subjects like this one, the brief insisted that any instruction about smoking be "truly educational" and "based on factual and full information." It should be "part of a total program of guidance on adult customs, which should include discussion of all aspects of modern living." Such programs should highlight "all areas of insufficient scientific knowledge" and not just provide "simple answers to complex questions." An exclusive focus on the "'dangerous' consequences" of smoking "might even serve to make the habit more attractive to immature minds by implying adventure." Since smoking was an "an adult custom," it was advisable to have parents "assume the primary responsibility of seeing that children are appropriately instructed in this."[117] In sum, schools should regard smoking and health instruction as the primary responsibility of parents, while any classroom teaching on this topic should include the industry's perspective on the scientific "controversy" involving smoking and disease.

The conference was closed to the press and non-invitees, and no official minutes of the meeting were released at the time.[118] The tobacco industry's view of this event is contained in a twelve-page memo chronicling the conference, most likely written by ITC's Norman Dann.[119] The tobacco industry representatives benefited from their "strategic" seating assignment, to the "immediate right-hand corner" of LaMarsh, meaning they could "get her attention almost immediately." Much of the first day was taken up with submissions from presenters. The remarks of the

CMA's R.M. Taylor "obviously indicated his anti-tobacco attitude." His CMA colleague Norman Delarue "became quite emotional" when describing the industry's report as an "attack on the medical profession as a whole." A.J. Philips, the statistician from NCI, criticized the statistical data in the tobacco industry's brief. LaMarsh asked provincial government representatives for their opinions on the association of smoking and cancer. Most expressed varying degrees of support for this thesis. The hardline position of British Columbia's Eric Martin was characterized as a "direct attack" on the industry; the Alberta and Saskatchewan health ministers were said to be "also of an extremist nature." From this airing of opinions, it was "apparent that all Provincial representatives accepted that some form of anti-cigarette smoking educational program should be developed, particularly for children."

The second day of the conference passed "with no locking of horns" among the participants. The memo described LaMarsh as believing it would be difficult to restrict cigarette advertising in Canada due to the "overflow" of American advertising in Canadian print and broadcast media. Instead of regulatory or legislative action related to warnings on cigarette packs, LaMarsh preferred stricter enforcement of the Tobacco Restraint Act to limit children's access to cigarettes. Keith then intervened to highlight the industry's "past cooperation in this regard and promised full and intensified cooperation in the future." The main outcome of the conference was the formation of two NHW-run committees on smoking and health, one on educational programs and the other on research initiatives. These meagre outcomes apparently did not sit well with the CMA and NCI representatives, who, according to the ITC account, "went away dissatisfied." After the conference, tobacco officials gave interviews to journalists, seen as a good "opportunity for the final word."[120] The ITC memo noted too that conference-goers had taken away most of the industry's printed materials left on information tables.

Among these materials were the results of a recent survey by Canadian Facts, commissioned by ITC for the conference. The national poll asked Canadians to choose "the one most important action the country should take in connection with smoking and health" from a list of three options. Forty-eight per cent chose "more research into the causes of cancer," 21 per cent picked "more publicity about the link between cancer and cigarettes," and 14 per cent selected "regulations to restrict smoking."[121] Respondents could select only one item, an artificial restriction since they were not mutually exclusive. In a differently designed survey, many might have chosen two or three options. Not surprisingly, a plurality of respondents chose the most affirmative option – supporting cancer research – rather than the negative option of "restricting" smoking or the pejoratively worded option of funding "more publicity" (rather than "more education"). Keith presented these survey results to the conference, emphasizing the greater popular support for funding cancer research versus the "more publicity" option. As Keith asked rhetorically: "Should the Government continue to intrude into individuals' private activities? Would money not be better devoted to trying to solve the basic problem of cancer and heart disease?"[122]

For tobacco executives, the National Conference on Smoking and Health came off as a major success. The Big Four cigarette makers had patched over their competitive differences to form a united front, led by ITC and assisted by US tobacco and public relations officials. Shortly after the conference, Keith wrote Devlin to praise the "cooperative and pleasant atmosphere" surrounding this exercise in solidarity, both before and during the conference.[123] (This co-operation occurred eight years before the formation of the Canadian Tobacco Manufacturers' Council in 1971, constituting, arguably, the origins of the CTMC.) During the conference, tobacco executives heard provincial health officials voice support for anti-smoking educational programs; however, the provinces carried little regulatory weight vis-à-vis tobacco, unlike Ottawa. And the limited funds allocated by LaMarsh for educational initiatives represented a tiny fraction of what the industry spent annually on cigarette advertising. The conference did not give rise to legislative or regulatory initiatives involving the industry, as cigarette executives had feared months earlier. The creation of the NHW working-group committees on smoking education and research likewise posed only minor risks to the industry. Two days after the conference, Keith had already contacted Carl Thompson at Hill & Knowlton to discuss the "approach that might be desirable to the [industry] membership and participation in the two committees that the Minister of Health will be establishing."[124]

CONCLUSION

Truly extraordinary was how quickly and adeptly Canadian tobacco firms repositioned the smoking-and-cancer millstone into a marketing opportunity, enlarging the industry's footprint and boosting company balance sheets. Dealt lemons, the industry made lemonade. By the mid-1950s, ITC-commissioned researchers were probing the health concerns and attitudes of smokers. In 1954, ITC released Matinée, which soon became the most popular filter brand on the market. Consumer researchers devised "brand personality indexes," among other marketing metrics, to assess the breadth and depth of health sentiment among smokers. By the late 1950s, ITC fully understood that commercial success hinged on developing and marketing cigarette brands that assuaged the health fears of smokers, especially women and young people.[125] Soon after arriving in Canada in 1957, Rothmans' O'Neil-Dunne came to the same realization. He authorized public service–type ads citing the cancer risks of cigarettes because past experience told him this was the "cheapest and easiest way of establishing new sales with a new brand" like Rothmans King-Size Filter, which touted a new-age filter and reduced tar. Rothmans' bid to establish a "cancer-free image," however, required competitor brands to wear the cancer label, which other companies, understandably, resisted. Explicit mentions of cancer and "safer" smoking in conjunction with cigarette filters and low-tar tobacco not only highlighted troubling facts for consumers, but boosted the prospect of state regulation of the industry. Not surprisingly, American, British, and Canadian tobacco executives closed ranks to pressure Rothmans Canada to end its "true facts" advertising campaign.

A similar coming together transpired in 1962 when ITC convinced fellow tobacco manufacturers to accept an industry-wide ban on tar and nicotine references in cigarette advertising. The motive here was fear of "socialist" state regulation of the industry, or, worse, a "Government Tobacco Monopoly" takeover of the sector. These concerns proved unfounded, as Canadian cigarette firms pursued strength in unity by having the industry speak with a single voice on smoking and health issues.[126] Industry executives successfully lobbied senior federal politicians and mandarins, while also circumventing health groups and government officials intent on curbing smoking. Canadian cigarette companies benefited from the experience, organizational skills, and knowledge of American tobacco and public relations executives, who crafted publicity campaigns and produced research briefs and reports promoting cigarette smoking as safe and socially beneficial. In the aftermath of the 1963 National Conference on Smoking and Health, the Canadian tobacco industry stood on much firmer terrain than many would have believed possible a decade earlier.

CHAPTER SIX

Marketing Bonanza

INTRODUCTION

Matinée advertising reflected key features of cigarette promotion in the 1960s. A filter brand launched by ITC in 1954 in the wake of the "cancer scare," Matinée maintained its health bona fides, touting an "exclusive Excello filter" and the tagline, "Canada's mildest cigarette." It came in king size as well, tagged by some as a healthier format.[1] In the late 1960s, ITC fused the brand's long-standing health appeal to premium marketing, offering smokers the chance to win up to $2,500 with each pack. Some ads in this campaign contained the names, addresses, and photographs of recent winners, testimonial endorsements from local residents that both corroborated cash pay-outs and upheld smoking as a shared cultural norm. "Switch to Matinée," the ads proclaimed, "first for the mildness, then for the money."[2] One campaign promoted a tongue-in-cheek "Loser" theme; winners of Matinée Money Chips were "losers," ordinary people typically unlucky in games of chance and life in general. One of these ads displayed a photo of Gloreen White of Eastern Passage, Nova Scotia, who "used to be a loser" and "never won anything." After switching to Matinée, she found herself $5,000 richer, now "a winner" in largesse and in life.[3] In the 1960s, premium brands appealed especially to lower-income smokers, who comprised a growing share of cigarette sales. The marketing appeal of the "Loser" campaign lay in its ability to tap into feelings of societal unfairness and "bad luck" often experienced by working people, while avoiding notes of condescension due to the ironic, "hip consumerist" tone of the ads.[4]

Countless other cigarette brands possessed hybrid appeals during the 1960s and early 1970s, an era remarkable for its bounty of product differentiation, marketing innovation, and advertising styles. Some of these developments, like filters and king-size formats, had begun in the 1950s; by the early 1970s, nine in ten cigarettes sold in Canada had filters, with many sold as Kings. The "health" sector of the cigarette market expanded in the 1960s to include "low-yield" brands like Belmont and Craven "A", promoted for their lower levels of tar and nicotine and enhanced filters. Tobacco firms developed and marketed these brands to assuage the health concerns of prospective and current smokers, providing the latter a "healthy" smoking option in lieu of quitting. The reputed health benefits of low-yield cigarettes were negated by "compensation," in which low-yield smokers consume more cigarettes, or inhale more deeply and more often, in order to attain accustomed to levels of tar and nicotine. Industry scientists conducted extensive research on compensation and fully understood these effects. In 1962 tobacco manufacturers agreed to ban explicit mentions of tar and health-related terms in cigarette advertising, in a bid to avert government regulation. But the agreement left intact implicit health messaging, allowing brands like Matinée Special Filter to use colour and imagery on cigarette packs and in advertising to generate and communicate favourable health associations. The many "Light" and "Mild" brands launched in the 1970s, especially Player's Light, contained marginally less tar and nicotine than their parent brands and generally avoided explicit health claims. But these brands sold well as smokers perceived them as offering comparative health benefits, along with, importantly, satisfying doses of tar and nicotine.

Three other developments galvanized the cigarette marketplace of the 1960s and early 1970s. The Matinée contest was one of dozens in the trade. This trend was not new; premiums and contest promotions first appeared in the 1930s, as discussed in chapter 1. But the breadth and intensity of gift and cash promotions in the 1960s threatened to destabilize the cigarette industry. A successful contest promotion could vault an obscure brand into the upper ranks of sales, spawning imitators. Premiums boosted sales, but industry executives regarded them with mixed feelings; while smokers might respond well to in-pack poker games or money chips, these types of promotions were expensive to run and tarnished the industry's public image. Government officials and health advocates denounced cash and gift incentives, citing their youth appeal. The second development involved sponsorship promotion, as cigarette firms rushed to embrace sports and cultural events as effective forms of marketing promotion. The appeal here was two-fold: sponsoring events like auto racing or skiing competitions allowed cigarette marketers to better target desired demographic groups, boosting brand identity and consumer appeal in a product sector that embraced market segmentation. Sponsorship also served a public relations function, exalting tobacco firms as socially responsible benefactors of amateur athletes, artists, and heritage preservationists, groups that were often short of funds. Third, cigarette makers began to identify and target younger teens as a valuable market segment. In 1962, ITC revamped its market research operations to collect data on people as young as fifteen. This research probed the smoking behaviours, health concerns, and pastimes of teenagers, enabling company marketers and advertisers to better appeal to this consumer segment, increasingly viewed as the keystone for capturing market share in the trade.

The tobacco industry's public handling of the smoking-and-health issue mirrored actions begun in the 1950s. Tobacco executives denied, frequently and emphatically, that credible medical evidence causally tied smoking to cancer or other serious illnesses. The science here, they claimed, remained "controversial" due to the paucity of quality research. Cigarette executives downplayed the health risks of smoking, comparing it to "risky" behaviours like entering a bathtub or driving a car, risks people willingly assumed for the accompanying benefits. Industry talking points on this issue appeared in newspaper articles, advice columns, and opinion pieces during the 1960s, highlighting the success of public relations efforts to influence news reporting and public discourse on smoking and health. Corporate disinformation campaigns and health-reassurance marketing contributed to Canadians' continued ambivalence about the health harms of cigarette use; in 1969, 54 per cent of regular smokers did not believe or realize that their own level of smoking constituted a health risk.[5] During this period, the views of scientists working in Canadian tobacco firms and their parent companies contrasted sharply with the public statements of industry executives about smoking and health. As early as 1958, company scientists discussed the serious prospect of cigarettes causing lung cancer, citing the presence of chemical carcinogens in tobacco smoke. In the early 1960s, scientists at Philip Morris and British American Tobacco called for safety improvements to the design of cigarettes to reduce the risk of contracting cancer. These views, conveyed in confidence and mostly in-house, fell largely on deaf ears as Canadian tobacco firms forged ahead with the twin-track strategy of public denial and health-reassurance marketing to manage and mitigate, mostly successfully, the smoking-and-health issue.

CIGARETTE MARKETING IN THE 1960S

Coupon and premium promotions proliferated during the 1960s.[6] Benson & Hedges' Mark Ten provided the template for this marketing trend that would transform cigarette promotion by 1970, as seen with the dozens of contests and coupon-incentive schemes offering gifts, cash vouchers, and prizes to customers. Coupons on the front flap of Mark Ten packages could be collected and redeemed for items like toasters, mink jackets, and even children's toys like dolls, tricycles, roller skates, and holster sets.[7] Mark Ten's share of the market rose from 1 per cent in 1963 to 6 per cent in 1969.[8] Belvedere gave away 15,000 watches to coupon holders and offered "instant gifts."[9] Matinée packages contained "money chips" that were redeemable for cash. Rothmans' Number 7 carried gift coupons and cash prizes. Peter Jackson featured contests with cash prizes, as did Macdonald's Export "A". Pay-outs for some promotions were as high as $25,000. Contest prizes ranged from coffee mugs to sports cars.[10] By 1969, brands featuring coupon incentives or contests accounted for about 60 per cent of sales, a market segment described as a "red-hot battle" and "all-out effort to attract new smokers."[11] Given the many financial incentives, it is not surprising that a 1969 marketing study found that coupon brands appealed disproportionately to "extremely lower class" and younger smokers.[12]

The promise of coupon brand promotion is exemplified by the case of ITC's Sweet Caporals. The brand had an old pedigree, dating back to the late 1800s, and had used "poker hand" promotions during the 1930s.[13] By the late 1960s, the brand's popularity had eroded considerably. In 1969, ITC reinvented "Sweet Caps" as a "poker-game" brand, offering cash prizes for winning hands. In just seven months, its market share jumped from 1 to 17 per cent. ITC's overall market share, which had previously dropped from about 50 per cent to under 40 per cent, experienced a sudden reversal of fortune. Sweet Caps spawned copycats. Rothmans Number 7 introduced a poker game with a $2,000 top prize and its Sportsman brand switched from offering gifts to cash certificates.[14]

Tobacco executives viewed the coupon trend as a mixed blessing. It boosted sales, but gift and prize money reportedly cost the industry $5 million in 1969. It also generated bad publicity. In 1970, the federal government charged Imperial Tobacco with fraudulent advertising, relating to a "$5 in every pack of New Casino" ad campaign. The company was found guilty and paid a fine of $3,000. Consumer and Corporate Affairs Minister Ron Basford was disturbed by the "excessive promotion" of coupon marketing, doubly so since "some of the tobacco companies are increasing their promotional advertising in anticipation of legislation preventing it. I think that is a most deplorable development."[15] Macdonald Tobacco vice-president Murray Mather described this marketing trend as an "awful nuisance" and one that "costs a lot of money." Rothmans president Wilmat Tennyson agreed: "We were not anxious to get in – and we are not particularly proud of the fact we are involved. We believe in quality before anything else." Speculation mounted that the coupon wave would swamp flagship brand holdouts like Rothmans King Size and Player's.[16] Tobacco executives saw coupon marketing as undermining the industry as a whole, but each firm feared the bottom-line consequences of a unilateral retreat.

King-size cigarettes similarly gained in popularity during this period. Rothmans started the king-size trend in the late 1950s when it heavily promoted a king-size version of its namesake brand.[17] The first Kings were 84 millimetres in length (compared to the 72 millimetre standard length), because federal taxes were higher for cigarettes 85 millimetres or longer. In 1962 Rothmans successfully lobbied Ottawa to rescind this tax differential.[18] This meant that longer cigarettes were taxed at the same rate, a point made flippantly by ITC president Paul Paré in 1965: "We could make a cigarette as big as three pounds without increasing the tax."[19] Cigarette makers launched many king-size brands during the 1960s, as seen with Rothmans' Stuyvesant and Craven "A" and ITC's Player's Filter Kings and

6.1 King-size cigarettes became popular during the 1960s. Their longer smoking time made them more harmful to smokers than regular-length cigarettes. du Maurier King-Size ad in the *Telegraph-Journal*, 17 September 1964.

Sweet Caporals. Benson & Hedges started a "length race" when it produced a 100-millimetre cigarette, Benson & Hedges 100s, touted as the "premium-length cigarettes at popular prices," for which the "extra puffs are on us."[20] Rothmans followed suit with its 100 millimetre Dunhill, as did Imperial Tobacco with Goldcrest. By 1968, king-size cigarettes were the choice of 45 per cent of smokers.[21]

For consumers, an 85 or 100 millimetre cigarette for the price of a regular-length one made economic sense (figure 6.1). But king-size cigarettes had a notable health drawback. The longer smoking time boosted the amount of tar and other carcinogens in the rear half of the cigarette. Canadians were also frugal smokers, as two studies in the late 1950s demonstrated, one appearing in the *British Medical Journal*.

Researchers collected samples of cigarette butts in Canada and the United States and found that Canadians on average smoked 68 per cent of a cigarette, compared to 62 per cent for Americans. Filtered cigarettes were puffed more than non-filtered ones, while "slightly more of the king-size is smoked than the regular size."[22]

The rise of filter cigarettes, begun in the early 1950s, continued unabated. From less than 2 per cent of the market in 1952, filtered smokes comprised 55 per cent of sales in 1962 and fully 87 per cent by 1971.[23] By then, filter cigarettes were the default choice for new smokers and those under thirty-five years of age. Consumers opting for filter cigarettes, as one journalist noted in 1958, were "disturbed by health stories and looking for protection." They were "ready to be sold a new idea anytime."[24] Press reports during the 1960s depicted advances in filter design as a form of technological salvation for concerned smokers. Scientifically engineered charcoal filters were praised for removing harmful agents and chemicals in tobacco smoke.[25] Benson & Hedges vice-president Antonio Toledo said in 1964 that "we are in the first phase of an entirely new generation of sophisticated filter systems," adding "there will be another breakthrough in a year or two." News stories played up research on charcoal and water filtration systems, with comparisons even made to the Turkish hookah.

SPONSORSHIP PROMOTION

Cigarette makers began investing heavily in sponsorship promotion of national sport competitions and cultural events during the 1960s. In 1961, Imperial Tobacco began sponsoring motor car racing, culminating six years later with the inaugural Player's Grand Prix, a Formula One event held in Montreal. Other ITC brands sponsored events. Matinée supported the Quebec Winter Carnival, du Maurier sponsored skiing competitions, and Peter Jackson was the brand sponsor for the Canadian Open Golf Tournament.[26] Benson & Hedges favoured arts sponsorship. In 1971 it launched an "Artwall" program, commissioning artists to paint murals in cities.[27] The company offered $2,000 scholarships to prison inmates to study music, literature, or visual arts at university upon release. In 1973, Benson & Hedges contributed $10,000 to the Canadian

Guild of Crafts for its biennial exhibition. Macdonald Tobacco sponsored La Tour de la Nouvelle-France, a five-day cycling race in Quebec, during the early 1970s.[28]

Rothmans was also active on this front. In 1961, Rothmans and Bee Hive Syrup co-sponsored skiing events in Collingwood, Ontario, which in part involved Rothmans vans ferrying injured skiers to hospital. The firm sponsored local horse shows and national competitions, on one occasion offering $200,000 to the Canadian Equestrian Team. During the 1960s, the company funded tennis tournaments, the National Ballet, and art galleries.[29] When the Rothmans Art Gallery opened in Stratford in 1967, former prime minister (and Rothmans chairman) Louis St Laurent presided at the dedication ceremony. Rothmans' "Special Events Caravan," a fleet of seven mobile broadcast studios, provided live broadcasts from cultural and sporting events.[30] In 1972, Rothmans founded the Craven Foundation to preserve heritage items and historical collections; its first undertaking was an exhibition of forty-seven antique cars which toured Ontario shopping centres.[31] Rothmans' Peter Stuyvesant brand featured a promotion in which one in every two hundred packages contained a coupon redeemable for an artwork valued between $250 and $400. "We want to sell cigarettes and we want to do something for Canadian artists," said vice-president of marketing Wilmat Tennyson in 1968, "and you've got to admit, this is a helluva dignified way to sell cigarettes."[32]

In early 1972, ITC established the du Maurier Council for the Performing Arts, headed by Canadian Senator Donald Cameron. The firm pledged $1 million to the Council to fund Canadian arts groups over five years. Isabelle Sauberli, an ITC media manager, stated that the program would "help enhance the du Maurier brand image" via a "soft sell" approach: "there will be no direct advertising. In effect, the groups supported by the program will be promoting an image themselves. There will be natural promotion; programs, press releases, receptions, announcements and so on." In its first year, the Council awarded $295,000 to twenty-one arts groups.[33] Soon after, the Council provided marketing expertise to grant holders, helping them design and distribute program covers, posters, show cards, and press kits, all of which bore the du Maurier Council name and logo. As one Council member said: "So many of the groups are small and have no facility to publicize their productions."[34]

The push for sponsorship promotion reflected a changing political environment. As ITC marketing vice-president Ian Murray underscored in 1970, as "government indicates its intention to restrict the industry, we must search for other marketing tools to remain competitive." Consequently, as one journalist observed, each tobacco firm was busy "dashing about trying frantically to put its name, or its brand's name, on just about any event the public participates in."[35] ITC president Paul Paré confirmed that sponsorship embodied a "soft sell" approach, a contrast to the intrusive nature of broadcast advertising. More importantly, it also offered a public relations benefit; the firm was seen as helping culture and sports organizations that had "difficulty finding support," which provided "an opportunity for us to put the names of our leading brands forward in an association that we like."[36] As one industry observer concluded, cigarette sponsorship made "it less likely – although no tobacco man admits it – for government to lean harder on the industry."[37]

HIGH-FILTRATION AND LOW-TAR BRANDS

In the 1960s, cigarette makers launched many "low-yield" brands, defined as those with enhanced filters or reduced levels of tar and nicotine. By 1968, the low-yield segment accounted for 12 per cent of the market.[38] Rothmans' Ransom brand touted its low-yield, Strickman filter. Imperial Tobacco followed suit with Richmond, a high-filtration brand, launched to "satisfy the health doubters." Benson & Hedges marketed Viscount, another strong-filter brand.[39] In 1969, Macdonald Tobacco released the low-tar brand Consols in western Canada with the ad slogan, "have a mild."[40] Cigarette manufacturers stepped up the marketing of low-yield cigarettes when smoking-related health issues were in the news. Benson & Hedges vice-president Antonio Toledo recounted to the trade how the firm had heavily promoted Belmont, its charcoal-filter brand, on the heels of the U.S. Surgeon General's report in 1964.[41] Anticipating a critical report on smoking by Ottawa in 1968, Rothmans was ready with full-page newspaper ads for Ransom.[42] In 1969, the federal government released a table listing the tar and nicotine levels of cigarette brands. An official from Vickers & Benson, the ad agency handling ITC's Matinée account, noted that after this government release rated Matinée King-Size Filters as very low in tar and nicotine, the brand's subsequent marketing "continue[d] to emphasize th[at] fact."[43] One tobacco executive in 1970 believed that low-yield brands offered high yields for the bottom line: "people smoke more as a reaction to the advertising of low tar and low nicotine content of cigarettes" because they viewed these products as safer, healthier choices.[44]

Industry market research explored in detail how health concerns moved some smokers to adopt low-yield brands. A 1969 Canadian Facts consumer survey for ITC rated brands on a "Safe for Health" scale, with Matinée and Craven "A" scoring highest.[45] In 1973, ITC conducted an analysis of cigarette marketing and smokers' health concerns. Drawing on company research, the report noted that "smoking and health pressures" had lowered smoking rates, but not yet overall sales. The incidence of male smoking, which had gradually declined over many years, was now in a holding pattern; but this would likely not continue *"if health pressures are not dramatically changed either in nature or in number."* The smoking rate for women had risen steadily during the past decade, but this would prove short-lived, the report underscored, if *"health concerns become more women-directed."* The long-term solution to smoking's health problem lay in formulating a "valid concept of the place of smoking in society and of the type of product that should be developed." This entailed replacing the concept of "safer cigarettes" with that of "safer smoking," which would "take into account all available knowledge about [the] smoker's behaviour, scientific knowledge of the constituents of smoke and their effects on smokers, and what practical avenues for change really exist."[46] In another report that year, ITC discussed marketing in relation to smoking and health concerns, with the prospect of introducing "moderately reduced [tar and nicotine] number brands," since "really low brands do not sell."[47]

The dilemma for the industry was that its advertising code banned explicit references to health in product promotion. How could firms appeal to the health worries of smokers without directly referencing health or physical well-being? British American Tobacco (BAT), ITC's parent company, issued guidelines for this in 1974.[48] The document noted that "on legal grounds alone, it will continue to be to the industry's advantage not to make explicit health claims." Instead, BAT companies like ITC were to make "increasingly competitive use of products for which health claims are implied." BAT-owned firms would also encourage their competitors "not to make explicit health claims" and would "discourage unsupportable health claims from any source."[49] In a 1974 planning document, ITC officials discussed the marketing challenge of describing the "benefits to the consumers when we cannot use the two words that best describe the concept – reduction in build-up of *Tar* and *Nicotine*." Advertising and promotion for reduced tar and nicotine cigarettes could only "imply a 'safer cigarette'" and not state this explicitly.[50]

ITC's market testing for Matinée "Special Filter," launched in 1976, found that this new brand was "perceived to be a very mild cigarette and better for your health."[51] Its development built upon ITC research revealing rising health awareness among smokers, 61 per cent of whom thought that cigarette smoking was "dangerous for anyone." The study's participants viewed Matinée Special Filter as having less tar and nicotine than Matinée Regular, even though nearly 70 per cent were unaware of actual tar and nicotine levels listed on the cigarette pack.[52] The brand's core messages of "mildness" and "health" were communicated most effectively by package design and advertising. "Image-type campaigns" like the one for Matinée Special Filter, ITC officials noted, could "often be more effective than words since the latter generally appeals to rational intelligence, whereas the former appeals to the sub-conscious." The brand's launch also provided a public relations benefit for ITC, as one official stressed: "the recent launch of Special Filter provided our sales force with a logical reply to the anti-smoking criticisms, 'You see, we are doing something about smoking and health. We are offering a safer cigarette.'"[53]

Similar considerations were evident during the planning and launch of Player's Light in 1976.[54] The new brand would have 14 milligrams of tar, while its marketing would emphasize a "mildness strategy" as compared to slightly higher-tar brands like Player's Filter and Export "A". In keeping with recent "Mild" and "Light" brand launches in the United States, the "mildness story" for Player's Light would be "only relative," since "14mg [of tar] is hardly a mild brand." There was, ITC marketers noted, "no milder version of a main younger starter brand on the market. Player's Light will fill this gap." Player's Light would "supply a 'safer' range extension of one of the two youngest, strongest, most masculine and popular starter brands in Canada."⁵⁵ Mild and Light brands like Player's Light proved especially popular in the late 1970s and 1980s; they successfully conveyed a healthier image than their namesake parent brand, while providing tar and nicotine at high-enough levels to deliver satisfying taste.⁵⁶

The success of health reassurance marketing is evidenced by a qualitative survey done for ITC in 1969.⁵⁷ Thirty-three per cent of respondents reported that "many of their friends had switched to milder brands, or from non-filter to filter type cigarettes," in lieu of quitting. One respondent, a stenographer from Mountain, Ontario, confirmed: "Oh, some of my friends have shifted brands, or tried filter, and some have tried to quit, but couldn't, so they went for the filter cigarettes, or low-tar type. I feel that their reasons are quite likely from a health viewpoint." Similarly, a building superintendent from Welland, Ontario, noted that "two of my family changed to filters because of fear of cancer and heart trouble, and some of my friends also smoke milder brands – for the same reason, I guess."⁵⁸ Twenty-seven per cent of respondents had switched brands more than once for health reasons. Nearly eight in ten smokers "credited the filter with performing a 'healthful' function." A construction worker from Sainte Eustache, Quebec, who had switched to Sportsman filter, added: "You know, if you can find a good filter brand like this one you can enjoy smoking again, without worrying so much about the health hazards."⁵⁹

COMPENSATION

To what extent did low-yield or high-filtration cigarettes provide health advantages to smokers? Industry research on compensation pointed to few, if any, tangible health benefits. (Compensation occurs when smokers switch to lower-yield cigarettes and then "compensate" for this change with deeper inhalation, extra puffs, or by smoking additional cigarettes.) Canadian cigarette firms began studying compensation in the early 1970s. In 1972, ITC scientist R.S. Wade wrote fellow BAT scientist D.G. Felton to discuss ITC's research on smoker compensation. The work to date showed that "when the nicotine content of a cigarette is reduced, smokers will alter their smoking patterns to try to obtain their normal nicotine intake, usually by taking more frequent puffs." By doing so, they "obtain a tar yield proportionately higher than that which the cigarette was designed to give." Smokers also smoked more cigarettes daily. Wade, citing research performed by Philip Morris and BAT, said that there was "considerable evidence" in support of the theory of nicotine compensation. He even thought it unwise for federal officials to encourage the use of low-yield brands since "compensation for lower nicotine can be expected to maintain higher tar intakes."[60]

In 1972, an ITC marketing program described the consumption of lower-tar and -nicotine cigarettes as a "function of the consumers' perception of the safety of the brand relative to its physiological delivery of a satisfying smoke." The volume of smoke inhaled was not reduced because "smokers adjust their physical smoking habit (the way they puff a cigarette) to compensate for a reduction of nicotine levels."[61] By the following year, ITC viewed compensation less as a theory than as an empirical fact. A discussion brief for a conference on smoking and health conference reported that:

> we are convinced that most smokers smoke to their own personal nicotine requirement, altering their pattern of puffing so as to extract and absorb the nicotine they require. If the nicotine delivery is low enough, they cannot change their smoking pattern enough to get satisfaction, and reject the brand. With a moderately low nicotine cigarette they simply take more puffs, or larger puffs and thereby increase their intake of harmful substances: tar, carbon monoxide, hydrogen cyanide, etc.[62]

A 1973 industry research proposal about smoking and health similarly discussed nicotine intake and compensation. Health-themed brands with lower levels of tar and nicotine still needed to consider the "user's need" for nicotine absorption. The "involuntary moderation" of enhanced filtration or air venting of smoke was of "limited merit" since smokers compensated with deeper inhalation, more puffs, or more cigarettes.[63]

Compensation helps to explain a paradox of cigarette consumption in the 1960s and 1970s: per-capita cigarette sales gradually rose, even while the overall smoking rate of the population declined slightly. ITC's W.T. Knox remarked on this trend in 1976, noting that there had been a "gradual erosion in incidence of smoking coincident with an almost offsetting increase in volume per smoker."[64] Consumers of low-yield cigarettes, accustomed to higher-yield brands, smoked more of these cigarettes to attain habituated levels of nicotine and tar. Compensatory smoking also meant that low-yield smokers received similar levels of tar and nicotine as those smoking regular cigarettes even when the same number of cigarettes were consumed, further negating any putative health advantage.[65]

CONSUMER RESEARCH AND TEENS

As mentioned earlier, the tobacco industry's advertising code of 1964 banned cigarette marketing and advertising to people under eighteen years of age. During the 1940s and 1950s, the cigarette marketplace had a decidedly adult orientation. Models in ads typically looked to be in their thirties or older, and scenes of adult sociability were a mainstay of industry advertising. Brand positioning, advertising, and trade press discourses characterized the cigarette market as being predominated by adult men, with a growing minority of adult women. This began to change in the 1960s as ITC moved to target younger consumers; in 1962, the semi-annual consumer survey done by Canadian Facts for ITC lowered its minimum age for respondents from eighteen to fifteen. In addition, the 1962 survey oversampled fifteen-to-nineteen-year-olds in order to improve the statistical reliability of interview data for this age group. "In recent studies," the report noted, "the basic sample of smokers 18 years and over has been 'beefed up' with an oversample of smokers under 20 years of age. In this study, this youthful oversample was achieved by simply extending the questionnaire to a standard sample down to 15 years of age."[66] The 1962 survey was also the first to gauge consumer interest in spectator sports like football, soccer, and auto racing. The latter proved especially popular among males aged fifteen to nineteen, 62 per cent of whom expressed interest, compared to just 37 per cent of all men. "Autosport," the report concluded, "is very definitely a youthful matter."[67] This Canadian Facts survey is notable for its methodological and analytical focus on people under age twenty, as evidenced by the detailed data produced on teen smoking behaviour, brand affinity, and sport interests.

Subsequent Canadian Facts surveys for ITC continued to examine teen smoking. In fall 1964, the company reported that the smoking rate among fifteen-to-nineteen-year-old males had climbed from 36 per cent in spring 1964 to 41 per cent six months later. For girls fifteen to nineteen, the corresponding increase was 25 to 31 per cent.[68] In this age group, 21 per cent of boys and 32 per cent of girls reported increased amounts of smoking compared with the previous year. Export "A" was the most popular brand among the fifteen-to-nineteen market segment. The survey report also noted how "teen-agers are the most receptive to" the idea that certain filter brands were safer than others. Another Canadian Facts survey in 1967 reported that "the general switch to filter cigarettes since 1961 has been spearheaded by smokers, both male and female, in the younger (15–19) age group." In 1967, 91 per cent of boys and 97 per cent of girls in the fifteen to nineteen age group smoked filter brands. The report concluded that in "terms of establishing brand loyalty among new smokers, the 15–24 age group is, of course, critical and is likely to remain so."[69]

Rothmans similarly compiled data on people as young as fifteen via consumer surveys it commissioned from Opinion Research Corporation International (ORC). In 1967, ORC conducted the first of its annual "Canadian Smoker" surveys. In the 1969 version, the first available to researchers, the minimum survey age was fifteen. ("Student" was also an occupational category in the survey.) The survey provided Rothmans with useful information on the fifteen- to nineteen-year-old market segment. Rothmans' brands captured 27 per cent of this group, second to Macdonald's 39 per cent share, owing to the popularity of Export "A" among youths. The report described Export "A" as a brand "with a high degree of social acceptability to the young people who smoke them."[70]

An ITC report in 1973 drew upon internal market research to describe how the smoking rate for boys aged fifteen to nineteen had remained at 46 per cent from 1963 to 1972, while the comparable rate for girls had climbed from 27 to 40 per cent. The smoking rate for all fifteen- to nineteen-year-olds stood at 44 per cent in 1972, which was "an all time high." (By comparison, the smoking rate for the adult population in 1972 was 46 per cent.)[71]

The report voiced concerns about potential inroads made by governments and medical authorities in reducing the social acceptability of smoking. But a contrasting "optimistic trend" involved the rising rates of smoking "among people aged 15–19, the youngest for which we have data." These teens had been "subjected to health concerns in classrooms virtually all their academic lives in addition to those pressures felt by adult Canadians." However, the report noted, there was "no suggestion of a fall off in [the smoking] incidence in this group and, in the past 2 years, there is even an indication of a substantial increase."[72]

ITC enlisted qualitative research to better comprehend youth culture and teen smoking. In 1975, it commissioned Creative Research Group to conduct focus groups with boys and girls between the ages of fifteen and eighteen concerning du Maurier, in a bid to make the brand more attractive to younger smokers.[73] Interviewers asked about various cigarette brands, with a focus on du Maurier, Belvedere, Export "A", and Player's Filter. They recorded feedback on sample ads shown to respondents. The study's final report offered advice on designing advertising creative. Male and female couples should be shown engaged in particular activities. The setting should have an "undercurrent of *excitement*"[74] and be something that "young people (particularly boys) would like to indulge." The activity should have "some physical accomplishment," be "slightly masculine" in nature, and one in "which girls could also participate." It should produce a "peaceful, tranquil, 'free' sort of feeling, not a hard, frenetic, sweaty, tiresome sort of feeling," meaning that sailing was more suitable than motor boating and bicycling better than jogging. The photo of the couple in the ad should occur just before or just after the activity and not during it.[75] ITC likely acted on these recommendations since creative research vice-president W.T. Wingrove later wrote an ITC official to discuss how "du Maurier has successfully extended its franchise and broadened it to include more younger smokers and more males."[76]

Consumer studies like these mined and analyzed the behaviour, attitudes, and values of Canadian teens. Survey reports typically contained dozens of pages of data tables and cross-tab analyses. By the early 1970s, ITC's storehouse of marketing data on teen smoking and youth consumption most likely surpassed that of any other organization – business, governmental, academic – in Canada. Daniel Cook describes child-directed market research as a "commercial epistemology," enabling various market and non-market actors to "see and apprehend children and childhood for specific purposes and towards particular ends."[77] "In order to sell the child," Cook writes, "one must of course know not a child as an individual, but the 'the child' as a type ... [an] amalgam of knowledge acquired and systematized through the gaze of various experts."[78] In the case of cigarette marketing to under-eighteen teens, consumer research constituted a powerful mode of "knowing," a *sine qua non* set of expert practices and technologies which both penetrated and ordered the inchoate terrain of youth culture and social identity. By accessing and codifying the views, needs, and opinions of teens, market research made possible practices like market segmentation, brand positioning, and package design and advertising that would resonate with their target markets.[79] ITC's later success in selling Player's Lights to teenage boys in the late 1970s and 1980s owes in part to the firm's extensive and sophisticated use of consumer market research.[80]

SEGMENTING THE MASS MARKET

The above developments in cigarette marketing (e.g., coupon and low-yield brands, targeting women and youths, etc.) highlight the shift from a mass market orientation to one characterized by market segmentation. Product promotion in a mass market employs a "shot gun" approach to marketing and advertising to reach and persuade as many people as possible. A classic illustration of this was the Ford Motor Company during the interwar years, when it focused on selling one affordable line of cars, the Model T, which, Henry Ford famously quipped, came in different colours "so long as they were black." The cigarette trade of the 1950s reflected this mass market orientation, where mostly undifferentiated products were sold to a wide cross-section of adults, largely uninfluenced by demographic variables like gender, class, or age. In the early 1950s, about six in ten Canadians smoked regularly. The sector was a duopoly with very limited competition. Two brands controlled nearly two-thirds of the market, appealing about equally to men and women, young and old, rich and poor. Most cigarettes were plain-end, standard-length, and made of bright-leaf tobacco.

The rise of market segmentation is well illustrated by the case of General Motors. Instead of selling one line of automobiles like Ford, GM marketed different lines based on price segments, with Chevrolet at the low end, Pontiac and Buick in the middle, and Cadillac at the top. By the 1950s, GM's sales had surpassed Ford's.[81] In that decade marketing experts like Wendell Smith and Pierre Martineau published ground-breaking articles delineating and promoting market segmentation as an optimal business strategy for many product sectors.[82] Consumer marketers, Daniel Pope notes, started to "divide up the broader market and design a campaign that could reach and attract a specific target audience with distinctive needs or desires."[83] By segmenting markets and targeting specific groups with different products marketers could increase sales, enhance consumer satisfaction, and boost profits. "Knowing the idiosyncrasies, attitudes, needs and 'hot buttons' of identified targets," Richard W. Pollay notes, "allows for product design and advertising that is far more likely to elicit favourable consumer responses."[84]

This new marketing strategy also reflected structural changes in the mass media. Traditional forms of mass media (general-interest magazines, television) were challenged by new forms of "segment-making" media, starting in the 1950s and 1960s. Radio ceded the "mass" audience to television and developed new station formats based on music flow and disc jockeys, with music programming aimed at particular, not general, audiences. Mass-circulation general-interest magazines like *Saturday Evening Post* and *Life* began losing money as magazine upstarts like *Psychology Today* and *Rolling Stone* launched, successfully targeting "slices of the population whose incomes, buying habits, and strong interests in particular subjects attracted national advertisers."[85] Marketers used quantitative and qualitative research to identify the needs and desires of different demographic and psychographic groups. Products and branding tailored to these groups gained competitive advantage in the marketplace.

By the mid-1960s, market segmentation characterized the Canadian cigarette industry. The arrival of foreign multinationals had ended the industry's prior duopoly, reshaping the market into a more competitive "Big Four" structure. In 1968, the two most popular brands (Export "A" and Rothmans) accounted for 24 per cent of sales,[86] much less than the 63 per cent total seen for the top two brands in 1950. The cigarette market of the

1960s offered: male brands (Export "A", Sportsman Filter); female brands (du Maurier, Matinée); "health" brands (Craven "A", Viscount); working-class brands (Mark Ten and other coupon brands); and brands with middle-class appeal (Rothmans King Size). More than seventy brands vied in a competitive and highly differentiated marketplace. Notably, the road to market segmentation began with the news about smoking and disease in the early 1950s and the industry's marketing response in the form of filter and, later, low-yield brands to reassure to smokers. While some of these smokers would later die from tobacco-related cancer and other diseases, the cruel irony remains that the "cancer scare" breathed new life – and marketing innovation – into a cigarette industry that had been largely placid for decades.

SMOKING AND HEALTH: US SURGEON GENERAL'S REPORT

On 11 January 1964, the US Surgeon General's Advisory Committee on Smoking and Health released its report, which had been favourably anticipated by cigarette makers. The US tobacco industry had been given a de facto veto over committee appointments. None of the committee's members were experts in tobacco-health science and about half were smokers. Two members, Maurice H. Seevers and Louis F. Fiser, had consulted previously for the tobacco industry. Despite all this, the report by Surgeon General Luther Terry offered disconcerting news for cigarette executives. The lung cancer death rate among male smokers was 1,000 per cent higher than that of non-smoking males. Cigarette smokers faced much higher risk for contracting coronary disease, emphysema, and bronchitis. "Cigarette smoking," the Terry report concluded, "contributes substantially to mortality from certain specific diseases and to the over-all death rate."[87] While the report proved less prescient in certain areas (e.g., classifying smoking as a "habit" and not an "addiction"), it nonetheless was a "turning point in the broader public recognition of tobacco hazards."[88] The Terry report, Brandt argues, was a watershed event that "ended any remaining medical and scientific uncertainty concerning the harmfulness of smoking." After 1964, remaining "core skeptics" of the smoking-causes-disease thesis were "almost exclusively tied to the industry," and increasingly "marginalized and de-legitimated."[89] Terry promised action to address this serious public health problem, citing possible measures like educational campaigns, health warnings on cigarette packages, and restrictions on advertising. The report's findings produced front-page news throughout Canada.[90]

Canadian tobacco executives soon attacked the Terry report. In a story in *La Presse*, ITC president John Keith said that "l'industrie canadienne du tabac considère le rapport sur la cigarette comme n'étant pas concluant." In the article, Keith was quoted as saying: "Il est clair que le rapport américain est essentiellement une interprétation des diverses et nombreuses études ou communications qui nous sont familières pour la plupart et qui sont à l'étude depuis un certain temps." Moreover, Keith said, the Terry report's recommendation for more research on smoking and cancer was "une attitude déjà adoptée par l'industrie au Canada."[91] At a shareholders meeting in April, Keith denied again that smoking was a cause of lung cancer or heart disease: "Despite the millions of words which have been written and the numerous statistical studies which have been made, the fact still remains that cigarette smoking has not been proven experimentally to be the cause of lung cancer, heart disease or other diseases with which it has been associated."[92] Rothmans vice-president Wilmat Tennyson also panned the Terry report because it "ne souligne point le fait qu'il n'y a aucune preuve réellement clinique que l'usage du tabac ait causé le cancer."[93]

The most far-ranging attack on the Terry Report came in an address by Tennyson to the Advertising and Sales Association in March 1964, as reported by the *Montreal Gazette*.[94] Tennyson's speech was titled "Smoking and Health: One Tobacco Man's Views," but its contents mirrored the industry's consensus view on this topic. The Surgeon General's report was a "model of the art of vague assertion, guilt by innuendo and easy conclusion." It failed to assess other probable causes of disease, for which the cigarette had become a convenient scapegoat. Auto exhaust and industrial pollution "may well be much more of a factor than smoking, in producing lung cancer." There was no clinical or laboratory evidence linking cancer to smoking and the report omitted studies on the "smoking Welsh mice" that lived longer than non-smoking ones. The report didn't account for higher lung cancer rates in cities than in rural areas. It failed to recognize that the quality of cigarette tobacco was now better than in past decades, since today "much more inorganic matter is removed from tobacco in modern manufacturing processes than ever before." The Terry report did not distinguish between the "modern filter cigarette" and its plain-end predecessors, when in fact the health measures between them were "growing each day with the development of improved selective filters." Tennyson asked: why did the Surgeon General not "find out and inform the public of the truth about modern filter cigarettes?" This was because the report was merely a "re-calculation of existing statistical surveys." What, Tennyson asked, is a statistician? "A man who draws straight lines to foregone conclusions from insufficient data." Smoking was dangerous, the report concluded, but, claimed Tennyson, the report inconsistently claimed that "most smokers suffer no serious impairment of health or shortening of life as a result of the habit," leaving smokers confused. The Terry report, Tennyson charged, had produced a state of affairs which had "reduce[d] medical research to publicity, speculation and judgment."[95]

Tennyson then weighed in against government officials. He characterized the efforts of Judy LaMarsh and provincial health ministers to publicize the risks of smoking as "gropingly amateurish," whose real motives were the pursuit of "considerable personal publicity – the life blood of the professional politician." He mocked the small amount ($40,000 per annum) that LaMarsh had assigned to fund research activities, a "laughable approach" when compared with the $7 million spent by the US industry on health-related research. Tennyson noted that the four largest cigarette makers in Canada spent $18 million annually on advertising and promotions, while contributing $420 million in federal taxes. And, yet, the Canadian government could only muster $40,000 per year for its research program? Moreover, some of these funds would go to "social study" research, assessing "why people smoked," as opposed to bench science on tobacco smoke itself.[96] Tennyson wondered why there was a "witch hunt against tobacco," when lung cancer "causes less than 2% of all deaths," a rate comparable to breast and prostate cancers, but the latter did not elicit "epidemic" headlines in newspapers. Cigarette makers were "concerned with the health of our fellow man and we would certainly voluntarily refrain from contributing to their detriment." But he also spoke about the responsibility to company shareholders and to ensuring the "economic welfare" of people in the cigarette trade, who should not suffer from the "irresponsible and hasty actions on the part of well-meaning but misguided people."[97]

The Canadian tobacco industry, however, did recognize that the public mood had changed after the Terry report. In June 1964, cigarette executives established the Cigarette Advertising Code, promoting industry self-regulation as both effective public policy and corporate social responsibility. The heads of ITC, Macdonald, Rothmans, and Benson & Hedges, which together controlled more than 98 per cent of the cigarette market, adopted the code, whose key planks concerned health and youth-smoking issues. The code required that no cigarette advertising "state that smoking the brand advertised promotes physical health, or that smoking a particular brand is better for health than smoking any other brand of cigarette." It stipulated that "all cigarette advertising shall be directed to adults," and that models in cigarette ads be at least twenty-five years of age. Advertising could not feature athletes or celebrities "whose major appeal" was with people under eighteen. Advertising could not "state or imply that cigarette smoking is essential to romance, prominence, success or personal advancement." The code banned cigarette ads on billboards that were "immediately adjacent" to elementary and secondary schools and banned ads on TV before 9:00 p.m.[98] The industry adopted the code with a strong eye to the federal government. Soon after its adoption, ITC president John Keith wrote LaMarsh to advise her of it, noting that the industry planned no "widespread publicity campaign about the Code."[99] During the 1960s and 1970s, cigarette executives repeatedly assured the public and government officials that their marketing and advertising targeted only adults over age eighteen. However, as discussed above, the cigarette industry routinely targeted under-eighteen teens via consumer research and marketing campaigns during these decades.

PUBLIC STATEMENTS, IN-HOUSE SCIENCE

In the early 1960s, ITC developed public relations "talking points" about smoking and health to handle related queries from members of the press and public. An ITC memo in October 1962 presented a series of company-sanctioned positions on this topic.[100] For example, a question like, "Why is there so much adverse publicity about smoking and health?," would be answered along these lines: "uninformed laymen and publicity seekers" sought "publicity by making 'anti-smoking' statements." There was also a "good number of other scientists who question[ed]" the smoking–cancer relationship who had "not sought or received equivalent publicity." The purpose here was to undermine the objectivity of news stories on smoking and cancer by portraying them as fear mongering or "sensational," whose real purpose was to sell newspapers or magazines. Company-issued positions held that smoking-is-harmful science was based on "statistical studies," not clinical or laboratory research, and that a "growing body of evidence" refuted the smoking–cancer causal thesis. The question, "Are filter-tip cigarettes 'safer' than unfiltered ones?," was to be answered by noting that since no credible evidence held that cigarettes were harmful, "it cannot be said that a filter may have any effect regarding health," only that "some filters are better at reducing smoke condensates." (However, as seen earlier, ITC's own market research clearly showed that most filter-cigarette smokers believed these cigarettes were healthier than plain-end ones.)

When asked about "hazards to smoking," the official response was to note that "every human action has its hazards, even taking a bath"; as such, people "should view smoking in its proper perspective." When asked what "Tobacco Inc" was doing to "help solve this health problem?," officials were to emphasize the industry's $300,000 donation to the National Cancer Institute in support of cancer research, while stressing that industry scientists worked closely with "independent scientific research teams on the lung cancer problem." The tobacco industry was acting in the best interests of consumers and the smoking public.

> We are interested in the continued improvement of the health of the public, we have said many times that we would like to be the first to know if there is anything in tobacco smoke that causes lung cancer. If there is, we should be able to remove it. However, intensive chemical tests have failed to uncover anything that would account for human cancer ... we and the smokers of Canada will probably have to live with anti-smoking publicity until the causes of lung cancer are discovered.[101]

The memo, and its appendix, provided many more "best practice" retorts: the "great majority" of smokers did not get lung cancer, while non-smokers did; far fewer women acquired lung cancer, despite rising rates of female smoking; smoking inhalation tests on lab animals had not resulted in lung cancer; "recent scientific research" pointed to viruses as causal agents of lung cancer. An aging population and improved diagnostic methods resulted in higher rates of lung cancer.[102] As well, tobacco firms never targeted non-smokers or children ("we do not advertise to children and do not wish to encourage children to smoke"), and only marketed "brand names to adults" who already smoked.[103]

Some of these industry talking points later appeared in news and opinion pieces following the release of the US Surgeon General's report. Writing in *Maclean's* in August 1964, physician W. Gifford-Jones advised heavy smokers "to quit worrying about it," since such anxiety would produce only "fearful hypochondriac smokers." Gifford-Jones held that the science linking smoking to cancer was "shaky" and had "huge flaws." Smoking eased tension and stress, which in turn kept in check ulcers and hypertension. He dismissed the Surgeon General report because he was "skeptical of the statistical approach to biological problems." He then cited more industry-friendly refrains in refuting smoking–cancer ties: some countries with high smoking rates had low lung cancer rates; diagnostic advances meant more detection of lung cancer and not higher existence of it; higher lung cancer rates in cities compared with rural areas pointed a causal finger at air pollution.[104]

In a similar vein, Evered Myers, writing in *Saturday Night*, chastised the "professional worry merchants, whose current big bogey is the cigarette-&-cancer scare." He conflated the Terry Report conclusion that smoking reduced life expectancy with what "your parents told you when they caught you with your first cigarette behind the woodshed," except that now "it's Big Brother speaking." Critics of cigarettes were "evangelical rather than scientific," who viewed smoking as an easy "scapegoat" for the manifold ills of modern society.[105] Another article in *Maclean's* offered a "surprising second look" at the "facts about cancer and smoking." Here again, industry talking points resounded: co-relation did not equal causation; lung cancer rates were inexplicably lower among pipe and cigar smokers than among cigarette enthusiasts; the evidence was statistical, not clinical or experimental; comparisons among countries found vast differences concerning smoking rates and lung cancer prevalence; urban pollution, especially coal smoke, was an unacknowledged cause of lung cancer. An examination of all relevant studies, and not just newspaper headlines, raised serious "doubts [as to] whether the cause of lung cancer has so simply been found." There was too much contradictory evidence.[106]

A *Financial Post* article reported on rising cigarette sales following an earlier downturn after the Surgeon General's report. When asked to comment, Rothmans president J.H. Devlin offered a fatalistic explanation: "the average man figures he has to die of something. Perhaps we will all die of cancer if we live long enough. Smoking is one of the minor pleasures of life, so people keep on doing it." The rest of the article mirrored the industry's script on smoking and health. A "number of medical experts" challenged "the flat judgement, based on statistical association, that cigarettes cause cancer and heart disease." In the article, TIRC's Clarence Little described how more than a decade of scientific research had still not provided a solid link between smoking and cancer or cardiovascular disease.[107]

Contrast these public statements with the views of scientists at the parent companies of Canadian tobacco firms. In spring 1958, three senior British American Tobacco executives conducted a fact-finding tour in the United States and Canada, meeting with tobacco executives and cancer researchers in universities or hospitals.[108] Their goal was to determine "the extent to which it is accepted that cigarette smoke 'causes' lung cancer." The answer to this question was clear. In their later report, the authors concluded that with one exception all of "the individuals whom we met believed that smoking causes lung cancer if by 'causation' we mean any chain of events which leads finally to lung cancer and which involves smoking as an indispensable link." The authors added that "there is no support for the view that in the same individual the tendency to smoke and to be susceptible to lung cancer are each independently an outward expression of some third unknown factor." The BAT report stated there was "general acceptance of the view that the most likely means of causation is that tobacco smoke contains carcinogenic substances present in sufficient quantity to provide lung cancer when acting for a long time in a sensitive individual." The authors concluded that "scientific opinion in U.S.A.

does not now seriously doubt that the statistical correlation is real and reflects a cause and effect relationship."

Also in 1958 BAT Chief Scientist Charles Ellis wrote Leo Laporte, his ITC counterpart, about smoking and cancer. Ellis thought it unlikely that there was "just one potent carcinogenic agent in smoke whose presence made it dangerous and whose removal would render smoke innocuous." Rather, he believed, the problem was of a more "general nature," more like a "long series of slight irritations which were only important when happening to a particularly susceptible person." The most likely solution lay in "reducing the tar while preserving the physiological effects and the taste, and hoping that the solution to our immediate problem will come from advance in our knowledge of cancer as a whole."[109] In his reply, Laporte agreed with Ellis that it was "unlikely that there is any one agent in smoke of sufficient concentration and of sufficient carcinogenic activity, the removal of which would still all criticism."

In a 1962 memo, Ellis wrote that BAT's "object must be to improve the safety of cigarette smoking." Part of this task involved discovering ways "to enable the smoker to absorb the nicotine he wants without the necessity of taking as much smoke into his lungs." It was a "tenable assumption" that if little or no smoke aerosol reached the lungs "there would be a marked reduction of damage to the lung, and of lung cancer." Researchers should investigate how to provide smokers with their "customary amount of nicotine" without the negative side-effects from inhaling cigarette smoke. He discussed various devices that might work, which included inhalers delivering nicotine without smoke aerosol reaching the lungs. It also might be possible, he wrote, to filter out most of the tar in cigarettes, while still delivering a sufficient amount of nicotine. New low-tar/high-nicotine tobacco strains "would obviously be safer to inhale." Researchers might also investigate how to speed up the absorption of nicotine in the mouth so as to reduce the need for inhalation.[110]

As early as 1961, Philip Morris scientist D.H. Wakeham voiced concerns about the health dangers of cigarette smoking. In a presentation to the firm's Research and Development Committee, he outlined the epidemiological evidence on smoking and lung cancer, stating that "these associations suggest that smoking may be a causative factor." Physiological studies of tobacco constituents painted on animals had resulted in "increased tumor frequency." Benzpyrene, a hydrocarbon found in tobacco, produced the highest number of tumours in mice. Wakeham proposed that the company begin research on reducing "the general level of carcinogenic substances in smoke," with the goal of producing "a medically acceptable cigarette." He estimated that such a research program would cost about $10 million and take seven to ten years to complete. This constituted a major research undertaking, but it was necessary since "carcinogens are found in practically every class of compounds in smoke." The proposed research program would probe such areas as "major precursors for carcinogens and/or cancer promoters," while also seeking to "discover mechanism[s] or conditions by which carcinogens are produced." Wakeham concluded by noting emphatically that a "*medically acceptable* low-carcinogen cigarette may be possible," but it would require the "TIME; MONEY; [and] UNFALTERING DETERMINATION" of the company.[111]

In 1964, soon after the release of the Surgeon General's report, Wakeham offered up more research ideas on smoking and health. A research program consisting of biomedicine, the chemical constituents of tobacco smoke, and filter technology could develop "cigarettes with distinguishing new product properties which are biologically approved on all major health questions." These new products, in turn, could be marketed and advertised "vigorously on the basis of studies so conducted." Wakeham believed the health question would form the "basis for competition in the industry" during the next few years. He advised against the denialist "common front approach of the industry," as exemplified by the Tobacco Institute and TIRC. He believed that the Surgeon General's report (which, Wakeham wrote, had "disclosed no vitiating errors of commission") would usher in an era of "health competition" in the cigarette industry, driven by technological innovation and commercial research. Philip Morris should embrace this future with the "same aggressiveness that it has shown in packaging innovation." Wakeham concluded with a bold call for action:

> If it is true that the onus of proof in the Smoking and Health issue has shifted to the tobacco industry, then the industry must come forward with evidence to show that its products, present and prospec-

tive, are not harmful. Medical research must be done for this purpose, as well as for judging the merit of work done outside the industry. The industry should abandon its past reticence with respect to medical research. Indeed, failure to do such research could give rise to negligence charges.[112]

Fellow Philip Morris scientist W.L. Dunn expressed similar views on this topic. In March 1964, he called on the company to boost research to develop cigarettes without "the properties that are alleged to have an adverse effect upon the health of the smoker." This program of research would evaluate "all the components of smoke," with the goal of "deleting those not meeting minimal acceptability requirements." Another approach, Dunn wrote, was to "abandon the usual conceptualization of the cigarette" and instead develop different products to deliver nicotine to consumers "while presenting none of the hazards to physical health which have been imputed to the cigarette as we now know it." Such a product would taste, smell, and inhale in ways similar to cigarettes. He envisioned a type of holder or container, similar to a pipe, but one looking more like a cigarette. This "surrogate cigarette" would "win medical endorsement," without sacrificing the nicotine-delivery needs of smokers and the psychosocial pleasures of smoking itself.[113]

PUBLIC OPINION, HEALTH, AND SMOKING

Even after the US Surgeon General's Report, Canadian public opinion on smoking and health remained ambivalent. In late 1964, the federal government commissioned a survey on awareness and belief concerning smoking and health hazards. While the poll found that 90 per cent were aware of public reports linking smoking to health problems, only 60 per cent responded affirmatively when asked, "Do you believe that cigarette smoking is a hazard to health?" (In the minds of respondents, this type of question wording could also include low-level health concerns like coughing and throat irritation.) When asked to identify specific diseases "reported" to have been associated with cigarette smoking, only 33 per cent mentioned lung cancer. (Similarly, awareness of "reported" diseases is not the same as believing such an association to be true.)[114] In 1966, the federal government discussed a poll it had commissioned on smoking cessation. Former smokers were asked to identify their main reasons for quitting cigarettes. Notably, only 4 per cent of respondents cited "fear of cancer," the same number of responses grouped under "miscellaneous." Nineteen per cent mentioned garden-variety health concerns like coughing, throat irritation, or difficulty breathing; 32 per cent of replies were grouped under "unspecified health reasons." While health-related topics comprised about two-thirds of replies, very few respondents cited diseases like lung cancer, heart disease, or emphysema, which had been medically shown to be the most harmful to smokers.[115]

Cigarette smokers continued to underestimate the health risks of cigarette smoking. A 1969 Rothmans survey on the smoking-and-health issue used two types of queries: current smokers were asked if smoking in general was dangerous to one's health and whether they thought "the number of cigarettes you currently smoke is dangerous to your health?" Twenty-four per cent maintained that smoking was not dangerous and another 23 per cent said that the amount they currently smoked was "probably not dangerous." Another 7 per cent were undecided, meaning that more than half of regular smokers (54 per cent) did not believe or realize that their level of cigarette smoking posed a significant health risk.[116] An ITC-commissioned marketing study in 1969 asked cigarette smokers to rank the health risks of cigarettes, pipes, and cigars. Only 5 per cent ranked cigarettes as the most dangerous of the three, with the majority citing cigars as least safe.[117] In the early 1970s, a sizeable portion of Canadians continued to misrepresent or doubt the health harms of smoking. A 1971 Canadian Gallup survey asked if cigarettes were "a cause" of cancer. While 58 per cent of respondents agreed, fully 42 per cent of respondents either disagreed or were undecided.[118] ITC market researchers also found that 46 per cent of smokers either disagreed with or were undecided as to whether "smoking is dangerous for anyone." Among French Canadian smokers, this figure was 58 per cent.[119] Survey results like these underscore the industry's success in marketing health reassurance to smokers, who continued to minimize the health risks of cigarette use. Tobacco companies effectively framed these risks as manageable, encouraging "concerned" smokers to take up one of the many low-yield or mild/light brands launched in the 1960s and 1970s.[120]

A Canadian Facts study in 1969 provides a social portrait of Cigarette Nation that reflects both continuity and change. Forty-six per cent of adults were regular smokers, a little more than 10 per cent lower than seen at the height of smoking's popularity in the early 1950s. Quebec had the highest rate of smoking (52 per cent), while prairie residents were the least inclined (41 per cent). The gradual decline in male smoking was offset somewhat by elevated smoking among women, especially those under age thirty. Fifty per cent of women between twenty and twenty-four smoked, as did an astounding 63 per cent of those aged twenty-five to twenty-nine, the summit age group for female smoking. Peak smoking for men occurred a little later, with 67 per cent of males between thirty and thirty-four smoking regularly. The survey report noted that the composition of smokers had begun to skew slightly more "lower class," the start of a trend that would see smoking strongly associated with lower socio-economic status by the 1990s. Conversely, smokers of king-size cigarettes were said to be a little more "upper class and better educated" than were smokers of regular-length cigarettes. Most consumers bought cigarettes in single packs (65 per cent), with 25 per cent opting for carton purchases. Cigarettes were bought mainly in supermarkets (24 per cent) and other types of grocery establishments, including variety stores (29 per cent). Only 9 per cent bought cigarettes in tobacco shops or newsstands.[121]

The above composite portrait is richly complemented by another consumer study conducted that year, illuminating social-psychological and cultural features of Canadian smoking society. In 1969, ITC commissioned Analytical Research (Canada) Limited, a motivation research firm,[122] to elicit and analyse the values and attitudes of smokers, along with the underlying motivations informing the decision making and behaviour of smokers.[123] Researchers compiled a sample of 180 smokers in Ontario, Quebec, and British Columbia, and then used in-depth, unstructured interviewing methods to probe beyond top-of-mind responses. The goal of motivational studies like these was to discern emotional cues and reflexes and assess how people "unknowingly" came to believe what they did about smoking, especially related to health issues. The study's 175-page report offers a vividly descriptive and analytical account of a smoking culture confronting key changes.

Pre-existing smoking culture, what the report called smoking's "Old Covenant," had centred on sociability and personal pleasure. Nearly all of the study's respondents "concurred that their smoking habits were initiated on a social level," and that smoking provided key "emotional satisfactions," described as "relaxing," "tasteful," and "increased contentment." Motivation research reports typically provide quotes from anonymous respondents to illustrate concepts and themes. A Trois-Rivières construction worker is quoted as describing smoking as a "source of great enjoyment, it gives me contentment, it takes away my sorrows ... it makes me feel good and in a good humor." A nurse from Longueil, Quebec, similarly stated that "smoking is part of our life like drinking coffee. I smoke with friends in company or at a party ...That's how I got started in the first place. It's a sociable habit." A homemaker from Brantford, Ontario, further added: "I associate smoking with sitting and talking to a group after we've had a good dinner at a restaurant ... It was friendly when I started, my friends did it and I wanted to start."[124]

But emergent challenges threatened the sociable culture of smoking, as seen by the comment of a Montreal office worker: "In the back of my mind I think I'll probably give it up within five years. For one thing, I think it will probably be socially unacceptable after awhile." He and others were worried about a future in which smoking was no longer a social attribute or a shared enjoyable pastime. Propelling this concern was the din of negative health news about cigarettes, producing malaise and foreboding among some smokers. Smokers, on the whole, remained ambivalent about the health question itself: "Respondents are not convinced that a health hazard exists as far as smoking is concerned, but neither are they convinced that it doesn't." While few contemplated quitting soon for health reasons, some worried that adverse news about smoking would impair its social acceptability, leading researchers to conclude that the "disapproval of peers apparently smarts more painfully than considerations of mortality."[125]

Researchers drew on interview data to construct three typologies of smokers: "Defiant," "Guilty," and "Intellectual." The "Defiant" group comprised 44 per cent of respondents. These smokers were largely unconcerned about smoking's health risks, even "patently ignoring them in most cases." Defiant smokers emphasized the pleasures of smoking and their ability to quit whenever they wanted, though they remained resolute in their desire to keep smoking. "Guilty" smokers formed 26 per cent of respondents; they harboured serious misgivings, even shame, about their smoking habit. A Burlington secretary described her smoking as "dirty, stupid, expensive and dangerous – but so far I can't stop!" She wished that authorities "would outlaw cigarettes, take them right off the market, and then I would HAVE to do without them." A Toronto publishing executive similarly said: "I've changed my brand, it is supposed to be 'milder' 'safer' but I know they are all bad. Or why would they go to all that trouble to change them?" Guilty smokers were thought most likely to leave the "smoking fraternity," since their guilt could only be fully absolved by quitting, and not just by switching to "safer" brands.[126]

The third segment, the "Intellectual" smokers, comprised 28 per cent of interviewees; they were neither blatantly dismissive of health concerns nor convinced that smoking was objectively dangerous, a "bad habit" that one must break. These smokers deployed logic, justifications, and evidence to assess the smoking-and-health issue in ways reminiscent of the discussion of motivated reasoning in chapter 4. They sought out supporting evidence while drawing selectively on past beliefs to reach conclusions that often minimized smoking's health harms. A Welland, Ontario, homemaker observed: "I've heard all the respiratory claims. It's supposed to put your blood pressure up, cause emphysema and all that, but I would say weed killer could do as much harm when you inhale it, or any of those things. I haven't met a sick smoker yet, nor one who takes these claims seriously." A beautician in Ottawa similarly stated: "I've read and heard said that cigarette smoking causes cancer, but I've also read of a child of four years old who died of lung cancer and she wasn't smoking, so how come cigarette smoking causes cancer?" Others attributed rising lung cancer deaths to air pollution. Many of these rationalizations and arguments mirrored those publicized by tobacco executives since the 1950s.[127]

In this period of flux and uncertainty, smokers were in search of a "New Covenant" to reanimate smoking. "The guiltless pleasure that [the smoker] enjoyed years ago in the pursuance of 'a good smoke' has disappeared."

Smokers were now in a "precarious limbo" between the "sanction of the old covenant" and a need for new ideas and social codes to shore up the cultural merits of smoking. One approach stressed a familiar theme: stress relief and psychological benefits. A London, Ontario, reporter underscored how there was "an awful lot of pressures pulling at you today, and like that doctor who's an expert on physical stress, Dr. Hans Selye, says: 'If you don't get rid of the tension with cigarettes it would probably eventually affect your body through actual disease' – like cancer, I guess. He figures smoking is the lesser of two evils." In this vein, smoking, by tackling nervous tension or psychological pressures, averted health problems rather than constituting a health hazard itself.[128]

But rationales and actions beyond stress management were also needed. Smokers, the report said, wanted manufacturers to do more to rejuvenate the image of smoking, while providing smokers a "product that [they] can enjoy without fear of physical or psychological reprisal." They wanted "dynamic advertising and promotional strategies" that would "represent the cigarette to the consumer as a valid product" and "restore the smoking environment to its former health." They wanted smoking to become both fun and therapeutic, enhancing both social life and psychological well-being. At times, this prospective social order for smoking sounded more like a chimera or nostalgic escapism than a serious attempt to resolve the cognitive dissonance of a habitual practice linked to deadly disease. For this "new covenant," smokers wanted cigarette makers to "restore innocence to [their] smoking pleasure, and exercise doubts that are undermining [their] enjoyment of it." They looked to manufacturers to provide them with "a safe smoke that will give [them] back [their] freedom of choice without fear of [their] peers' disapproval, or the prospect of an untimely demise."[129]

CONCLUSION

Smokers wanted the pall enshrouding cigarettes to dissipate, rendering smoking once again an uncontested source of personal enjoyment and social engagement. In the meantime, many would hedge their bets by smoking brands perceived as safer. The tobacco industry understood this, as seen with its strategy to sell doubt and hope to smokers.[130] When the Royal College of Physicians and the US Surgeon General released reports on the health harms of smoking, industry executives publicly lambasted them as shoddy science, while simultaneously boosting advertising for low-yield brands selling the hopeful message of health reassurance. This point is highlighted by a complaint made by Benson & Hedges to an industry body concerning advertising for Rothmans' Craven "A" Special Mild, a so-called health brand. The lettering in the government-issued health warning in the ads, Benson & Hedges maintained, was too large – done in a 15-point font instead of the stipulated 10-point size. In so doing, Rothmans was "making a conscious decision to add greater impact to the health warning," turning the warning into a "marketing tool" to "get around the industry agreement of not using tar and nicotine in advertising."[131] Ironically, some of the frankest assessments of the smoking and health issue came from industry scientists. On many occasions, company scientists raised concerns about the health harms of smoking, even calling on their firms to research and market tobacco products that would deliver nicotine to people in ways safer than cigarettes. All the while, tobacco executives continued to declare publicly that no credible scientific evidence causally linked cigarette smoking to lung cancer or other diseases.

A similar divide between public utterance and private action characterized the industry's relationship to teen smoking. While cigarette executives publicly portrayed the cigarette market as an adults-only affair, industry marketing practices routinely targeted people as young as fifteen, as seen in consumer research commissioned by ITC. These large sample surveys provided statistically reliable measures of smoking prevalence, brand preference, media and leisure time consumption, and health awareness. They generated a large body of data on teen smoking–related behaviour to inform marketing planning and execution. ITC marketers worked to understand the "why" of teen smoking and the dynamics of social acceptability underpinning the practice among youths. Evident here was another dual-track stratagem of the cigarette industry: the industry's public actions and proclamations, like the Cigarette Advertising Code, affirmed the reputable ideal of an adults-only cigarette market. Industry marketing practices, however, like surveying people as young as fifteen, reflected a commercial imperative that teens were the crucial "starter smokers," who often stayed loyal to their initial regular brand well past the teen years. While capturing the teen market became vital for commercial success in the cigarette business, the public repudiation of this fact by industry officials became as important in staving off public criticism and unwanted government regulation of the cigarette trade.

CHAPTER SEVEN

The View from Ottawa

INTRODUCTION

In March 1967, National Health and Welfare (NHW) Minister Allan MacEachen spoke in Toronto about his government's approach to smoking and health. While he recognized that a large body of scientific research linked cigarettes to lung cancer and other diseases, many people, nonetheless, still chose to smoke. Should Ottawa's response then be to make "smoking an offense?," he asked. Such a move, along with severe restrictions on cigarette promotion, violated basic tenets of liberal thought and governance: the proper role of the state was to "inform and educate" people, since the decision to smoke was fundamentally a "question of personal responsibility." Governments should only supply the necessary facts so that people would "know the risks they take when they smoke." This was because the "only really effective remedy" for unhealthy behaviours like smoking entailed people "making up their own minds" to curtail or quit these habits. He added: "Today we hear a lot of people clamouring for governments to do this, and do that legislation in a Quixotic effort to stuff a statute book in a vacuum that can only be filled by the exercise of personal responsibility."[1] Government intervention was both ineffective and unwarranted meddling in the private lives of citizens.

MacEachen's views were in keeping with those of Justice Minister Pierre Trudeau, who soon after introduced an omnibus bill to legalize divorce, therapeutic abortion, birth control, gambling, and homosexuality, among other measures. The bill died on the order paper when the federal election of 1968 was called. But after the election, Trudeau, now prime minister, reintroduced the bill, which became law in 1969. The Criminal Code Reform Act, C-150, has been rightly called historic, marking, as Suzanne Morton notes, the "evolution of liberal thought from a preoccupation with private property to an increased emphasis on moral autonomy and individual freedom."[2] Trudeau had famously defended the omnibus bill by proclaiming "there's no place for the state in the bedrooms of the nation." The legislation formed part of Trudeau's "Just Society," to be realized via political, economic, and legal reforms. His government would promote individual liberty, ensuring Canadians were no longer "bound up by standards of morality which have nothing to do with law and order but which have to do with prejudice and religious superstition."[3] Canadians adults, and not the state, would determine the merits of playing the lottery or acting on same-sex attraction.

Less known is that Bill C-150 broadened state powers in a few areas, notably involving firearms and impaired driving. The rationale here was public safety, since irresponsible gun owners and drunk drivers could potentially harm others besides themselves. Might a similar rationale support state curbs on cigarette promotion or smoking in general? Or should the liberal doctrine of limited state involvement in the private affairs of citizens guide federal policy on cigarettes and health? In the 1960s and early 1970s, parliamentarians, federal health bureaucrats, and cabinet ministers debated how best to promote the public health goal of reduced smoking while respecting liberal freedoms and personal choice. Health warnings on cigarette packs and restrictions on tobacco marketing and advertising featured prominently in this discussion. Supporters of stronger state controls on the cigarette industry included a multi-party group of MPs, many of whom tabled private member bills to ban cigarette advertising, reduce tar and nicotine levels in cigarettes, and require health warnings on packages. Senior mandarins in NHW pushed for similar regulations on the cigarette industry. They typically had medical or scientific backgrounds and were highly cognizant of the empirical evidence connecting smoking to serious illness. They monitored the tobacco trade closely, meeting often with cigarette executives, which in turn made them skeptical about industry self-regulation to promote the interests of public health.

A strong proponent of government action was John Munro, who succeeded MacEachen as NHW minister in 1968. A heavy smoker troubled by his inability to quit, Munro took up this file with more drive and conviction than had any previous minister (or, indeed, any future one until the late 1980s). He directed a parliamentary standing committee, led by Liberal MP Gaston Isabelle, to investigate and hold hearings on the cigarette industry with respect to smoking and health; the committee's report recommended many legislative and regulatory moves to restrict cigarette advertising and alert smokers to the health risks of tobacco use. In 1970, Munro secured Cabinet approval for a bill (C-248) bearing many of the Isabelle Report recommendations, including a total ban on cigarette advertising. Bill C-248, however, languished after first reading, and the Trudeau government soon after abandoned it. The demise of Bill C-248 resulted in part from the liberal orientation of key cabinet ministers, for whom decisions on socially controversial subjects like smoking (or gambling or homosexuality) were best left to individuals, not the state. To do otherwise meant upholding an anachronistic view of smoking and society, one informed by notions of vice or personal weakness in which the state acted to preserve community standards or serve as the moral guardian of the nation. Just as the Trudeau-era state would no longer police the pleasures of the bedroom, nor should it come substantially between Canadians and their cigarettes.

Politics turns as much on marshalling constituencies as it does on fulfilling first principles. And here the tobacco industry, once again, proved second to none. But for a brief period, the Canadian industry spoke in a single voice on smoking and health in its dealings with the federal government. It solicited and benefited from the involvement of foreign tobacco firms and public relations experts. American executives from the Tobacco Industry Research Committee, Hill & Knowlton, the Tobacco Institute, and Philip Morris liaised regularly with their Canadian counterparts. These US officials provided strategic advice, drafted reports and submissions, and secured expert witnesses for parliamentary hearings. Under the leadership of ITC president Paul Paré, the cigarette industry pieced together a coalition of tobacco unions, growers, and retailers, whose members lobbied elected representatives and cabinet ministers. During the fight against C-248, this coalition widened to include marketing and advertising trade associations, ad agencies, and newspaper and magazine publishers. Representatives from these groups wrote government officials and testified before parliamentary hearings denouncing the proposed ban on cigarette advertising. Newspaper and magazine executives characterized the ban as an attack on freedom of the press, and their opposition proved especially influential with key members of Trudeau's Cabinet. While polling showed that a majority of Canadians backed the proposed cigarette advertising ban, the formidable phalanx of industry groups opposing this measure eventually won the day, quashing C-248 and leaving intact most avenues of cigarette promotion.

HEALTH WARNINGS AND TAR AND NICOTINE LEVELS

In May 1965, ITC vice-president Leo Laporte and Norman Dann, ITC's manager of public relations, met with NHW Deputy Minister G.D.W. Cameron to discuss health warnings on cigarette packages, which ITC opposed. According to Laporte and Dann, Cameron himself viewed this approach as "unrealistic" and "silly." Cameron preferred to wait and see what happened in the United States with warning labels and their effect on smoking levels. In any event, said Cameron, there would be no "precipitous action" without prior consultation with the industry.[4] Soon after, J.N. Crawford replaced the retiring Cameron as deputy minister at NHW. During a November 1965 meeting, Laporte raised the issue of warning labels, to which Crawford responded that in his personal experience he did "not think that anyone read anything on a label." According to an ITC account of this meeting, Crawford illustrated this point by saying that the only time his wife had "shown a preference for one cigarette against another was when there was a requirement to match the colour of her dress." Based on this encounter, Laporte and Dann concluded that "Dr. Crawford's attitude is that any health labelling on cigarettes would have no effect on usage." But they also underscored that Crawford had less expertise than Cameron in smoking and health matters, making it likely that he would rely more on the advice of staff in this area. They concluded that "there will be value in reaffirming and developing further our relationships with" more junior members of his staff. The memo duly noted that Crawford smoked Edgeworth pipe tobacco and that his secretary smoked Buckingham cigarettes.[5]

In January 1966, ITC executives met with Crawford and Allan MacEachen, the new minister of National Health and Welfare. ITC president John Keith conveyed the industry's opposition to health warnings on packages: the "theory that smoking is a health hazard is based essentially on statistical studies which we do not accept as proof of a causal relationship and therefore, we could not agree with the implications of a warning message and would not, for our part, voluntarily follow the American pattern." Crawford countered that NHW accepted this statistical evidence as proof that smoking was a health hazard and that the department sought to discourage cigarette smoking, which could involve the use of warning labels. MacEachen asked Keith to present the matter to the tobacco industry's Ad Hoc Committee, which comprised the heads of the four largest companies and dealt with smoking and health issues, to see if the industry would agree voluntarily to health warnings on packages "rather than forcing such a measure by legislation." ITC officials came away from the meeting believing that Crawford and MacEachen, both relatively new to their positions, relied heavily on the advice of junior NHW staff who favoured stronger curbs on smoking and cigarette promotion.[6]

The hardline position of NHW staff members like E.A. Watkinson, director general of health services, is revealed in a memo he wrote for Crawford in August 1966. In reviewing a tobacco industry brief that opposed warning notices on packages, Watkinson lambasted the industry's claim that flimsy "statistical" evidence supported the smoking–cancer thesis: "The evidence regarding the health hazards of cigarette smoking is now overwhelming. It has come from numerous studies carried out in several countries and is accepted by major bodies, governmental and scientific, of responsible informed opinion throughout the world." There was little scientific doubt that "smoking contributes to the production of cancer, heart disease, and bronchitis and emphysema." Watkinson criticized the industry for how it equated public health efforts to educate people about the harms of smoking with "religious" attacks on the "evils" of smoking seen in the early 1900s. The industry opposed warning labels, he wrote, because it understood that these would adversely affect sales. In the absence of voluntary moves by the industry, he advocated for new legislation.[7] Plans for such legislative action, however, did not materialize in the following weeks.[8]

Instead, Ottawa sought to measure and publicize tar and nicotine levels in cigarettes, in the hope that smokers would gravitate towards brands with lower readings. NHW staff wrote to cigarette manufacturers advising them of this, and Keith and others indicated their initial compliance.[9] The Ad Hoc Committee approved the hiring of an outside scientist to measure tar and nicotine levels and make these results available to NHW.[10] MacEachen wrote a memo for Cabinet in support of requiring cigarette packages and advertising to include nicotine and tar levels, and, on 11 May 1967, Cabinet approved this measure.[11] ITC officials then began to set up roadblocks. During a meeting with Crawford, Laporte and Dann advised him of the many "practical technical problems" associated with this initiative.[12] Crawford wrote MacEachen suggesting they hold off on the legislation due to expected administrative and enforcement difficulties. He advised instead that the matter be given to the Committee on Public Health in the House of Commons.[13]

On 13 July 1967, the Ad Hoc Committee met to discuss this issue. Keith asked whether "we wait for government action or should we take some initiative before government action is taken?" The consensus view was to try and "guide the government in any action it might take." The industry would continue to oppose health warnings and tar and nicotine levels on packages. Members discussed the Advertising Code, which, to date, had "served its purpose in holding a line of defense for a number of years," but now, however, certain of its provisions "no longer st[ood] up to public opinion." Since much cigarette advertising on television had "a strong appeal to teen-agers – under 18," it was thought that TV advertising placed the industry "in an indefensible and unrealistic position." After discussion, a consensus emerged to consider "some Canadian-oriented response to broadcast advertising (radio & T.V.) in the context of total North American action." In effect, the industry opted to do nothing; they would wait and see how this issued first played out in the United States.[14]

When Keith next met with MacEachen and senior NHW staff in November 1967, the mood of the department had soured considerably. Writing Macdonald president May Stewart, Keith described how he was "disturbed at the change in attitude of the Deputy Minister and his staff. Previously they had appeared to be sympathetic to the tobacco industry, but this has changed."[15] NHW staff told Keith that the industry "was not behaving in a responsible manner toward the smoking and health problem." They were especially troubled by the advent and heavy promotion of 100 mm king-size cigarettes. They were also disturbed by the acceleration of coupon and premium promotions, which, NHW officials maintained, were "attractive to children." The tobacco industry was "not living up to the spirit" of its Advertising Code. MacEachen said that he was under pressure from his staff to act on this, telling Keith that a bill on the matter had been prepared. He was willing to hold off on this if the industry provided suitable voluntary actions which included: "a program of moderation; alteration in our advertising approach; elimination or price differential on 100mm cigarettes; and whether we would voluntarily show tar and nicotine contents on labels."[16] Keith took MacEachen's terms to the Ad Hoc Committee, whose members agreed to comply with much of this: they would raise prices on 100 mm brands; they would co-operate with tar and nicotine testing of cigarettes and the later publishing of these results, including on cigarette packages; they would develop a moderation campaign to discourage young people from smoking; and they would restrict televised cigarette advertising to 10:00 p.m. and later.[17] Of course, these moves were "voluntary" in the barest sense only, since they materialized only after the threat of legislation.

The industry, however, soon backtracked on these promises. Keith notified MacEachen in January 1968 that Benson & Hedges had quit the Ad Hoc Committee, making industry-wide agreement difficult to achieve. (According to Keith, the departure of Benson & Hedges was due to the concern of its parent company, Philip Morris, that "any concessions they make in Canada will be used against them in the U.S.")[18] For the time being, industry leaders could deliver on only one item: the 10:00 p.m. start time for televised cigarette ads. The other measures would be delayed, Keith indicated, since the exit of Benson & Hedges from the Ad Hoc Committee "could well place us in an invidious competitive position."[19] In May 1968, MacEachen met with the "Big Four" presidents in Montreal, seeking to find a way forward. Rothmans vice-president W. Tennyson supported co-operation with the government, but not if it placed them at a competitive disadvantage vis-à-vis holdout Benson & Hedges. He opposed as well "irresponsible and unnecessary restrictions" like US-style warning labels. MacEachen asked them to consider the removal of 100 mm cigarettes from the market, since it was "the one thing that bugs his Departmental people more than anything else." Benson & Hedges president Antonio Toledo offered a flat "No."

MacEachen then laid out the required terms for the industry to avoid legislation. Benson & Hedges must rejoin the Ad Hoc Committee and all parties needed to adopt the following: a 10:00 p.m. start time for TV advertising, an NHW-run system of tar and nicotine testing, an industry-sponsored moderation campaign, and higher prices for 100 mm cigarettes.[20] Soon after, Benson & Hedges did rejoin the Ad Hoc Committee, but members would agree only to the tar and nicotine testing provisions and only consider for further discussion the other measures.[21] This intransigence in part reflected a political calculus: Pierre Trudeau had recently been elected leader of the Liberal Party and a federal election, slated for 25 June, was currently underway. Cigarette executives could well be dealing with a different minister come the summer. The 1968 federal election was the fourth in the past six years, a period of political instability (and ministerial changeover) that arguably benefited the tobacco industry.

Industry opposition to government direction was again evident at the Ad Hoc Committee meeting on 30 July 1968. Members opposed "voluntary restraint" involving broadcast advertising, and did not back a moderation program.[22] In order to have greater control over the content of research projects, committee members opted to examine the feasibility of establishing an "institute" that would serve as an industry "vehicle for research on problems of smoking and health."[23] Previously, in December 1966, William Shinn, a lawyer in the US law firm of Shook, Hardy & Bacon, which worked closely with American tobacco companies, and Alexander Holtzman, legal counsel for Philip Morris, had visited Hans Selye in Montreal to discuss industry funding of his research on external stress and disease and the role of cigarette smoking in alleviating stress.[24] In late 1967, ITC had established "Project S & H" ("Smoking and Health") to prepare for future industry appearances at government hearings. Laporte, Dann, and N. MacDonald from Public & Industrial Relations were to handle the "political field" operations. The drafters of the brief's scientific sections would "undoubtedly use the services of Carl Thompson of Hill & Knowlton," since that PR firm had been "largely responsible for the preparation of our brief on scientific perspectives" at the Conference on Smoking and Health in 1963. Project S & H would also "seek whatever information and guidance we can obtain from the Council for Tobacco Research in New York, as well as from our friends in the U.S. and, if necessary, the U.K."[25] In February 1968, Thompson reported back to Dann that he had begun work on the project but that it was "taking much more time than I had originally hoped, primarily because it has meant going through many more papers and analyzing them and also double checking on everything possible that was Canadian."[26]

PARLIAMENTARY VOICES

During the 1960s, more than twenty private member's bills were introduced to restrict cigarette marketing or fund anti-smoking programs. Many were sponsored by NDP MP Barry Mather, a passionate critic of smoking since his election in 1962. Another outspoken opponent was Tory MP and physician Philip Rynard, who since the late 1950s had spoken out in the Commons about the health dangers of smoking. In May 1963, Rynard invoked a recent British Medical Association statement on smoking and lung cancer, asking NHW Minister Judy LaMarsh what the government would do "to make teen-agers and others aware of the connection between cigarette smoking and cancer of the lung."[27] Shortly after, he highlighted the scale of this growing epidemic: "cancer of the lung kills more people than any other single disease. It kills more people than all the traffic accidents and drownings occurring across Canada each year."[28] Mather sought, unsuccessfully, to have 31 May designated as Non-Smoking Day, as the British Columbia government had done.[29] Soon after LaMarsh's statement on smoking in the Commons in June 1963, Mather introduced a private member's bill with stringent controls on cigarette labelling, packaging, and advertising. A year later, he presented a similar bill.[30]

Private member's bills rarely become law, and those targeting tobacco proved no exception. But members' questions to ministers proved effective in highlighting some of the contradictions of Ottawa's handling of the tobacco file. A favourite approach by Mather was to request how much the government derived from tobacco taxes alongside what it spent on anti-smoking measures. In the 1967–68 fiscal year, tobacco taxes totalled $461,266,414, while $200,389 was spent on "combatting cigarette-induced disease and/or on smoking and health education."[31] When the CBC declined to follow the BBC and refuse cigarette advertising, NDP MP David Orlikow tabled figures showing that the CBC earned $1.2 million from this source in 1964, compared to just $100,000 by CTV.[32] In 1967, Mather called on Ottawa to adopt the "Fairness Doctrine" of US broadcasting and require Canadian television stations to air anti-smoking messages in proportion to the volume of cigarette advertising.[33] In 1968–69, Ottawa gave $536,160 in subsidies to tobacco growers, more than twice the $239,649 it spent on smoking-related research and health education.[34] When Imperial Tobacco sponsored skiing competitions, which also received federal funding, Mather objected forcefully in the Commons.[35]

Alongside Mather, Rynard, and Orlikow were other critical voices in Parliament. Ontario Tory MP William Howe pressed for more public health spending to combat smoking, while underscoring the government's conflicting interests in the matter: "we find the government has set up a fund to examine and report on the effects ... of the use of tobacco ... and on the other ... we find another area crying for assistance to produce more of this product."[36] Howe introduced private member's bills to limit tar and nicotine levels in cigarettes and to bring the industry under the control of the Food and Drug Directorate, where it could be more tightly regulated.[37] Liberal MP Antonio Yanakis tabled two private member bills in 1967 to curtail cigarette advertising and mandate the package warning – "Warning-Smoking may endanger your health."[38] H.W. Herridge, the NDP member from Kootenay West, highlighted the recent resolution from the Union of B.C. Municipalities criticizing tobacco advertising, calling on Ottawa to "eliminate, modify or deglamorize all forms of tobacco advertising."[39] Liberal MP W.K. Robinson introduced a bill containing stringent limits on tar (8 milligrams) and nicotine (0.5 milligrams) levels in cigarettes.[40] Support for tobacco control measures spanned party lines; Liberals, Tories, and New Democrats sponsored bills to reduce or eliminate cigarette advertising, lower nicotine and tar levels in cigarettes, and require health warnings on packages.

JOHN MUNRO AND THE ISABELLE COMMITTEE

The strongest force for tobacco control in government came with John Munro's appointment as NHW minister in July 1968.[41] An unwilling chain-smoker, he spoke often and movingly about his difficulties in quitting cigarettes (figure 7.1). Munro soon became an ardent proponent of tighter restrictions on cigarette marketing and smoking in general. A November 1968 meeting in Ottawa between ITC's Leo Laporte and E.A. Watkinson from NHW revealed the department's newfound vigour to rein in the industry. Watkinson told Laporte that because the industry "continued to show a lack of public responsibility by continuing its advertising policies and promotional devices," the department was left with few other choices.[42] In December, Munro wrote Prime Minister Pierre Trudeau about the need to move beyond the "education" approach with smoking and instead act to "curb this dangerous practice." He described the many private member's bills on smoking that had been presented in the Commons, some of which included health warnings and advertising bans.[43] Munro then moved to have the Standing Committee on Health, Welfare and Social Affairs, chaired by Liberal MP Dr Gaston Isabelle, investigate smoking and health. The Isabelle Committee included both vehement anti-smoking MPs like Barry Mather and tobacco-belt MPs who were industry boosters. Munro opened the committee's hearings on 19 December 1968 with a statement supporting restrictions on cigarette advertising, package warnings, and mandated caps on tar and nicotine. Macdonald Tobacco president David Stewart later described this turn of events as a "major attack" on the industry, one that "was like Pearl Harbour [*sic*]."[44]

The industry plotted its "defence" at an extraordinary meeting of the Ad Hoc Committee, held on 29 January 1969.[45] Along with Canadian company presidents, attendees included Alexander Holtzman, legal counsel for Philip Morris, David Hardy, a lawyer for the Tobacco Institute, and Carl Thompson from Hill & Knowlton, the public relations firm.[46] At the

7.1 National Health and Welfare Minister John Munro was a strong advocate for tobacco control measures. In 1970, he introduced Bill C-248, which would have imposed strong curbs on cigarette marketing. However, strong opposition from the tobacco industry and media and advertising interests prevented the bill from moving beyond first reading. Photo of John Munro (second from left) in 1968.

meeting, participants discussed preparations for the Isabelle Committee hearings. Because Gaston Isabelle was deemed a "poor administrator," the worry was that someone on the committee like Mather might in fact become the "effective" chairman. ITC president Paul Paré, who chaired the meeting, "referred to Imperial Tobacco's historic and enforced position of

7.2 During the 1960s and 1970s, Imperial Tobacco president Paul Paré led the tobacco industry's efforts to thwart government restrictions on cigarette promotion. Paul Paré, 1965.

industry representative in this matter of all-industry concern" (figure 7.2). Preparations for the Isabelle hearings would take place with "maximum input" from "Messrs. Hardy and Holtzman." Relevant information and materials would be "directed to Carl Thompson who would work to a two-week deadline for referral of a total brief final draft to the Ad Hoc Committee." The PR firm Public & Industrial Relations would handle press relations, as it had done at the LaMarsh conference in November 1963. Hardy underscored that officials south of the border had a close eye on the Isabelle Committee: "the U.S. industry and the Tobacco Institute viewed the current Canadian situation as extremely important." He stressed the concerns of "reciprocal influences" and the prospect that the hearings might influence American public opinion. US industry lawyers would work alongside Thompson and other public relations experts to strengthen the Canadian industry for its fight with Ottawa.[47]

The following month, Carl Thompson moved to "escalate" the American industry's response to the mounting critical tone of the Isabelle Committee. He enlisted "more manpower" from the "Hardy-Shinn-Holtzman group," to build contacts with expert witnesses and develop "material specifically on some issues that have been raised."[48] Shortly after, David Hardy, tasked with the "marshalling of expert witnesses" for the Isabelle hearings, had contacted twelve experts, later securing ten of these as scientific witnesses.[49] Hill & Knowlton officials completed a draft of the brief in mid-February, and Thompson was then "scheduled to review the total brief" with ITC's Leo Laporte. Both Thompson and Hardy attended sessions of the Isabelle Committee in Ottawa and "as a result of their observations both gentlemen contributed useful advice on strategy to Canadian members of the Ad Hoc Committee."[50] In March, Holtzman encountered a problem when Hans Selye refused to appear before the Isabelle Committee because the industry "had declined to support his proposal more than a year ago."[51] That problem was quickly resolved when the Ad Hoc Committee agreed to provide Selye with $150,000 over three years to fund his "Stress and Relief from Stress" project; the US Council for Tobacco Research provided another $150,000 for this research.[52] (Selye later appeared as an industry expert witness at the Isabelle Committee.) Thompson encountered problems with the briefs from the Ontario Flue-Cured Tobacco Marketing Board and the National Association of Tobacco and Confectionary Distributors. Their handling of "medical and scientific matters," Thompson wrote, was done "very ineptly and probably harmfully," and so required revisions.[53]

Indeed, the level of co-operation among US and Canadian officials proved so extensive and mutually rewarding that Paré proposed to Holtzman that it be formalized: "Your thought about establishing some sort of communications network among countries which are under mounting pressures of anti-smoking legislation is sound. Certainly the idea of some coordinating activity for North America is part of our thinking here. This could be a first step to wider communications as suggested in your letter."[54] This type of co-operation superseded marketplace competition; Paré made this suggestion not to an official of BAT-affiliated Brown & Williamson, but to the legal counsel for Philip Morris, the parent company of Benson & Hedges, its Canadian competitor.[55]

BAT, the parent company of ITC, was also interested in Canadian developments. In March 1969, the corporation sent a memo to the presidents of its affiliated companies to advise them of the Isabelle proceedings. The year 1969 was becoming a "crucial year" with respect to "increasing opposition to smoking." Developments involving the Isabelle hearings and elsewhere would "no doubt influence governments and health authorities in other countries and the tobacco industry must everywhere be prepared to meet changes in local attitudes to the smoking and health problem." In August 1969, G.C. Hargrove, head of public relations at BAT, issued a memo to the heads of affiliated companies in order to apprise them of ITC's handling of the Isabelle Committee, depicting it as a model for other companies in the event that they "face similar situations at some future date." The memo summarized the actions of ITC and other industry officials in their struggle with government officials and medical authorities. The industry acted in unison, under the rubric of the Ad Hoc Committee. Tobacco unions, tobacco growers, and tobacco trade people applied political pressure on "MPs and other influential people with whom they had local connections." Expertise was provided by professional public relations executives (e.g., Hill & Knowlton) and US industry lawyers, all with "previous experience of finding favourable evidence in this field." A "special law-science team headed by a senior partner of a U.S. firm of lawyers" worked to secure expert witnesses for the Isabelle hearings. These experts were "well known to the American lawyers assisting the Industry, most of them having already given evidence in Smoking and Health court cases in the U.S.A." The industry's ad agencies liaised with the Canadian Advertising Association to influence the "preparation of their submission." Public relations people compiled a list of journalists who in the past had written on smoking and health. "A comprehensive mailing list was thus available to which every release or information document was sent." During crucial days of the hearings, PR firms monitored radio and TV news broadcasts to enable the industry to respond quickly to breaking news.[56]

Extensive preparation went into Paul Paré's appearance (and accompanying policy papers) before the Isabelle Committee on 5 June 1969, where he represented Canadian cigarette manufacturers.[57] Paré situated the current attacks on smoking within the historical context of nineteenth-century moral crusaders who sought to ban cigarettes. The goal of "anti-smoking forces" today, Paré said, was the "strangulation of the tobacco economy – from farmers through retailers – and the eventual elimination of the use of tobacco." Paré cited the views of scientists, many of whom had appeared before the committee, who refuted smoking–disease causation: "Those who claim they have found the answer in tobacco smoking are relying more on prejudice than scientific evidence, while hiding behind the guise of appearing to serve the public interest." The critics of cigarettes were only partially informed, with many having fallen into the trap of promulgating "extreme and unsubstantiated propaganda" about the "so-called evils of smoking." If anti-smoking legislation were enacted, Paré asked, then where would it end? "Aspirin? Automobiles? Milk? Alcohol? Eggs?" Anti-cigarette laws would lead to a "new concept of governmental control over millions of individuals," where the state would soon be "telling people what they should eat for breakfast, lunch and dinner."[58]

Paré highlighted the "major research programs" funded by tobacco firms: "If there are ways to make cigarettes 'safer' – though safer than what we don't know as yet – or 'better' in any other way, believe me, we will utilize those methods. We will not wait for or need legislation to do so." Tobacco firms had donated $300,000 to the Respiratory Research Laboratory at McGill University to "learn more about chronic bronchitis and emphysema." They had similarly funded "studies on stress to be conducted in Canada," largely by Selye. Paré criticized smoking education programs in schools, which used "much material with which we disagree and which is such an unfair representation of the issues that its effectiveness is being questioned even by those using the materials." The Canadian tobacco industry, according to Paré, had a stellar record of close co-operation with the federal government, and, through its long-standing support of research, had "diligently sought answers to the unsolved health problems."[59]

Paré made similar public statements during the fall of 1969. A press release for a Paré speech to a meeting of the tobacco trade highlighted the "tens of millions of dollars" spent on health-related research by tobacco firms in the United States, Britain, and Canada. These studies showed that tobacco was not a causal factor for various "health problems." Moreover, Paré said, some of this "research is showing beneficial aspects of tobacco use for some people," affirming that the "beneficial aspects" of smoking were "a reality that must be recognized."[60] Later, in a Vancouver radio interview, Paré repeated these points. Many "world famous scientists" had refuted the smoking–cancer link, determining instead that variables like stress and genetics were important causal factors. He underscored that these scientists were "not, in any way, subservient to us," failing to mention the industry's long-standing financing of such research. When asked about studies where mice painted with tobacco tar had contracted cancer, Paré responded that "you can do the same thing with tomato ketchup or orange juice." Asked about a study in which pregnant rats exposed to cigarette smoke had given birth to smaller babies, Paré replied: "is having smaller babies a bad thing, do you know? I think there was a study done in Winnipeg by a doctor which demonstrated that smaller babies was probably a good thing; the baby has a better chance to live ... [and] to grow normally."[61] Paré not only defended tobacco against charges that it caused disease, but also espoused the benefits of cigarette smoking for temperamental and psychological well-being – and even lower birth weights.

In December 1969, the Isabelle Committee issued its report, which contained hard-hitting recommendations for the cigarette industry. The report recommended an immediate spending freeze on all promotional expenditures. It called for a complete ban, within one year, on cigarette sampling and all coupon and premium incentives. Within this one-year time frame, televised cigarette ads would cease before 10:00 p.m., and health warnings and tar and nicotine levels would appear on cigarette packages, ads, and vending machines. Within two years, there would be a ban on all broadcast advertising and on "non-brand name" advertising in remaining print and outdoor media. In four years' time, there would be a "complete elimination of all cigarette promotional activities."[62] Not surprisingly, Paré denounced these recommendations, calling them an "arbitrary destruction of an important segment of our economy" and "a dangerous and intolerable precedent for our free enterprise system."[63] During a January 1970 meeting with Munro, Paré said he regarded the Isabelle recommendations as laying the groundwork for the "elimination of the Industry."[64] Despite the severity of these recommendations, members of the Ad Hoc Committee at their next meeting would move only to voluntarily restrict broadcast advertising and to end cigarette sampling and campus-based advertising.[65]

BILL C-248 ("THE CIGARETTE PRODUCTS ACT")

In June 1970, the federal Cabinet discussed a report from Munro advocating legislation to ban all cigarette advertising except in magazines and on billboards. The proposed legislation would incorporate many of the key recommendations of the Isabelle Report, including an end to contest and coupon promotions and prescribed caps on tar and nicotine levels in cigarettes. Some in Cabinet questioned the merits of an advertising ban. Labour Minister Bryce Mackasey believed it would "probably just lead to new forms of advertising." Charles Drury, Treasury Board president, thought it contradictory to promote informed individual choice on the one hand while prohibiting advertising on the other. In the end, Cabinet agreed to the ban on coupon and premium promotions and to maximum levels of tar and nicotine. It approved in principle a ban on broadcast and newspaper advertising, with the proviso that Minister of Consumer and Corporate Affairs Ron Basford, who opposed the measure, consider "whether it would be useful to have an examination into the whole issue of [cigarette] advertising, its effects and costs."[66]

But Cabinet did not again address the matter for eight months, due, in part, to the October Crisis, which preoccupied the government in late 1970. At the Cabinet meeting on 18 February 1971, Munro again pressed for stiffer regulations on the cigarette industry. After a brief discussion, Cabinet agreed to the proposed legislation restricting tar and nicotine levels and agreed to a ban on cigarette advertising on radio and television and in newspapers.[67] When next before Cabinet, on 6 May 1971, the draft bill now also included a ban on billboard and magazine advertising, which seemingly exceeded the scope of Cabinet's previous direction on this matter. Members debated the fact that American cigarette ads could still run in US magazines sold in Canada, which, some felt, would disadvantage the Canadian magazine industry. Magazine publishers "would be very disturbed" by the ban and, along with newspaper owners, would challenge it forcefully. Cabinet ministers noted the double standard in which Ottawa subsidized tobacco exports while seeking to "abolish promotion of domestic use of tobacco products." After much debate, Munro managed to carry the day, and Cabinet agreed to introduce a bill after 30 May to "prohibit the promotion by any means whatsoever of the sale of any cigarette product."[68] On 10 June, Munro introduced Bill C-248, "The Cigarette Products Act," in the Commons, a landmark bill that would ban all forms of cigarette advertising, impose maximum limits on tar and nicotine levels in cigarettes, and require tar and nicotine readings on packages, along with this warning: "Warning: Danger to Health Increases with Amount Smoked" and "Avoid Inhaling."[69]

The matter was not fully settled, however. A month earlier Cabinet Secretary R.G. Robertson advised Prime Minister Pierre Trudeau that a cigarette ad ban would place the Canadian periodical industry in "a very precarious financial position." Maclean-Hunter Limited had recently reported a loss of "approximately $723,000 on the publication of Maclean's, le Maclean, Chatelaine, and the French Chatelaine." Robertson had done an informal survey of advertising in the latest editions of magazines in the Privy Council Office, reporting that *Maclean's* "contained three full pages of cigarette advertising out of a total of approximately fifteen and the advertising ratio was approximately the same in Saturday Night." He thought that Secretary of State Gérard Pelletier, whose portfolio included cultural industries like magazines, should advise Munro of the policy implications. If a tobacco ad ban included magazines then a position paper was needed to assess the impact this would have on the magazine industry.[70] Both Pelletier and Trudeau were advised of Robertson's views, with the prime minister asking Pelletier to speak to Munro about the matter.[71] It is not known whether the two spoke about this, but at a subsequent Cabinet meeting dealing with the Munro bill, Pelletier, a close confidante of Trudeau's, indicated that he would support the bill only "on the understanding that it would be brought for first reading only prior to the Summer recess." He noted that if "protests from the publications industry were serious enough to justify the action, the Bill might be amended in the House." Cabinet agreed that Bill C-248 would be "introduced for first reading only at this time."[72] This reflects what Patrick Brennan observed in his study of twentieth-century Liberal–press relations; print news media continued to heavily influence Ottawa policymakers even while broadcast news operations and audiences grew in size.[73]

Facing stringent legislative restrictions on cigarette promotion, would the tobacco industry now consider voluntary concessions that it had refused to make in the past? The answer to this question had, in part, been furnished by BAT, when a year earlier it advised the presidents of associated companies on how best to handle difficult circumstances related to smoking and health.[74] The ten-page memo advised companies not to "provoke the legislation we seek to avoid." The "over-riding policy" of BAT was to "discourage and delay" legislation, in order to "allow maximum time for research to establish the precise relationship between cigarette smoking and lung cancer and other diseases." When restrictive legislation was a possibility, as was the case in Canada, then "negotiation should be pursued to its limits, both within the industry and between the industry and the medical authorities and government, in order to fend off anti-smoking legislation."[75]

Canadian cigarette makers also faced competing pressures from US tobacco officials. At a September 1971 meeting of the Canadian Tobacco Manufacturers' Council (formerly the Ad Hoc Committee), David Hardy, legal counsel to the Tobacco Institute, voiced concerns about groups in the United States that were "pushing for prohibition." These anti-smoking forces were "well organized on an international basis in contrast to the industry which is handling the problem on what might be termed 'a regional basis.'" In Hardy's view, given that "anti-smoking forces will continue to press for more and more restrictions, voluntary action by the industry should ... be the least possible."[76]

In the end, the Canadian industry chose the BAT path of tactical retreat. In September 1971, Canadian cigarette makers moved to voluntarily end all cigarette advertising on radio and television, effective 1 January 1972.[77] Soon after, the industry agreed to additional measures: future advertising spending would remain at 1971 levels, adjusted for inflation; the warning – "The Department of National Health and Welfare advises that danger to health increases with amount smoked" – would appear on cigarette packages; product giveaways, coupon promotions, and sampling would be sharply curtailed; cigarette tar levels would be capped at 22 milligrams and nicotine yields at 1.6 milligrams. By most measures, the industry's moves were modest. A broadcast ad ban and mandatory warning labels already existed in the United States. About 70 per cent of cigarette marketing expenditures went to non-broadcast areas like print and outdoor advertising and sponsorship promotion, all of which were left untouched by the industry's move. Only four of the dozens of cigarette brands in the marketplace were impacted by the new limits on tar and nicotine levels.[78]

The key provision of Bill C-248 proved popular with the public. In August 1971, a Gallup poll reported that 50 per cent of Canadians supported a ban on all cigarette advertising, while 40 per cent were opposed and 10 per cent undecided.[79] But publishers and advertisers remained strongly opposed to Munro's bill. Tobacco firms spent nearly $20 million on advertising in 1970, so it should not surprise that advertising interests lobbied hard to defeat C-248. In August 1971, a delegation from the Outdoor Advertising Association of Canada met with Munro. Other groups signed on to oppose the bill, including the Canadian Advertising Advisory Board, the Canadian Advertising and Sales Association, the Association of Canadian Advertisers, the Magazine Advertising Bureau of Canada, and the Institute of Canadian Advertising.[80] In September, representatives from media and advertising organizations met with senior NHW officials to outline their concerns. Taking up the cause on the media side were the Canadian Daily Newspaper Publishers Association (CDNPA), the Canadian Community Newspapers Association, the Magazine Publishers Association, the Radio Sales Bureau, and the Canadian Association of Broadcasters. Their briefs stressed the economic downside of a cigarette ad ban, highlighting potential job losses in the media and advertising sectors. By September 1971, Canada's main advertising, broadcasting, magazine, and newspaper interests stood shoulder-to-shoulder against C-248.[81]

For some, like the CDNPA, the ostensible issue was press freedom. In an October brief to the government, the CDNPA characterized a ban on cigarette advertising as "a serious abridgement of the fundamental right of the Canadian citizen to be informed." Lost income was not the main concern, since cigarette lineage accounted for about 1 per cent of newspaper ad revenues. Rather, the CDNPA claimed, press freedom was at stake: "there is no difference between freedom to disseminate information in news columns and the freedom to disseminate information through advertising, with the same responsibility for honesty, good taste and legal implications." Instead of a blanket ban, it advocated controls on the "content and form" of tobacco ads; the CDNPA opposed "persuasion" in cigarette ads but not the factual portrayal of "information." For example, cigarette ads should not associate smoking with good health, but they could present factual information about the product or depict package illustrations: "persuasion could be removed and information about the product remain."[82] A brief by the Association of Canadian Advertisers (ACA) argued that any product legally produced, sold, and taxed should be free to advertise. The ban, by depleting operating revenues, could derail smaller publications and, in turn, curtail the range of ideas and viewpoints necessary for a vibrant democracy: "The free press concept," the ACA wrote, "is realizable mainly through revenues to mass media from advertising."[83]

In keeping with Pelletier's prior stipulation, Munro's bill did not advance beyond first reading. It languished at the committee stage, and by mid-1972 reports circulated that C-248 had been shelved for good.[84] Bill C-248 was ultimately defeated by lukewarm support in Cabinet, the opposition of newspaper, magazine, and advertising groups, and the skilful lobbying of the Canadian tobacco industry, which included its pre-emptive move to voluntarily adopt some of the more benign provisions of Munro's bill. The demise of C-248 was a lost opportunity for the nascent forces of tobacco control, both nationally and internationally. In 1970, only two countries – Italy and the USSR – had adopted total bans on cigarette advertising, though other nations had implemented partial ad bans, mostly involving radio and television.[85] Studies have since confirmed the importance of total advertising bans for lowering smoking rates. Partial ad restrictions, like the voluntary broadcast ban of Canadian cigarette makers, generally do not reduce tobacco consumption since they merely result in more advertising migrating to remaining media outlets.[86]

CONCLUSION

The volatile political climate of the 1960s worked against serious government action on the cigarette file. While prime minister from 1963 to 1968, Lester Pearson led only minority governments, which accentuated his "chronic indecisiveness."[87] Four federal elections occurred between 1962 and 1968, and each new government produced a different minister at

NHW, a rate of turnover which abetted the industry's goal of fighting government regulation and preserving the status quo. Liberal governments during these years were engrossed in social policy initiatives, notably the Canada Pension Plan, the Canada Assistance Plan, and national medicare. The latter, which proved highly contentious, was not fully settled until 1972 when Quebec joined the program. Terrorist acts by members of the Front de libération du Québec preoccupied Ottawa lawmakers for months during the early 1970s. While many opposition MPs and NHW mandarins pressed for greater curbs on tobacco advertising, these views were not widely held within the federal Cabinet, the locus of political power in the Westminster system. The NHW portfolio did not attract high-ranking cabinet ministers. The party's progressive wing, which included Judy LaMarsh, was on the outs after the 1965 election, and her replacement at NHW, Allan MacEachen, was, like LaMarsh, a "junior minister" who "did not carry much clout in Cabinet."[88] John Munro, the dogged, if ultimately unsuccessful, champion of harsher restrictions on the cigarette trade, was himself a thirty-seven-year-old junior minister when given the NHW job in 1968. With the exception of Munro, smoking and health remained a low priority for Liberal governments. When, in 1963, a reporter asked LaMarsh if the government would advertise to promote its anti-smoking message, she responded that "scare advertising" was "not effective."[89] The $600,000 committed to smoking reduction over five years was "ludicrously small," one critic noted. The $80,000 allotted annually to educational programs amounted to "less than *one twelfth* of the amount tobacco companies spend *each year* on CBC radio and TV"; Ottawa's anti-smoking efforts resembled "a mosquito trying to knock out a tank."[90]

It bears noting that Montreal was the centre of the Canadian tobacco industry and the political base of the federal Liberals; Trudeau, along with other powerful Cabinet colleagues like Charles Dury, Gérard Pelletier, and André Ouellet, represented Montreal ridings.[91] Cigarette manufacturers employed thousands in the city, a fact well known to Montreal politicians at all levels. Finally, while not discussed in Cabinet, there remains the subtext of the hundreds of millions of dollars that flowed annually into federal coffers from cigarette taxes. David Sim, deputy minister of National Revenue, noted this when writing an ITC executive in 1964: "We are, of course, placed in a rather anomalous situation ourselves, bearing in mind our interest in revenue which is obviously being prejudicially affected by the activities of another branch [NHW] of Government."[92] Government success in reducing smoking had the downside of trimming federal revenues resulting in possible cuts to program spending, the lifeblood of politicians.

The above points, along with effective organizing and lobbying by the tobacco industry, provide partial explanations for the absence of substantive regulations on the cigarette trade. Another factor concerns the limitations of liberal individualism for addressing public health issues like smoking. For Liberal ministers like MacEachen, Drury, and others, notions of individual free will, consumer sovereignty, and personal responsibility informed understandings of cigarette use, a viewpoint also shared by many Canadians. For them, smoking was a social habit that users freely adopted and who also bore personal responsibility for its negative consequences. "The liberal body" of the Trudeau era, Cormack and Cosgrave note, constituted a "legitimate site of pleasures as long as those pleasures [did] not infringe on the rights and pleasures of others." Smoking was one of those pleasures.[93] Difficulties related to smoking cessation concerned psychological conditioning rather than physiological compulsion. Smokers, health authorities, and government officials during the 1960s and early 1970s generally did not view cigarette smoking as addictive. Even the landmark Surgeon General's report of 1964 used the nomenclature of habituation, equating smoking with regular coffee drinking rather than, say, the pharmacodynamics of heroin addiction. Not until the 1980s did health experts fully understand and accept the addictive nature of nicotine and cigarette use, shifting smoking from a socio-cultural paradigm to a medical one.[94] It was also during the 1980s that a scientific consensus emerged over second-hand cigarette smoke posing a serious health risk to non-smokers with sustained exposure, recasting the meaning of smoking as "less a free choice than a toxic intrusion, a pollution of personal space."[95] The rhetorical edifice of liberal individualism and personal responsibility now crumbled in the face of involuntary personal use and the health harms inflicted on innocent third parties.[96] As well, federal officials were largely unaware of troubling industry practices discussed in previous chapters. Had they and the public known more about health-reassurance branding, compensation, and the target marketing of teens, it is not hard to imagine a changed political climate more conducive to tougher regulations on the industry.[97]

The stillborn C-248 represents an ironic frontispiece. Liberal politicians cited individual freedom and personal responsibility to justify limited state action on the smoking-and-health file, while Canadian and US cigarette executives used the same language to defend their right to sell a product linked to serious disease and premature death.[98] The same era that saw one of health care's finest moments – the creation of national state-sponsored medical insurance – also saw continued government complacency towards cigarette smoking, which would become the country's leading public health problem, killing 40,000 Canadians annually by the 2010s, many of whom would have started smoking in the 1960s or 1970s.

Conclusion

In June 1972, Imperial Tobacco Canada president Paul Paré delivered an upbeat speech to executives from British American Tobacco gathered in Montreal.[1] With the recent defeat of Bill C-248, Paré believed there was "no ground for pessimism despite the smoking and health controversy." His optimistic view of the cigarette industry centred on a few factors: Canada's legal system banned "contingency lawsuits by 'ambulance chasers,'" negating a potential threat to industry from the courts;[2] the industry's relations with the federal Liberal government were strong, anchored by its "large contributions to government tax coffers";[3] tobacco farmers wielded political clout in tobacco-growing areas; and the industry was on good terms with "our adversaries in the anti-smoking fraternity developed as a result of our own industry concern and initiative." Here he underscored industry funding of health research in areas like respirology and cardiology, noting that cigarette firms had "bought scientific instruments for disease treatment in hospitals essentially to demonstrate our goodwill and sense of responsibility."[4] The campaign to quash Bill C-248, which "benefitted enormously from the special resources" of British and American parent companies, had afforded the industry "many freedoms of action." Distilleries and breweries, Paré said, had operated profitably for decades while contending with social controversy and government regulation. Cigarette makers could do likewise. The smoking and health "controversy" would remain an ongoing issue. But this was fully manageable, as indeed the industry had been demonstrating since the early 1950s.[5] Paré's positive outlook was not out of place. During the post–"cancer scare" years, cigarette sales in Canada had soared, from 17.1 billion in 1950 to 53.2 billion in 1972. Per-capita daily consumption of cigarettes, a measure that controls for population growth, had ballooned by 92 per cent during this period.[6]

Born in 1922, Paré's own life paralleled the meteoric rise of the cigarette. As a Quebec teen in the 1930s, he likely witnessed developments described in this book. By the 1930s, the cigarette had shed its bohemian and effete image and was well on its way to displacing pipes and cigars as the predominant form of smoking in Canada. Cigarette smoking imbued the routines and customs of male (and increasingly female) socializing. Cigarettes signified up-to-the-minute modernity and social desirability, especially in urban areas. They appeared increasingly wherever people congregated and fraternized and were ubiquitous on the Big Screen and on billboards. During these years, Paré's future employer, Imperial Tobacco Company (ITC), Canada's largest tobacco firm, was attacked repeatedly by journalists and politicians for restraint-of-trade practices and price fixing, damaging the company's reputation. To restore its social legitimacy, ITC launched a multi-year public relations ad campaign touting the firm's beneficence to consumers, retailers, and government officials. A key development during this decade was the advent of menthol and filtered brands, marketed to address smokers' complaints about coughing and throat irritation. Cigarette filters promised a technological solution for these minor health ailments by removing so-called impurities and irritants from tobacco smoke. When, in the 1950s, tobacco firms launched more filter brands to assuage smokers' health anxieties over lung cancer, they could draw on product developments and marketing know-how originating in the 1930s.

During the Second World War, Paré served in the Royal Canadian Navy, where he would have experienced the vibrant military smoking culture described in chapter 2. The importance that Ottawa placed on cigarettes during the war is evidenced by its decision not to ration cigarettes, unlike many other consumer products. Cigarettes were non-discretionary goods, vital for boosting morale on the home front and among soldiers serving abroad. Provisioning troops with cigarettes, typically via gift-exchange networks, became a national duty, an expression of patriotism and heartfelt desire to support kin, kith, or home-town enlistee. The overwhelming consensus was that cigarettes promoted the social and psychological well-being of soldiers, both in the bunk house and on the field of combat. Canadian troops sent letters and thank-you cards expressing gratitude for these cigarettes, which in turn engendered forms of reciprocal obligation and mutual attachment benefiting both donor and recipient. Cigarette fundraising drives by businesses, service clubs, and schools in support of area-resident soldiers fighting overseas strengthened the latter's ties to local community and nation. Gift cigarettes were routinely shared with fellow troops, enhancing camaraderie and social cohesion within military units. By war's end, cigarette smoking had achieved an exalted sense of social standing among Canadian soldiers abroad and those back home supporting them.

When Paré first joined Imperial Tobacco in 1949, Cigarette Nation was ascendant. About 60 per cent of adults smoked cigarettes and smoking was a widely accepted cultural norm, praised for enhancing social interaction, stress relief, and cognitive operation. Whether as relaxant in a tavern or stimulant during an overnight shift, cigarettes functioned differently depending on the context. Cigarettes infused the reflexive project of identity formation and self presentation. The assumed benefits of cigarette smoking were far-ranging and broadly shared. It should not surprise then that people inhabiting this smoking culture might be skeptical of medical reports linking cigarette use to lung cancer, a typically fatal disease. Put aside for the moment the issue of nicotine addiction, which as popular understanding and scientific concept did not prevail widely until the 1980s. Quitting smoking produced social and psychological hardships beyond the physiological effects of nicotine withdrawal. It carried the risk of social isolation if those quitting avoided outings with smoking friends at the bowling alley or the tavern in order to avoid temptation and relapse. Quitting might upset relations with a smoking spouse or produce tension and conflict at family gatherings where most people smoked. Smoking-related mannerisms infusing the modern project of identity formation and self projection now needed to be replaced with something else. The social and psychological costs of quitting meant that many smokers were cognitively biased to dismiss or discount the view that cigarettes were a major cause of lung cancer. Many smokers adopted modes of motivated reasoning to minimize or negate the health risks of smoking in ways that seemed logical and self-convincing. Abetting this cognitive process were the many news stories and opinion columns appearing during the 1950s and 1960s which cast doubt on the smoking–cancer thesis or extolled the social and psychological benefits of smoking.

Cigarette manufacturers promoted this cognitive process with the use of health-reassurance marketing, which transformed the Canadian cigarette trade starting in the mid-1950s. Until then, the cigarette market was largely homogeneous; nearly all cigarettes came in plain-end format, were uniform in length, and offered similar levels of tar and nicotine. The industry's response to smokers' health concerns was to launch and heavily promote filter brands, initially popular with women and youths. Smokers (wrongly) viewed filter cigarettes as safer than plain-end ones, an understanding the industry encouraged, especially Rothmans and ITC. By the early 1960s health-themed marketing had become a staple of the cigarette trade. When well-publicized reports by the Royal College of Physicians or the US Surgeon General elevated the health concerns of smokers, cigarette makers responded with increased marketing for filter and low-tar "health" brands like Vantage. In the mid-1970s, the industry expanded this approach by launching "Mild" and "Light" brands like Player's Light. These cigarettes contained marginally less tar and nicotine than their namesake parent brands; but they sold well because smokers regarded them as safer alternatives to these and other brands. In the 1960s, industry scientists studied the process of smoker compensation. Their research showed that smokers switching to low-yield brands for their perceived health benefits were in fact consuming tar and nicotine at much higher rates than those listed on the cigarette packages. To compensate for lower delivery, people smoked more cigarettes, or puffed more often and more deeply, to attain accustomed levels of tar and nicotine. For consumers, this consumption pattern negated any potential health benefit; for the industry, it was fortuitous, since smokers smoked more cigarettes in search of customary levels of tar and nicotine, thus boosting sales and profits. Health-reassurance marketing also served to thwart or delay quit attempts, keeping fearful smokers within the ranks of Cigarette Nation.

By the time Paul Paré assumed the role of vice-president of marketing at ITC in 1964, the company had begun to target youths with cigarette promotion. Starting in the early 1960s, ITC consumer surveys of teens as young as fifteen produced a large storehouse of data on smoking-related behaviour, serving up detailed knowledge on youth culture and social identity. By accessing and codifying the attitudes, needs, and idiosyncrasies of teens, industry market research made possible practices like market segmentation, brand positioning, and package design and advertising that would resonate with this target market. In the 1970s, tobacco companies, especially ITC, ran focus groups with teens to illuminate underlying motivations and attitudes related to smoking and particular cigarette brands. Industry marketers probed the "when," "why," and "how" features of teen smoking and the dynamics of social acceptability underpinning the practice. Market research on youths revealed themes (e.g., independence, freedom) which resonated strongly with teens, and cigarette makers ensured that branding and advertising for relevant brands incorporated these messages and related imagery. By the mid-1970s, cigarette makers understood that success with the teen "starter" market was a pre-condition for building long-term brand share. Tobacco executives routinely denied, especially to government officials, that they marketed to under-eighteen youths. But teen-oriented marketing was a staple feature of the cigarette industry, reflecting a perceived commercial imperative that securing teen consumers was vital for a brand's long-term growth and profitability.

For decades after 1953, Canadian tobacco executives denied repeatedly and publicly that cigarette smoking caused serious illness. When, in the early 1950s, scientific studies reported on smoking's links to lung cancer, industry officials dismissed these findings. They disparaged the epidemiological evidence as merely "statistical" and not properly clinical or experimental; they claimed that air pollution, viruses, and occupational hazards accounted for growing rates of lung cancer. Industry executives lambasted smoking-related reports by the US Surgeon General and other reputable organizations as biased, speculative, and faulty. They dismissed anti-smoking health authorities as publicity-seeking zealots. To generate industry-friendly science, they funded outside researchers to secure findings challenging the relationship between smoking and disease. They sponsored tangential research so that the industry could publicize its own support of scientific inquiry aimed at solving the "controversy" of smoking and health (when in fact the wider scientific community had solved this "controversy" by the late 1950s). This campaign of science denial, coupled with health-reassurance marketing, served to confuse Canadians about the risks of smoking. As late as 1971 when Gallup asked Canadians if cigarettes were a cause of cancer, fully 42 per cent of respondents disagreed or were unsure.[7] The industry's efforts constituted an extreme form of "manipulative publicity," designed to smother the "knowledge resources upon which informed citizen consent depends."[8] While industry executives issued these refutations publicly, company scientists expressed mounting concerns about the carcinogenicity of cigarette smoking in internal correspondence. Starting in the late 1950s, scientists at ITC and parent companies like BAT and Philip Morris voiced varying degrees of support for the view that cigarette smoking and cancer were causally related. Scientists like BAT's S.J. Green and ITC's Robert Gibb stated repeatedly that it was no longer tenable for the industry to ignore the strong scientific consensus that cigarettes were very harmful to health.

The Canadian tobacco industry's handling of the smoking and health issue was a highly collaborative undertaking. Industry groups like the Ad Hoc Committee met regularly to adopt collective responses to the health issue, as seen with the Cigarette Advertising Code of 1964. This common-front approach was used to combat state regulation of cigarette marketing and to undermine information campaigns on the health harms of smoking. As well, Canadian cigarette makers relied heavily on American tobacco executives and public relations experts, starting in 1962. Officials from the Tobacco Industry Research Committee (TIRC), Philip Morris, the public relations firm Hill & Knowlton, and US law firms worked closely with their Canadian counterparts on the smoking and health file. These Americans helped to prepare industry testimony and write submissions for parliamentary hearings and government conferences, while also assisting with media outreach and other public relations activities. This cross-border co-operation proved especially important during the industry's dealings with the Isabelle Committee in 1969 and the successful campaign to defeat Bill C-248.

One could situate the above actions within the history of public relations, a form of corporate publicity begun in the early 1900s by Ivy Lee and others to persuade ordinary citizens that public and corporate interest were commensurate.[9] But this would be only partially accurate. A helpful interpretive lens is suggested by David Courtwright's description of the

TIRC as "a smoothly running disinformation machine."[10] The industry's coordinated program of public deception, which would span four decades, invokes state propaganda, or even Orwell's Ministry of Truth, as much as it does corporate advertising promoting the social benefits of low corporate taxes. This is because the tobacco industry did not aim to change public opinion on an issue for which legitimate debate was possible; rather it worked to eradicate the very basis for knowing what constituted empirical fact and expert knowledge. The incessant attacks on mainstream smoking science, coupled with industry funding of decoy research, served to diminish people's capacity to evaluate risk, weigh evidence, and make informed decisions. Smoking remained safe, industry talking points bellowed, because the scientist jurors were still deliberating – as they would be until the 1990s. Buttressing this denialist doctrine was a form of industry Newspeak, where terms like "medical controversy," "benefits of smoking," and "freedom of choice" were marshalled to drown out discourse on lung cancer and heart disease. All of this, Robert Proctor argues, amounted to an elaborate exercise in "agnotology," or ignorance creation, characterized by the industry trifecta of "feigning its *own* ignorance of hazards, while simultaneously affirming the *absence of definite proof* in the scientific community, while also doing all it could to *manufacture ignorance on the part of the smoking public.*"[11] The Big Lie of Big Tobacco would factor greatly in the massive death toll of cigarette smoking – an estimated 100 million people globally during the twentieth century.[12]

This story, sadly, does not end with tobacco. As Naomi Oreskes and Erik M. Conway show, the "Tobacco Strategy" of doubt-mongering and science repudiation became the template for later industry attacks on the science of climate change. During the 1980s and 1990s, scientist-for-hire allies of the US tobacco industry like Frederick Seitz and S. Fred Singer pivoted to "fight the facts and merchandise doubt" about the science of global warming.[13] In the age of Trump, campaign slogans like "Trump Digs Coal" and US withdrawal from the Paris Agreement underscore the endurance and political appeal of climate science denial. Indeed a core feature of Trumpism involves the routine rejection of expert knowledge – social, legal, economic, and scientific. Filling this gap is the strongman spectacle of rote lying as statecraft, self-dealing, and the "fake news" labelling of unfavourable press coverage, no matter how credible the source.[14] While historical explanations for the rise of Trump are many, it bears noting that for decades after 1950 the tobacco industry constructed and promulgated its own "post-truth" social reality, disseminating reams of "alternative facts" about the science of smoking and health to unsuspecting Americans and Canadians.

＊＊

If, as the saying goes, "the personal is political," then a prime illustration of this concept is the modern cigarette. This book describes far-ranging social, commercial, and political events and structural changes underpinning mounting cigarette sales and cultural modes of smoking. It also makes sense of my own personal experience and family history. I began this book describing my ten-year-old self buying cigarettes for my mother at a neighbourhood store during the 1970s. This act, not uncommon for that time,[15] could not have happened without massive changes to the retailing of cigarettes. Starting in the 1940s, cigarette selling branched out from tobacconist shops to encompass such venues as grocers, supermarkets, restaurants, vending machines, and, most importantly, variety stores. The latter were prime hang-out spots for kids like me and my friends. There we bought popsicles and chips, read comics and *Mad Magazine*, and popped wheelies in the store parking lot. Older teens would come to buy cigarettes, sometimes lingering to smoke them near us. These scenes, as much as parents smoking in the home, served to normalize cigarette use for children and adolescents, since variety stores functioned as important youth cultural spaces, alongside their commercial roles. Cigarette retailing had come a long way from the adults-only tobacconist shops of the 1930s.

Other examples highlight my family's ties to developments described in this book. Both of my grandfathers smoked cigarettes, a habit they took up in earnest while serving abroad in the Canadian Army during the Second World War. While a teen in a Quebec pulp and paper mill town in the 1950s, my father and his friends would rip off the filters on cigarettes before smoking them, expressions of masculine swagger and social defiance. Not long after, Imperial Tobacco would conduct research on youths like him, exploring the relationship between masculinity, teen longing, and filtered cigarettes. When health officials complained about postwar working women foregoing healthy meals for smokes and coffee, they could have been addressing my Quebec aunt who often joked about Pepsi, fries, and cigarettes being her go-to fuel. After high school I travelled for a year, spending time on a kibbutz in Israel, where I became friends with a man who had previously lived in Winnipeg and had fond memories of smoking Export "A" cigarettes. I got my father to mail me a couple of cartons and presented him with my own "gift of cigarettes." Not unlike those wartime soldiers discussed above, this act engendered much gratitude, reciprocal obligation, and social bonding, highlighted by a standing offer to join his family for Friday-night Shabbat dinners.

More than anyone else in my family, my mother's life was closely bound up with cigarettes and smoking. Oddly, she started smoking relatively late, in her early twenties. A stay-at-home working-class mom of two toddlers in the late 1960s, she socialized with other moms in the townhouse complex where we lived. On one occasion, someone gave her a cigarette, which she reluctantly smoked. Arriving home shortly after, she promptly threw up in a bucket near the front door. But she went back for the company – and the cigarettes that came with it – to alleviate the pressures and social isolation of parenting. I think of my mom when reading Penny Tinkler's account of the appeal of smoking for working-class women, a habit offering "a means of coping with stress, of mitigating the boredom and monotony of being housebound and, on a practical level, of managing childcare responsibilities and delineating time for relaxation."[16] She was by no means alone in this respect; 63 per cent of Canadian women between twenty-five and twenty-nine smoked in 1969.[17] After she divorced in the early 1970s, cigarettes became part of her newfound working life, smoking while typing or filing, and later on in the company's smoking room or its outside "butt hut," where she and fellow smokers congregated. On the social front, cigarettes dotted the "Keno Nights" and dinner parties that she loved to attend, features of her vibrant and friend-filled personal life. As her health concerns mounted in the 1980s, she turned to the many "Mild" and "Light" brands that were offering health reassurance. Gone were the solid red du Maurier packages, replaced by the softer, more soothing hues of packages for Matinée Extra Mild or Craven "A". She cycled through these "health" brands, such that each time I visited home for the holidays there seemed to be a different one on the coffee table. Her quit attempts began soon after, with some lasting days and others a few months. Years later, I found her membership card for a smoking cessation group she had joined, whose oath read: "Because I believe tobacco is detrimental to my health, and illness due to smoking would both jeopardize the security of those I love and hinder further service to my community, I hereby choose to cease smoking from this day forward." She signed this pledge on 25 February 1983, but not until the late 1990s, in her early fifties, did she manage to quit smoking for good, closing a fraught thirty-year chapter of her life. In her later years, she regarded quitting cigarettes as one of the hardest and proudest achievements of her life.

When, in her early seventies, she received a cancer diagnosis there was some initial relief that it did not appear to be smoking related. It was breast cancer, not lung cancer, and luckily caught early. After minor surgery, the treatment plan called for a moderate program of chemotherapy followed by radiation. The general prognosis was good. But near the end of her chemotherapy sessions, her breathing worsened. On the day of her final chemo appointment, in April 2017, she was instead admitted to hospital to undergo tests, which revealed damage to her lung tissue. She remained in hospital receiving a series of antibiotics and antiviral drugs, but her condition deteriorated and she was later moved to the intensive care unit. Her final weeks were painful and agonizing, a succession of CPAP and BIPAP breathing masks, steroid doses, oxygen supplements, and intubation. The hospital staff, who worked hard to save her life, concluded that this was a rare case of chemotherapy-induced interstitial lung disease, producing widespread scarring of her lung tissue. While unexpected and atypical in one sense, her final weeks would have been all too familiar to many Canadians. For hers, in many ways, was a smoker's death, not unlike that experienced by thousands of Canadians annually due to lung cancer or chronic obstructive pulmonary diseases.

Notes

INTRODUCTION

1 Ans Nicolaides-Bouman, Nicholas Wald, Barbara Forey, and Peter Lee, eds, *International Smoking Statistics: A Collection of Historical Data from 22 Economically Developed Countries* (Oxford: Oxford University Press, 1993), 61–2.
2 Canadian Institute of Public Opinion [CIPO] press release, "City Life Conducive to Cigarette Smoking," 25 May 1949.
3 Propel Centre for Population Health Impact, *Tobacco Use in Canada: Patterns and Trends, 2019 edition* (Waterloo, ON: University of Waterloo, 2019), 13.
4 Graham D. Taylor, *A Concise History of Business in Canada* (Toronto: Oxford University Press, 1994); Graham D. Taylor, *The Rise of Canadian Business* (Toronto: Oxford University Press, 2009); Don Nerbas, *Dominion of Capital: The Politics of Big Business and the Crisis of the Canadian Bourgeoisie, 1914–1947* (Toronto: University of Toronto Press, 2013); Joseph E. Martin, *Relentless Change: A Casebook for the Study of Canadian Business History* (Toronto: University of Toronto Press, 2009); Shirley Tillotson, *Give and Take: The Citizen-Taxpayer and the Rise of Canadian Democracy* (Vancouver: UBC Press, 2017); Catherine Carstairs, Bethany Philpott, and Sara Wilmshurst, *Be Wise! Be Healthy: Morality and Citizenship in Canadian Public Health Campaigns* (Toronto: University of Toronto Press, 2018); Graham Broad, *A Small Price to Pay: Consumer Culture on the Canadian Home Front, 1939–45* (Vancouver: UBC Press, 2013).
5 Christopher Dummitt, *The Manly Modern: Masculinity in Postwar Canada* (Vancouver: UBC Press, 2007); Christine Ramsay, ed., *Making It Like a Man: Canadian Masculinities in Practice* (Waterloo, ON: Wilfrid Laurier University Press, 2011); Jeffery Vacante, *National Manhood and the Creation of Modern Quebec* (Vancouver: UBC Press 2017); Peter Gossage and Robert Rutherdale,

eds, *Making Men, Making History: Canadian Masculinities across Time and Place* (Vancouver: UBC Press, 2018).

6 For examples, see Robert A. Campbell, *Sit Down and Drink Your Beer: Regulating Vancouver's Beer Parlours, 1925–1954* (Toronto: University of Toronto Press, 2001); Craig Heron, *Booze: A Distilled History* (Toronto: Between the Lines, 2003); Craig Heron, "The Boys and Their Booze: Masculinities and Public Drinking in Working-class Hamilton, 1890–1946," *Canadian Historical Review* 86, no. 3 (2005): 411–52; Robert Rutherdale, "'I'm a lousy father': Alcoholic Fathers in Postwar Canada and the Myths of Masculine Crises," in *Making Men, Making History: Canadian Masculinities across Time and Place*, ed. Peter Gossage and Robert Rutherdale (Vancouver: UBC Press, 2018): 409–26.

7 The best illustration of this occurs in Bryan D. Palmer's lively survey of the 1960s. While the text does not discuss cigarette smoking, cigarettes adorn the hands of many of the activists and protesters in the book's photo plates. My personal favourite – my father is a former smoker and postal union leader – is of a young postal worker walking a picket line in 1968. In the hand holding his sign ("On Strike for Better Wages") burns a cigarette. Palmer, *Canada's 1960s: The Ironies of Identity in a Rebellious Era* (Toronto: University of Toronto Press, 2009). On the relationship between workplace smoking rights and labour militancy, see Gregory Wood, "'The Justice of a Rule That Forbids the Men Smoking on Their Jobs': Workers, Managers, and Cigarettes in World War II America," *Labor: Studies in Working-Class History of the Americas* 13, no. 1 (2016): 11–39.

8 Daniel Miller, *Consumption and Its Consequences* (Cambridge: Polity 2012), 91.

9 See Franca Iacovetta, Valerie J. Korinek, and Marlene Epp, eds, *Edible Histories, Cultural Politics: Towards a Canadian Food History* (Toronto: University of Toronto Press, 2012); James Opp, "Branding 'the Bay/la Baie': Corporate Identity, the Hudson's Bay Company, and the Burden of History in the 1960s," *Canadian Historical Review* 96, no. 2 (June 2015): 223–56; Catherine Carstairs and Steve Penfold similarly document how patriotically national brands like Roots and Tim Hortons had decidedly Ontario-centric origins. Carstairs, "'Roots' Nationalism: Branding English Canada Cool in the 1980s and 1990s," *Histoire sociale/Social History* 39, no. 77 (2006): 235–55; Penfold, *The Donut: A Canadian History* (Toronto: University of Toronto Press, 2008).

10 For the United States, see especially Lizabeth Cohen, *A Consumers' Republic:*

The Politics of Mass Consumption in Postwar America (New York: Vintage, 2003): and Charles F. McGovern, *Sold American: Consumption and Citizenship, 1890–1945* (Chapel Hill: University of North Carolina Press, 2006).

11 Bettina Liverant, *Buying Happiness: The Emergence of Consumer Consciousness in English Canada* (Vancouver: UBC Press, 2018), 13. It bears mentioning that Liverant does not discuss French-speaking Canada.

12 Donica Belisle, *Retail Nation: Department Stores and the Making of Modern Canada* (Vancouver: UBC Press, 2011), 11–12. While Michael Dawson's study of public debates on expanded shopping hours focuses on Victoria and Vancouver, he frames his study as illuminating the "the historical development of consumerism in Canada and about Canadian society more generally." *Selling Out or Buying In?: Debating Consumerism in Vancouver and Victoria, 1945–1985* (Toronto: University of Toronto Press, 2018), 7.

13 Penfold, *The Donut*, 15.

14 Matthew Hilton, *Smoking in British Popular Culture, 1800–2000* (Manchester: Manchester University Press, 2000), 241.

15 For examples, see Sally H. Clarke, *Trust & Power: Consumers, the Modern Corporation & the Making of the United States Automobile Market* (New York: Cambridge University Press, 2007); Tom McCarthy, *Auto Mania: Cars, Consumers, and the Environment* (New Haven, CT: Yale University Press, 2007); Kristina Wilson, "Like a 'Girl in a Bikini Suit' and Other Stories: The Herman Miller Furniture Company, Gender and Race at Mid-Century," *Journal of Design History* 28, no. 2 (April 2015): 161–81; Einav Rabinovitch-Fox, "[Re]fashioning the New Woman: Women's Dress, the Oriental Style, and the Construction of American Feminist Imagery in the 1910s," *Journal of Women's History* 27, no. 2 (Summer 2015): 14–36.

16 The Canadian Letters and Images Project, https://www.canadianletters.ca/. This project is based in the History Department of Vancouver Island University.

17 On this point, see Daniel J. Robinson, *The Measure of Democracy: Polling, Market Research, and Public Life* (Toronto: University of Toronto Press, 1999); "Imperial Tobacco, Market Research, and Canadian Teens, 1960–1988," in *Advertising, Consumer Culture, and Canadian Society*, ed. Kyle Asquith (Toronto: Oxford University Press, 2018), 53–70.

18 Létourneau c JTI-MacDonald Corp., 2015 QCCS 2382; see the "Canadian

Tobacco Industry" collection in The Truth Tobacco Industry Documents project, hosted by the UCSF Library and Center for Knowledge Management, https://www.industrydocuments.ucsf.edu/tobacco/.

19 See Kerry Segrave, *Women and Smoking in America, 1880–1950* (Jefferson, NC: McFarland, 2005); Pamela E. Pennock, *Advertising Sin and Sickness: The Politics of Alcohol and Tobacco Marketing 1950–1990* (Dekalb: Northern Illinois University Press, 2007); Allan M. Brandt, *The Cigarette Century: The Rise, Fall, and Deadly Persistence of the Product That Defined America* (New York: Basic Books, 2007); Robert N. Proctor, *Golden Holocaust: Origins of the Cigarette Catastrophe and the Case for Abolition* (Berkeley: University of California Press, 2011); Peter Benson, *Tobacco Capitalism: Growers, Migrant Workers and the Changing Face of a Global Industry* (Princeton, NJ: Princeton University Press, 2012); Elizabeth Crisp Crawford, *Tobacco Goes to College: Cigarette Advertising in Student Media, 1920–1980* (Jefferson, NC: McFarland, 2014); Laura D. Hirshbein, *Smoking Privileges: Psychiatry, the Mentally Ill, and the Tobacco Industry in America* (New Brunswick, NJ: Rutgers University Press, 2015); Gregory Wood, *Clearing the Air: The Rise and Fall of Smoking in the Workplace* (Ithaca, NY: ILR Press, 2016).

20 Penny Tinkler, *Smoke Signals: Women, Smoking and Visual Culture* (Oxford: Berg, 2006); Matthew Hilton, *Smoking in British Popular Culture 1800–2000* (Manchester: Manchester University Press, 2000); Virginia Berridge, *Marketing Health, Smoking and the Discourse of Public Health in Britain, 1945–2000* (Oxford: Oxford University Press, 2007).

21 Jarrett Rudy, *The Freedom to Smoke: Tobacco Consumption and Identity* (Montreal and Kingston: McGill-Queen's University Press, 2005); Sharon Anne Cook, *Sex Lies and Cigarettes: Canadian Women, Smoking, and Visual Culture, 1880–2000* (Montreal and Kingston: McGill-Queen's University Press, 2012); Rob Cunningham, *Smoke & Mirrors: The Canadian Tobacco War* (Ottawa: IDRC, 1996); and Cheryl Krasnick Warsh, "The Canadian Cigar and Tobacco Journal in the Forties: A Remembrance," *Social History of Alcohol and Drugs* 21, no. 1 (Fall 2006): 23–49.

22 Kenneth Lipartito, "Reassembling the Economic: New Departures in Historical Materialism," *American Historical Review* 121, no. 1 (February 2016): 126, 135, 138. See, too, Lipartito, "Connecting the Cultural and the Material in Business History," *Enterprise & Society* 14, no. 4 (December 2013): 686–704.

23 Daniel Miller, *Stuff* (Cambridge: Polity Press, 2010), 155. Some of the contra-

dictions and paradoxes discussed in this book include: the "cancer scare" served not as a *brake* on the cigarette industry but as an *accelerant*, engendering new market segments and cigarette brands related to health awareness; while medical evidence confirming smoking–cancer causality mounted so too did the per-capita consumption of cigarettes in Canada until the early 1980s; the "progressive" federal Liberal government of the late 1960s that decriminalized homosexuality, citing individual liberal freedoms, also used this same logic to reject restrictions on the "freedom" to market and advertise a highly harmful product.

CHAPTER ONE

1 "W.H. Wright Becomes Owner of the Globe," *Toronto Daily Star*, 15 October 1936, 1, 3. Along with tobacco-related accounts listed in the *Canadian Periodical Index*, this paper draws on cigarette-related content found in digitized historical newspapers such as the *Toronto Daily Star* and the *Globe and Mail*. Researchers also examined every issue of *Marketing Magazine*, Canada's main advertising trade journal, for the 1930s.
2 du Maurier Filter ads, *Globe and Mail*, 10 December 1936, 17; 21 December 1936, 7.
3 Cassandra Tate, *Cigarette Wars: The Triumph of the "The Little White Slaver"* (New York: Oxford University Press, 1999), 4; Lee J. Alston, Ruth Dupré, and Tomas Nonnenmacher, "Social Reformers and Regulation: The Prohibition of Cigarettes in the United States and Canada," *Explorations in Economic History* 39, no. 4 (October 2002): 432.
4 Rob Cunningham, *Smoke & Mirrors: The Canadian Tobacco War* (Ottawa: IDRC, 1996), 37; Alston et al., "Social Reformers," 430–1.
5 Sharon Anne Cook, *Sex Lies and Cigarettes: Canadian Women, Smoking, and Visual Culture, 1880–2000* (Montreal and Kingston: McGill-Queen's University Press, 2012) Allan M. Brandt, *The Cigarette Century: The Rise, Fall, and Deadly Persistence of the Product that Defined America* (New York: Basic Books, 2007), 110.
6 Jarrett Rudy, *The Freedom to Smoke: Tobacco Consumption and Identity* (Montreal and Kingston: McGill-Queen's University Press, 2005), 132–4.
7 Per-capita annual cigar consumption declined from 31.6 in 1920 to 19 in 1928. Dominion Bureau of Statistics (DBS), *Statistical Handbook of Canadian Tobacco* (Ottawa: King's Printer, 1947), 40.

8 Rudy, *Freedom to Smoke*, 132, 141. See also H.E. Stephenson and Carlton McNaught, *The Story of Advertising in Canada* (Toronto: Ryerson Press, 1940), 196–204.
9 Economic downturn does not fully explain these results. Canada's gross national product declined by 8 per cent from 1929 to 1939, while per-capita cigarette consumption increased by 24 per cent during these years. *Statistical Handbook of Canadian Tobacco* (1947), 40.
10 M.C. Urquhart and K.A.H. Buckley, eds, *Historical Statistics of Canada* (Toronto: Macmillan, 1965), 130; *Statistical Handbook of Canadian Tobacco* (1947), 40.
11 *Historical Series of Tobacco Statistics* (Ottawa: Dominion Bureau of Statistics, 1950), 7.
12 For cigarette "health marketing" during the 1960s, see Daniel J. Robinson, "Marketing and Regulating Cigarettes in Canada, 1957–1971," in *Les Territoires de l'entreprise*, ed. Claude Bellevance and Pierre Lanthier (Quebec: Laval University Press, 2004), 245–63.
13 "Canada in Danger of a Dictatorship," *Toronto Daily Star*, 10 April 1934, 23.
14 "Profits Surpass All Money Paid Tobacco Growers," *Toronto Daily Star*, 24 April 1934, 1–2; "Growers Poor, Companies Rich, Say Tobacco Men," *The Globe*, 25 April 1934, 2.
15 "Profits of Millions by Tobacco Concern Disclosed to Probe," *The Globe*, 4 May 1934, 1, 3.
16 "Charges Tobacco Firm Depressed Prices by Delay," *Toronto Daily Star*, 8 May 1934, 1–2.
17 "Huge Bonuses for Imperial Tobacco Officials," *The Globe*, 9 May 1934, 1.
18 "Tobacco Dividends $32,000,000, 1929–1933," *Toronto Daily Star*, 9 May 1934, 1, 2.
19 "Advance Budget Tip-Off Charged by Witness," *The Globe*, 11 May 1934, 1. Newspaper accounts of this caught the attention of federal Liberal leader Mackenzie King. Library and Archives Canada [LAC], Mackenzie King Diary, 11 May 1934.
20 "Claim Reign of Terror Exists in Tobacco Trade," *Toronto Daily Star*, 16 May 1934, 9.
21 "Ruthless Methods against Retailers Alleged at Probe," *The Globe*, 16 May 1934, 2.

22 "No Light on 'Budget Leak' Given by Cahan, Matthews," *Toronto Daily Star*, 17 May 1934, 12.
23 Joanne Burgess, "Mortimer Davis" entry, *Dictionary of Canadian Biography*.
24 Howard Cox, *The Global Cigarette: Origins and Evolution of British American Tobacco 1880–1945* (Oxford: Oxford University Press, 2000), 101; Burgess, "Mortimer Davis."
25 Cox, *Global Cigarette*, 103.
26 Rudy, *The Freedom to Smoke*, 126–7, 129.
27 Ibid., 124–5.
28 Burgess, "Mortimer Davis."
29 "Tuckett's Tobacco (Hamilton) and ITC (Montreal)," *Marketing Magazine*, 24 May 1930, 319.
30 Cox, *Global Cigarette*, 106; Rudy, *Freedom to Smoke*, 126.
31 Robert Craig Brown and Ramsay Cook, *Canada 1896–1921: A Nation Transformed* (Toronto: McClelland and Stewart, 1974), 91–2.
32 Lloyd G. Reynolds, *The Control of Competition in Canada* (Cambridge: Harvard Studies in Monopoly and Competition, 1940), 136–7.
33 Michael Bliss, *A Living Profit: Studies in the Social History of Canadian Business, 1883–1911* (Toronto: McClelland and Stewart, 1974), 40.
34 Bliss, *A Living Profit*, 33–54. On urban utilities and the monopoly question, see Christopher Armstrong and H.V. Nelles, *Monopoly's Moment: The Organization and Regulation of Canadian Utilities, 1830–1930* (Philadelphia: Temple University Press, 1986).
35 John Herd Thompson and Allen Seager, *Canada 1922–1939: Decades of Discord* (Toronto: McClelland and Stewart, 1986), 258–9.
36 Canada. *Report of the Royal Commission on Price Spreads* (Ottawa: King's Printer, 1937), 308–15.
37 Larry A. Glassford, *Reaction and Reform: The Politics of the Conservative Party under R.B. Bennett, 1927–1938* (Toronto: University of Toronto Press, 1992): 149.
38 Glassford, *Reaction and Reform*, 157; P.B. Waite, *In Search of R.B. Bennett*. (Montreal and Kingston: McGill-Queen's University Press, 2012), 221.
39 *Report of the Royal Commission on Price Spreads*, 13.
40 Ibid., 51.
41 Ibid.

42 "Tobacco Industry Is Lacking Balance, Says Mass Report," *The Globe*, 13 April 1935, 14.
43 *Report of the Royal Commission on Price Spreads*, 54.
44 Ibid., 265.
45 Ibid., 266.
46 Glassford, *Reaction and Reform*, 158.
47 Ibid., 165–6; P.B. Waite, *In Search of R.B. Bennett*, 209.
48 Glassford, *Reaction and Reform*, 166.
49 Thompson and Seager, *Canada 1922–1939*, 266.
50 For a discussion of anti-democratic views by prominent Canadian businessmen, see Don Nerbas, *Dominion of Capital: The Politics of Big Business and the Crisis of the Canadian Bourgeoisie, 1914–1947* (Toronto: University of Toronto Press, 2013).
51 Roland Marchand, *Creating the Corporate Soul: The Rise of Public Relations and Corporate Imagery in American Big Business* (Berkeley: University of California Press, 1998), 45.
52 Karen S. Miller, *The Voice of Business: Hill & Knowlton and Postwar Public Relations* (Chapel Hill: University of North Carolina Press, 1997), 10–12.
53 Inger L. Stole, *Advertising on Trial: Consumer Activism and Corporate Public Relations in the 1930s* (Urbana: University of Illinois Press, 2006), 99.
54 Robert Jackall and Janice M. Hirota, *Image Makers: Advertising, Public Relations, and the Ethos of Advocacy* (Chicago: University of Chicago Press, 2000), 39.
55 H.A. Batten, president of N.W. Ayer & Son, quoted in "Calls on Business to Rebuild Faith," *New York Times*, 29 April 1937, 30; See also Marchand, *Creating the Corporate Soul*, 204–5; Scott M. Cutlip, *The Unseen Power: Public Relations. A History* (Hillsdale, NJ: Lawrence Erlbaum, 1994), 526–7. In 1934, Seagram launched what would become North America's longest-running institutional advertising campaign. See Daniel J. Robinson, "'The Luxury of Moderate Use': Seagram and Moderation Advertising, 1934–1955," in *Communicating in Canada's Past: Essays in Media History*, ed. Daniel J. Robinson and Gene Allen (Toronto: University of Toronto Press, 2009), 109–139.
56 ITC ad, *The Globe*, 28 January 1935, 10; Notably, these ads ran in the *Globe* when the paper did not accept cigarette advertising, underscoring the perceived difference between brand and institutional advertising.
57 For commentary in the advertising trade press on the broader public relations thrust of this campaign see *Marketing Magazine* (untitled), 2 February 1935, 5.

58 ITC ad, *Globe*, 12 February 1935, 3.
59 ITC ads, *Toronto Daily Star*, 11 March 1935, 12; *Toronto Daily Star*, 25 March 1935, 10.
60 ITC ad, *Toronto Daily Star*, 8 April 1935, 12.
61 *Toronto Daily Star*, 29 April 1935, 12.
62 *Toronto Daily Star*, 14 May 1935, 14.
63 *Toronto Daily Star*, 20 May 1935, 12, and 3 June 1935, 22. For similar advertising in interwar America, see Marchand, *Creating the Corporate Soul*, 164–248.
64 Canada, *Report of the Royal Commission on Price Spreads*, 378, 364.
65 Marchand, *Creating the Corporate Soul*, 15, 21–2.
66 *Toronto Daily Star*, 8 July 1935, 9.
67 *Toronto Daily Star*, 7 October 1935, 14.
68 *Toronto Daily Star*, 21 October 1935, 16. Wholesaler and retailer margins on cigarettes were slim. In 1930, the manufacturer "value at factory" for a twenty-pack of cigarettes was 19.5 cents (which included a 12-cent excise duty), which most often retailed for 25 cents. In 1938, owing to a 33 per cent reduction of the cigarette excise tax, the "value at factory" cost dropped to 15.4 cents, with advertised retail prices for twenty-packs typically at 20 or 25 cents. DBS, *Statistical Handbook of Canadian Tobacco* (Ottawa: DBS, 1941), 12; Department of Labour, *An Investigation into an Alleged Combine in the Distribution of Tobacco Products* (Ottawa: Department of Labour, 1939), 6.
69 *Toronto Daily Star*, 4 November 1935, 13.
70 *Toronto Daily Star*, 11 November 1935, 14.
71 *Toronto Daily Star*, 18 March 1936, 14, and 22 April 1936, 7.
72 *Toronto Daily Star*, 20 May 1936, 9.
73 *Toronto Daily Star*, 22 July 1936, 5.
74 *Toronto Daily Star* 24 June 1936, 9.
75 *Toronto Daily Star*, 26 August 1936, 9.
76 Sally H. Clarke, Naomi R. Lamoreaux, and Steven W. Usselman, "Introduction" in Clarke, Lamoreaux, Usselman, eds, *The Challenge of Remaining Innovative: Insights from Twentieth-Century American Business* (Stanford, CA: Business Books, 2009), 7.
77 Jeffrey L. Meikle, *American Plastic: A Cultural History* (New Brunswick, NJ: Rutgers University Press, 1995), 63
78 *Toronto Daily Star*, 24 March 1937, 5.
79 Robert N. Proctor, *Golden Holocaust: Origins of the Cigarette Catastrophe and the Case for Abolition* (Berkeley: University of California Press, 2011), 66–8.

80 Mary Vipond, *The Mass Media in Canada* (Toronto: James Lorimer, 1989), 24.
81 The listed brands were Sweet Caporals, Player's, Turret, Winchester, Cameo Menthol, and Gold Flake.
82 For one example, see "Women Smokers to Cause Decline in World's Health," *Toronto Daily Star*, 21 July 1928, 1.
83 Brandt, *Cigarette Century*, 117.
84 Ibid., 124.
85 Ibid., 125.
86 Procter, *Golden Holocaust*, 155–70.
87 For examples, see "Local Doctors Scoff at New Smoking Evil," *Toronto Daily Star*, 23 June 1930, 30; "Don't See Cigarettes Causing Lip Cancer," *Toronto Daily Star*, 9 March 1934, 13. For a humour-inflected version of this, see "The Doctor's Opinion That Tobacco Causes Your Trouble Would Be More Impressive if His Cigarette Didn't Smell So Good," *Toronto Daily Star*, 25 September 1933, 17.
88 Cited in Procter, *Golden Holocaust*, 158.
89 Brandt, *Cigarette Century*, 124.
90 "Imperial Tobacco Copy Buttonholes Smokers," *Marketing*, 11 February 1939, 7.
91 See Karen S. Miller, *The Voice of Business*, 121–48; Brandt, *Cigarette Century*, 159–207.
92 ITC ad, *Toronto Daily Star*, 3 September 1935, 16.
93 Canada, Department of Trade and Commerce, *Food Products, Beverages, Rubber, Tobacco and Miscellaneous Manufacturers* (Ottawa: Department of Trade and Commerce, 1941), 149.
94 Frederick Wright, "Propagating a New Agricultural Industry," *Canadian Magazine*, August 1928, 16–17; Bruce M. Pearce, "Tobacco – And Wealth," *Saturday Night*, 10 January 1931, 21; J.E.T. Musgrave, "Canadian Tobacco," *Canadian Geographical Journal*, June 1934, 277–89.
95 Canada, *Historical Series of Tobacco Statistics* (Ottawa: Dominion Bureau of Statistics, 1950), 13. On improved relations between tobacco farmers and manufacturers, see "Kirkwood Speaking," *Marketing*, 13 May 1939, 10
96 Canada, DBS, *Historical Series of Tobacco Statistics*, 35. See also Sam Sheldon, "Ontario's Flue-Cured Tobacco Industry: The Southern United States Legacy," *American Review of Canadian Studies* 18, no. 2 (1988): 195–212. Edward Dunsworth's account of labour militancy among Ontario tobacco

workers in the late 1930s fails to connect these actions to relevant business and political contexts, such as ITC's tobacco buying practices and the Price Spreads Royal Commission. "Green Gold, Red Threats: Organization and Resistance in Depression-Era Ontario Tobacco," *Labour/Le Travail* 79 (Spring 2017): 105–42.

97 Frederick Edwards, "Mister, I'm Singing!" *Maclean's*, 15 March 1939, 20–2, 34.
98 Ibid., 20.
99 Ibid.
100 Urquhart and Buckley, eds, *Historical Statistics of Canada*, 478, 466. Canada, Department of Trade and Commerce, *Food Products, Beverages, Rubber, Tobacco and Miscellaneous Manufacturers* (Ottawa: Department of Trade and Commerce, 1941), 142; "Quebec Unique in Tobacco Industry," *Canadian Cigar and Tobacco Journal*, April 1944, 6.
101 *Historical Statistics of Canada*, 466.
102 Department of Trade and Commerce, *Food Products, Beverages, Rubber, Tobacco and Miscellaneous Manufacturers*, 142.
103 *Historical Statistics of Canada*, 356, 366.
104 Ibid., 463.
105 *Statistical Handbook of Canadian Tobacco* (1947), 43; *Historical Statistics of Canada*, 197.
106 *Toronto Daily Star*, 18 November 1935, 12.
107 For example, in 1946 tobacco excise duties, while much higher at $98.2 million, totalled just 4 per cent of the $2.4 billion raised in federal tax revenues. *Statistical Handbook of Canadian Tobacco* (1947), 42; *Historical Statistics of Canada*, 197.
108 On the history of taxation in twentieth-century Canada, see Shirley Tillotson, *Give and Take: The Citizen-Taxpayer and the Rise of Canadian Democracy* (Vancouver: UBC Press, 2017). This account, however, does not mention tobacco-related taxation.
109 Reginald Whitaker, *The Government Party: Organizing and Financing the Liberal Party of Canada, 1930–58* (Toronto: University of Toronto Press, 1977).
110 "History of Federal Ridings since 1867," http://www.parl.gc.ca/About/Parliament/FederalRidingsHistory/hfer.asp?Language=E&Search=G. On the fundraising difficulties of the Conservative Party in Montreal during the early 1940s, see J.L. Granatstein, *The Politics of Survival: The Conservative Party of Canada, 1939–1945* (Toronto: University of Toronto Press, 1967), 49–50, 71–2.

111 "History of Federal Ridings since 1867." Tory fortunes changed in the 1945 federal election when the party took five of these ridings.
112 *Historical Statistics of Canada*, 208–9.
113 *Historical Series of Tobacco Statistics* (1950), 41.
114 *Statistical Handbook of Canadian Tobacco* (1947), 40.
115 Stephenson and McNaught, *The Story of Advertising in Canada*, 204.
116 "Address Cigarette Copy to Women," *Marketing*, 25 June 1927, 530.
117 Ibid.
118 *Marketing*, 12 May 1928, 410.
119 Ads for Diva cigarettes, made with Egyptian tobacco and targeting high-society women, ran in the magazine *Le Journal de Françoise* in the early 1900s. Rudy, *Freedom to Smoke*, 152–3.
120 Rudy, *Freedom to Smoke*, 160–1. In Britain, full-blown cigarette advertising directed at women also began in the late 1920s, although there were a few instances of such marketing in the early 1910s. Penny Tinkler, *Smoke Signals: Women, Smoking and Visual Culture in Britain* (Oxford: Berg, 2006), 57. For a discussion of how women still may have found male-centred cigarette advertising appealing, see Cheryl K. Warsh, "Smoke and Mirrors: Gender Representation in North American Tobacco and Alcohol Advertisements before 1950," *Social History* 31 (1998): 183–222.
121 "Flapper's Puff Gains Power," *Toronto Daily Star*, 15 March 1930, 26.
122 Library and Archives Canada [LAC], Mackenzie King Diary, 10 June 1933, 2.
123 "Gowns for Co-Eds New Rule at Queen's," *Toronto Daily Star*, 14 November 1934, 26.
124 Cook, *Sex, Lies and Cigarettes*, 177.
125 Rudy, *Freedom to Smoke*, 150.
126 "Women Now Enjoy Smoke Walking on City Streets," *Toronto Daily Star*, 13 July 1937, 26.
127 Cook, *Sex, Lies and Cigarettes*, 174.
128 Ibid., 174–5.
129 Sweet Caporals ad, *Toronto Daily Star*, 13 December 1938, 3.
130 Ted Magder, "A 'Featureless' Film Policy: Culture and the Canadian State," in *Communication History in Canada*, ed. Daniel J. Robinson, 2nd ed. (Toronto: Oxford University Press, 2009), 272–81.
131 Rudy, *Freedom to Smoke*, 162.
132 Tinkler, *Smoke Signals*, 123, 121.

133 Iain Gately, *La Diva Nicotina: The Story of How Tobacco Seduced the World* (New York: Simon & Schuster, 2001), 248.
134 Tinkler, *Smoke Signals*, 127.
135 Richard Klein, *Cigarettes Are Sublime* (Durham, NC: Duke University Press, 1993), 9; Tate, *Cigarette Wars*, 138; Brandt, *Cigarette Century*, 87; more generally see Proctor, *Golden Holocaust*, 62–6.
136 Rudy, *Freedom to Smoke*, 163.
137 Tinkler, *Smoke Signals*, 60.
138 Gold Flake ad, *Toronto Daily Star*, 19 October 1935, 14.
139 K.L. Lum, J.R. Polansky, R.K. Jackler, and S.A. Glantz, "Signed, Sealed and Delivered: 'Big Tobacco in Hollywood, 1927–1951," *Tobacco Control* 17 (2008): 313–323. Other actors included Clark Gable, Joan Crawford, Carole Lombard, Robert Montgomery, Barbara Stanwyck, Robert Taylor, and Spencer Tracy.
140 "Historical Statistics of Canada," Statistics Canada, Table A67-69, "Population, Rural & Urban," http://www.statcan.gc.ca/pub/11-516-x/sectiona/4147436-eng.htm#1.
141 Rudy, *Freedom to Smoke*, 122.
142 Miss de Peyster advice column, *Toronto Daily Star*, 9 May 1934, 25.
143 Eaton's ad, *Toronto Daily Star*, 12 March 1936, 51.
144 Life Savers ad, *Toronto Daily Star*, 7 September 1933, 10; Wrigley's ad, *Toronto Daily Star*, 22 April 1937, 3.
145 Elizabeth Arden ad, *Toronto Daily Star*, 6 February 1935, 18; Kellogg's Asthma Relief ad, *Toronto Daily Star*, 18 May 1938, 24.
146 Eaton's ad, *Toronto Daily Star*, 12 August 1937, 42. One modern-day comparison is "Cappuccino Brown."
147 Dress ad, *Toronto Daily Star*, 28 April 1939, 24.
148 Classified ad, "Motor Cars," *Toronto Daily Star*, 5 December 1930, 41.
149 Eaton's ad, *Toronto Daily Star*, 15 September 1938, 29.
150 Ida Jean Kain, "Transverse Stretch Said Best Way to Slim Waist," *Toronto Daily Star*, 21 October 1939, 22.
151 Frigidaire ad, *Toronto Daily Star*, 30 June 1931, 5.
152 Uptown Tire ad, *Toronto Daily Star*, 22 May 1940, 18.
153 Knox Gelatine ad, *Toronto Daily Star*, 26 April 1939, 9.
154 Aqua Velva ad, *Toronto Daily Star*, 7 March 1935, 23.
155 Cigarette premium promotions also existed in the early 1900s. See Rudy, *Freedom to Smoke*, 128–9.

156 *Marketing Magazine*, 13 May 1933, 5; 5 September 1925, 134.
157 ITC catalogue, "Gifts for Poker Hands," September 1935, in author's possession. ITC ad ("Save the Poker Hands"), *The Globe*, 13 July 1936, 18. In the UK, coupon trading, Hilton notes, had "transformed the cigarette trade" by the mid-1930s, rising from 4 per cent of the market in 1927 to 33 per cent in 1933. Matthew Hilton, *Smoking in British Popular Culture, 1800–2000* (Manchester: Manchester University Press, 2000), 108.
158 "'Run' Develops on Premium Stores of Tobacco Companies," *Marketing*, 10 August 1935, 1; ITC ads, *Toronto Daily Star*, 30 August 1935, 6; 7 September 1935, 4.
159 Macdonald Blends ads, *Toronto Daily Star*, 13 September 1929, 16; 29 October 1929, 10; 5 November 1929, 34; 4 March 1930, 13; Grads ad, *Toronto Daily Star*, 11 September 1934, 8; My Fortune ad, *Toronto Daily Star*, 13 July 1931, 10.
160 For a parallel with Wrigley's use of premiums, see Daniel J. Robinson, "Marketing Gum, Making Meanings: Wrigley in North America, 1890–1930," *Enterprise & Society* 5, no. 1 (2004): 22–4. On the rise of premium marketing, see Wendy A. Woloson, "Wishful Thinking: Retail Premiums in Mid-Nineteenth-Century America," *Enterprise & Society* 13, no. 4 (2012): 790–831.
161 *Marketing Magazine*, 30 January 1932, 70; Turret ads, *Toronto Daily Star*, 27 January 1932, 15; 5 February 1932, 14.
162 *Marketing Magazine*, 19 November 1932, 213; Turret ads, *Toronto Daily Star*, 13 April 1932, 13; 25 April 1932, 5.
163 Draegerman ad, *Globe and Mail*, 20 January 1937, 7.
164 British Consols ad, *Toronto Daily Star*, 9 January 1933, 11.
165 Turret ad, *Toronto Daily Star*, 5 March 1932, 12; "Cueists Play for Trophy," *Toronto Daily Star*, 7 March 1932, 7.
166 "Interesting Photographic Series for Cigarettes," *Marketing*, 18 February 1933, 9.
167 Philip Morris ads, *Toronto Daily Star*, 14 December 1936, 9; 4 January 1937, 10; 1 February 1937, 9; 15 February 1937, 9; 8 March 1937, 10; Philip Morris ads, *Globe and Mail*, 4 January 1937, 19; 1 February 1937, 17.
168 Buckingham ads, *Toronto Daily Star*, 1 May 1931, 13; 9 December 1938, 19; 16 May 1939, 13.
169 Buckingham ad, *Toronto Daily Star*, 16 July 1930, 4; Frank Bagnall, "Thrill Theme Ties up with News Events," *Marketing*, 13 September 1930, 125–6.
170 Buckingham ads, *Toronto Daily Star*, 20 July 1939, 16; 17 April 1939, 9.

171 Buckingham ads, *Toronto Daily Star*, 4 July 1932, 8; 7 November 1938, 11; 21 November 1938, 5.
172 Oxford ad, *Toronto Daily Star*, 24 April 1933, 23.
173 Roxy ads, *Toronto Daily Star*, 2 May 1932, 10; 15 April 1932, 13.
174 Allenburys ad, *Toronto Daily Star*, 10 November 1932, 34; Smith Brothers ad, *Toronto Daily Star*, 29 March 1935, 29; Zubes ad, *Toronto Daily Star*, 19 October 1937, 8.
175 Denicotea ads, *Toronto Daily Star*, 20 October 1933, 12; 25 October 1933, 8; 6 November 1933, 26.
176 Brandt, *Cigarette Century*, 244.
177 Proctor, *Golden Holocaust*, 498.
178 Spuds ads, *Toronto Daily Star*, 20 September 1932, 13; 4 October 1932, 14.
179 This ad's headline read, "What Is the Irritant in Cigarette Smoke?" Spuds ad, *Toronto Daily Star*, 21 November 1935, 21; Spuds ad, *London Free Press*, 5 May 1936, 6.
180 Spuds ad, *Toronto Daily Star*, 16 April 1936, 5.
181 Spuds ads, *Toronto Daily Star*, 12 September 1938, 11; 12 January 1939, 3; 20 February 1939, 23; 27 February 1939, 5.
182 Cameo ad, *London Free Press*, 5 May 1936, 5; Cameo ad, *Toronto Daily Star*, 9 December 1938, 11. The department store Simpson's issued its own menthol brand, "Artik," whose package featured an arctic landscape. Artik ad, *Toronto Daily Star*, 8 February 1935, 20.
183 Macdonald's Menthol ads, *London Free Press*, 1 April 1935, 14; *Toronto Daily Star*, 27 March 1935, 13.
184 De Reszke ad, *Toronto Daily Star*, 8 August 1935, 21.
185 Proctor, *Golden Holocaust*, 343.
186 Craven "A" ads, *London Free Press*, 2 June 1937, 3 (original emphasis); *Toronto Daily Star*, 20 September 1937, 3; 22 March 1938, 9; In Britain, Carreras used a similar advertising appeal for Craven "A," noting that the brand had been granted a "certificate" from the "Institute of Hygiene for Quality and Purity." Hilton, *Smoking in British Popular Culture*, 99.
187 Craven "A" ad, *Toronto Daily Star*, 25 May 1937, 3.
188 Macdonald ad, *Globe and Mail*, 17 February 1937, 19.
189 See "Lice on House Plants," *Toronto Daily Star*, 9 November 1935, 6; 7 August 1935, 7.
190 du Maurier ads in *Globe and Mail*, 21 December 1936, 7; 13 January 1937, 7; 1

February 1937, 5; du Maurier ads in *Toronto Daily Star*, 21 December 1938, 8; 31 May 1939, 13.
191 du Maurier ad, *Globe and Mail*, 1 February 1937, 5.
192 du Maurier ad, *Toronto Daily Star*, 31 May 1939, 13. For other ads see *Globe and Mail*, 21 December 1936, 7; 13 January 1937, 7; 1 February 1937, 5; *London Free Press*, 1 June 1937, 5; *Toronto Daily Star*, 21 December 1938, 8.
193 Proctor, *Golden Holocaust*, 343.
194 du Maurier ads, *Globe and Mail*, 21 December 1936, 7; 13 January 1937, 7.
195 Marc H. Choko and Joanne Burgess, *Imperial Tobacco Canada: 1908–2008* (Montreal: Imperial Tobacco, 2008), 270. This commemorative history is highly sanitized. For example, the health risks of cigarette smoking, and the firm's various responses, are not discussed.
196 Miss de Peyster advice column, *Toronto Daily Star*, 28 January 1935, 23.
197 "Women Now Enjoy Smoke Walking on City Streets," *Toronto Daily Star*, 13 July 1937, 26.
198 Kenneth Lipartito, "Connecting the Cultural and the Material in Business History," *Enterprise & Society* 14, no. 4 (December 2013): 703.
199 On the moderation ethos and alcohol, see Robinson, "The Luxury of Moderate Use," 109–39, and Lisa Jacobsen, "Navigating the Boundaries of Respectability and Desire: Seagram's Advertising and the Meanings of Moderation after Repeal," *Social History of Alcohol and Drugs* 26, no. 2 (Summer 2012): 122–46.
200 du Maurier ad, *Toronto Daily Star*, 14 June 1937, 11.
201 Robinson, "Marketing and Regulating Cigarettes in Canada, 1957–1971," 250. Robert Proctor similarly notes that filtered cigarettes in the United States comprised only about 1 per cent of the market during most of the 1940s, but by 1960 they accounted for half of all sales. Proctor, *Golden Holocaust*, 343, 347.

CHAPTER TWO

1 The Canadian Letters and Images Project [Letters], W. Martyn to Mother, 8 February 1941, https://www.canadianletters.ca/.
2 Letters, G. Dennison to Parents, 20 March 1944.
3 Letters, James Baker, 21 October 1941.
4 Letters, James Baker, 12 December 1941; 18 November 1944.

5 Letters, Stanley H. Winfield, memoir (1945).
6 Letters, Winfield memoir (1945). See too J.L. Granatstein, *The Best Little Army in the World: The Canadians in Northwest Europe, 1944–1945* (Toronto: HarperCollins, 2015), 153, 245, 251–2.
7 Cheryl Krasnick Warsh, "The Canadian Cigar and Tobacco Journal in the Forties: A Remembrance," *Social History of Alcohol and Drugs* 21, no. 1 (Fall 2006): 30.
8 Matthew Hilton, "Smoking and Sociability," in *A Global History of Smoking*, ed. Sander L. Gilman and Zhou Zun (London: Reaktion, 2004), 132 .
9 Per-capita cigarette sales rose from 630 in 1939 to 1,255 in 1945. Dominion Bureau of Statistics, *Historical Series of Tobacco Statistics* (1950), 45.
10 C.P. Stacey and Barbara M. Wilson, *The Half-Million: The Canadians in Britain* (Toronto: University of Toronto Press, 1987), xi.
11 Library and Archives Canada [LAC], Amicus # 633357, "Tax Free Smokes for Our Forces," *Canadian Cigar and Tobacco Journal* [CCTJ] (April 1944): 10. While in combat, Canadian soldiers received seven low-quality cigarettes ("often made in India from what seemed to be factory sweepings") daily, as part of their "compo pack" rations. Granatstein, *Best Little Army*, 150.
12 David Cheal, "Gifts in Contemporary North America," in *Gift Giving: A Research Anthology*, ed. Cele Otnes and Richard F. Beltramini (Bowling Green: Bowling Green State University Popular Press, 1996), 89.
13 Jacques Godbout with Alain Caillé, *L'esprit du don* (Paris: La Découverte, 1992); Maurice Godelier, *The Enigma of the Gift* (Chicago: University of Chicago Press, 1999). See too the insightful essay by Avner Offer, "Between the Gift and the Market: The Economy of Regard," *Economic History Review* 50, no. 3 (August 1997): 450–76.
14 Aafke E. Komter, *Social Solidarity and the Gift* (Cambridge: Cambridge University Press, 2005), 8.
15 For historical works on gift exchange practices in the early modern period, see Natalie Zemon Davis, *The Gift in Sixteenth-Century France* (Madison: University of Wisconsin Press, 2000); James G. Carrier, *Gifts and Commodities: Exchange and Western Capitalism since 1700* (New York: Routledge, 1995); Ilana Krausman Ben-Amos, *The Culture of Giving: Informal Support and Gift-Exchange in Early Modern England* (Cambridge: Cambridge University Press, 2008). On Aboriginal–settler relations, see Thomas S. Dye, "Gift Exchange

and Interpretations of Captain Cook in the Traditional Kingdoms of the Hawaiian Islands," *Journal of Pacific History* 46, no. 3 (December 2011): 275–99; Karin Velez, "'A sign that we are related to you': The Transatlantic Gifts of the Hurons of the Jesuit Mission of Lorette, 1650–1750," *French Colonial History* 12 (2011): 31–44; Cary Miller, "Gifts as Treaties: The Political Use of Received Gifts in Anishinaabeg Communities, 1820–1832," *American Indian Quarterly* 26, no. 2 (Spring 2002): 221–45; Jennifer Thigpen, "'You Have Been Very Thoughtful Today': The Significance of Gratitude and Reciprocity in Missionary-Hawaiian Gift Exchange," *Pacific Historical Review* 79, no. 4 (November 2010): 545–72. For a nineteenth-century work, see John Hamer, "English and American Giving: Past and Future Imaginings," *History and Anthropology* 18, no. 4 (December 2007): 443–57; Ellen Litwicki's focus is on the early twentieth century. "From the 'ornamental and evanescent' to 'good, useful things': Redesigning the Gift in Progressive America," *Journal of the Gilded Age & Progressive Era* 10, no. 4 (2011): 467–505. For an intellectual history of gift-exchange theory from the eighteenth century until the early 1900s, see Harry Liebersohn, *The Return of the Gift: European History of a Global Idea* (New York: Cambridge University Press, 2011).

16 Leonard Wong, Thomas A. Kolditz, Raymond A. Millen, and Terrence M. Potter, *Why They Fight: Combat Motivation in the Iraq War* (Carlisle Barracks, PA: Strategic Studies Institute, 2003); David K. Vaughan and William A. Schum, "Motivation in the U.S. Narrative Accounts of the Ground War in Vietnam," *Armed Forces & Society* 28 (2001): 7–31. For a counter-perspective on the importance of social cohesion to combat effectiveness, see Robert J. MacCoun, Elizabeth Kier, and Aaron Belkin, "Does Social Cohesion Determine Motivation in Combat?: An Old Question with an Old Answer," *Armed Forces & Society* 32, no. 4 (July 2006): 646–54.

17 Komter, *Social Solidarity and the Gift*, 21.

18 Bank of Canada Inflation Calculator, http://www.bankofcanada.ca/rates/related/inflation-calculator/. There was limited rationing in Canada during the last year of the First World War.

19 Desmond Morton and J.L. Granatstein, *Victory 1945: Canadians from War to Peace* (Toronto: HarperCollins, 1995), 76–93; Magda Fahrni, "Counting the Costs of Living: Gender, Citizenship, and a Politics of Prices in 1940s Montreal," *Canadian Historical Review* 83, no. 4 (December 2002): 483–504; Matthew J. Bellamy, "'To Ensure the Continued Life of the Industry': The

Public Relations Campaign of the Ontario Brewers during WWII," *Histoire sociale / Social History* 48, no. 97 (2015): 403–23.
20 Graham Broad, *A Small Price to Pay: Consumer Culture on the Canadian Home Front, 1939–45* (Vancouver: UBC Press, 2013), 7.
21 Cigarettes, like nearly all goods, were subject to price controls and faced shortages of packaging-related materials. See "Further Economies in Tobacco Packaging Ordered by W.P.T.B.," *CCTJ* (November 1943): 5. Notably, the most comprehensive account of domestic consumption during the Second World War does not mention tobacco or cigarettes. Broad, *A Small Price to Pay*.
22 "Highlight Items in War Budget," *Toronto Daily Star*, 25 June 1940, 1.
23 "Nicotine, Liquor, Letters Clubs to Add $46,200,000," *Toronto Daily Star*, 3 March 1943; Jeffrey A. Keshen, *Saints, Sinners, and Soldiers: Canada's Second World War* (Vancouver: UBC Press, 2004), 112.
24 Ottawa raised taxes on so-called "sin" products like playing cards, beer, and chewing gum. "Liquor, Tobacco, Pop, Cards Feel New Budget's Weight," *Toronto Daily Star*, 24 June 1942, 3; "Current Cigarette Advertising Shows Considerable Copy Variety," *Marketing*, 5 August 1944, 2–3.
25 Keshen, *Saints, Sinners and Soldiers*, 112.
26 Jeff Keshen, "One for All or All for One: Black Marketing in Canada, 1939–1947," in *The Good Fight: Canadians and World War II*, ed. J.L. Granatstein and Peter Neary (Toronto: Copp Clark, 1995), 278; LAC, "Post Office Determined to Stop Illegal Mailing of Cigarettes," *CCTJ* (October 1943): 10.
27 Dominion Bureau of Statistics, *Statistical Handbook of Canadian Tobacco* (1947), 39.
28 "Smokes – For the Men behind the Guns," *CCTJ* (February 1944): 9.
29 Ottawa, *House of Commons Debates*, 26 November 1940, 438.
30 Jarrett Rudy, *The Freedom to Smoke: Tobacco Consumption and Identity* (Montreal and Kingston: McGill-Queen's University Press, 2005), 132–3.
31 Stag ad, *London Free Press*, 6 October 1915, 7.
32 "Cigarets a Treat to Wounded Soldiers," *Toronto Daily Star*, 5 June 1915, 2.
33 Letter to Editor, "Smoking at the Front," *Toronto Daily Star*, 23 June 1915, 5.
34 "Cigarets Necessity, Capt. Julia Henshaw," *Toronto Daily Star*, 2 November 1917, 4.
35 "Is Crowding Out Doctrine of the Lord?," *Toronto Daily Star*, 11 June 1918, 2.
36 Rudy, *Freedom to Smoke*, 137.
37 Desmond Morton, *When Your Number's Up: The Canadian Soldier in the First*

World War (Toronto: Random House, 1993), 140. For the UK experience, see Michael Reeve, "Special Needs, Cheerful Habits: Smoking and the Great War in Britain, 1914–18," *Cultural and Social History* 13, no. 4 (2016): 483–501.

38 Tim Cook, *At the Sharp End: Canadians Fighting the Great War 1914–1916* (Toronto: Viking, 2007, 249.
39 Rudy, *Freedom to Smoke*, 141.
40 Army Club ad, *Toronto Daily Star*, 6 November 1918, 20.
41 Rudy, *Freedom to Smoke*, 132.
42 Lake St Louis Historical Society [LSLHS], Macdonald Tobacco Collection, Box MT 8, file 105, ad photo for Canadian Legion cigarettes; Box 2, file WMS 108, W.L. Mackenzie to W.M. Stewart (4 May 1943); Box 17, file 17.39 C.W. Taylor to Messrs. Marks (7 February 1944).
43 Player's Navy Cut ads, *London Free Press*, 6 September 1941, 3; 2 April 1942, 4.
44 Player's Navy Cut ad, *New World Illustrated*, September 1944, 21.
45 Wings ads, *London Free Press*, 5 February 1940, 14; 2 October 1940, 24.
46 Macdonald ad, *London Free Press*, 3 November 1943, 14.
47 Warsh, "Canadian Cigar and Tobacco Journal," 16.
48 "ITC direct merchandising offer," *Marketing*, 3 February 1940, 8.
49 Sweet Caporals ad, *London Free Press*, 5 October 1941, 4.
50 LSLHS, Macdonald Collection, Box MT-8; Macdonald ad, *Montreal Standard*, 16 March 1940, no page; Macdonald ad, *The Legionary*, August 1943, 20.
51 F. Trant letter to editor, "Smokes for Soldiers," *Toronto Daily Star*, 10 July 1941, 6.
52 LAC, "Cigarettes Vial to Lads Overseas," CCTJ (February 1944): 30. On the historical rise of giving pragmatic, useful gifts, see Litwicki, "From the 'ornamental and evanescent' to 'good, useful things,'" 482–96.
53 LAC, "League Has Sent 73,000,000," CCTJ (March 1944): 14.
54 Serge Marc Durflinger, *Fighting from Home: The Second World War in Verdun, Quebec* (Vancouver: UBC Press, 2006, 59.
55 "Smokes Going Forth for Horse Guards," *Toronto Daily Star*, 10 March 1942, 22.
56 "Small Arms Guild," *Toronto Daily Star*, 10 January 1942, 21; "120,000 Cigarettes Shipped to Fliers," *Toronto Daily Star*, 22 April 1942, 25; Bingo ad, *Toronto Daily Star*, 5 July 1943, 11; "I.O.D.E. War Service Record is Reviewed at Meeting," *Toronto Daily Star*, 2 June 1943, 25; cricket match ad, *Toronto Daily Star*, 18 August 1944, 11.

57 "Event at Temagami Aids Bomb Victims," *Toronto Daily Star*, 29 August 1941, 10.
58 "Send 831,700 Smokes to Boys Over There," *Toronto Daily Star*, 17 April 1942, 8.
59 "Club Auction of English Fags Nets $18.50 for Cigarette Fund," *Toronto Daily Star*, 19 May 42, 8; "Donation Day Is Set for Cigarette Fund," *Toronto Daily Star*, 1 September 1943, 8.
60 "Beverly Veterans Send Boys Smokes," *Toronto Daily Star*, 19 February 1943, 2; "Ayr Holds Carnival for Cigarette Fund," *Toronto Daily Star*, 9 March 1943, 2. See too, "Paris Sends Army a Million Smokes," *CCTJ* (October 1943): 22; and "Soo Legion Smoke Fund Big Success," *CCTJ* (October 1943): 30.
61 "Raises $8,000," *CCTJ* (August 1944): 22; "New Smoke Fund," *CCTJ* (August 1944): 24; "Held Tag Day," *CCTJ* (July 1944): 26.
62 Western University, The Ley and Lois Smith War, Memory, and Popular Culture Research Collection [WMPCRC], Major Rev. Mike Dalton, "Personal War Diary, 1939–1946" (entries for 9 March 1942; 7 May 1942).
63 William MacFarlane, letter to the editor, *Toronto Daily Star*, 26 March 1943, 6.
64 "Saying It with Smokes," *CCTJ* (December 1943): 6.
65 WMPCRC, *Maple Leaf News*, July 1943, 8–9.
66 "50,000 Cigarettes Bought for Troops," *Toronto Daily Star*, 29 April 1942, 16.
67 "Students in Oakville Plan Theatre Nights," *Toronto Daily Star*, 30 November 1942, 8.
68 "Fags, Comforts for Troops Aim of Forest Hill Fair," *Toronto Daily Star*, 6 April 1944, 4.
69 Durflinger, *Fighting from Home*, 62, 25.
70 Ibid., 59.
71 Ibid., 127.
72 Ibid., 66. On US companies' involvement in community initiatives and events during the war, see Roland Marchand, *Creating the Corporate Soul: The Rise of Public Relations and Corporate Imagery in American Big Business* (Berkeley: University of California Press, 1998), 316–56.
73 WMPCRC, Overseas League Tobacco Fund ad, *New World Illustrated*, December 1942, 38. On wartime cigarette drives in the United States, see Gregory Wood, "'The Justice of a Rule That Forbids the Men Smoking on Their Jobs': Workers, Managers, and Cigarettes in World War II America," *Labor: Studies in Working-Class History of the Americas* 13, no. 1 (2016): 17–23.

74 Letters, F. Scandiffio to Esther, 25 January 1942; Scandiffio to Millie, 29 January 1942.
75 Letters, F. Scandiffio to Millie, 29 June 1942; F. Scandiffio to Esther/Millie, 9 October 1942.
76 Letters, F. Scandiffio to "Sis," 19 December 1942.
77 Letters, K. Butler to Mother, 23 January 1940; 4 September 1940.
78 Letters, W. Martyn to Father, 10 September 1943; 4 April 1943.
79 Letters, H. Davis to Aunt, 18 February 1942; H. Davis to Mother, 7 June 1944.
80 Letters, G. Turpin to Family, 2 June 1944; see too Granatstein, *Best Little Army*, 149.
81 Archives of Ontario [AO], RG 9-7-8 Ontario House, file "Cigarettes-Acknowledgements," Private Kinnart to G. Drew, 17 August 1944.
82 For examples, see "Life Saved by Tin of Smokes," CCTJ (September 1944): 9; "Tanks Guided by Cigarette" (October 1944): 11.
83 Warsh, "Canadian Cigar and Tobacco Journal," 9.
84 "Her Parting Gift Saved Flier Friend's Life," *Toronto Daily Star*, 11 May 1942, 3.
85 Historica Canada, The Memory Project, Stuart Vallieres interview, http://www.thememoryproject.com/.
86 Letters, F. Scandiffio to E. McKnight, 10 May 1942.
87 Memory Project, Arthur Haley interview.
88 Tu Thanh Ha, "Obituary: How Blowing Smoke Rings Saved a PoW's life," *Globe and Mail*, 16 May 2014.
89 AO, RG 9-7-8, Ontario House, file "Cigarettes-Acknowledgements," W.J. Brooks/R. Graham to Ontario People, 5 July 1944.
90 AO, RG 9-7-8, Ontario House, file "Cigarettes, 1944–1946," J. Armstrong to G. Drew, 18 July 1944; Armstrong transposed part of Keller's note in his letter; see too, LAC, "Smokes Greatest Morale Builder," CCTJ (August 1944): 18. One recent study found that US military personnel who experienced combat later consumed cigarettes and alcohol at higher rates than soldiers who did not experience combat. Resul Cesur, Alexander Chesney, and Joseph J. Sabia, "Combat Exposure, Cigarette Consumption, and Substance Use," *Economic Inquiry* 54, no. 3 (2016): 1705–26.
91 WMPCRC, Sweet Caporal ad, *Canadians All* (Autumn 1944): 54.
92 "Smokes – For the Men behind the Guns," CCTJ (February 1944): 8.
93 Letters, Jack Andrews memoir.
94 Letters, J. Baker to Mother (8 May 1942).

95 Memory Project, David Simpson interview.
96 Letters, K. Butler to "Wannie," 12 February 1940.
97 Letters, A. Morlidge to "Folks," 15 May 1942; see also, LAC, "Many Thanks for the Cigarettes," *CCTJ* (June 1945): 20.
98 On this point, see Offer, "Between the Gift," 455.
99 Memory Project, Harold Hall interview.
100 Richard S. Malone, *A Portrait of War, 1939–1943* (Toronto: Collins, 1983), 154.
101 "Boys Over There Prefer Our Fags," *CCTJ* (October 1943): 30; "Canadian Smokes Acutely Needed," *CCTJ* (February 1944): 30 "Canadian Cigarettes Are Still Scarce in Overseas Army Camps," *CCTJ* (January 1945): 12.
102 Letters, E. Loney to Mother, 29 November 1944.
103 Letters, W. Martyn to Father, 4 April 1943.
104 Letters, W. Orval to Mother, 2 February 1944; Gould to Mother, ca May 1944.
105 Letters, W. Watson to "Folks," 18 March 1944.
106 Malone, *Portrait of War*, 104–5.
107 LAC, "Tax Free Smokes for Our Forces," *CCTJ* (April 1944): 10.
108 "The Boys Need the Smokes More in France Than in England," *Marketing*, 24 June 1944, 22; "Canada's Armed Forces in Italy Will Get Cigarettes via Fast New System," *CCTJ* (June 1944): 1
109 British civilians also complained about the taste of wartime cigarettes; one account described a brand as tasting like "the sweepings from the factory floor and smelled like you were burning dead dogs on a garden bonfire." "Cigarette" recollection in BBC History archive, WW2 People's War, https://www.bbc.co.uk/history/ww2peopleswar/stories/25/a2226025.shtml; see too https://www.bbc.co.uk/history/ww2peopleswar/stories/45/a2884845.shtml.
110 Letters, W. Martyn to Mother, 27 June 1940; W. Martyn to Father, 6 January 1941; H. Davis to Mother, 2 December 1941; K. Butler to Mother and Father, 4 September 1940; "Canada's Smokers Are Still Ahead," *CCTJ* (April 1944): 20.
111 Letters, E. Bryer to Edgar, 4 September 1943.
112 Letters, G. Dennison to "Folks," 2 March 1944; see too Dennison's letters on 13 March 1944; 21 May 1944; 7 June 1944.
113 Letters, W. Watson to Family, 1 April 1944.
114 Letters, A. Gould to Mother and Father, 23 May 1944 and 31 May 1944.
115 Letters, H. Hansell to Mother, 1 August 1943.
116 "Sure-Fire Method Sends Cigarettes," *CCTJ* (December 1944): 38.
117 Letters, B. Turpin to Family, 25 July 1944 and 1 October 1944.

118 Accordingly, this differs from the form of consumer nationalism discussed by Catherine Carstairs in "'Roots' Nationalism: Branding English Canada Cool in the 1980s and 1990s," *Histoire Sociale / Social History* 39 (2006): 235–55.
119 See Patricia Cormack and James F. Cosgrave, *Desiring Canada: CBC Contests, Hockey Violence, and Other Stately Pleasure* (Toronto: University of Toronto Press, 2013), 77–9.
120 Letters, Morlidge to Family, 2 July 1942; F. Scandiffio to Millie, 29 June 1942; P. Scandiffio to Esther, 8 August 1942.
121 Letters, P. Scandiffio to Esther and Bill, 8 August 1942; G. Turpin to Family, 1 October 1944.
122 Letters, P. Scandiffio to Esther and Bill, 5 November 1942.
123 Letters A. Nelson to Mother, 6 December 1942.
124 Letters, W. Bell to Mother and Father, 14 June 1942; W. Bell to Mother, 8 July 1942.
125 http://www.veterans.gc.ca/eng/remembrance/history/second-world-war/canada-netherlands.
126 Amsterdam, Nederlands Instituut voor Oorlogsdocumentatie [NIOD], Collectie 244 – dagboeken; no. 1562; Mulder, Steven W. (Diary, 14 April 1945), 12. Special thanks to Astrid Van den Bossche who provided this translation. The original Dutch is: "Vanavond sprak ik met een Canadese captain (3 sterretjes op de epauletten). Hij zei dat de Canadezen voor 100% volunteers waren, the only country in the world without conscription [original in English]. Hij vond het prachtig om juist in de bezette landen te vechten en dan de bevolking te zien juichen. Hij vond het echter niet in de haak dat de Canadezen altijd moesten vechten en de Engelsen als bezettingstroepen dienst deden. Na Frankrijk, Belgie en Nederland bevrijd te hebben wou hij nog graag naar Denmark, waarna hij vanaf nu gerekend over 3 maanden hoopt thuis te zijn. Hij krijgt per maand 2000 sigaretten: 1000 van zijn vrouw en 100 van de 'firma.' Hij rookt 20 sigaretten per dag en geeft de rest weg. De beste tabak is voor het leger. De bevolking in Canada krijgt een mindere soort. Nu, op zaterdag, leest hij de kranten die op donderdag in Londen gedrukt zijn. De soldaten en officieren zijn haast niet van elkaar te onderscheiden, alleen sterren van stof op de epauletten."
127 NIOD, Collectie 244 – dagboeken; No 1565; Jeanne Teding van Berkhout-Tutein Nolthenius, 34.
128 Michiel Horn, "More than Cigarettes, Sex and Chocolate: The Canadian

Army in the Netherlands, 1944–1945," *Journal of Canadian Studies* 16 (Fall-Winter 1981): 156–73, at 156.

129 For examples, see Norman Phillips and J. Nikerk, *Holland and the Canadians, with 150 Photographs* (Amsterdam: Contact Pub. Co. 1946), 68, 69; Hen Bollen and Paul Vroemen, *Het einde van vijf jaar terreur in Nederland/The End of Five Years of Terror in Holland* (Zaltbommel: Europese Bibliotheek 1990), 127–8.

130 David Kaufman and Michiel Horn, *De Canadezen In Nederland, 1944–1945: een bevrijdingsalbum* (Laren: Luitingh, 1981, 88.

131 Kaufman and Horn, *De Canadezen In Nederland, 1944–1945*, 89. Original photo caption, in Dutch, is: "De vriendschappelijke relaties tussen soldaten en burgers werden aangemoedigd. Een van de beste methoden om contact te leggen was het aanbieden van sigaretten, en die konden er bij de Canadezen altijd wel van af."

132 NIOD; collectie 616, Collectie Europese voorwerpen inv. no. 717. Forrest C. Pogue, a US combat historian serving in France, wrote about American soldiers being beset by children asking for "cigarettes, candy or chewing gum" and how nearly any stop produced "requests for cigarettes." He wrote: "We did our best to play the role of liberators, and we finally hit on the device of wrapping up two or three cigarettes and a piece of candy in paper bundles and tossing them to people along the road. I ... got rid of several cartons that way." Forest C. Pogue, *Pogue's War: Diaries of a WWII Combat Historian* (Lexington: University Press of Kentucky, 2001), 197, 209.

133 Offer, "Between the Gift and the Market," 451.

134 http://tulipfestival.ca/about/tulip-legacy. Of note, Queen Wilhelmina and other members of the Dutch Royal Family took refuge in Ottawa from 1940 to 1945.

135 Bollen and Vroemen, *Het einde van vijf jaar terreur in Nederland*, 130.

136 Horn, "More Than Cigarettes," 158, 162; see too Samy Mesli, "'Free us from our Liberators': l'armée canadienne et la libération des Pays-Bas (1944–1946)," *Bulletin d'histoire politique* 21, no. 3 (2013), 24–31.

137 "Dutchmen Promised 20 Fags per Week," CCTJ (September 1945): 10.

138 Horn, "More Than Cigarettes," 162–3.

139 Letters, Winfield memoir (1945).

140 Amsterdam, Stadsarchief Amsterdam [SA], Archive # 15030; Inventory # 85397, Johan Luger and G.H. Wallagh, "All about Amsterdam" (Amsterdam: W.L. Salm, 1945), 4.

141 Ibid., 43.
142 Pogue, *Pogue's War*, 231.
143 Ibid., 232; for other accounts, see "French Forced to Smoke the Butts," CCTJ (October 1944): 28; and "Strange Mixtures in Paris Smokes," CCTJ (November 1944): 20.
144 Charles Lynch, "Cigarettes Buy Car, Hose in Berlin's Black Market," *Toronto Daily Star*, 29 October 1945, 15. On the underground economy in Berlin in 1945–46, see Kevin Conley Ruffner, "You Are Never Going to Be Able to Run an Intelligence Unit: SSU Confronts the Black Market in Berlin," *Journal of Intelligence History* 2, no. 2 (December 2002): 1–20.
145 Mark Wyman, *DPs: Europe's Displaced Persons, 1945–1951* (Ithaca, NY: Cornell University Press, 1998), 115.
146 Letters, L. Lindsay to W.M. Mouat, 18 September 1943. On Canadian POWs, see Jonathan F. Vance, *Objects of Concern: Canadian Prisoners of War through the Twentieth Century* (Vancouver: UBC Press, 1994).
147 WMPCRC, ad, "Smokes for Prisoners of War," *Toronto Daily Star*, 15 March 1943, 3; Macdonald ads, *Canadian Prisoners of War Relatives Association*, newsletter (October 1943): 27; and (January 1944, 27).
148 Keshen, *Saints, Sinners, and Soldiers*, 240.
149 WMPCRC *Canadian Prisoners of War Relatives Association*, newsletter (October 1943): 27.
150 WMPCRC, *The Prisoner of War*, Newsletter (Jan.-Feb. 1944): 2.
151 WMPCRC, *Canadian Prisoners of War Relatives Association*, newsletter (October 1943): 18.
152 "Gifts Other Than Smokes a Waste," CCTJ (August 1944): 24.
153 WMPCRC, John Colwell (Stalag Luft 3, Sagan, German), diary entries, 10 February 1944 to 23 May 1944; see especially pp. 19 and 43.
154 Hal Lehrman, "Star Meets Canadians Saved, Fed by Russians," *Toronto Daily Star*, 25 March 1945, 1, 2.
155 Mack Lynch, ed., *Salty Dips*, vol. 3 (Ottawa: Naval Association of Canada, 1988), 153–4.
156 Ruth Latta, ed., *The Memory of All That: Canadian Women Remember World War II* (Burnstown, ON: General Store Publishing House, 1992), 97. The interviewee is Norah Forster.
157 Charles Roland, *Long Night's Journey into Day: Prisoners of War in Hong Kong and Japan, 1941–1945* (Waterloo, ON: Wilfrid Laurier University Press, 2001), 105.

158 WMPCRC, "Prison Can Be Fun," a memoir by Paul Ramage, pp. 59, 61.
159 Larry Allen, *Encyclopedia of Money*, 2nd ed. (Santa Barbara: ABC-CLIO, 2009), 320–1.
160 "Cigarettes Used as Money in Camps," CCTJ (December 1944), 22; Keshen, *Saints*, 241.
161 Hal Lehrman, "Star Meets Canadians Saved, Fed by Russians," *Toronto Daily Star*, 25 March 1945, 1, 2; LAC, "Our Cigarettes Used for Money," CCTJ (July 1944): 6.
162 William Kinmond, "If We Could Light It, Pronto We Burned It," *Toronto Daily Star*, 16 May 1945, 99.
163 Roland, *Long Night's Journey*, 104.
164 LAC, "Canadian Smokes Are Lifesavers," CCTJ (November 1945): 12; "Fags Capital in Jap Prison Camps," CCTJ (May 1946): 33.
165 Roland, *Long Night's Journey*, 104.
166 Ibid., 103, 105.
167 Ibid., 105, 104. Walter W. Igersheimer experienced something similar as a German-Jewish refugee in a wartime internment camp near Sherbrooke, Quebec: "You must understand that to have cigarettes or chocolate in camp is like having gold in the bank. Whatever the fluctuating prices of other items, the value of cigarettes and chocolate remains constant. It is a safe investment for which people pay heavily. For two months, we are without a canteen. For two months, the older men are raving and clamouring for tobacco. They would sell their last shirt, willingly do your chores, sometimes pleading with you for hours, and promising to pay you back twentyfold as soon as they get cigarettes sent from the States." Igersheimer, *Blatant Injustice: The Story of a Jewish Refugee from Nazi Germany Imprisoned in Britain and Canada during World War II* (Montreal and Kingston: McGill-Queen's University Press, 2005), 54–5.
168 Letters, John McGuire Taylor memoir, n.d. (POW in Stalag Luft III).
169 Letters, E. Bell to Family, 31 October 1944.
170 Paul Fussell, *Wartime: Understanding and Behavior in the Second World War* (New York: Oxford University Press, 1989), 145.
171 Komter, *Social Solidarity*, 22.
172 Ibid., 191; see too Karen Sykes, *Arguing with Anthropology: An Introduction to Critical Theories of the Gift* (London: Routledge, 2005), 1.
173 For example, this can be seen with the postwar attempts by veterans to allow

cigarette smoking on streetcars, which typically invoked their wartime experiences with cigarettes. See "Smoker Denounces Crabs Who Seek to Ban Public Smoking," *CCTJ* (April 1946): 9; "Letter Writer Has Say on Smoking," *CCTJ* (April 1947): 41.

174 Ted Barris and Alex Barris, *Days of Victory: Canadians Remember, 1939–1945* (Toronto: Macmillan, 1995), 128.

CHAPTER THREE

1 "City 'Laughing Stock' Balfour Claims, Urges Sunday Cigarette Sale," *Toronto Daily Star*, 21 January 1949, 23.
2 Canadian Institute of Public Opinion (CIPO), poll release, "City Life Conducive to Cigarette Smoking" (25 May 1949). In author's possession.
3 Jason Hughes, *Learning to Smoke: Tobacco Use in the West* (Chicago: University of Chicago Press, 2003), 58.
4 See Anthony Giddens, *Modernity and Self-Identity: Self and Society in the Late Modern Age* (Stanford: Stanford University Press, 1991).
5 Ans Nicolaides-Bouman, Nicholas Wald, Barbara Forey, and Peter Lee, eds., *International Smoking Statistics: A Collection of Historical Data from 22 Economically Developed Countries* (Oxford: Oxford University Press, 1993), 62, 64.
6 Dominion Bureau of Statistics, *Statistical Handbook of Canadian Tobacco* (Ottawa, 1947), 36, 38.
7 Nicolaides-Bouman et al., eds, *International Smoking Statistics*, 62, 64.
8 M.C. Urquhart and Kenneth Buckley, eds, *Historical Statistics of Canada* (Cambridge: Cambridge University Press, 1965), 478.
9 Ibid., 482; Wald et al., eds, *International Smoking Statistics*, 62, 64.
10 Urquhart and Buckley, *Historical Statistics*, 466.
11 Ibid.
12 Ibid., 85.
13 "Consumer Survey Shows 68 p.c. Men, 39 p.c. Women Are Cigarette Smokers," *Canadian Cigar and Tobacco Journal [CCTJ]* (July 1947): 9.
14 CIPO press release, "City Life Conducive to Cigarette Smoking," 25 May 1949.
15 CIPO press release, "Cigarette Habit Shows No Signs of Dying Out," 29 December 1951; "Fumez-vous la cigarette?," *La Presse*, 29 December 1951, 22.
16 Archives of Ontario [AO], Elliott Research Collection, F 245-20-0-4.1 Elliott-Haynes Report, "National Survey of Consumer Brand Switching Habits in the

Canadian Cigarette Market," (November 1950). On consumer research conducted by Elliott-Haynes, see Daniel J. Robinson, *The Measure of Democracy: Polling, Market Research, and Public Life 1930–1945* (Toronto: University of Toronto Press, 1999), 139–40.

17 AO, Elliott-Haynes Report (1950), Table 1.
18 AO, Elliott-Haynes Report (1950), Table 1a.
19 Matthew Hilton, *Smoking in British Popular Culture 1800–2000* (Manchester: Manchester University Press, 2000), 235.
20 Player's ads, *La Presse*, 20 June 1953, 17, 56.
21 Wynne Thomas, "How a King-Sized Sales Campaign Upset a Highly Competitive Market," *Marketing*, 3 October 1958, 36–7.
22 On the history of mass marketing see Richard S. Tedlow, *New and Improved: The Story of Mass Marketing in America* (New York: Basic Books, 1990); Susan Strasser, *Satisfaction Guaranteed: The Making of the American Mass Market* (New York: Pantheon, 1989); Daniel J. Robinson, "Marketing Gum, Making Meanings: Wrigley in North America, 1890–1930," *Enterprise & Society* 5, no. 1 (March 2004): 4–44.
23 Steve Penfold, *The Donut: A Canadian History* (Toronto: University of Toronto Press, 2008): 11.
24 Philip Morris ad, *Toronto Daily Star*, 27 January 1948, 9.
25 Sweet Caporals ad, *Toronto Daily Star*, 10 January 1949, 14.
26 The first of these surveys available to researchers took place in 1955.
27 Canadian Facts [CF] Survey, "Study No. 4 Canadian Smoking Habits and Smokers' Attitudes toward Major Cigarette Brands, July-Aug 1955" (for ITC), https://www.industrydocumentslibrary.ucsf.edu/tobacco/docs/kkmv0223.
28 CF Survey, "Study No. 4 Canadian Smoking Habits and Smokers' Attitudes toward Major Cigarette Brands, July-Aug 1955," (for ITC) (1–4, 8) https://www.industrydocumentslibrary.ucsf.edu/tobacco/docs/kkmv0223.
29 CF Survey, "Study No. 4 Canadian Smoking Habits and Smokers' Attitudes toward Major Cigarette Brands, July-Aug 1955" (for ITC), 12, https://www.industrydocumentslibrary.ucsf.edu/tobacco/docs/kkmv0223. On Export, see Timothy Dewhirst, "Gender, Extreme Sports, and Smoking: A Case Study of Export 'A' Cigarette Brand Marketing," in *Sexual Sports Rhetoric: Global and Universal Contexts*, ed. Linda K. Fuller (New York: Peter Lang, 2010), 263–75.
30 Christopher J. Grieg, "Boys' Underachievement in School in Historical Perspective," in *Canadian Men and Masculinities: Historical and Contemporary*

Perspectives, ed. Christopher J. Grieg and Wayne J. Martino (Toronto: Canadian Scholars' Press, 2012), 99–115; see too Mary Louise Adams, *The Trouble with Normal: Postwar Youth and the Making of Heterosexuality* (Toronto: University of Toronto Press, 1997); and Mona Gleason, *Normalizing the Ideal: Psychology, Schooling, and the Family in Postwar Canada* (Toronto: University of Toronto Press, 1999).

31 Christopher J. Grieg, "Boys' Underachievement in School in Historical Perspective: Exploring Masculinity and Schooling in the Postwar Era, 1945–1960," in *Canadian Men and Masculinities: Historical and Contemporary Perspectives*, ed. Christopher J. Grieg and Wayne J. Martino (Toronto: Canadian Scholars' Press, 2012), 101.

32 Christopher Dummitt, *The Manly Modern: Masculinity in Postwar Canada* (Vancouver: UBC Press, 2007): 22

33 CF Survey, "Study No. 5 Canadian Smoking Habits and Smokers' Attitudes, Sept–Oct 1956," (for ITC), table 39, https://www.industrydocumentslibrary.ucsf.edu/tobacco/docs/jkmv0223.

34 Hughes, *Learning to Smoke*, 40, 58, 129.

35 "Smuggled Cigarettes Go to Veterans," CCTJ (July 1948): 9; "Confiscated Cigarettes for D.V.A. Hospitals," CCTJ (February 1949): 8; "La Légion envoie 250,000 cigarettes à nos troupes," *La Presse*, 15 February 1951, 33; "Ontario Sends 1,000,000 Cigarettes to Servicemen," CCTJ (February 1955): 20.

36 Sharon Anne Cook, *Sex, Lies, and Cigarettes: Canadian Women, Smoking, and Visual Culture, 1880–2000* (Montreal and Kingston: McGill-Queen's University Press, 2012), 124–5.

37 "If You Take My Advice," *Toronto Daily Star*, 28 April 1947, 23.

38 For elaboration on this topic, see B. Poland, K. Frolich, R.J. Haines, E. Mykhalovskiy, R. Rock, and R. Sparks, "The Social Context of Smoking: The Next Frontier in Tobacco Control?" *Tobacco Control* 15, no. 1 (February 2006): 59–63.

39 William Leiss, Stephen Kline, Sut Jhally, Jacqueline Botterill, and Kyle Asquith, *Social Communication in Advertising*, 4th ed. (New York: Routledge, 2018), 231.

40 See Raymond Williams, *Culture and Society* (London: Chatto and Windus, 1958) and *The Long Revolution* (London: Chatto and Windus, 1961). Members of the Birmingham School of Cultural Studies later adopted this position, studying everyday items like dime-store novels or Graceland kitsch in order to understand the relationship between popular culture and social power.

41 CF Survey, "Study No. 5 Canadian Smoking Habits and Smokers' Attitudes, Sept–Oct 1956" (for ITC), https://www.industrydocumentslibrary.ucsf.edu/tobacco/docs/jkmv0223.

42 Gregory Wood, "'The Justice of a Rule That Forbids the Men Smoking on Their Jobs': Workers, Managers, and Cigarettes in World War II America," *Labor: Studies in Working-Class History of the Americas* 13, no. 1 (2016): 11–39; see too Gregory Wood, "'Habits of Employees': Smoking, Spies, and Shop Floor Culture at Hammermill Paper Company," *Journal of Social History* 45, no. 1 (Fall 2011): 99–100; and Gregory Wood, *Clearing the Air: The Rise and Fall of Smoking in the Workplace* (Ithaca, NY: ILR Press, 2016).

43 "La cigarette de moins en moins fumée," *La Presse*, 1 March 1954, https://www.industrydocumentslibrary.ucsf.edu/tobacco/docs/fqjc0223.

44 Hughes, *Learning to Smoke*, 90, 40, 93.

45 "Fire Chief Urges Yeggmen 'Not to Smoke on the Job,'" *Toronto Daily Star*, 17 November 1945, 1.

46 "Modern Girl Does Eat More," *Toronto Daily Star*, 12 January 1946, 30; for similar commentary see Dept. of Pensions and National Health, *Smoking* (Ottawa: King's Printer, 1940), 8.

47 "Cigarette, Coffee No Lunch, She Says," *Toronto Daily Star*, 4 March 1948, 29.

48 "Blames Smokes, Doughnuts for Hidden Hunger in Many," *Toronto Daily Star*, 27 April 1949, 2.

49 See Jackson Lears, *Fables of Abundance: A Cultural History of Advertising in America* (New York: Basic Books, 1994), 141–4; Daniel J. Robinson, "Marketing Gum, Making Meanings: Wrigley in North America, 1890–1930," *Enterprise & Society* 5, no. 1 (March 2004): 26–31.

50 Jocelyn Szczepaniak-Gillece, "Smoke and Mirrors: Cigarettes, Cinephilia, and Reverie in the American Movie Theater," *Film History* 28, no. 3 (2016): 90.

51 Allan M. Brandt, "From Nicotine to Nicotrol: Addiction, Cigarettes, and American Culture," in *Altering American Consciousness: The History of Alcohol and Drug Use in the United States, 1800–2000*, ed. Sarah W. Tracey and Caroline J. Acker (Amherst: University of Massachusetts Press, 2004), 386.

52 CF Survey, "Study No. 5 Canadian Smoking Habits and Smokers' Attitudes , Sept-Oct 1956" (for ITC), table 39, https://www.industrydocumentslibrary.ucsf.edu/tobacco/docs/jkmv0223.

53 Cook, *Sex, Lies, and Cigarettes*, 255.

54 "War Brides' Smoking One Rift Cause – Bride," *Toronto Daily Star*, 27 November 1946, 21.

55 Penny Tinkler, *Smoke Signals: Women, Smoking and Visual Culture* (Oxford: Berg, 2006), 145–6.
56 "Nicotine and the Tobacco Habit," *CCTJ* (September 1945): 34.
57 Sweet Caporals ad, *Toronto Daily Star*, 16 April 1948, 21.
58 Pall Mall ad, *Le Soleil*, 16 November 1950, 14; "New Pall Mall Ads Stress 'Relaxation' from Smoking," *Marketing*, 2 December 1950, 21.
59 Pall Mall ad, *Toronto Daily Star*, 14 November 1950, 14.
60 JoAnne Brown, *The Definition of a Profession: The Authority of Metaphor in the History of Intelligence Testing, 1890-1930* (Princeton, NJ: Princeton University Press, 1992); Ellen Herman, *The Romance of American Psychology: Political Culture in the Age of Experts* (Berkeley: University of California Press, 1995).
61 Mary J. Wright, "The CPA: The First Ten Years," *Canadian Psychologist* 15, no. 2 (April 1974): 112; Mary J. Wright and C. Roger Myers, *History of Academic Psychology in Canada* (Toronto: C.J. Hogrefe, 1982), 15–16, 81–5; Robinson, *Measure of Democracy*, 94–125.
62 Mona Gleason, "Psychology and the Construction of the 'Normal' Family in Postwar Canada, 1945–60," *Canadian Historical Review* 78, no. 3 (September 1997): 446.
63 "Curing the Jitters," *Toronto Daily Star*, 19 July 1951, 6.
64 CF Survey, "Study No. 5 Canadian Smoking Habits and Smokers' Attitudes, Sept–Oct 1956" (for ITC), https://www.industrydocumentslibrary.ucsf.edu/tobacco/docs/jkmv0223.
65 See Brandt, "From Nicotine to Nicotrol."
66 Anthony Giddens, *Modernity and Self-Identity: Self and Society in the Late Modern Age* (Stanford, CA: Stanford University Press, 1991), 81; see too Hilton, *Smoking in British Popular Culture*, 11.
67 Ernest Dichter, *The Psychology of Everyday Living* (New York: Barnes & Noble, 1947); Ronald Fullerton, "Ernest Dichter: The Motivational Researcher," in *Ernest Dichter and Motivation Research: New Perspectives on the Making of Post-War Consumer Culture*, ed. Stefan Schwarzkopf and Rainer Gries (New York: Palgrave Macmillan, 2010), 58–74.
68 Erving Goffman, *The Presentation of Self in Everyday Life* (Garden City, NY: Doubleday Anchor, 1959), 129. The first edition of this book was published in 1956.
69 Ibid., 127.
70 Tinkler, *Smoke Signals*, 215.

NOTES TO PAGES 96–100

71 Hughes, *Learning to Smoke*, 97, 15; emphasis in original.
72 On how individual being is "constantly re-created through a strategy of display" involving consumer goods, see Daniel Miller, *Stuff* (Cambridge: Polity Press, 2010), 19.
73 Library and Archives Canada [LAC] Mackenzie King Diary (20 April 1946), http://www.bac-lac.gc.ca/eng/discover/politics-government/prime-ministers/william-lyon-mackenzie-king/Pages/item.aspx?IdNumber=29495&.
74 "War Brides' Smoking One Rift Cause – Bride," *Toronto Daily Star*, 27 November 1946, 21.
75 CF Survey, "Study No. 4 Canadian Smoking Habits and Smokers' Attitudes toward Major Cigarette Brands, July–Aug 1955," (for ITC), table 2, https://www.industrydocumentslibrary.ucsf.edu/tobacco/docs/kkmv0223.
76 "If You Take My Advice," *Toronto Daily Star*, 21 December 1949, 32.
77 "Klondike Kate," *Le Devoir*, 23 March 1950, 5; emphasis added. See too Paul Davidson, "Nothing New about Smoke Getting in Eyes of Feminine Smokers," *Saturday Night*, 13 January 1945, 102.
78 "Les fumeuses ont gagné leur point," *La Presse*, 30 October 1950, 6.
79 Hughes, *Learning to Smoke*, 119, 124.
80 Cook, *Sex, Lies, and Cigarettes*, 260.
81 Ibid., 187–8.
82 Ibid., 266.
83 "Is This True?," *Toronto Daily Star*, 13 August 1947, 6.
84 Cook, *Sex, Lies, and Cigarettes*, 287. For other historical works on women and smoking, see Rosemary Elliot, *Women and Smoking since 1890* (New York: Routledge, 2007); Penny Tinkler, *Smoke Signals: Women, Smoking and Visual Culture in Britain* (Oxford: Berg, 2006); Kerry Segrave, *Women and Smoking in America, 1880–1950* (Jefferson, NC: McFarland, 2005).
85 Elizabeth Crisp Crawford, *Tobacco Goes to College: Cigarette Advertising in Student Media, 1920–1980* (Jefferson, NC: McFarland, 2014): 9.
86 Hughes, *Learning to Smoke*, 124.
87 Teen smoking rose steadily during the 1950s and 1960s, which is examined more in later chapters. Tinkler also notes, for Britain, that the "trend towards smoking in adolescence became increasingly apparent in the postwar decades." Tinkler, *Smoke Signals*, 187.
88 "Clinique de l'École des Parents du Québec," *Le Devoir*, 26 April 1950, 5. Coincidentally, Jean-Yves Blais, the lead plaintiff in the Quebec class action which

resulted in a $15 billion judgment in 2015 for smokers who contracted lung cancer, began smoking in 1950 at age ten. twitter.com/CTVBeauchemin/status/1101610008951828480?s=19.

89 Dan Boland, "Smoking by Minors," *Toronto Daily Star*, 26 October 1948, 6.
90 "Trustees Decline to Act Regarding Young Smokers," *Toronto Daily Star*, 22 October 1948, 16. The Board voted down the motion (11–5).
91 "Teen-Age Smoking," *Toronto Daily Star*, 18 November 1952, 6.
92 "Children's Cigarettes," *Toronto Daily Star*, 12 December 1952, 6.
93 "High School Students Big Potential Puffers," *Marketing*, 23 December 1955, 17. Various newspapers reported on these findings. For examples, see "Many Students Heavy Smokers," *Telegraph-Journal*, 27 December 1955; "16 per cent des étudiants de high school sont des fumeurs de cigarettes," *La Presse*, 3 January 1956, 39. In 1959, John Godden, a medical school professor at Dalhousie University, attributed rising rates of teen smoking to the "powerful, aggressive and irresponsible" tobacco industry, whose advertising is "aimed at creating an illusion in young minds that the cigaret is a requirement for acceptance as a mature, admired, successful young adult." "Blames Teen Cigaret Habit on Illusion," *Toronto Daily Star*, 6 June 1959, 2.
94 On retailing history in Canada, see David Monod, *Store Wars: Shopkeepers and the Culture of Mass Marketing, 1890–1939* (Toronto: University of Toronto Press, 1996); Donica Belisle, *Retail Nation: Department Stores and the Making of Modern Canada* (Vancouver: UBC Press, 2011).
95 Cheryl Krasnick Warsh, "*The Canadian Cigar and Tobacco Journal* in the Forties: A Remembrance," *Social History of Alcohol and Drugs* 21, no. 1 (Fall 2006): 35–6.
96 Ibid., 42.
97 "Toys Are a 'Natural,'" *CCTJ* (March 1954): 12.
98 "Increase Your Hallowe'en Sales!," *CCTJ* (September 1954): 8.
99 "Ten Sales Tips," *CCTJ* (January 1954): 10.
100 "Doll Sales Are Excellent," *CCTJ* (October 1955): 7; "Sell More *Toys* and *Games* this Christmas," *CCTJ* (November 1954): 8.
101 "Are You on the Davy Crockett 'Bandwagon'?," *CCTJ* (September 1955): 7.
102 Kool-Aid ad, *CCTJ* (January 1955): 11.
103 "Toys, Viewmasters, Great Sellers," *CCTJ* (December 1955): 10.
104 "Trustees Decline to Act Regarding Young Smokers," *Toronto Daily Star*, 22 October 1948, 16.

105 Marcel Martel, *Canada the Good: A Short History of Vice since 1500* (Waterloo, ON: Wilfrid Laurier University Press, 2014): 141. British shopkeepers also routinely sold cigarettes to under-age teens. Hilton, *Smoking*, 239.
106 "Food Stores Now the Nation's #1 Seller of Cigarettes," *Marketing*, 26 August 1950, 1; see too "Cigarette Industry in Midst of Major Changes," *Marketing*, 25 April 1953, 1; on the rise of US grocery stores and supermarkets, see Tracey Deutsch, *Building a Housewife's Paradise: Gender, Politics, and American Grocery Stores in the Twentieth Century* (Chapel Hill: University of North Carolina Press, 2010).
107 Urquhart and Buckley, *Historical Statistics of Canada*, 571.
108 "You've Got to Sell by the Carton!," CCTJ (February 1954): 8.
109 "Health and Beauty Aid Profits," *Canadian Cigar, Tobacco and Variety Journal [CCTVJ]* (March 1956): 8; "The Untapped Field of Cosmetics," CCTVJ (March 1956): 10; "Trade News," CCTVJ (April 1956): 13.
110 Editorial, "Between the Lines," CCTVJ (April 1956): 18. Notably, in 1955 Canada's Dominion Bureau of Statistics stopped tracking tobacco store sales as a stand-alone category, instead lumping these sales into the "all other retail" category. Urquhart and Buckley, *Historical Statistics*, 571.
111 "Trade News," CCTVJ (April 1956): 13. See too "Youngsters Can Become Good Customers," *Tobacco, Confectionery and Variety Journal* (August 1958): 13–14.
112 "Canadian Cigarette Advertising Allures without Superlatives' Aid," *Marketing*, 23 October 1948, 8.
113 "Players Uses Variant of Navy Theme," *Marketing*, 23 February 1946, 4.
114 Larry R. Greene, "When 'Buckingham' Blended Cigarette Caught On, Competition Entered Field," *Marketing*, 6 October 1951, 16–17; "W.C. Macdonald Again Using Posters," *Marketing*, 1 June 1946, 14.
115 "Interesting New Series Launched," *Marketing*, 21 May 1949, 3.
116 "New Theme for Player's," *Marketing*, 31 March 1951, 3.
117 "Tobacco Awakening," *Marketing*, 1 December 1951, 24.
118 "First Sign of Its Kind in Canada," *Marketing*, 26 August 1950, 4.
119 "Trade News Roundup," CCTJ (September 1954): 12.
120 "Guy Lombardo Radio Show," *Marketing*, 5 June 1948, 15.
121 "ITC Sponsors New Show, 'Bold Venture,'" *Marketing*, 10 February 1951, 4.
122 "Two New Radio Shows for Player's Cigarettes," *Marketing*, 11 October 1952, 1.
123 Player's ad, *Toronto Daily Star*, 15 October 1955, 30.
124 "ITC/Sweet Cap Sponsors 'Smoke Rings of Memory,'" *Marketing*, 21 July 1951, 4.

125 "ITC Purchases New 1/4 Hour Transcribed Radio Program – 'Saddle Rockin' Rhythm,'" *Marketing*, 17 September 1949, 3; "ITC Sponsors New Radio Program – 'Smiley Burnett Show,'" *Marketing*, 21 April 1951, 3; "'Smiley Burnett' Show Renewed with ITC Sponsoring Ogden's," *Marketing*, 23 February 1952, 12.

126 "Interesting New Series Launched," *Marketing*, 21 May 1949, 3.

127 CF Survey, "Study No. 4 Canadian Smoking Habits and Smokers' Attitudes toward Major Cigarette Brands, July–Aug 1955," 21, 26–7, https://www.industrydocumentslibrary.ucsf.edu/tobacco/docs/kkmv0223.

128 For examples, see Roland Marchand, *Advertising the American Dream: Making Way for Modernity, 1920–1940* (Berkeley: University of California Press, 1985); Russell Johnston, *Selling Themselves: The Emergence of Canadian Advertising* (Toronto: University of Toronto Press, 2001); Paul Rutherford, *Endless Propaganda: The Advertising of Public Goods* (Toronto: University of Toronto Press, 2000).

129 While not discussed in this section, which focuses exclusively on Macdonald Tobacco, ITC also promoted its brands in local communities in other venues besides sports facilities.

130 Lake St Louis Historical Society [LSLHS], Montreal, Macdonald Tobacco, [MT] box 4, file 10, Stanfield to Macdonald, 27 July 1945.

131 LSLHS, MT, box MT-4, file 4.6; Geary to Macdonald, 19 February 1947; Geary to Macdonald, 3 April 1947.

132 LSLHS, MT, file MT 4.5, Stanfield to Macdonald, 24 November 1948.

133 LSLHS, MT, file, MT 4.4, Geary to Macdonald, 17 August 1949.

134 LSLHS, MT, file MT 4.2, Stanfield to Macdonald, 9 April 1951; file MT 4.3, Geary to Macdonald, 25 September 1950. ITC also supplied and advertised on arena clocks. See "Imperial Tobacco Co. Presents New Time Clock," *CCJT* (April 1948): 12.

135 LSLHS, MT, file 8, Stanfield to Macdonald, 5 December 1946; file MT 4.6, Geary to Macdonald, 26 February 1947; file MT 4.1, Stanfield to Macdonald, 12 February 1952.

136 LSLHS, MT, box MT 4, file MT 4.6, Geary to Macdonald, 16 April 1947; file MT 4.6, Geary to Macdonald, 30 July 1947.

137 LSLHS, MT, box MT 4, file MT 4.6, Geary to Macdonald, 3 June 1947.

138 LSLHS, MT, box MT 4, file MT 4.6, Geary to Macdonald, 20 August 1947.

139 LSLHS, MT, box MT 4, file MT 4.3, Geary to Macdonald, 12 April 1950.

140 LSLHS, MT, box MT 4, file MT 4.6, Geary to Macdonald, 15 October 1947; file MT 4.2, Stanfield to Macdonald, 5 October 1951.
141 LSLHS, MT, box MT 4, file 8, Stanfield to Macdonald, 25 September 1946; file 8, Stanfield to Macdonald, 16 November 1946.
142 LSLHS, MT, box MT 4, file MT 4.6, Geary to Macdonald, 29 January 1947; file MT 4.6, Geary to Macdonald, 16 April 1947; file MT 4.6, Geary to Macdonald, 30 April 1947; file MT 4.6, Geary to Macdonald, 21 May 1947; file MT 4.6, Geary to Macdonald, 16 July 1947; file MT 4.5, Geary to Macdonald, 7 January 1948; file MT 4.5, Geary to Macdonald, 17 March 1948; file MT 4.2, Stanfield to Macdonald, 20 August 1951; file MT 4.1, Stanfield to Macdonald, 28 March 1952.
143 LSLHS, MT, box MT 4, file 8, Stanfield to Macdonald, 16 November 1946.
144 Robert Putnam discusses the waning of league bowling after the 1950s in his study of declining civic engagement among Americans. *Bowling Alone: The Collapse and Revival of American Community* (New York: Simon & Schuster, 2000).
145 On the history of bowling see Ian MacMillan, "Strikes, Bogeys, Spares, and Misses: Pin-Boy and Caddy Strikes in the 1930s," *Labour/Le Travail* 44 (Fall 1999): 149–90; Peter Ester, "Still Bowling Together: Social Capital of Dutch Protestant Immigrant Groups in North America," *European Contributions to American Studies* 64 (2006): 21–31; Mark Voight and Sandy Hansell, "Bowling in Southeastern Michigan," *Michigan Jewish History* 54 (Fall 2014): 36–47.
146 William Fong, *Sir William C. Macdonald: A Biography* (Montreal and Kingston: McGill-Queen's University Press, 2007), 172–276. On corporate philanthropy more generally see Bettina Liverant, "The Incorporation of Philanthropy: Negotiating Tensions between Capitalism and Altruism in Twentieth Century Canada," *Journal of the Canadian Historical Association* 20, no. 1 (2009): 191–220.
147 Peter Gage entry, *Eye on the Trials* blog, http://tobaccotrial.blogspot.com/search/label/Gage.
148 Roland Marchand, *Creating the Corporate Soul: The Rise of Public Relations and Corporate Imagery in American Big Business* (Berkeley: University of California Press, 1998), 1, 183–4.
149 Marchand, *Creating the Corporate Soul*, 361–2.
150 Ibid., 183–4. See too Archie B. Carroll, Kenneth J. Lipartito, James E. Post, and Patricia H. Werhane, *Corporate Responsibility: The American Experience* (Cambridge: Cambridge University Press, 2012), 195–229; Rowena Olegario

and Christopher McKenna, "Introduction: Corporate Reputation in Historical Perspective," *Business Historical Review* 87 (Winter 2013): 643–54.
151 Powell Smily, "Canadian Tobacco Has Come of Age," *Canadian Business*, September 1946, 90–2.
152 Ibid., 94.
153 Canadian Broadcasting Corporation [CBC] Archives. "CBC News Roundup" (3 September 1947). http://www.cbc.ca/archives/entry/harvest-time-in-tobacco-country; see too "Where There's Smoke," *Canadian Business*, November 1952, 2, 4.
154 H.G. Bowley, "Tobacco: The Economics of a National Habit," *Saturday Night*, 24 July 1954, 21, 26.
155 Ibid., 26.
156 "Smoker's Utopia," CCTJ (February 1946): 22.
157 "Tobacconists Suffer in Halifax Riot," CCTJ (June 1945): 8.
158 "Fags Are Necessity For Women – Judge," *Toronto Daily Star*, 14 July 1951, 3.
159 "Smokers of the World," CCTJ (November 1946): 12.
160 "La princesse Margaret fume," *La Presse*, 28 March 1950, 35.
161 "Duchess Prefers Cigaret to Drink," *Toronto Daily Star*, 25 August 1954, 3.
162 "Le tabac, une herbe magique," *La Presse*, 18 August 1953, 4.
163 "Smoked for a Century Says 109-Year Oldster," CCTJ (November 1954): 22; see too "103 Years Old, Smokes Pound Tobacco a Week," CCTJ (January 1955): 18; "Centenarians Smoked All Their Lives," CCTJ (March 1955): 14.
164 "Smallwood Smoke Precedent-Making at Ottawa Meeting," *Toronto Daily Star*, 11 January 1950, 1.
165 Urquhart and Buckley, *Historical Statistics*, 466, 478; Statistics Canada, "Section F: Gross National Product, the Capital Stock and Productivity," https://www150.statcan.gc.ca/n1/en/pub/11-516-x/pdf/5500096-eng.pdf?st=B1yi9uvi.
166 Penfold, *The Donut*, 193.
167 Marchand, *Creating the Corporate Soul*, 361; see too David L. Deephouse and Suzanne M. Carter, "An Examination of Differences between Organizational Legitimacy and Organizational Reputation," *Journal of Management Studies* 42, no. 2 (2005): 329–60; Rowena Olegario and Christopher McKenna, "Introduction: Corporate Reputation in Historical Perspective," *Business History Review* 87 (Winter 2013): 643–54.
168 Giddens, *Modernity and Self-Identity*, 181, 186.

169 Richard Klein, *Cigarettes Are Sublime* (Durham, NC: Duke University Press, 1993), 9.
170 Ibid., 16.
171 Keith Walden, *Becoming Modern in Toronto: The Industrial Exhibition and the Shaping of a Late Victorian Culture* (Toronto: University of Toronto Press, 1997), 5.

CHAPTER FOUR

1 Dominion Bureau of Statistics, *Statistical Handbook of Canadian Tobacco* (Ottawa: King's Printer, 1947), 43; M.C. Urquhart and K.A.H. Buckley, eds, *Historical Statistics of Canada* (Toronto: Macmillan, 1965), 197.
2 *Statistical Handbook of Canadian Tobacco* (1947): 42.
3 "Early Diagnosis and Treatment Can Reduce Cancer Mortality," *Toronto Daily Star*, 5 March 1949, 6.
4 Canadian Institute of Public Opinion [CIPO] news release, "One in Four Say Lung Cancer Caused by Cigarette Smoking" (21 July 1954), https://www.industrydocumentslibrary.ucsf.edu/tobacco/docs/jybh0223.
5 "Liquor, Tobacco, Pop, Cards Feel New Budget's Weight," *Toronto Daily Star*, 24 June 1942, 3; "Current Cigarette Advertising Shows Considerable Copy Variety," *Marketing*, 5 August 1944, 2–3.
6 "New Budget Is a Disappointment to Many in the Tobacco Trade," *Canadian Cigar and Tobacco Journal* [CCTJ] (July 1946): 7; "Time for 'Wartime' Taxes to Go," CCTJ (May 1947): 50.
7 "Time for 'Wartime' Taxes to Go," CCTJ (May 1947): 50 ; "There's No Time Like the Present," CCTJ (June 1947): 46.
8 Letter to Editor, *Toronto Daily Star*, 14 March 1949, 6.
9 "'Nuisance Taxes' Gone, See 'Pop,' Candy Sold at Old Price Level," *Toronto Daily Star*, 23 March 1949, 25.
10 "Surcharge de 20.p.c. à l'impôt sur le revenu," *Le Soleil*, 11 April 1951, 1; "Le fumeur mis à contribution," *La Presse*, 11 April 1951, 3.
11 "Protestation contre la taxe des tabacs," *La Presse*, 12 December 1951, 23.
12 "43 cents pour un paquet de 20 cigarettes," *La Presse*, 17 April 1951, 3.
13 "Makes Own Cigarette" *Toronto Daily Star*, 9 October 1951, 99.
14 "Price of Cigarettes," *Toronto Daily Star*, 3 October 1951, 99.
15 "20-For-30c 'Fags' Industry Seeks Ottawa Action," *Toronto Daily Star*, 19 January 1952, 15.

16 "Bon espoir de baisse partielle de la taxe sur les cigarettes," *Le Devoir*, 19 February 1952, 3; "Taxes excessives sur les cigarettes," *La Presse*, 25 February 1952, 26.
17 "Les points saillants du budget de l'hon. Abbott," *Le Soleil*, 9 April 1952, 1; "Baisse de 3 cents sur les cigarettes," *Le Soleil*, 9 April 1952, 1.
18 "L'Imperial Tobacco est fort désappointée," *La Presse*, 10 April 1952, 2.
19 "Les taxes sur le tabac sont trop élevées," *La* Presse, 14 August 1952, 29.
20 "1,500 Tobacco Growers Demand Ottawa Cut Cigarette Tax 9 Cents," *Toronto Daily Star*, 13 December 1952, 27.
21 "Tabac moins cher; revenus augmentés," *La Presse*, 21 November 1952, 19.
22 "May Take 2 Weeks for 4-Cent Tax Cut to Reach Smokers," *Toronto Daily Star*, 20 February 1953, 1; "Le prix des cigarettes trop élevé," *La Presse*, 1 February 1954, 8.
23 "La cigarette canadienne," *Le Soleil*, 28 January 1953, 4.
24 "Au sujet des cigarettes," *Le Soleil*, 11 December 1951, 4.
25 "750,000 cigarettes saisies près de la frontière hier soir," *La Presse*, 8 November 1951, 3.
26 "La contrebande des cigarettes est active," *Le Soleil*, 15 November 1951, 3.
27 "Claims Smugglers Active Peddling Fags in Toronto," *Toronto Daily Star*, 6 December 1951, 29.
28 "Old Rum Runners Had Nothing on Fag Smugglers," *Financial Post*, 8 December 1951, 3.
29 "La contrebande des cigarettes," *Le Soleil*, 26 November 1951, 9.
30 "Le prix des cigarettes trop élevé," *La Presse*, 1 February 1954, 8.
31 "La contrebande des cigarettes diminue," *La Presse*, 5 June 1954, 77. Ottawa would again cut tobacco taxes in the 1990s in response to increased contraband trading of cigarettes. Marcel Martel, *Canada the Good: A Short History of Vice since 1950* (Waterloo, ON: Wilfrid Laurier University Press, 2014), 145; see too Robert N. Proctor, *Golden Holocaust: Origins of the Cigarette Catastrophe and the Case for Abolition* (Berkeley: University of California Press, 2011), 52–5.
32 This observation is somewhat speculative, owing to the paucity of historical scholarship on this topic. For example, Shirley Tillotson's historical account of taxation for this period does not mention cigarette smuggling. See *Give and Take: The Citizen-Taxpayer and the Rise of Canadian Democracy* (Vancouver: UBC Press, 2017).

33 "Fire Danger," *Toronto Daily Star*, 26 September 1949, 6.
34 "Smoking on Hill Buses," *Toronto Daily Star*, 15 April 1950, 6.
35 "Smoking in Buses," *Toronto Daily Star*, 4 October 1949, 6.
36 "Smoking in T.T.C. Buses," *Toronto Daily Star*, 1 June 1950, 6.
37 "Want to Prohibit Smoking in Larger Toronto Stores," *Toronto Daily Star*, 22 January 1948, 2; smoking and fire safety was a recurring issue in the *Toronto Daily Star*. See "Soothing Fag Is Branded as Toronto's No. 1 Arsonist," *Toronto Daily Star*, 10 April 1945, 2; "Careless Smokers Still Setting Fires," *Toronto Daily Star*, 25 March 1946, 28; "67-Year-Old Woman Burns to Death, Blame Her Fallen Cigarette," *Toronto Daily Star*, 9 May 1950, 25; "Too Many Cigarette Fires," *Toronto Daily Star*, 20 February 1951, 6.
38 "Smoking in Buses," *Toronto Daily Star*, 15 July 1952, 6.
39 "Dislikes Toronto Habits," *Toronto Daily Star*, 22 February 1950, 6.
40 Gordon Huston letter, "Smoking on Hill Buses," *Toronto Daily Star*, 15 April 1950, 6.
41 "Smoking in Theatres," *Toronto Daily Star*, 2 September 1948, 6.
42 "The Careless Smoker," *Toronto Daily Star*, 7 November 1949, 6.
43 "Approves Smoking Ban," *Toronto Daily Star*, 26 March 1951, 6.
44 Letter to editor in *Hamilton Spectator*, reprinted as "Smoker Denounces Crabs Who Seek to Ban Public Smoking," *CCTJ* (April 1946): 9.
45 On liberalism and cigarette smoking in Britain and Canada, see Matthew Hilton, *Smoking in British Popular Culture 1800–2000* (Manchester: Manchester University Press, 2000), and Jarrett Rudy, *The Freedom to Smoke: Tobacco Consumption and Identity* (Montreal and Kingston: McGill-Queen's University Press, 2005).
46 Letter to editor in *Hamilton Spectator*, reprinted as "Letter Writer Has Say on Smoking," *CCTJ* (April 1947): 8.
47 On this see Blake D. Poland, "The 'Considerate' Smoker in Public Space: The Micro-Politics and Political Economy of 'Doing the Right Thing,'" *Health & Place* 6 (2000): 1–14.
48 "Careless with Ashes," *Toronto Daily Star*, 24 September 1946, 6; "Clean, Bland Insists, Hall Is No Museum," *Toronto Daily Star*, 5 November 1948, 7.
49 "Schools and Smoking," *Toronto Daily Star*, 13 February 1947, 6.
50 "Trop de fumeurs dans des classes," *Le Soleil*, 11 March 1953, 28.
51 Allan M. Brandt, *The Cigarette Century: The Rise, Fall, and Deadly Persistence of the Product That Defined America* (New York: Basic Books, 2007), 127–8.

52. Ernest L. Wynder and Evarts A. Graham, "Tobacco Smoking as a Possible Etiologic Factor in Bronchiogenic Carcinoma," *Journal of the American Medical Association* 143, no. 4 (27 May 1950): 329–36, and Evarts A. Graham, "Primary Carcinoma of the Lung," *Diseases of the Chest* 18, no. 1 (July 1950): 1–9; Brandt, *Cigarette Century*, 133

53. Richard Doll and A. Bradford Hill, "Smoking and Carcinoma of the Lung," *British Medical Journal* 2, no. 4682 (30 September 1950): 739–48; Brandt, *Cigarette Century*, 141.

54. E. Cuyler Hammond and Daniel Horn, "Tobacco and Lung Cancer," *Proceedings of the National Cancer Conference*, vol. 2 (American Cancer Society, 1953), 871–5; E. Cuyler Hammond et al., "The Relationship between Human Smoking Habits and Death Rates," *Journal of the American Medical Association* 155, no. 15 (1954): 1316–28.

55. Brandt, *Cigarette Century*, 146. For press coverage of the Hammond and Horn findings, see "Coffin Nails Indeed," *Toronto Daily Star*, 24 June 1954, 6.

56. Ernest L. Wynder, Evarts A. Graham, and Adele B. Croninger, "Experimental Production of Carcinoma with Cigarette Tar," *Cancer Research* 13, no. 12 (1953): 855–64.

57. Brandt, *Cigarette Century*, 148.

58. "Early Diagnosis and Treatment Can Reduce Cancer Mortality," *Toronto Daily Star*, 5 March 1949, 6.

59. "Heavy Cigarette Smoking Linked to Lung Cancer," *Toronto Daily Star*, 24 October 1949, 16.

60. Alton Blakeslee, "Scientists Test Smoking in Relation to Cancer," *Toronto Daily Star*, 18 July 1950, 19.

61. "Trace Lung Cancer to Heavy Smoking," *Toronto Daily Star*, 29 September 1950, 1.

62. "Heavy Cigarette Use Increases Risk – U.S.," *Toronto Daily Star*, 9 December 1953, 2; "Link Cigarette to Lung Cancer Scientists Sure," *Toronto Daily Star*, 3 February 1954, 3.

63. Editorial, "Smoking and Health," *Toronto Daily Star*, 20 November 1952, 6.

64. Editorial, "Cancer and Cigarettes," *Toronto Daily Star*, 31 August 1953, 6.

65. Editorial, "Cancer and Smokers," *Toronto Daily Star*, 19 October 1953, 6.

66. Editorial, "Cancer in the Air?," *Toronto Daily Star*, 11 November 1953, 6.

67. Editorial "More Research Needed," *Toronto Daily Star*, 18 December 1953, 8.

68 Roger Williams Riis, "Est-il vraiment mauvais de fumer?," *Sélection du Reader's Digest*, April 1950, 21–30.
69 Riis wrote: "Nombre de médecins sont persuadés que le benzo-pyren, élément essentiel de ce goudron, est plus dangereux pour les gros fumeurs que la nicotine, bien qu'il soit un irritant plutôt qu'un poison." Ibid., 23.
70 Ibid., 29.
71 Courtney Ryley Cooper, "J'ai cessé de fumer," *Sélection du Reader's Digest*, August 1950, 83–6; see too Roy Norr, "Le cancer et le tabac," *Sélection du Reader's Digest*, January 1953, 72–3; Clarence William Lieb, "Peut-on éliminer les poisons de la cigarette?," *Sélection du Reader's Digest*, January 1954, 26–8.
72 Robert H. Feldt, "This Is the Truth about Tobacco," *Maclean's*, 1 November 1943, 10, 38–40.
73 "Smokers Not So Bad after All," CCTJ (March 1946): 20; reprinted from the *New York Times*.
74 E.L. Chicanot, "You May Puff Peacefully while Doctors Disagree," *Saturday Night*, 28 August 1948, 32.
75 Irvin S. Koll, "Is Tobacco Injurious?," CCTJ (March 1949): 20, cited in Cheryl Krasnick Warsh, "*The Canadian Cigar and Tobacco Journal* in the Forties: A Remembrance," *Social History of Alcohol and Drugs* 21, no. 1 (Fall 2006): 28
76 "Le tabac contiendrait quatre vitamines 'B,'" *Le Soleil*, 7 September 1951, 15.
77 Dr T.R. Van Dellen, "Proof Said Lacking in Cancer of the Lung," *Toronto Daily Star*, 21 January 1952, 4.
78 Sydney Katz, "Can Cigarettes Kill You?," *Maclean's*, 1 April 1954, 9–11, 86–8.
79 Donald G. Cooley, "Who Says Smoking Causes Lung Cancer?," *True* Magazine, July 1954, 18–19.
80 H.G. Bowley, "Tobacco: The Economics of a National Habit," *Saturday Night*, 24 July 1954, 26.
81 P.G. Wodehouse, "Smokers of the World, Unite," *Saturday Night*, 25 September 1954, 12, 13.
82 "Smoke Moderately This M.D. Advises," *Toronto Daily Star*, 1 December 1954, 21. Rienhoff was later among the first members of the Scientific Advisory Board of the US industry-sponsored Council for Tobacco Research, begun in 1964. See H. Ramm to A. Galloway (26 October 1972), https://www.industry documents.ucsf.edu/tobacco/docs/#id=lshp0081.
83 "Denies Smoking Is the Cause of Lung Cancer," *Telegraph-Journal*, 14 October

1954; see too "Test City Air Pollution Link in Lung Cancer," *Toronto Daily Star*, 30 June 1954, 21.
84 "Heart Sufferers Should Not Smoke" *Telegraph-Journal*, 23 June 1955, 1.
85 "Bad Air Said Possible Cause of Lung Cancer," *Toronto Daily Star*, 18 August 1954, 21. See too "Blame Diesel Fumes, Not Cigarets, in Lung Cancer," *Toronto Daily Star*, 3 June 1955, 2; "Smoking, Cancer Link Not Found in British Tests," *Toronto Daily Star*, 12 July 1955, 2; "Lack Evidence Fags, Cancer Related – Doctor," *Toronto Daily Star*, 11 August 1955, 27.
86 "Le tabac ne causerait aucun cancer au poumon," *La Presse*, 14 July 1955, 23, https://www.industrydocumentslibrary.ucsf.edu/tobacco/docs/nhdf0223; "La cigarette est inoffensive pour les gens en santé," *La Presse*, 22 May 1956, https://www.industrydocumentslibrary.ucsf.edu/tobacco/docs/pnkc0223.
87 Sharon Anne Cook, "'Smokin' in the Boys' Room': Girls' Absence in Anti-Smoking Educational Literature," in *Out of the Ivory Tower: Feminist Research for Social Change*, ed. Andrea Martinez and Meryn Stuart (Toronto: Sumach Press, 2003), 31, 34–5.
88 Helen Shacter, Harold Johns, and Archibald McKie, *You're Growing Up* (Toronto: W.J. Gage, 1955), 214 (original emphasis); cited in Cook, "Smokin' in the Boys' Room," 34.
89 "Laws against Cigarets?" *Toronto Daily Star*, 12 June 1959, 6.
90 Sara Wilmshurst, "'Tobacco Truths': Health Magazine, Clinical Epidemiology, and the Cigarette Connection," *Canadian Bulletin of Medical History* 32, no. 1 (2015): 163–80. On the Health League of Canada, see Catherine Carstairs, Bethany Philpott, and Sara Wilmshurst, *Be Wise! Be Healthy!: Morality and Citizenship in Canadian Public Health Campaigns* (Toronto: University of Toronto Press, 2018).
91 Wilmshurst, "Tobacco Truths," 163, 168, 169.
92 Hilton, *Smoking in British Popular Culture*, 7.
93 Ibid., 219, 240–1.
94 Létourneau c JTI-MacDonald Corp., 2015 QCCS 2382, David H. Flaherty, "Expert Report of David H. Flaherty" (4 January 2011), https://www.industrydocumentslibrary.ucsf.edu/tobacco/docs/qhwb0223; and Jacques Lacoursière, "Rapport d'expertise: sur la connaissance populaire des risques associés à la consommation de tabac" (December 2010), https://www.industrydocumentslibrary.ucsf.edu/tobacco/docs/qkwb0223. For a critique of such historical evidence, see Robert N. Proctor, "Everyone Knew but No One Had Proof:

Tobacco Use of Medical History in U.S. Courts, 1990–2002," *Tobacco Control* 15, Suppl. IV (2006): iv117–25.

95 Paul F. Lazarsfeld and Robert K. Merton, "Mass Communication, Popular Taste, and Organized Social Action," in *The Communication of Ideas*, ed. Lyman Bryson (New York: Harper), 99.

96 See Peter Simonson and Gabriel Weimann, "Critical Research at Columbia: Lazarsfeld's and Merton's 'Mass Communication, Popular Taste, and Organized Social Action,'" in *Canonic Texts in Media Research*, ed. Elihu Katz, John Durham Peters, Tamar Liebes, and Avril Orloff (Cambridge: Polity Press, 2003), 12–38.

97 CIPO press release, "City Life Conducive to Cigarette Smoking" (25 May 1949), in author's possession.

98 CIPO press release, "Cigarette Habit Shows No Signs of Dying Out" (29 December 1951).

99 Ibid.

100 Simpson's ad, *Toronto Daily Star*, 26 March 1945, 11.

101 du Maurier ad, *Toronto Daily Star*, 26 November 1946, 13.

102 du Maurier ad, *Toronto Daily Star*, 30 October 1951, 12; and other du Maurier ads in *Toronto Daily Star*, 22 April 1949, 4; 28 March 1950, 10.

103 Craven "A" ad, *Toronto Daily Star*, 17 February 1950, 31.

104 Viceroy ad, *Toronto Daily Star*, 29 May 1951, 4; "Imperial Tobacco Introduces New Brand," *Marketing*, 9 June 1951, 17.

105 See photos in CCTJ (March 1945): 7; and *Toronto Daily Star*, 7 March 1945, 21. See too Aeleah Soine and Sioban Nelson, "Selling the (Anti-) Smoking Nurse: Tobacco Advertising and Commercialism in the *American Journal of Nursing*," *Journal of Women's History* 30, no. 3 (2018): 82–106.

106 "Smuggled Cigarettes Go to Veterans," CCTJ (July 1948): 9; "Confiscated Cigarettes for D.V.A. Hospitals," CCTJ (February 1949): 8.

107 Lake St Louis Historical Society [LSLHS], Montreal, Macdonald Tobacco, [MT] box 4, file 7, Stanfield to Macdonald Inc., 28 January 1946; file MT 4.3, Stanfield to Macdonald, 6 January 1950; file MT 4.2, Stanfield to Macdonald, 12 February 1951; file MT 4.4, Geary to Macdonald, 12 January 1949.

108 LSLHS, MT, box 4, file 8, Stanfield to Macdonald, 3 December 1946; file MT 4.3, Geary to Macdonald, 10 July 1950; file MT 4.2, Stanfield to Macdonald, 25 May 1951.

109 LSLHS, MT, file MT 4.5, Geary to Macdonald, 4 March 1948; file MT 4.3, Geary

to Macdonald, 16 February 1950; file MT 4.2 Stanfield to Macdonald, 2 January 1951; file MT 4.4, Geary to Macdonald, 3 March 1949.

110 LSLHS, MT, file MT 4.1 Stanfield to Macdonald, 23 May 1952; file MT 4.1, Stanfield to Macdonald, 11 January 1952.

111 J. Ayre to W.M. Stewart, 12 August 1948, https://www.industrydocuments library.ucsf.edu/tobacco/docs/npyn0222; LSLHS, MT, file MT 4.1, Stanfield to Macdonald, 28 November 1952); G. Gordon to W. Stewart (19 December 1952), https://www.industrydocumentslibrary.ucsf.edu/tobacco/docs/ypyn0222.

112 "La cigarette de moins en moins fumée," *La Presse*, 1 March 1954, https://www.industrydocumentslibrary.ucsf.edu/tobacco/docs/fqjc0223.

113 Canadian Facts [CF] Survey, "Study No. 4 Canadian Smoking Habits and Smokers' Attitudes toward Major Cigarette Brands, July-August 1955" (for ITC), https://www.industrydocumentslibrary.ucsf.edu/tobacco/docs/kkmv0223.

114 CF Survey (July-August 1955), 1, https://www.industrydocumentslibrary.ucsf.edu/tobacco/docs/kkmv0223.

115 CF Survey (July-August 1955), 2–3, https://www.industrydocumentslibrary.ucsf.edu/tobacco/docs/kkmv0223.

116 Ans Nicolaides-Bouman et al., eds, *International Smoking Statistics: A Collection of Historical Data from 22 Economically Developed Countries* (Oxford: Oxford University Press, 1993), 62.

117 Stephen Branch, "Filters Prove They're Here to Stay," *Financial Post*, 27 May 1961, 7; "Still Trend to Filter Smokes," *Marketing*, 5 October 1962, 10. Filter brands grew at a similar rate in the United States, from less than 2 per cent of the market in 1952 to nearly 60 per cent in 1960. Pamela E. Pennock, *Advertising Sin and Sickness: The Politics of Alcohol and Tobacco Marketing 1950–1990* (Dekalb: Northern Illinois University Press, 2007), 101.

118 CF Survey (July-August 1955), p. 5, table 16, https://www.industrydocuments library.ucsf.edu/tobacco/docs/kkmv0223.

119 CF Survey (July-August 1955), 8, https://www.industrydocumentslibrary.ucsf.edu/tobacco/docs/kkmv0223.

120 Placing the onus on individuals to smoke "healthily" by moderating their own cigarette consumption reflects Foucault's idea of "governmentality," in which social risks like cigarette-caused illness become the individual's responsibility and the domain of self-care. See Thomas Lemke, "'The Birth of Bio-Politics': Michel Foucault's Lectures at the Collège de France on Neo-Liberal

Governmentality," *Economy and Society* 30, no. 2 (2001): 190–207; and Nikolas Rose, *Inventing Our Selves: Psychology, Power, and Personhood* (Cambridge: Cambridge University Press, 1996).

121 Barbara Clow, *Negotiating Disease: Power and Cancer Care, 1900–1950* (Montreal and Kingston: McGill-Queen's University Press, 2001), 12.

122 Clow, *Negotiating Disease*, 18. In the best-selling novel *Love Story* (1970), and the later popular film based on the novel, the protagonist "Jenny" is struck with leukemia. But this news is initially kept from her by her doctor and lover. IMDb "Love Story" (1970), https://www.imdb.com/title/tt0066011/plotsummary?ref_=tt_stry_pl#synopsis.

123 James T. Patterson, *The Dread Disease: Cancer and Modern American Culture* (Cambridge: Harvard University Press, 1987), 69.

124 "Afraid of Cancer, Doctor Takes Life," *Telegraph-Journal*, 6 August 1954, 1.

125 Clow, *Negotiating Disease*, 17, 33.

126 Patterson, *The Dread Disease*, 69. Similar attitudes about cancer prevailed in Britain. See Hilton, *Smoking in British Popular Culture*, 235–6.

127 CIPO news release, "One in Four Say Lung Cancer Caused by Cigarette Smoking" (21 July 1954). Unfortunately, the press release did not provide specific figures for this; https://www.industrydocumentslibrary.ucsf.edu/tobacco/docs/jybh0223; "Cigarette et cancer pulmonaire," *La Presse*, 21 July 1954, https://www.industrydocumentslibrary.ucsf.edu/tobacco/docs/fqkb0223.

128 Brandt, *Cigarette Century*, 157.

129 Ibid.; see too Proctor, *Golden Holocaust*, 307, 338.

130 For examples, see C.S. Taber and M. Lodge, "Motivated Skepticism in the Evaluation of Political Beliefs," *American Journal of Political Science* 50, no. 3 (2006): 755–69; David P. Redlawsk, Andrew J.W. Civettini, and Karen M. Emmerson, "The Affective Tipping Point: Do Motivated Reasoners Ever 'Get It'?," *Political Psychology* 31, no. 4 (2010): 563–93.

131 Ziva Kunda, "The Case for Motivated Reasoning," *Psychological Bulletin* 108, no. 3 (1990): 480–98.

132 Ibid., 483.

133 Ibid., 490.

134 H.H. Kassarjian and J.B. Cohen, "Cognitive Dissonance and Consumer Behavior," *California Management Review* 8 (1965): 55–64, cited in Kunda, "The Case for Motivated Reasoning," 489.

135 Patrick W. Kraft, Milton Lodge, and Charles S. Taber, "Why People 'Don't

Trust the Evidence': Motivated Reasoning and Scientific Beliefs," *Annals of the American Academy of Political and Social Science* 658, no. 1 (March 2015): 130–1.

136 Nicolaides-Bouman et al., eds, *International Smoking Statistics*, 61–2.

137 For examples, see C. Carpenter and P.J. Cook, "Cigarette Taxes and Youth Smoking: New Evidence from National, State and Local Youth Risk Behavior Surveys," *Journal of Health Economics* 27, no. 2 (2008): 287–99; S. Ahmad and G.A. Franz, "Raising Taxes to Reduce Smoking Prevalence in the U.S.: A Simulation of the Anticipated Health and Economic Impacts," *Public Health* 122, no. 1 (2008): 3–10. The West German government also cut cigarette taxes to curb tobacco black markets and promote domestically produced cigarettes. Rosemary Elliot, "Smoking for Taxes: The Triumph of Fiscal Policy over Health in Postwar West Germany, 1945–55," *Economic History Review* 65, no. 4 (November 2012): 1450–74.

138 For examples of early relevant research, see Takeshi Hirayama, "Nonsmoking Wives of Heavy Smokers Have a Higher Risk of Lung Cancer: A Study from Japan," *British Medical Journal* (Clinical Research Ed.) 283, no. 6296 (1981): 183–5; Pelayo Correa, Elizabeth Fontham, Linda Williams Pickle, Youping Lin, and William Haenszel, "Passive Smoking and Lung Cancer," *The Lancet* 322, no. 8350 (1983): 595–7.

139 Nicolaides-Bouman et al., eds, *International Smoking Statistics*, 62.

CHAPTER FIVE

1 "Tobacco Shares Plunge on New Cancer Charges," *Toronto Daily Star*, 10 December 1953, 13.

2 "Cigarette Sales Down 4.6 Per Cent in U.S.," *Canadian Cigar and Tobacco Journal* (February 1955): 22; Pamela E. Pennock, *Advertising Sin and Sickness: The Politics of Alcohol and Tobacco Marketing 1950–1990* (Dekalb: Northern Illinois University Press, 2007), 98.

3 Ans Nicolaides-Bouman, Nicholas Wald, Barbara Forey, and Peter Lee, eds, *International Smoking Statistics: A Collection of Historical Data from 22 Economically Developed Countries* (Oxford: Oxford University Press, 1993), 62

4 Nicolaides-Bouman et al., eds, *International Smoking Statistics*, 61–2.

5 "Why So Many New Cigarette Brands?" *Marketing*, 16 June 1961, 16, 18; Clive Baxter, "Battle for Smokers to Be Hotter in '61," *Financial Post*, 21 January 1961, 20.

6 Hill & Knowlton memo, "Preliminary Recommendations for Cigarette Manu-

facturers" (24 December 1953), https://www.industrydocumentslibrary.ucsf.edu/tobacco/docs/lggd0124. See too Karen S. Miller, *The Voice of Business: Hill & Knowlton and Postwar Public Relations* (Chapel Hill: University of North Carolina Press, 1999), 121–46; David T. Courtwright, "'Carry on Smoking': Public Relations and Advertising Strategies of American and British Tobacco Companies since 1950," *Business History* 47, no. 3 (July 2005): 421–6.

7 For Canadian examples of this favourable reporting, see "U.S. Tobacco Firms Study Cancer Theory," *Montreal Star*, 4 January 1954, 8; "U.S. Fag-Makers Organize Fight Lung Cancer Story," *Toronto Daily Star*, 2 January 1954, 25; "To Probe Cigarette Effects," *Toronto Daily Star*, 4 January 1954, 6.

8 "Frank Statement" ad, cited by Alan M. Brandt, *The Cigarette Century: The Rise, Fall, and Deadly Persistence of the Product That Defined America* (New York: Basic Books, 2007), 170–1.

9 Ibid., 160, 175.

10 "Cancer Is Complicated Doubts Smoking Cause," *Toronto Daily Star*, 25 February 1954, 31.

11 For examples see, "Keep Smoking, Forget Cancer Scare – Writer," *CCTJ* (January 1955): 21; "U.K. Cancer Report," *Tobacco and Variety Journal* (August 1956): 20; "Smoking Influence Disputed," *Montreal Gazette*, 9 October 1959.

12 "Smoking Also Causes Heart Disease," *Toronto Daily Star*, 18 July 1957, 2.

13 "Smoking, Cancer Linked by U.S. Health Service," *Telegraph-Journal*, 28 November 1959, 19.

14 "Lack Evidence Fags, Cancer Related – Doctor," *Toronto Daily Star*, 11 August 1955, 27; on Berkson's ties to the tobacco industry, see Robert N. Proctor, *Golden Holocaust: Origins of the Cigarette Catastrophe and the Case for Abolition* (Berkeley: University of California Press, 2011), 436, 467.

15 "Link 'Voice Box' Cancer to Any Kind of Smoke," *Toronto Daily Star*, 7 December 1955, 7.

16 "Say Cigaret Makers Suffer Less Cancer," *Toronto Daily Star*, 14 November 1957, 5.

17 "Discovery of More Lung Cancer Deaths Shows Need for Research in Tobacco Use," *Montreal Gazette*, 25 February 1954), https://www.industrydocumentslibrary.ucsf.edu/tobacco/docs/xfch0223.

18 "Tobacco Man Disputes 'Dry-Cleaning' Claims," *Toronto Daily Star*, 29 July 1957, 35; see too "If Danger There We Want to Find It – Tobacco Firm," *Toronto Daily Star*, 15 July 1958, 7.

19 "Cigar Firm's Boss Likes Canada Already, Not Cigars," *Montreal Gazette*, 3 June 1961, 9.
20 "U.S. Fag-Makers Organize Fight Lung Cancer Story," *Toronto Daily Star*, 2 January 1954, 25.
21 "Aucun indice reliant la cigarette au cancer," *La Presse*, 23 November 1954, https://www.industrydocumentslibrary.ucsf.edu/tobacco/docs/lsywo223. (Translation: "I can say without fear of contradiction that cigarette opponents to date have not been able to support their theory with any substantial proof. Rather, they are merely content to base their 'claims' on the association of ideas … To date, no results identified in intensive research have succeeded in establishing a direct relationship between lung cancer and cigarette smoke.")
22 "Tobacco Company Head Attacks Cancer Society," *CCTJ* (February 1955): 22.
23 On the US experience, see Robert N. Proctor, "Agnotology," in *Agnotology: The Making & Unmaking of Ignorance*, ed. Proctor and Londa Schiebinger (Stanford, CA: Stanford University Press, 2008), 11–17; Naomi Oreskes and Erik M. Conway, *Merchants of Doubt: How a Handful of Scientists Obscured the Truth on Issues from Tobacco Smoke to Global Warming* (New York: Bloomsbury, 2010), 13–35; and Courtwright, "'Carry on Smoking,'" 421–2.
24 BAT, "Notes on Chairman's Committee, 1956" (meetings on 11 January 1956 and 6 February 1956), https://www.industrydocuments.ucsf.edu/docs/qxdd0214.
25 "New Cigarets to Compete for Smoke $$," *Marketing*, 19 April 1957, 1–2; Clive Baxter and Rodney Touche, "Fight Has Only Started in Cigarette Sales War," *Financial Post*, 22 March 1958, 25.
26 Wynne Thomas, "How a King-Sized Sales Campaign Upset a Highly Competitive Market," *Marketing*, 3 October 1958, 36–7.
27 Clive Baxter, "Battle for Smokers to Be Hotter in '61," *Financial Post*, 21 January 1961, 20.
28 "Why Small Cigarette Firms Plan Merger," *Financial Post*, 19 May 1962, 38.
29 "Why So Many New Cigarette Brands?," *Marketing*, 16 June 1961, 16,18; Clive Baxter, "Battle for Smokers to Be Hotter in '61," *Financial Post*, 21 January 1961, 20.
30 "About the Author" description, 1979, https://www.industrydocumentslibrary.ucsf.edu/tobacco/docs/xmhg0017.
31 Rothmans ad, *Globe and Mail*, 21 June 1958, 3.

32 Rothmans ad, *Toronto Daily Star*, 13 August 1958, 8.
33 Létourneau c JTI-MacDonald Corp., 2015 QCCS 2382; P. O'Neil-Dunne to R.A. Irish, 23 July 1958, exhibit 917.
34 Létourneau c JTI-MacDonald; P. O'Neil-Dunne to R.A. Irish, 23 July 1958, exhibit 917.
35 Létourneau c JTI-MacDonald; P. O'Neil-Dunne to R.A. Irish, 23 July 1958, exhibit 917.
36 "British Cigarette Maker Finds Lung Cancer Linked to Smoking," *New York Times*, 29 July 1958, https://www.industrydocumentslibrary.ucsf.edu/tobacco/docs/#id=thnv0223. Other US articles on this topic include: "The Filter War," *Time*, 11 August 1958, and "Rothmans Admits Cigaret-Cancer Tie," *Advertising Age*, 25 August 1958; "Rothmans Believes Smoking Can Remain Safe," *Advertising Age*, 29 September 1958, 70. For Canadian reporting on this, see "Un expert anglais admet le danger de la cigarette pour le cancer du poumon," *La Presse*, 31 July 1958, 39.
37 TIRC press release, 31 July 1958, https://www.industrydocumentslibrary.ucsf.edu/tobacco/docs/rxnv0223. TIRC Chairman Timothy V. Hartnett did not mention O'Neil-Dunne by name, referring to him as a "South African tobacco company's sales representative" in Canada.
38 O'Neil-Dunne to Sydney Rothman, 7 August 1958, https://www.industrydocumentslibrary.ucsf.edu/tobacco/docs/kncb0223.
39 O'Neil-Dunne to All Group Co-ordinators, 25 August 1958, https://www.industrydocumentslibrary.ucsf.edu/tobacco/docs/#id=xglv0223.
40 O'Neil-Dunne to All Group Co-ordinators, 25 August 1958, https://www.industrydocumentslibrary.ucsf.edu/tobacco/docs/#id=xglv0223.
41 O'Neil-Dunne to T. Hartnett, 9 September 1958, https://www.industrydocumentslibrary.ucsf.edu/tobacco/docs/jglv0223.
42 O'Neil-Dunne to A. Rupert, 11 December 1958, https://www.industrydocumentslibrary.ucsf.edu/tobacco/docs/nglv0223.
43 "About the Author" description, 1979, https://www.industrydocumentslibrary.ucsf.edu/tobacco/docs/xmhg0017; Patrick O'Neil-Dunne post, *Eye on the Trials* blog (6 November 2012), http://tobaccotrial.blogspot.com/search?q=Devlin.
44 See Daniel J. Robinson, *The Measure of Democracy: Polling, Market Research, and Public Life, 1930–1945* (Toronto: University of Toronto Press, 1999), 28–32.

45 Canadian Facts [CF] Survey, "Study No. 4 Canadian Smoking Habits and Smokers' Attitudes toward Major Cigarette Brands, July-Aug 1955" (for ITC), https://www.industrydocumentslibrary.ucsf.edu/tobacco/docs/kkmv0223.

46 CF, "Study No. 6, Canadian Smoking Habits and Smokers' Attitudes, Sept-Oct 1957" (for ITC), https://www.industrydocumentslibrary.ucsf.edu/tobacco/docs/mkmv0223.

47 CF, "Study No. 7: Canadian Smoking Habits and Smokers' Attitudes, Dec 1958-Jan 1959" (for ITC), https://www.industrydocumentslibrary.ucsf.edu/tobacco/docs/lkmv0223.

48 In 1959, 57 per cent of women smoking tailor-made cigarettes used filter brands, compared with 30 per cent of men. "Study No. 7," https://www.industrydocumentslibrary.ucsf.edu/tobacco/docs/lkmv0223.

49 CF, "Study No. 4, July-Aug 1955," https://www.industrydocumentslibrary.ucsf.edu/tobacco/docs/kkmv0223.

50 CF, "Study No. 6, Sept-Oct 1957," https://www.industrydocumentslibrary.ucsf.edu/tobacco/docs/mkmv0223.

51 CF, "Study No. 7, Dec 1958-Jan 1959," https://www.industrydocumentslibrary.ucsf.edu/tobacco/docs/lkmv0223.

52 Ibid. In 1962, University of Toronto chemist George Wright, whose research on cigarette smoke was funded by Canadian tobacco firms, publicly debunked the view of filters conferring health benefits to smokers: "A few years ago the numbers game started with filters. This one cuts down tar 15 per cent so the next one cuts it down 20 per cent. This is ridiculous. The only way to reduce the risk 15 per cent is to cut down smoking by 15 per cent. You could carry a pair of scissors around and cut 15 per cent of the cigaret off." "Filters Don't Help Smoker," *Toronto Daily Star*, 18 March 1963, 1.

53 CF, "Study No. 7, December 1958-January 1959," https://www.industrydocumentslibrary.ucsf.edu/tobacco/docs/lkmv0223.

54 CF, "Study No. 7, December 1958-January 1959." The health-related questions in the survey were:

Ask if agree or disagree with each of these statements:

1. Filter tips are safer for your health than plain ends.

2. (If agree with above) Some filters are safer for your health than other filters.

8. Some cigarette companies are really trying to lick the health problem.

(If agrees: Which companies are really trying to lick the health problem?) https://www.industrydocumentslibrary.ucsf.edu/tobacco/docs/lkmv0223.

55 Cf, "Study No. 7, December 1958-January 1959," https://www.industrydocumentslibrary.ucsf.edu/tobacco/docs/lkmv0223.

56 Ibid.

57 Ibid. On filter-and-health cigarette marketing in the US, see Proctor, *Golden Holocaust*, 340–56.

58 Canada, *House of Commons Debates* (16 December 1953), 970–1, https://www.industrydocumentslibrary.ucsf.edu/tobacco/docs/rskg0223.

59 G.D.W. Cameron to N. McKinnon, 21 December 1953, https://www.industrydocumentslibrary.ucsf.edu/tobacco/docs/npch0223.

60 G.D.W. Cameron to Minister, 27 January 1954, https://www.industrydocumentslibrary.ucsf.edu/tobacco/docs/nrch0223.

61 L.C. Laporte memo, "Smoking and Health" (27 January 1954). In this memo, Laporte writes that he and Keith had told Cameron that a "larger number of doctors and scientists have questioned the significance of this [smoking–cancer] evidence" and that "research has indicated a number of possible causes of lung cancer such as atmospheric pollution." As well, there was "no proof that lung cancer in any human being is traceable to tobacco in any form." https://www.industrydocumentslibrary.ucsf.edu/tobacco/docs/ppvb0223.

62 ITC letter to O.H. Warwick, 3 March 1954. Eleven firms signed this agreement: Allied Cigar Corporation, Benson & Hedges (Canada) Ltd, Central Tobacco Mfg Co. Ltd, La Compagnie de Tabac Trans-Canada, General Cigar Company Ltd, B. Houde & Grothe Ltd, Imperial Tobacco Company of Canada Ltd, W.C. Macdonald, Inc., Rock City Tobacco Co. (1936) Ltd, H. Simon & Sons, Ltd, Tuckett Tobacco Company Ltd. With the exception of Tuckett, all were Quebec-based companies. https://www.industrydocumentslibrary.ucsf.edu/tobacco/docs/lrch0223.

63 "Canadian Tobacco Industry Provides Funds for Support of Research in Lung Cancer," *Canadian Cancer Society Newsletter* (April 1954): 3–4, https://www.industrydocumentslibrary.ucsf.edu/tobacco/docs/ffch0223.

64 "Aucune preuve que la cigarette cause le cancer," *Le Devoir*, 30 April 1955, 1. (Translation: "To date, it has not been possible to cause cancer in guinea pigs with cigarette tar; but the research experience has not reached a stage where

we can draw definitive conclusions.") https://www.industrydocuments library.ucsf.edu/tobacco/docs/sfhn0222. On Selye, see Mark P. Petticrew and Kelley Lee, "The 'Father of Stress' Meets 'Big Tobacco': Hans Selye and the Tobacco Industry," *American Journal of Public Health* 101, no. 3 (March 2011): 411–18. On favourable press coverage of the industry's donation to NCI, see "Smoking and Health," *Toronto Daily Star*, 11 March 1954, 6; H.G. Bowley, "Tobacco: the Economics of a National Habit," *Saturday Night*, 24 July 1954, 26.

65 Report of Royal College of Physicians of London, *Smoking and Health: Of Smoking in Relation to Cancer of the Lung and Other Diseases* (March 1962), 43, 56, https://www.industrydocumentslibrary.ucsf.edu/tobacco/docs/qplg0223.

66 L. Laporte memo, 27 February 1962, https://www.industrydocumentslibrary.ucsf.edu/tobacco/docs/gqvb0223.

67 ITC press release, 7 March 1962, https://www.industrydocumentslibrary.ucsf.edu/tobacco/docs/zpvb0223. For press coverage of Wood's statement see "Rien de nouveau dans le rapport de Londres (Wood)," *Le Soleil*, 7 March 1962, 15; "Aucune preuve nouvelle pour appuyer cette affirmation," *Le Devoir*, 8 March 1962, 5.

68 "Statement by Dominion Council of Health on Smoking and Health" (April 1962), https://www.industrydocumentslibrary.ucsf.edu/tobacco/docs/mtbh0223.

69 L. Laporte memo, 4 January 1963, https://www.industrydocumentslibrary.ucsf.edu/tobacco/docs/hsvb0223.

70 "Statement by Dominion Council of Health on Smoking and Health" (April 1962), https://www.industrydocumentslibrary.ucsf.edu/tobacco/docs/mtbh0223.

71 ITC, "Draft Notes on Meeting Held at Royal Montreal Golf Club, August 2, 1962," 15 August 1962, https://www.industrydocumentslibrary.ucsf.edu/tobacco/docs/ntgb0223.

72 ITC memo, "Notes & Comments re: Tar Advertising Situation" (9 October 1962), https://www.industrydocumentslibrary.ucsf.edu/tobacco/docs/jfbb0223. US tobacco firms had voluntarily agreed to ban references to tar and nicotine in cigarette advertising in 1960. Pennock, *Advertising Sin and Sickness*, 110.

73 ITC memo, "Notes & Comments re: Tar Advertising Situation" (9 October 1962), https://www.industrydocumentslibrary.ucsf.edu/tobacco/docs/jfbb0223.

74 E. Wood to President, Macdonald Tobacco, 12 October 1962, https://www.industrydocumentslibrary.ucsf.edu/tobacco/docs/kpnv0223.

75 Ibid. Wood sent a version of this letter to the presidents of six other tobacco companies, including Benson & Hedges (Canada) and Rothmans of Pall Mall Canada.

76 J. Devlin to E. Wood, 18 October 1962, https://www.industrydocumentslibrary.ucsf.edu/tobacco/docs/kfbb0223.

77 ITC memo, "Suggested Opening Paragraphs" (29 October 1962), https://www.industrydocumentslibrary.ucsf.edu/tobacco/docs/zzvb0223.

78 "Policy Statement by Canadian Tobacco Manufacturers on the Question of Tar, Nicotine and Other Smoke Constituents That May Have Similar Connotations" (12 October 1962). Signatories to the agreement were Edward Wood (ITC); May B. Stewart (Macdonald Tobacco); J.H. Devlin (Rothmans); and Robert Leahy, Benson & Hedges). Officials from Rock City Tobacco, B. Houde & Grothe, Tuckett Tobacco, and Trans Canada Tobacco also endorsed the agreement. https://www.industrydocumentslibrary.ucsf.edu/tobacco/docs/lfbb0223.

79 E. Wood to W. Monteith, 12 October 1962, https://www.industrydocumentslibrary.ucsf.edu/tobacco/docs/gfbb0223.

80 ITC memo to E.C. Wood, 24 October 1962, https://www.industrydocumentslibrary.ucsf.edu/tobacco/docs/ffbb0223.

81 E. Wood to R. Dobson, 29 October 1962, https://www.industrydocumentslibrary.ucsf.edu/tobacco/docs/nfbb0223.

"Minutes of Meeting of Nucleus Committee of the C.M.A. Committee on Cancer" (25 January 1963), https://www.industrydocumentslibrary.ucsf.edu/tobacco/docs/ysbh0223.

83 D. Cameron to K. Charron, 29 January 1963, https://www.industrydocumentslibrary.ucsf.edu/tobacco/docs/nsbh0223.

84 NHW memo, "Report of Departmental Committee on Smoking and Health" (for discussion at Dominion Council of Health Meeting on 24 April 1963), https://www.industrydocumentslibrary.ucsf.edu/tobacco/docs/tgkg0223.

85 ITC presentation to Canadian Medical Association, May 1963, https://www.industrydocumentslibrary.ucsf.edu/tobacco/docs/trvb0223.

86 ITC presentation to Canadian Medical Association (May 1963), https://www.industrydocumentslibrary.ucsf.edu/tobacco/docs/trvb0223.

87 Proctor, *Golden Holocaust*, 232–5.

88 Brandt, *Cigarette Century*, 159–207.
89 "CMA Considers Lung Cancer-Tobacco Question at Toronto Council Session," *Montreal Gazette*, 12 June 1963.
90 "Tobacco Firm to 'Go Along' on Any Law," *Montreal Gazette*, 13 June 1963, 42.
91 P.E. Bryden, *Liberal Politics and Social Policy, 1957–1968* (Montreal and Kingston: McGill-Queen's University Press, 1997), 80–1.
92 Judy LaMarsh, *Memoirs of a Bird in a Gilded Cage* (Toronto: McClelland and Stewart, 1968), 52.
93 Library and Archives Canada [LAC], RG2, Series A-5-a, vol. 6253, Cabinet Conclusions, 4 June 1963; J. LaMarsh Memo to Cabinet, "The Effect of Smoking on Health," 4 June 1963, https://www.industrydocumentslibrary.ucsf.edu/tobacco/docs/kqnw0223. See also Daniel J. Robinson, "Marketing and Regulating Cigarettes in Canada, 1957–1971," in *Les Territoires de l'entreprise*, ed. Claude Bellavance and Pierre Lanthier (Quebec: Laval University Press, 2004), 252.
94 Canada, *House of Commons Debates*, 17 June 1963, 1214.
95 J. Keith memo to E. Wood, N. Dann, L. Laporte, 19 June 1963, https://www.industrydocumentslibrary.ucsf.edu/tobacco/docs/zrvb0223.
96 L. Laporte memo, "Smoking and Health," 28 June 1963, https://www.industrydocumentslibrary.ucsf.edu/tobacco/docs/mjbb0223.
97 L. Laporte memo, "Smoking and Health," 28 June 1963, https://www.industrydocumentslibrary.ucsf.edu/tobacco/docs/mjbb0223.
98 LaMarsh, *Memoirs of a Bird*, 51.
99 J. Keith to J. Devlin, 22 July 1963, https://www.industrydocumentslibrary.ucsf.edu/tobacco/docs/lrvb0223.
100 J. Keith to J. LaMarsh, 29 July 1963, https://www.industrydocumentslibrary.ucsf.edu/tobacco/docs/zqvb0223.
101 ITC, "Notes on a Meeting at the Royal Montreal Golf Club on 14 Aug" (23 August 1963), https://www.industrydocumentslibrary.ucsf.edu/tobacco/docs/ptgb0223.
102 A. Bass to M. Cramer, 23 September 1963, https://www.industrydocumentslibrary.ucsf.edu/tobacco/docs/fzgd0040.
103 ITC, "Notes on a Meeting at the Royal Montreal Golf Club on 14 Aug" (23 August 1963), https://www.industrydocumentslibrary.ucsf.edu/tobacco/docs/ptgb0223.

NOTES TO PAGES 175–6

104 A. Duffin to A. Holtzman, 9 December 1969, https://www.industrydocuments library.ucsf.edu/tobacco/docs/znhd0114. See alsol R. Leahy to G. Weissman, 1 October 1963, https://www.industrydocumentslibrary.ucsf.edu/tobacco/docs/yypb0175.
105 See L. Laporte memo, "Smoking and Health," 1 November 1963, https://www.industrydocumentslibrary.ucsf.edu/tobacco/docs/yrcb0223.
106 D. Sim to E. Wood, 19 August 1963, https://www.industrydocumentslibrary.ucsf.edu/tobacco/docs/pqvb0223.
107 Curiously, Judy LaMarsh did not mention the conference in her 367-page memoir (*Memoirs of a Bird in a Gilded Cage*) covering her years serving in the federal Cabinet.
108 Macdonald Tobacco's sole representative was Rene Fortier. "Canadian Conference on Smoking and Health, List of Participants, 25–26 November 1963," https://www.industrydocumentslibrary.ucsf.edu/tobacco/docs/ggch0223.
109 Ibid.
110 J. LaMarsh, "Statement Regarding Proposals for Government Action" (25 November 1963), https://www.industrydocumentslibrary.ucsf.edu/tobacco/docs/qrbh0223; "Agenda of Canadian Conference on Smoking and Health, 25–26 November 1963," www.industrydocumentslibrary.ucsf.edu/tobacco/docs/prbh0223.
111 Ad hoc Committee of Canadian Tobacco Industry. Presentation to Conference on Smoking and Health, 25–6 November 1963, https://www.industrydocumentslibrary.ucsf.edu/tobacco/docs/srcb0223.
112 "Statement by the Canadian Public Health Association on Cigarette Smoking and Health," to National Conference on Smoking and Health, 25–26 November 1963), https://www.industrydocumentslibrary.ucsf.edu/tobacco/docs/xgkg0223.
113 O. Warwick (NCIC) Statement to Conference on Smoking and Health, 25 November 1963, https://www.industrydocumentslibrary.ucsf.edu/tobacco/docs/xhkg0223. In contrast, the presentation by the Department of National Health and Welfare, at close to one hundred total pages, approximated the length of the tobacco industry brief. See NHW, "Smoking and Health: A Presentation of the Department of National Health and Welfare" (25 November 1963), https://www.industrydocumentslibrary.ucsf.edu/tobacco/docs/stkg0223.

114 Copies of this brief were later sent to "all members of the medical profession in Canada." J. Keith to J. Devlin, 24 December 1963, https://www.industry documentslibrary.ucsf.edu/tobacco/docs/hqcb0223.

115 Ad Hoc Committee of Canadian Tobacco Industry, presentation to Conference on Smoking and Health, 25–6 November 1963, https://www.industry documentslibrary.ucsf.edu/tobacco/docs/srcb0223.

116 "Text of Remarks by Leo Laporte to Conference on Smoking and Health" (25 November 1963), https://www.industrydocumentslibrary.ucsf.edu/tobacco/docs/jhcb0223. See too Public & Industrial Relations press release, "Summary of Presentation by Canadian Tobacco Industry" (25 November 1963), https://www.industrydocumentslibrary.ucsf.edu/tobacco/docs/hrcb0223.

117 Ad Hoc Committee of Canadian Tobacco Industry, "School Programs on Tobacco Use," submitted to Conference on Smoking and Health, 25–6 November 1963, https://www.industrydocumentslibrary.ucsf.edu/tobacco/docs/xphb0223.

118 For NHW accounts of the conference, see "National Conference on Smoking and Health 25 November 1963," https://www.industrydocumentslibrary.ucsf.edu/tobacco/docs/frcb0223; and "Notes: Canadian Conference on Smoking and Health, Second Day" (26 November 1963), https://www.industry documentslibrary.ucsf.edu/tobacco/docs/hylb0223.

119 "Notes on the Canadian Conference on Smoking and Health, Nov 25–26, 1963," https://www.industrydocumentslibrary.ucsf.edu/tobacco/docs/yqcb0223. This unsigned document was most likely written by Norman Dann, ITC's manager of public relations.

120 Ibid.

121 Canadian Facts, "Report of an Opinion Survey on Smoking and Health" (November 1963), https://www.industrydocumentslibrary.ucsf.edu/tobacco/docs/hkmv0223.

122 "Notes: Canadian Conference on Smoking and Health, Second Day" (26 November 1963), https://www.industrydocumentslibrary.ucsf.edu/tobacco/docs/hylb0223.

123 J. Keith to J. Devlin, 27 November 1963, https://www.industrydocuments library.ucsf.edu/tobacco/docs/mqcb0223.

124 Ibid. ITC's Norman Dann and G.J. McDonald, research coordinator at Rothmans, were later appointed to NHW's Technical Advisory Committee on

Heath Education Concerning Smoking and Health. https://www.industry documentslibrary.ucsf.edu/tobacco/docs/lgch0223.

125 Pamela E. Pennock similarly argues that the US tobacco industry benefited from the health scare of the 1950s, as cigarette advertisers "stepped into the role of consoler and medical authority, 'generously' helping Americans overcome their apprehension about smoking." *Advertising Sin and Sickness*, 102.

126 David Miller and William Dinan similarly characterize "unity of communication and action" and building "alliances amongst different corporate factions" as hallmark features of effective corporate public relations. *A Century of Spin: How Public Relations Became the Cutting Edge of Corporate Power* (London: Pluto Press, 2008), 5–6.

CHAPTER SIX

1 Robert N. Proctor, *Golden Holocaust: Origins of the Cigarette Catastrophe and the Case for Abolition* (Berkeley: University of California Press, 2011), 351.

2 Matinée ad, *Telegraph-Journal*, 13 July 1967, 11.

3 Matinée ad, *Telegraph-Journal*, 11 July 1968, 12. For similar Matinée ads, see *Telegraph-Journal*, 6 June 1967, 15; 24 May 1968, 7; and 31 May 1968, 12.

4 On hip consumerist advertising in the 1960s, see Thomas Frank, *The Conquest of Cool: Business Culture, Counterculture, and the Rise of Hip Consumerism* (Chicago: University of Chicago Press, 1997). On working-class people, gambling, and luck, Suzanne Morton insightfully observes: "Most people had a keen realization that they were living against the odds. Even if the economic system loaded the dice against most working-class Canadians, the act of visiting a bookmaker ... was an expression of hope ... [The acts of] buying tickets and placing bets made a great deal of sense for people who recognized that everyday survival meant taking chances, and at times the act of living required not only courage but a great deal of luck." *At Odds: Gambling and Canadians, 1919–1969* (Toronto: University of Toronto Press, 2003), 65.

5 ORC International, "The Canadian Smoker, 1969: A National Consumer Study for Rothmans of Pall Mall Canada" (December 1969), 115, https://www.industrydocumentslibrary.ucsf.edu/tobacco/docs/gmhb0223.

6 As discussed in chapter 1, coupon and premium cigarette marketing also took place during the 1930s.

7 "Premium Fag Merchandise via Mark Ten's Coupons," *Marketing*, 10 May 1963, 1.

8   Susan Carson and Ed Patrick, "All-Out War Rages in Promo Cigs," *Marketing*, 14 February 1969), 1, 33.
9   "Watch How Time Sells Belvedere," *Marketing*, 10 August 1962, 2.
10 "B&H's Turnabout for Mark Ten Down-to-Earth Campaign," *Marketing*, 31 May 1968, 1, 27; Peter Bartha, "Promoting Cigarets," *Commentator*, 13 (March 1969), 30.
11 Carson and Patrick, "All-out war…," *Marketing*, 14 February 1969, 1.
12 Canadian Facts [CF], "8M Survey," for ITC (August 1969), https://www.industrydocumentslibrary.ucsf.edu/tobacco/docs/zrfb0223. Penny Tinkler also describes British cigarette makers marketing coupon brands to working-class smokers. *Smoke Signals: Women, Smoking and Visual Culture* (Oxford: Berg, 2006), 202.
13 Sweet Caporals ad, *Toronto Daily Star*, 28 October 1933, 12.
14 David Bentley, "Tobacco Games Banned," *Financial Post*, 6 June 1970.
15 Canada, *House of Commons Debates* (15 January 1970), 2418; (4 February 1970), 3209; (4 June 1970), 7714; Tom Messer, "Imperial Fined $3,000 for Misleading Ads," *Marketing*, 26 October 1970, 1; Rob Cunningham, *Smoke & Mirrors: The Canadian Tobacco War* (Ottawa: IDRC, 1996), 57–8.
16 David Bentley, "Prizes Turn Costly for Tobacco Firms," *Financial Post*, 6 December 1969).
17 "English Cigarette Comes to Canada," *Marketing*, 22 February 1957, 1.
18 "Plenty of Smoke Billows in Battle of the 'Kings,'" *Financial Post*, 24 March 1962, 48.
19 "Imperial Moves Player's into the King-Size Team," *Marketing*, 30 April 1965, 14.
20 "$250,000 Launch for Extra-Length Cigarette," *Marketing*, 24 March 1967, 1, 48.
21 CF, "8M Survey," for ITC (August 1969), https://www.industrydocumentslibrary.ucsf.edu/tobacco/docs/zrfb0223.
22 Robert Marjoribanks, "Smoke 'Em Shorter because of Taxes?," *Financial Post*, 30 May 1959. Claire Halliday, "Why High School Students Smoke," *Saturday Night*, 23 January 1960, 35.
23 Stephen Branch, "Filters Prove They're Here to Stay," *Financial Post*, 27 May 1961, 7; "Still Trend to Filter Smokes," *Marketing*, 5 October 1962, 10; "Coupon and Premium Cigarettes Get a King-Size Knockout," *Marketing*, 25 October 1971, 22.
24 Clive Baxter and Rodney Touche, "Fight Has Only Started in Cigarette Sales War," *Financial Post*, 22 March 1958, 25.

25 "Exciting Promise of Charcoal in the New Cigarette Filter," *Financial Post*, 13 July 1963, 11.
26 John Fell, "Cultural, Sports Groups to Benefit from Ban on Cigarette Advertising," *Financial Post*, 29 January 1972, 34
27 Ibid.
28 Ibid. For an international overview of sports sponsorship by tobacco firms, see Proctor, *Global Holocaust*, 88–117.
29 "Rothmans Join Bee Hive in Promoting Ski Meet," *Marketing*, 24 February 1961, 60; Fell, "Cultural, Sports Groups," 34
30 "Mobile Studio Fleet Boosts Rothmans," *Marketing*, 23 February 1968, 40; "Rothmans Helps with Art Gallery," *Marketing*, 11 August 1967, 8.
31 "Benson and Hedges Offers Scholarship to Convicts," *Marketing*, 24 May 1971, 6; "B&H $10,000 to Arts," *Marketing*, 12 November 1973, 2.
32 "Now You Can Puff Way to a Work of Art," *Toronto Daily Star*, 13 September 1968, 27.
33 "Imperial Tobacco Pledges Million Dollars for Arts," *Marketing*, 3 January 1972, 23; "Du Maurier Arts Council Hands Out $295,000 This Year," *Marketing*, 8 May 1972, 24.
34 "'Double' the Costs for du Maurier on Arts Venture," *Marketing*, 1 October 1973, 6.
35 "What Will Tobacco Industry Do?" *Marketing*, 3 August 1970, 8–9.
36 "Cigarette Marketing: Adjusting to Ottawa's New Rules, *Executive*, September 1971, 62.
37 Fell, "Cultural, Sports Groups," 34.
38 "There Sits Stately Imperial," *Monetary Times*, December 1968, 20.
39 "Big Three Clash over Low-Yield Filter Cig. Claims," *Marketing*, 14 June 1968, 1; "There Sits Stately Imperial," *Monetary Times*, December 1968, 20; Richmond and Viscount were also king-size brands.
40 "Big Campaign for New Cig. Launch," *Marketing*, 7 July 1969, 14.
41 "A David Cracks the Cigarette Goliath," *Marketing*, 31 March 1967, 30–1.
42 "Health Minister's Warnings Not Worrying Cig. Industry," *Marketing*, 29 November 1968, 1, 29.
43 Susan Carson and Ed Patrick, "All-Out War Rages in Promo Cigs." *Marketing*, 14 February 1969, 1, 33. In addition to encouraging Canadians to adopt low-tar cigarettes, if they could not quit, the federal government promoted agricultural research on developing low-tar tobacco leaf strains. NHW news release,

"Fourth Report on Cigarette Tar-Nicotine Conent" (2 February 1971), https://www.industrydocuments.ucsf.edu/tobacco/docs/#id=nrnv0223.

44 Basil Jackson, "Warnings Ignored: Tobacco Sales Up," *Financial Post*, 17 October 1970, 3.

45 CF, "8M Survey," for ITC (August 1969), https://www.industrydocumentslibrary.ucsf.edu/tobacco/docs/zrfb0223.

46 ITC, "Smoking and Health: Analysis and Recommendations" (n.d., ca. early 1973), https://www.industrydocumentslibrary.ucsf.edu/tobacco/docs/zgyv0223; emphasis in original.

47 "Discussion of Agenda: Montreal S&H Conference" (March 1973), https://www.industrydocumentslibrary.ucsf.edu/tobacco/docs/rphb0223; ITC, "Smoking and Health: Analysis and Recommendations" (n.d., ca early 1973), https://www.industrydocumentslibrary.ucsf.edu/tobacco/docs/zgyv0223.

48 BAT, "Smoking and Health" (July 1974), https://www.industrydocumentslibrary.ucsf.edu/tobacco/docs/mzyv0223.

49 BAT, "Smoking and Health" (July 1974), https://www.industrydocumentslibrary.ucsf.edu/tobacco/docs/mzyv0223.

50 ITC, "Project Gatwick" (n.d. ca September 1974), https://www.industrydocumentslibrary.ucsf.edu/tobacco/docs/xjwb0223.

51 S. Baxter to A. Kalhok et al., 11 June 1976, https://www.industrydocumentslibrary.ucsf.edu/tobacco/docs/zkxb0223.

52 S. Baxter to A. Kalhok et al., 11 June 1976, https://www.industrydocumentslibrary.ucsf.edu/tobacco/docs/zkxb0223.

53 A. Kalhok, "Minutes of Meeting on Smoking and Health, May 6, 1976" (10 May 1976), https://www.industrydocumentslibrary.ucsf.edu/tobacco/docs/mqyv0223. On the American industry's use of colour and package design to convey positive health meanings, see Proctor, *Golden Holocaust*, 408, 415–17.

54 In 1971, Philip Morris launched Marlboro Lights, the first of the "Lights extension" brands. Marlboro Lights sold very well and by the end of the 1970s every major US cigarette maker had at least one "Lights" brand. Proctor, *Golden Holocaust*, 409.

55 ITC, "Project Pel" (Planning for launch of Player's Light) (n.d. ca early 1976), https://www.industrydocumentslibrary.ucsf.edu/tobacco/docs/zqfb0223.

56 R.W. Pollay and Tim Dewhirst, "The Dark Side of Marketing Seemingly 'Light' Cigarettes: Successful Images and Failed Fact," *Tobacco Control* 11 (Suppl. 1) (March 2002): i18–i31.

57 Analytical Research (Canada) Inc. [for ITC], "Contemporary Consumer Attitudes toward Cigarettes, Smoking and Health" (August 1969), https://www.industrydocumentslibrary.ucsf.edu/tobacco/docs/xngb0223.
58 Ibid., 57.
59 Ibid., 75, 94–5
60 ITC, R. Wade to D. Felton, 24 March 1972, https://www.industrydocumentslibrary.ucsf.edu/tobacco/docs/zjdh0202. See too Christopher Proctor, *Sometimes a Cigarette Is Just a Cigarette* (London: Sinclair-Stevenson, 2003), 160–1
61 ITC Report, "Project 'Gatwick': Position Report" (June 1972), https://www.industrydocumentslibrary.ucsf.edu/tobacco/docs/nskv0223.
62 "Discussion of Agenda: Montreal S&H Conference" (March 1973), https://www.industrydocumentslibrary.ucsf.edu/tobacco/docs/rphb0223.
63 CTMC, "Smoking and Health Research Proposals" (August 1973), https://www.industrydocumentslibrary.ucsf.edu/tobacco/docs/qmvb0223. On compensation and scientists at Philip Morris, see Proctor, *Golden Holocaust*, 374–6.
64 W. Knox memo, "Benefits of Smoking – A Canadian View" (October 1976), https://www.industrydocumentslibrary.ucsf.edu/tobacco/docs/rghb0223.
65 N.L. Benowitz, S.M. Hall, R.I. Herning, P. Jacob 3rd, R.T. Jones, and A.L. Osman, "Smokers of Low-Yield Cigarettes Do Not Consume Less Nicotine," *New England Journal of Medicine* 309 (1983): 139–42; N.L. Benowitz and P. Jacob 3rd, "Nicotine and Carbon Monoxide Intake from High- and Low-Yield Cigarettes," *Clinical Pharmacology and Therapeutics* 36, no. 2 (August 1984): 265–70; National Cancer Institute, *Risks Associated with Smoking Cigarettes with Low Machine-Measured Yields of Tar and Nicotine – Monograph 13* (Bethesda: USDHHS, 2001); Lynn T. Kozlowski et al., "Smokers' Misperceptions of Light and Ultra-Light Cigarettes May Keep Them Smoking," *American Journal of Preventative Medicine* 15, no. 1 (July 1998): 9–16.
66 CF, "Study No. 11: June 1962," Foreword. Handwritten notes on page 29A of this report suggest that the practice of including fifteen-, sixteen-, and seventeen-year-olds in this annual survey may have begun in 1960 (1962, n11, 29A), https://www.industrydocumentslibrary.ucsf.edu/tobacco/docs/gkmv0223.
67 Ibid.
68 CF, "Study No. 13B: Canadian Smoking Habits and Smokers' Attitudes" (Fall 1964), https://www.industrydocumentslibrary.ucsf.edu/tobacco/docs/glmv0223.
69 CF, "Memorandum on Trends in Cigarette Smoking in Canada" (1967),

https://www.industrydocumentslibrary.ucsf.edu/tobacco/docs/ypkv0223. See also CF, "Study No. 15A: Canadian Smoking Habits and Smokers Attitudes, vol. 1: Cigarette Smoking" (Spring 1966), https://www.industrydocumentslibrary.ucsf.edu/tobacco/docs/flmv0223.

70 ORC International, "The Canadian Smoker, 1969: A National Consumer Study for Rothmans of Pall Mall Canada" (December 1969), https://www.industrydocumentslibrary.ucsf.edu/tobacco/docs/gmhb0223.

71 Imperial Tobacco Limited (hereafter ITC, "Smoking and Health: Analysis and Recommendations" [ca early 1973], CTIC, UCSFL, https://www.industrydocumentslibrary.ucsf.edu/tobacco/docs/zgyv0223.

72 ITC, "Smoking and Health, 1973"; emphasis in original.

73 Creative Research Group (CRG), "Du Maurier and Young People: An Initial Exploration," 24 September 1975, CTIC, UCSFL, https://www.industrydocumentslibrary.ucsf.edu/tobacco/docs/hxgb0223.

74 Ibid.; emphasis in original.

75 Ibid.

76 W.T. Wingrove to J. Woods, 29 March 1976, https://www.industrydocumentslibrary.ucsf.edu/tobacco/docs/lnpd0223.

77 Daniel T. Cook, "Commercial Epistemologies of Childhood: 'Fun' and the Leveraging of Children's Subjectivities and Desires," in *Inside Marketing: Practices, Ideologies, Devices*, ed. Detlev Zwick and Julien Cayla (Oxford: Oxford University Press, 2011), 258.

78 Daniel T. Cook, "The Other 'Child Study': Figuring Children as Consumers in Market Research, 1910s–1990s," *Sociological Quarterly* 41, no. 3 (2000): 499.

79 Richard W. Pollay, "Targeting Youth and Concerned Smokers: Evidence from Canadian Tobacco Industry Documents," *Tobacco Control* 9 (2000): 138.

80 Daniel J. Robinson "Imperial Tobacco, Market Research, and Canadian Teens, 1960–1988," in *Advertising, Consumer Culture, and Canadian Society*, ed. Kyle Asquith (Toronto: Oxford University Press, 2018), 53–70. For similar events in the UK, see Daniel O'Neill, "'People Love Player's': Cigarette Advertising and the Teenage Consumer in Post-War Britain," *Twentieth Century British History* 28, no. 3 (September 2017): 414–39.

81 On General Motors, see Richard S. Tedlow, *New and Improved: The Story of Mass Marketing in America* (New York: Basic Books, 1990), 112–81; Sally H. Clarke, *Trust and Power: Consumers, the Modern Corporation, and the Making*

of the United States Automobile Market (Cambridge: Cambridge University Press, 2007).

82 Lizbeth Cohen, *A Consumers' Republic: The Politics of Mass Consumption in Postwar America* (New York: Vintage, 2003), 295.

83 Daniel Pope, *The Making of Modern Advertising* (New York: Basic Books, 1983), 259.

84 Pollay, "Targeting Youth and Concerned Smokers," 138.

85 Joseph Turow, *Breaking Up America: Advertisers and the New Media World* (Chicago: University of Chicago Press, 1997), 30.

86 CF, "8M Survey" for ITC (August 1969), https://www.industrydocuments library.ucsf.edu/tobacco/docs/zrfb0223.

87 "Cigarette Smoking Seen as Grave Health Hazard," *Telegraph-Journal*, 13 January 1964, 1.

88 Proctor, *Golden Holocaust*, 238. Proctor also highlights shortcomings in the Surgeon General's report, notably its failure to recognize nicotine as addictive (236–7). On the development and impact of the Terry Report see Richard Kluger, *Ashes to Ashes: America's Hundred-Year Cigarette War, the Public Health, and the Unabashed Triumph of Philip Morris* (New York: Vintage Books, 1997), 238–62; Christopher J. Bailey, "From 'Informed Choice' to 'Social Hygiene': Government Control of Cigarette Smoking in the US," *Journal of American Studies* 38 (2004): 41–65.

89 Brandt, *Cigarette Century*, 224, 229.

90 For examples, see "Cigarets Are Major Cause of Lung Cancer: U.S. Report," *Toronto Daily Star*, 11 January 1964, 1; "Cigarette Smoking Seen as Grave Health Hazard," *Telegraph-Journal*, 13 January 1964, 1; "La cigarette cause le cancer!" *La Presse*, 13 January 1964, 1; "Les dangers de la cigarette," *Le Devoir*, 12 January 1964, 1

91 "Au Canada, la réaction au rapport sur la cigarette est la même qu'aux. E.-U." *La Presse*, 13 January 1964, 1. (Translation: Keith "said in a statement in Montreal that the Canadian tobacco industry views the report on cigarettes as inconclusive." In the article, Keith was quoted as saying: "It is clear that the American report is essentially an interpretation of the many and diverse studies or accounts that are familiar to us for the most part and have been under consideration for some time… an approach already adopted by the industry in Canada.")

92 "Cigarette Smoking Said Not Proved Cause of Diseases," *Telegraph-Journal*, 9 April 1964, 13, 15.
93 "L'offensive contre la cigarette: 'insinuations et conclusions hâtives,'" *La Presse*, 16 March 1964, 2. (Translation: it "does not refute the fact that there is no real clinical evidence that smoking causes cancer.")
94 "Smoke Report Not So Hot – Tobacco Man," *Montreal Gazette*, 13 March 1964, 7.
95 W. Tennyson speech, "Smoking and Health: One Tobacco Man's Views," to Advertising and Sales Association in Montreal (12 March 1964), https://www.industrydocumentslibrary.ucsf.edu/tobacco/docs/rglv0223.
96 Ibid.
97 Ibid.
98 "Canadian Cigarette Advertising Code" (16 June 1964), http://legacy.library.ucsf.edu/tid/zrc54e00. Many of the code's provisions were similar to those of the US Cigarette Advertising Code enacted just two months earlier, in April 1964. Pamela E. Pennock, *Advertising Sin and Sickness: The Politics of Alcohol and Tobacco Marketing 1950–1990* (Dekalb: Northern Illinois University Press, 2007), 126.
99 J. Keith to J. LaMarsh, 29 June 1964, https://www.industrydocumentslibrary.ucsf.edu/tobacco/docs/pfbb0223.
100 ITC, "Smoking and Health Memorandum" (October 1962), https://www.industrydocumentslibrary.ucsf.edu/tobacco/docs/nzvb0223.
101 Ibid.
102 ITC, "Appendix to Smoking and Health Memorandum" (October 1962) https://www.industrydocumentslibrary.ucsf.edu/tobacco/docs/mzvb0223.
103 ITC, "Smoking and Health Memorandum" (October 1962), https://www.industrydocumentslibrary.ucsf.edu/tobacco/docs/nzvb0223.
104 W. Gifford-Jones, "For the Sake of Argument," *Maclean's*, 22 August 1964, 48.
105 Evered Myers, "Cigarettes and the Hysteria Hazard," *Saturday Night*, July 1964, 22–3.
106 C. Harcourt Kitchin, "A Surprising Second Look at Those 'Facts' about Cancer and Smoking," *Maclean's*, 17 December 1966, 21, 25–6.
107 "Cancer Controversy Rising – So Are Cigarette Sales," *Financial Post*, 24 October 1964, 17.
108 BAT. H. Bentley, D. Felton, and W. Reid, "Report on Visit to U.S.A. and Canada: 17th April –12th May 1958," https://www.industrydocumentslibrary.ucsf.edu/tobacco/docs/gygb0223.

109 C. Ellis to L. Laporte, 7 March 1958, https://www.industrydocumentslibrary. ucsf.edu/tobacco/docs/tnvc0199. On Ellis's work at BAT, see the account by former BAT scientist Christopher Proctor, *Sometimes a Cigarette Is Just a Cigarette*, 70–3, 80–4. Proctor describes the research program led by Ellis in these terms: "The idea was, through chemistry, to build a greater knowledge of tobacco smoke under the working hypothesis that smoking caused lung cancer and that product modifications could either reduce or eliminate the risks" (80).

110 C. Ellis memo, "The Health Problem and Objectives in Research on Cigarette Design" (28 May 1962), https://www.industrydocumentslibrary.ucsf.edu/tobacco/docs/gghd0040. One year later, Herbert A. Gilbert secured a US patent for an early type of e-cigarette, a battery-powered device that heated (non-nicotine) liquid, turning it into a vapour for inhalation. Gilbert envisioned that people would use the device, which he called "The Smokeless," to help quit cigarette smoking; in the end, he was unable to convince a company to manufacture the product. See April White, "Plans for the First E-Cigarette Went up in Smoke 50 Years Ago," *Smithsonian* 49, no. 8 (December 2018): 6.

111 H. Wakeham presentation to PM R&D Committee (15 November 1961), https://www.industrydocumentslibrary.ucsf.edu/tobacco/docs/xfkj0045; emphasis in original.

112 H. Wakeham, memo "Smoking and Health: Significance of the Report of the Surgeon General's Committee to Philip Morris Incorporated" (18 February 1964), https://www.industrydocumentslibrary.ucsf.edu/tobacco/docs/hzlw0181.

113 W.L. Dunn memo (5 March 1964), https://www.industrydocumentslibrary.ucsf.edu/tobacco/docs/jgfd0040.

114 Canadian Facts Survey for NHW (Spring 1965), https://www.industrydocumentslibrary.ucsf.edu/tobacco/docs/fqbh0223; https://www.industrydocumentslibrary.ucsf.edu/tobacco/docs/nych0223; L. Pett to H. Colburn (15 June 1965), https://www.industrydocumentslibrary.ucsf.edu/tobacco/docs/lych0223; NHW press release for Canadian Facts Survey (31 August 1965), https://www.industrydocumentslibrary.ucsf.edu/tobacco/docs/fgbb0223.

115 NHW press release, "Million Canadian Cigarette Smokers Quit" (8 December 1966), https://www.industrydocumentslibrary.ucsf.edu/tobacco/docs/tsnw0223.

116 ORC International, "The Canadian Smoker, 1969: A National Consumer Study for Rothmans of Pall Mall Canada" (December 1969), 115, https://www.industrydocumentslibrary.ucsf.edu/tobacco/docs/gmhb0223.

117 Analytical Research (Canada) Inc., "Contemporary Consumer Attitudes toward Cigarettes, Smoking and Health" (August 1969), 68, https://www.industrydocumentslibrary.ucsf.edu/tobacco/docs/xngb0223.

118 "La cigarette est une cause du cancer pour 58% des Canadiens," *La Presse*, 15 September 1971, A18. For a similar discussion of polling results showing Americans' uncertainty over smoking's causal relationship to cancer, see Proctor, *Golden Holocaust*, 307–15.

119 CF Survey, "Canadian Smoking Habits and Smokers' Attitudes: Cigarettes, Cigars and Pipes" (Spring 1972), https://www.industrydocumentslibrary.ucsf.edu/tobacco/docs/qsfb0223. A 1998 retrospective look at US Gallup polls on smoking and health by two Gallup officials concluded there was "a high degree of public doubt and confusion about the dangers of smoking in the 1950s and 60s. There may have been widespread awareness of the *controversy* over smoking, but public *belief* that smoking was linked to lung cancer trailed far behind this general awareness of the controversy." Lydia Saad and Steve O'Brien, "The Tobacco Industry Summons Polls to the Witness Stand," paper presented to annual meeting of the American Association for Public Opinion Research (15 May 1998), https://www.industrydocumentslibrary.ucsf.edu/tobacco/docs/htgg0072.

120 On popular perceptions that "light" and "mild" brands are healthier, see David Hammond and Carla Parkinson, "The Impact of Cigarette Design on Perceptions of Risk," *Journal of Public Health* 31 (2009): 345–53.

121 CF, "8M Survey" (August 1969), https://www.industrydocumentslibrary.ucsf.edu/tobacco/docs/zrfb0223.

122 On post-1950 motivation research, see Stefan Schwarzkopf and Rainer Gries, eds, *Ernest Dichter and Motivation Research: New Perspectives on the Making of Post-War Consumer Culture* (London: Palgrave MacMillan, 2010).

123 Analytical Research (Canada) Inc., "Contemporary Consumer Attitudes toward Cigarettes, Smoking and Health" (August 1969), https://www.industrydocumentslibrary.ucsf.edu/tobacco/docs/xngb0223.

124 Ibid., 18, 42.

125 Ibid., 43, 45, 135.

126 Ibid., 28, 32.

127 Ibid., 38–9.

128 Ibid., 24, 11, 136. The tobacco industry funded (and publicized) Selye's research on the relationship between stress and smoking.

129 Ibid., 13, 20, 155.
130 Proctor lists fourteen ways in which the US tobacco industry created doubt about the health harms of smoking. *Golden Holocaust*, 290–2.
131 R.W. Bulmer to N. McDonald, 20 April 1977, https://www.industrydocuments library.ucsf.edu/tobacco/docs/szvb0223.

CHAPTER SEVEN

1 Excerpt of Allan J. MacEachen Speech, Toronto (4 March 1967), https://www.industrydocumentslibrary.ucsf.edu/tobacco/docs/zhcb0223.
2 Suzanne Morton, *At Odds: Gambling and Canadians, 1919–1969* (Toronto: University of Toronto Press, 2003), 195.
3 George Bain interview with Trudeau in the *Globe and Mail*, 22 May 1968, cited in Paul Stevens and John T. Saywell, "Parliament and Politics," in Saywell ed., *Canadian Annual Review for 1968* (Toronto: University of Toronto Press, 1969), 41. On Trudeau and liberalism, see Rainer Knopff, "Pierre Trudeau and the Problem of Liberal Democratic Statesmanship," *Dalhousie Review* 60, no. 4 (Fall 1980): 712–26; Reg Whitaker, *A Sovereign Idea: Essays on Canada as a Democratic Community* (Montreal and Kingston: McGill-Queen's University Press, 1992), 132–62.
4 L. Laporte & N. Dann memo on meeting with G.D.W. Cameron, 11 May 1965, https://www.industrydocumentslibrary.ucsf.edu/tobacco/docs/rjbb0223.
5 L. Laporte memo on meeting with NHW deputy minister, 8 November 1965, https://www.industrydocumentslibrary.ucsf.edu/tobacco/docs/fjbb0223.
6 L. Laporte memo on meeting with NHW minister, 11 January 1966, https://www.industrydocumentslibrary.ucsf.edu/tobacco/docs/zybb0223.
7 E.A. Watkinson to J. Crawford, 11 August 1966, https://www.industrydocu mentslibrary.ucsf.edu/tobacco/docs/psnw0223.
8 H. Colburn to L. Pett, 28 September 1966, https://www.industrydocuments library.ucsf.edu/tobacco/docs/lqlb0223.
9 L. Pett to J. Keith, 5 October 1966; J. Keith to L. Pett, 12 October 1966, https://www.industrydocumentslibrary.ucsf.edu/tobacco/docs/jybb0223; https://www.industrydocumentslibrary.ucsf.edu/tobacco/docs/frch0223.
10 L. Laporte memo on meeting with L.B. Pett on 1 November 1966 (10 November 1966); L. Laporte to J. Keith, 10 November 1966, https://www.industry documentslibrary.ucsf.edu/tobacco/docs/ynbb0223.
11 Memorandum to the Cabinet, "Consumer Information on Cigarette Smoke

Tar and Nicotine Content" (13 April 1967), https://www.industrydocuments
library.ucsf.edu/tobacco/docs/hywh0223; Library and Archives Canada [LAC],
Cabinet Conclusions (11 May 1967), http://www.bac-lac.gc.ca/eng/discover/
politics-government/cabinet-conclusions/Pages/image.aspx?Image=e000837
354&URLjpg=http%3a%2f%2fcentral.bac-lac.gc.ca%2f.item%3fop%3dimg%
26app%3dcabinetconclusions%26id%3de000837354&Ecopy=e000837354.

12 L. Laporte & N. Dann memo on meeting with J.N. Crawford on 14 June 1967 (22 June 1967), https://www.industrydocumentslibrary.ucsf.edu/tobacco/docs/tgcb0223.

13 J. Crawford to A. MacEachen, 11 July 1967, https://www.industrydocuments library.ucsf.edu/tobacco/docs/yswh0223.

14 Meeting of Smoking & Health Ad Hoc Committee of Canadian Tobacco Manufacturers on 11 July 1967 (13 July 1967), https://www.industrydocuments library.ucsf.edu/tobacco/docs/mtdb0223.

15 J. Keith to M. Stewart, 3 November 1967, https://www.industrydocuments library.ucsf.edu/tobacco/docs/jtdb0223.

16 ITC memo on meeting with Drs Crawford and Watkinson on 1 November 1967 (2 November 1967), https://www.industrydocumentslibrary.ucsf.edu/tobacco/docs/mmbh0223.

17 J. Keith to A. MacEachen, 28 November 1967, https://www.industrydocuments library.ucsf.edu/tobacco/docs/qqch0223.

18 W. Tennyson to J. Devlin, 10 May 1968, https://www.industrydocuments library.ucsf.edu/tobacco/docs/tflv0223.

19 J. Keith to A. MacEachen, 23 January 1968, https://www.industrydocuments library.ucsf.edu/tobacco/docs/pqch0223.

20 W. Tennyson to J. Devlin, 10 May 1968, https://www.industrydocuments library.ucsf.edu/tobacco/docs/tflv0223.

21 Minutes of Ad Hoc Committee Meeting on 23 May 1968 (24 May 1968), https://www.industrydocumentslibrary.ucsf.edu/tobacco/docs/gsdb0223.

22 The industry's perennial rejection of "moderation" advertising is somewhat inexplicable. Moderation advertising, as seen with the long-running successful campaign by Seagram, not only fostered corporate goodwill but, if applied to the cigarette sector, would carry an implicit message that individual smokers, and not tobacco firms or governments, were responsible for protecting society against any possible harms associated with "immoderate" cigarette

use. See Daniel J. Robinson, "'The Luxury of Moderate Use': Seagram and Moderation Advertising, 1934–1955," in *Communicating in Canada's Past: Essays in Media History*, ed. Daniel J. Robinson and Gene Allen (Toronto: University of Toronto Press, 2009), 109–39; Lisa Jacobsen, "Navigating the Boundaries of Respectability and Desire: Seagram's Advertising and the Meanings of Moderation after Repeal," *Social History of Alcohol and Drugs* 26, no. 2 (Summer 2012): 122–46.

23 Minutes of Ad Hoc Committee Meeting on 30 July 1968 (14 August 1968), https://www.industrydocumentslibrary.ucsf.edu/tobacco/docs/trdb0223.

24 W. Shinn to D. Hardy, 29 December 1966, https://www.industrydocumentslibrary.ucsf.edu/tobacco/docs/lnfb0223.

25 L. Laporte memo, "Project S&H" (ca 1967), https://www.industrydocumentslibrary.ucsf.edu/tobacco/docs/fphb0223.

26 C. Thompson to N. Dann, 12 February 1968, https://www.industrydocumentslibrary.ucsf.edu/tobacco/docs/tmlv0223.

27 *House of Commons Debates* (14 April 1959), 2673; (23 May 1963), 175.

28 *Debates* (28 May 1963), 395–6.

29 *Debates* (29 May 1963), 419.

30 *Debates* (17 June 1963), 1214; (29 May, 1964), 3763–4.

31 *Debates* (16 October 1968), 1201. This was up from the $387,574,859 raised from tobacco taxes in 1962–63. *Debates* (11 December 1963), 5687.

32 *Debates* (1 March 1965), 11815; (31 March 1965), 12998; (7 February 1966), 777.

33 *Debates* (6 November 1967), 3959.

34 *Debates* (5 October 1970), 8728.

35 *Debates* (21 March 1968), 7884.

36 *Debates* (28 July 1964), 6101. For analysis of this contradiction in the United States, see Kraig Larkin, "A World of Pleasure: Tobacco Promotion and Health in the American Market Empire," *Social History of Alcohol & Drugs* 30, no. 1 (December 2016): 75–96; Sarah Milov, "Smoking as Statecraft: Promoting American Tobacco Production and Global Cigarette Consumption, 1947–1970," *Journal of Policy History* 28, no. 4 (2016), 707–35.

37 *Debates* (18 December 1968), 4095; (4 December 1969), 1582.

38 *Debates* (28 February 1967), 13605; (29 May 1967), 650.

39 *Debates* (16 October 1967), 3161.

40 *Debates* (30 January 1969), 4932.

41 For a celebratory biography of Munro, see Sherry Sleightholm, *Munro* (Ancaster: Sleightholm Publishing, 1984)
42 L. Laporte memo on meeting with Dr Watkinson on 27 November 1968 (28 November 1968), https://www.industrydocumentslibrary.ucsf.edu/tobacco/docs/smlv0223.
43 J. Munro to P. Trudeau, 16 December 1968, https://www.industrydocumentslibrary.ucsf.edu/tobacco/docs/tfnw0223.
44 Létourneau c JTI-MacDonald; David Stewart, Year-End Report of the President (13 January 1969), exhibit 1485.15.
45 Minutes of meeting of Ad Hoc Committee of the Canadian Tobacco Manufacturers (29 January 1969), https://www.industrydocumentslibrary.ucsf.edu/tobacco/docs/ypwb0223.
46 Thompson and TIRC head Timothy Hartnett had previously met with ITC officials in Montreal to help coordinate the Canadian industry's handling of smoking and health issues in the wake of the Surgeon General's report. Discussion topics included Hans Selye, the University of Montreal researcher who had received industry funding for his research on stress. Selye's research was of "definite value," especially since the US industry had recently started to fund more research in cardiovascular and psychological areas. Attendees also discussed setting up an "informal scientific committee in Canada," in the event that the National Cancer Institute did not support enough projects favoured by the tobacco industry. N. Dann, "Notes on a Meeting Held at Royal Montreal Golf Club" (17 August 1964), https://www.industrydocumentslibrary.ucsf.edu/tobacco/docs/ytvb0223.
47 Minutes of meeting of Ad Hoc Committee of the Canadian Tobacco Manufacturers (29 January 1969), https://www.industrydocumentslibrary.ucsf.edu/tobacco/docs/ypwb0223. When the Tobacco Institute sent Paré a position paper on the "Cigarette Controversy" for use in Canada, it recommended that "it be put forward as the Canadian industry's work product and not be attributed to the U.S. industry or the Tobacco Institute." A.Y. to P. Paré, 21 January 1969, https://www.industrydocumentslibrary.ucsf.edu/tobacco/docs/shdd0024.
48 C. Thompson memo, 19 February 1969, https://www.industrydocumentslibrary.ucsf.edu/tobacco/docs/hlwm0116; C. Thompson to A. Holtzman, 20 February 1969, https://www.industrydocumentslibrary.ucsf.edu/tobacco/

docs/glwm0116. Holtzman later described the Canadian industry's report to the Isabelle Committee as "principally the work of Carl Thompson, with Messrs. Shinn, Noel and myself acting as contributing editors." A. Holtzman to A. Duffin, 12 December 1969, https://www.industrydocumentslibrary. ucsf.edu/tobacco/docs/tnhd0114.

49 N. Dann to P. Paré, 4 March 1969, https://www.industrydocumentslibrary. ucsf.edu/tobacco/docs/yrdb0223; P. Paré to J. Bennett, 19 June 1969, https:// www.industrydocumentslibrary.ucsf.edu/tobacco/docs/yzxx0013. On the Tobacco Institute's profuse recommendation of David Hardy to Paul Paré, see A.Y. to P. Paré, 24 January 1969, https://www.industrydocumentslibrary. ucsf.edu/tobacco/docs/fzxf0135. Many of the industry's scientific witnesses had prior financial ties to the US tobacco industry, notably its Council for Tobacco Research (CTR). Milton Rosenblatt had received industry funding since the 1950s. Victor Buhler and Theodor Sterling received Special Projects funds from the CTR. Sheldon Sommers was both a member of the CTR's Scientific Advisory Board and its research director. See Proctor, *Golden Holocaust*, 467, 278, 269–70.

50 N. Dann to P. Paré, 4 March 1969, https://www.industrydocumentslibrary. ucsf.edu/tobacco/docs/yrdb0223.

51 A. Holtzman to F. Decker, 10 March 1969, https://www.industrydocuments library.ucsf.edu/tobacco/docs/mnfb0223.

52 L. Laporte to H. Selye, 26 March 1969, https://www.industrydocumentslibrary. ucsf.edu/tobacco/docs/hpnv0223.

53 C. Thompson to C. Batten, 17 April 1969, https://www.industrydocuments library.ucsf.edu/tobacco/docs/tyhb0223.

54 P. Paré to A. Holtzman, 29 July 1969, https://www.industrydocumentslibrary. ucsf.edu/tobacco/docs/mrdb0223. See also P. Smith to P. Paré, 9 June 1969, https://www.industrydocumentslibrary.ucsf.edu/tobacco/docs/kkfk0136.

55 See Mira Wilkins, "Multinational Enterprises and the Varieties of Capitalism," *Business History Review* 84, no. 4 (2010): 638–45. Wilkins describes the two-way flow, between home and host operations, of such matters as technical and managerial know-how and cultural norms of conducting business. In this case, the "know-how" from Philip Morris flowed to the Canadian industry as a whole, and not just its Canadian subsidiary.

56 G. Hargrove to "All No. 1s of Associated Companies" (28 August 1969), https://

www.industrydocumentslibrary.ucsf.edu/tobacco/docs/hlwb0223. See too ITC ("KMC") to G. Hargrove (22 August 1969), T0395.

57 See "Position Papers," 1 through 4: https://www.industrydocumentslibrary.ucsf.edu/tobacco/docs/lgwb0223; https://www.industrydocumentslibrary.ucsf.edu/tobacco/docs/ngwb0223; https://www.industrydocumentslibrary.ucsf.edu/tobacco/docs/pgwb0223; https://www.industrydocumentslibrary.ucsf.edu/tobacco/docs/zgwb0223.

58 Paul Paré statement to Isabelle Committee (5 June 1969), https://www.industrydocumentslibrary.ucsf.edu/tobacco/docs/fzgb0223.

59 Paul Paré statement to Isabelle Committee (5 June 1969), https://www.industrydocumentslibrary.ucsf.edu/tobacco/docs/fzgb0223.

60 ITC press release of Paul Paré speech to National Association of Tobacco and Confectionary Distributors (8 October 1969), https://www.industrydocumentslibrary.ucsf.edu/tobacco/docs/qjfb0223.

61 Létourneau c JTI-MacDonald; transcript of radio interview of Paul Paré by Jack Wasserman (8 October 1969), trial exhibit, 25A.

62 "Report of the Standing Committee on Health, Welfare and Social Affairs" (18 December 1969), https://www.industrydocumentslibrary.ucsf.edu/tobacco/docs/hzgb0223.

63 "P. Paré TV Statement – CBC 11 PM News, 18 December 1969," https://industrydocuments.library.ucsf.edu/tobacco/docs/#id=sffc0107.

64 L. Laporte, memo on meeting with NHW Minister, on 16 Jan 1970 (19 January 1970), https://www.industrydocumentslibrary.ucsf.edu/tobacco/docs/frdb0223.

65 L. Laporte memo on meeting of NHW and Ad Hoc Committee Officials, on 19 Feb 1970 (26 February 1970); "Notes for the Minister Justifying Legislative Measures to Reduce the Hazards of Cigarette Smoking" (27 April 1970); P. Paré to J. Munro, 4 May 1970, https://www.industrydocumentslibrary.ucsf.edu/tobacco/docs/sqdb0223; https://www.industrydocumentslibrary.ucsf.edu/tobacco/docs/lkch0223; https://www.industrydocumentslibrary.ucsf.edu/tobacco/docs/pqdb0223.

66 LAC, *Cabinet Conclusions* (18 June 1970), http://www.bac-lac.gc.ca/eng/discover/politics-government/cabinet-conclusions/Pages/image.aspx?Image=e000002395&URLjpg=http%3a%2f%2fcentral.bac-lac.gc.ca%2f.item%3fop%3dimg%26app%3dcabinetconclusions%26id%3de000002395&Ecopy=e000002395.

67 LAC, *Cabinet Conclusions* (18 February 1971), http://www.bac-lac.gc.ca/eng/discover/politics-government/cabinet-conclusions/Pages/item.aspx?IdNumber=1382.
68 *Cabinet Conclusions* (6 May 1971). https://www.bac-lac.gc.ca/eng/discover/politics-government/cabinet-conclusions/Pages/item.aspx?IdNumber=1689.
69 NHW press release, "Bill Would Ban All Cigarette Advertising and Promotion" (10 June 1971), https://www.industrydocumentslibrary.ucsf.edu/tobacco/docs/tfvb0223.
70 R. Robertson to P. Trudeau, 12 May 1971, https://www.industrydocumentslibrary.ucsf.edu/tobacco/docs/zfnw0223.
71 P. Trudeau to G. Pelletier, 13 May 1971, https://www.industrydocumentslibrary.ucsf.edu/tobacco/docs/xgnw0223; https://www.industrydocumentslibrary.ucsf.edu/tobacco/docs/hgnw0223.
72 *Cabinet Conclusions* (7 June 1971), https://www.bac-lac.gc.ca/eng/discover/politics-government/cabinet-conclusions/Pages/item.aspx?IdNumber=1848.
73 Patrick H. Brennan, *Reporting the Nation's Business: Press–Government Relations during the Liberal Years* (Toronto: University of Toronto Press, 1994), ix.
74 G. Hargrove to P. Paré, 12 June 1970; G. Hargrove, "To All No. 1s of Associated Companies: Smoking and Health" (ca June 1970), https://www.industrydocumentslibrary.ucsf.edu/tobacco/docs/txyv0223; https://www.industrydocumentslibrary.ucsf.edu/tobacco/docs/fjyv0223.
75 G. Hargrove to P. Paré, 12 June 1970; G. Hargrove, "To All No. 1s of Associated Companies: Smoking and Health" (ca June 1970), https://www.industrydocumentslibrary.ucsf.edu/tobacco/docs/txyv0223; https://www.industrydocumentslibrary.ucsf.edu/tobacco/docs/fjyv0223.
76 Minutes of CTMC meeting (8 Sept. 1971), https://www.industrydocumentslibrary.ucsf.edu/tobacco/docs/lzcb0223.
77 Paul Paré/CTMC press release (21 Sept. 1971). In June 1970, the industry had agreed to end most in-pack coupon and premium promotions: https://www.industrydocumentslibrary.ucsf.edu/tobacco/docs/lpdb0223.
78 "Big 4 Cigarette Firms Seek Deal with Munro," *Marketing*, 27 September 1971, 2.
79 "50% Support Plan to Ban All Cigarette Advertising," *Toronto Star*, 4 August 1971, 7.
80 "Battle Hotting Up against that Ban on Smoking Ads," *Marketing*, 16 August 1971, 15.

81 "Delay Ad Ban, Munro Urged," *Marketing*, 20 September 1971, 35; "Cig Ban Threatens 250 Ad Jobs," *Marketing*, 4 October 1971, 4. In 1969, Rothmans had withheld a full-page ad in the *Toronto Telegram* after that paper ran a series of stop-smoking stories. "Paper Runs Smoking Series Big Cigarette Ad Withheld," *Toronto Daily Star*, 16 January 1969, 42.

82 "CDNPA Urges Softening of Cigarette Ad Ban," *Marketing*, 1 November 1971, 30, 32.

83 "ACA Warns Munro on Cig Ad Ban," *Marketing*, 6 December 1971, 2.

84 Dave MacLaren, "Anti-Smoke Legislation Shelved," *Delhi News Record*, 26 July 1972, https://www.industrydocumentslibrary.ucsf.edu/tobacco/docs/qrch0223. See too Rob Cunningham, *Smoke and Mirrors: The Canadian Tobacco War* (Ottawa: IDRC, 1996), 59–60.

85 Munro memo to Cabinet, "Cigarette Smoking and the Health of Canadians: Legislative and Other Action at Federal Level" (27 April 1970), https://www.industrydocumentslibrary.ucsf.edu/tobacco/docs/hxmv0223.

86 Henry Saffer and Frank Chaloupka, "The Effect of Tobacco Advertising Bans on Tobacco Consumption," *Journal of Health Economics* 19 (2000): 1117–37.

87 P.E. Bryden, *Planners and Politicians: Liberal Politics and Social Policy, 1957–1968* (Montreal and Kingston: McGill-Queen's University Press, 1997), 163.

88 Ibid., 162.

89 John Morgan, "Ottawa Vetoes Anti-Smoke Ads," *Marketing*, 29 November 1963, 1. Tellingly, there is no mention of smoking and health in Judy LaMarsh's autobiography. See *Memoirs of a Bird in a Gilded Cage* (Toronto: McClelland and Stewart, 1969).

90 "LaMarsh vs. Le Weed: More Smoke than Fire," *Maclean's*, 17 April 1965, 1; emphasis in original.

91 ITC executives maintained close ties to the federal Liberal Party during the 1970s and 1980s. During the Quebec referendum in 1980, Paul Paré campaigned strongly for the "No" side, while ITC also donated $50,000 to the federalist side. Paul Paré obituary, "Paul Pare: Lawyer Led Tobacco Firm through Diversification," *Globe and Mail*, 28 February 1996, E6.

92 D. Sim to J. Calder, 7 July 1964, https://www.industrydocumentslibrary.ucsf.edu/tobacco/docs/tzvb0223.

93 Patricia Cormack and James F. Cosgrave, *Desiring Canada: CBC Contests, Hockey Violence, and Other Stately Pleasures* (Toronto: University of Toronto Press, 2013), 8.

94 See Allan M. Brandt, "From Nicotine to Nicotrol: Addiction, Cigarettes, and American Culture," in *Altering American Consciousness: The History of Alcohol and Drug Use in the United States, 1800–2000*, ed. Sarah W. Tracey and Caroline Jean Acker (Amherst: University of Massachusetts Press, 2004), 383–402; Proctor, *Golden Holocaust*, 326.

95 Proctor, *Golden Holocaust*, 302.

96 Matthew Hilton similarly argues that popular rejection of the smoking-and-harm message in Britain during the 1960s owed in part to "older liberal ideals of independence and individuality which opposed state-sponsored campaigns to direct personal consumption." *Smoking in British Popular Culture 1800–2000* (Manchester: Manchester University Press, 2000), 181.

97 Allan M. Brandt similarly argues that equating smoking with individual liberty and consumer sovereignty does not take into account actions by US tobacco companies (e.g., political lobbying, denials of smoking's health harms and addictiveness, manipulating data, etc.) that undermined freedom of choice. *The Cigarette Century: The Rise, Fall, and Deadly Persistence of the Product that Defined America* (New York: Basic Books, 2007).

98 For the United States, see Pamela E. Pennock, *Advertising Sin and Sickness: The Politics of Alcohol and Tobacco Marketing 1950–1990* (Dekalb: Northern Illinois University Press, 2007), 130–1; for a more general account of how American business leaders conflated individual freedoms with free markets after 1945 to rescind New Deal liberal and social reforms, see Kim Phillips-Fein, *Invisible Hands: The Making of the Conservative Movement from the New Deal to Reagan* (New York: W.W. Norton, 2009).

CONCLUSION

1 Paul Paré speech, "Smoking and Health Controversy in Canada" (6 June 1972) at BAT Conference in Montreal, https://www.industrydocumentslibrary.ucsf.edu/tobacco/docs/jyvb0223.

2 This view would prove short-lived. In 1998, lawyers filed a class-action lawsuit against Canadian tobacco makers, on behalf of Quebec residents who contracted lung cancer or became addicted to nicotine. In March 2019, the Quebec Court of Appeal unanimously upheld a lower court's $15 billion judgment against the industry.

3 In the early 1950s, Paré had worked as an executive assistant to federal Liberal cabinet minister Brooke Claxton.

4 Paré was personally involved with many health organizations. During his career, he served as governor of St Mary's Hospital of Montreal and the Douglas Hospital Corporation. He was an honorary member of the Canadian Association for Children's Surgery and a member of the Advisory Board of the Palliative Care Centre of the Royal Victoria Hospital. "A Tribute to the Great Montrealers: Paul Paré," Chambre de Commerce du Montréal Métropolitain, http://grandsmontrealais.ccmm.qc.ca/en/47/.

5 P. Paré speech, "Smoking and Health Controversy in Canada" (6 June 1972) at BAT Conference in Montreal, https://www.industrydocumentslibrary.ucsf.edu/tobacco/docs/jyvb0223.

6 Ans Nicolaides-Bouman, Nicholas Wald, Barbara Forey, and Peter Lee, eds, *International Smoking Statistics: A Collection of Historical Data from 22 Economically Developed Countries*. (Oxford: Oxford University Press, 1993), 60–2

7 "La cigarette est une cause du cancer pour 58% des Canadiens," *La Presse*, 15 September 1971, A18.

8 Sue Curry Jansen, *Stealth Communications: The Spectacular Rise of Public Relations* (Cambridge: Polity, 2017): 5

9 On the rise of public relations see Scott M. Cutlip, *The Unseen Power: Public Relations, A History* (Hillsdale, NJ: Lawrence Erlbaum Associates, 1994); Karen S. Miler, *The Voice of Business: Hill & Knowlton and Postwar Public Relations* (Chapel Hill: University of North Carolina Press, 1999); Cynthia Lee Henthorn, *From Submarines to Suburbs: Selling a Better America 1939–1959* (Athens: Ohio University Press, 2006); David Miller and William Dinan, *A Century of Spin: How Public Relations Became the Cutting Edge of Corporate Power* (London: Pluto Press, 2008); Jansen, *Stealth Communications*.

10 David T. Courtwright, "'Carry on Smoking': Public Relations and Advertising Strategies of American and British Tobacco Companies since 1950," *Business History* 47, no. 3 (July 2005): 423.

11 Robert N. Proctor, "Agnotology," in Proctor and Londa Schiebinger, eds, *Agnotology: The Making and Unmaking of Ignorance* (Stanford, CA: Stanford University Press, 2008), 13–14; italics in original.

12 Robert N. Proctor, *Golden Holocaust: Origins of the Cigarette Catastrophe and the Case for Abolition* (Berkeley: University of California Press, 2011), 549.

13 Naomi Oreskes and Erik M. Conway, *Merchants of Doubt: How a Handful of Scientists Obscured the Truth on Issues from Tobacco Smoke to Global Warming*

(New York: Bloomsbury, 2010), 6, 35. On this general theme, see also David Michaels, *Doubt Is Their Product: How Industry's Assault on Science Threatens Your Health* (New York: Oxford University Press, 2008); Marion Nestle, *Soda Politics: Taking on Big Soda (and Winning)* (New York: Oxford University Press, 2015), and David Michaels, *The Triumph of Doubt: Dark Money and the Science of Deception* (New York: Oxford University Press, 2020).

14 CNN reporter Daniel Dale has systematically documented the accelerating pace of Donald Trump's lying. In 2017, Trump averaged three false claims per day, rising to an average of eight per day during 2018. By November 2019, Trump's average was ten false claims per day. See Dale tweet (14 November 2019), https://twitter.com/ddale8/status/1195033506440712198?s=09; Dale and Tara Subramaniam, "With a Focus on Ukraine, Trump Made 67 False Claims Last Week," *CNN.com* (14 November 2019), https://amp.cnn.com/cnn/2019/11/14/politics/fact-check-trump-november-67-false-claims/index.html.

15 In the 1970s, I had friends who also bought cigarettes for their parents at local stores. While writing this book, I heard from others who similarly bought cigarettes – sometimes with a parental note – for moms and dads during this period. Jesse Thistle similarly describes doing this as a child in Brampton in the 1980s. *From the Ashes: My Story of Being Metis, Homeless, and Finding My Way* (Toronto: Simon & Schuster, 2019), 61–4.

16 Penny Tinkler, *Smoke Signals: Women, Smoking and Visual Culture* (Oxford: Berg, 2006), 206.

17 Canadian Facts, "8M Survey," for ITC (August 1969), https://www.industrydocumentslibrary.ucsf.edu/tobacco/docs/zrfb0223.

Index

Note: Page numbers in italics refer to images.

Abbott, Douglas, 120, *121*
Ad Hoc Committee of the Canadian Tobacco Industry, 168, 221–4, 227, 230, 231, 233. *See also* Canadian Tobacco Manufacturers' Council
air pollution (as cause of cancer), 127, 131, 132, 149–51, 170, 205–6, 213, 305n61
American Cancer Society, 127, 128, 141, 150
American cigarettes, 6, 41; advertising of, 27, 105, 178, 234; smuggling of, 50, 120–2
American Tobacco Company (US), 19, 29, 35
American Tobacco Company of Canada (ATCC), 19
Andrews, Jack (soldier), 60
anti-smoking educational campaigns, 169, 177–9, 225, 226, 232
anti-smoking legislation, 219, 230, 232. *See also* Bill C-248; health warnings on cigarette packages
anti-trust legislation, 20–1
Army Club brand cigarettes, 52–3
Association of Canadian Advertisers (ACA), 238

Baker, James (soldier), 45–6, 60
Barnes, I.M. (soldier), *137*
Belisle, Donica, 6
Bell, Elmer (soldier), 76
Bell, William (soldier), 66
Belmont brand cigarettes, 183, 190
Belvedere brand cigarettes, 151, 152, 165, 185, 197

Bennett, R.B., 21–2
Benson & Hedges 100s brand cigarettes, 187
Benson & Hedges Canada, 152, 167–8, 215, 223–4
Bill C-150, 218
Bill C-248, 14, 219–20, 234–8
Black Cat brand cigarettes, 83, 86, *88*, 151
black markets: in Canada, 50, 117, 120–2; in wartime Europe, 46, 69, 70–1, 78, 300n137
Bliss, Michael, 21
Boer War, 51
bowling alleys, 109–10
brand loyalty, 37, 86
Brandt, Allan M., 9, 29, 93, 126, 148, 200
Brennan, Patrick, 235
British American Tobacco Company Limited (BAT), 20, 191–2, 206–7, 230–1, 236
British Consols brand cigarettes, 37, 54, 108
Broad, Graham, 49
Brooks, W.J. (soldier), 59
Bryer, Edward (soldier), 65
Buckingham brand cigarettes, 39, 83, 105, 106, 221
Butler, Karl (soldier), 58, 60

Camels brand cigarettes, 27
Cameo brand cigarettes, 41, 262n81
Cameron, G.D.W., 160–2, 169, 171, 172, 220
Canadian Cancer Society, 166
Canadian Cigar and Tobacco Journal (*CCTJ*), 58, 59, 102–4, 112, 113, 130
Canadian Daily Newspaper Publishers Association (CDNPA), 237–8
Canadian Facts (market research firm),

157–8; 1955 survey, 85–6, 137–8; 1956 survey, 87, 93, 94; 1959 survey, 158–60; 1962 survey, 195–6; 1963 survey, 178–9; 1964 survey, 196; 1967 survey, 196; 1969 survey, 191, 211
Canadian Letters and Images Project, 8
Canadian Medical Association (CMA), 152, 160–1, 163, 164, 169, 170
Canadian Pacific Railway, 89, 99
Canadian Public Health Association, 176
Canadian Tobacco Manufacturers' Council (CTMC), 179, 236
cancer, prevailing views of, 118, 140–1
cancer and smoking. *See* smoking–cancer link
"cancer scare." *See* smoking–cancer link
Carousel brand cigarettes, 151
CBC, 226
Cheal, David, 48
chewing tobacco, 51
cigarette advertising: aimed at women, 32–4, 42, 264n120; military themes in, 52–4; on radio and television, 106, 222, 223, 233, 234, 236; references to tar and nicotine, 147, 165–8, 180, 192; restrictions on, 203, 223, 219, 234–5, 237–8; sports-related, 39, 107–10. *See also* health marketing
Cigarette Advertising Code, 203, 222–3
cigarette brands. *See individual brands (e.g., du Maurier)*
cigarette consumption and sales: by age, 80, 84, 98, 137–8, 211; by gender, 80, 82, 83, 86, 137; per capita, 4, 16, 32, 82, 138, 145, 269n9. *See also* Canadian Facts; Gallup polls on smoking
cigarette fundraising, 54–6, 56
cigarette industry. *See* industry donations; industry scientists; public relations advertising; sponsorship promotion
Cigarette Products Act, the. *See* Bill C-248
cigarette smoking: in Hollywood films, 34–5; and mild health concerns, 134–5; perceived benefits of, 50, 81, 87, 92–4, 130, 212, 214; popular attitudes toward, 15–16; in public, 119, 122–6, 143; and self-identity, 95–6, 115; by women, 81, 95–100, 124, 137, 157–9; at work, 88, 90, 91, 92, 92–3, 99; by youth, 100–2, 104, 158, 195–8
cigar smoking, 16, 32, 35, 82, 124, 210, 257n7

cinematic smoking, 34–5
Clow, Barbara, 141
cognitive dissonance, 142
Colwell, John (soldier), 73
Combines Investigation Act of 1910, 20–1, 23
Committee on Price Spreads and Mass Buying, 18, 19, 21, 22
common knowledge thesis, 134
compensatory smoking, 193–5
Consols brand cigarettes, 190
consumer nationalism, 65
consumer surveys. *See* Canadian Facts; market research
contest promotions. *See* premium promotions
contraband cigarettes, 120–2, 136, 292n31
Conway, Erik M., 248
Cook, Daniel, 197
Cook, Sharon Anne, 10, 33, 99–100, 132
Cook, Tim, 52
Cormack, Patricia, 240
Cosgrave, James, 240
Council for Tobacco Research (US), 225, 230, 295n82, 325n49
coupons. *See* premium promotions
Courtwright, David, 247–8
Craven "A" brand cigarettes, 41, 135, 146, 151, 165, 167, 183, 191; Craven "A" Special Mild, 215
Crawford, J.N., 220–2

Dalton, Rev. Mike (soldier), 54–5
Dann, Norman, 164, 174, 176, 177, 220, 222, 224
Davis, Henry (soldier), 58
Delhi, Ontario, 30, 112
Denek, Thomas (soldier), 73
Dennison, Gordon (soldier), 65
De Reszke brand cigarettes, 41
Devlin, J.H., 157, 167, 174, 176, 206
Dichter, Ernest, 95
Doll, Richard A., 126–7
Doll and Hill study, 126–8
Dominion Council of Health (DCH), 163–4
Draegerman brand cigarettes, 37
Drury, Charles, 173, 234, 239
du Maurier brand cigarettes, 41, 42, 159, 159, 187, 189, 197, 200; du Maurier filter, 15, 43, 135, 136

INDEX

du Maurier Council for the Performing Arts, 189
Dummitt, Christopher, 86
Dunhill brand cigarettes, 187
Dunn, W.L., 209
Durflinger, Serge Marc, 56
Dwernichuk, Steve (soldier), 55

Elliott-Haynes survey (1950), 83
Ellis, Charles, 207
English cigarettes, 7, 64–5, 275n109
Export brand cigarettes, 41, 83–4, 86, 106, 137; Export "A," 160, 196–7, 199, 200

Famille Plouffe, La, 106
federal government: private member's bills on smoking, 225–7; revenues from tobacco taxation, 31, 112, 117, 202, 226, 263n107; spending on smoking research, 171, 202, 226; subsidies to tobacco growers, 226
filter cigarettes, 41–2, 135, 138, 157–8, 183, 268n201, 298n117, 304n48
Financial Post, 206

Gage, Peter, 110
Gallup polls on smoking: 1949 results, 80, 82–3, 135; 1951 results, 83, 135; 1954 results, 90, 137, 138, 140, 141; 1971 results, 210, 237, 247
Giddens, Anthony, 95, 115
gift cigarettes. *See under* soldiers
gift exchange theory, 47–8
Gleason, Mona, 93
Globe and Mail, 15, 78
Godbout, Jacques, 48
Godelier, Maurice, 48
Goffman, Erving, 95
Goldcrest brand cigarettes, 187
Gold Flake brand cigarettes, 35, 39, 52, 67, 262n81
Goodson, James (soldier), 59
Gould, Albert (soldier), 65
Grads brand cigarettes, 37
Graham, Evarts, 126, 127, 129, 141
Graham, R. (soldier), 59
Great War, 16, 49, 51, 52, 270n18
Guinea Gold brand cigarettes, 36

Haley, Arthur (soldier), 59
Hall, Harold (soldier), 64

Hamil, Franklin (soldier), 65
Hammond, E. Cuyler, 127
Hanmer, Hiram R., 29
Hansen, Harry (soldier), 65
Hardy, David, 227, 229, 230, 236
Hartnett, Timothy V., 155, 156, 164, 174, 303n37, 324n46
Health (magazine), 132–3, 143
health marketing, 17–18, 29, 39–42, 135, 146, 154–6, 182, 183, 191–3, 203
health warnings on cigarette packages, 178, 215, 218, 220–2, 226–7, 233, 235, 236
Hill, A. Bradford, 126, 127
Hill & Knowlton (PR firm), 24, 147, 148, 164, 165, 174, 225
Hilton, Matthew, 7, 9, 47, 133
Holtzman, Alexander, 224, 227, 230
Home, W.J. (soldier), 75
Horn, Daniel, 127
Horn, Michiel, 68, 69
Hughes, Jason, 81, 87

Imperial Tobacco Canada (ITC), 17–26, 106, 160, 165–6, 186, 328n91. *See also* Canadian Facts
Imperial Tobacco Company of Great Britain and Ireland, 18–20
industry donations, 51, 136–7, 161–2, 204, 232
industry scientists, 26, 193, 204, 206, 215, 247, 248, 304n52. *See also* Council for Tobacco Research; Selye, Hans
inflation, 49, 69
institutional advertising. *See* public relations advertising
International Cancer Congress (ICC), 153
Isabelle, Gaston, 219, 227–8
Isabelle Committee, 227–33, 247
Isabelle Report, 219, 233, 234

Keith, John M., 160–4, 171–4, 176, 178, 179, 201, 203, 221–3
Keller, R.F.L. (soldier), 59
Kennedy, W.W., 23
Keshen, Jeffrey, 72
King, William Lyon Mackenzie, 23, 33, 97
King George's Navy brand cigarettes, 53
king-size cigarettes, 153, 155, 186, 187, 211, 223
Komter, Aafke E., 48–9, 78
Kunda, Ziva, 141–2

LaMarsh, Judy, 171–4, *172*, 176–8, 202, 225, 239
Laporte, Leo, 160–5, 171, 173, 176, 177, 207, 220, 222, 224, 230
Leahy, Robert J., 150, 176
Legion brand cigarettes, 53, 54
LeRoy, Jack (soldier), 72
Liberal Party of Canada, 31–2
Lipartito, Kenneth, 10
Little, Clarence Cook, 148–9, 165, 206
Liverant, Bettina, 6
Loney, Edward (soldier), 64
Lord's Day Act, 80
low-tar ("low-yield") cigarettes, 152, 153, 168, 183, 190–3
Lucky Strikes brand cigarettes, 35
lung cancer. *See* smoking–cancer link

Macdonald's Menthol brand cigarettes, 41
Macdonald Tobacco, 51, 83, 107–11, 136–7, 152
MacEachen, Allan, 217, 221–4, 239
machine-rolled cigarettes, 15, 26
Maclean's (magazine), 129, 131, 134, 205, 235
Maitland, Bill (soldier), 58
Malone, Richard S. (soldier), 64
Marchand, Roland, 111, 114–15
Marketing (magazine), 20, 102, 104, 105
market research, 82, 83, 101, 157–60, 191, 192, 197–8, 210–12. *See also* Canadian Facts
market segmentation, 198–200
Mark Ten brand cigarettes, 152, 185, 200
Marlboro Lights brand cigarettes, 314n54
Martin, Paul, 160, 161, 174
Martyn, William (soldier), 58, 64
Mather, Barry, 225–8
Matinée brand cigarettes, 138, *139*, 146, 157–9, 182, 190–1, 200; Matinée Cork, 102; Matinée King-Size Filters, 191; Matinée Special Filter, 183, 192
Mauss, Marcel, 47–8
Mayor's Cigarette Fund (MCF), 55
media effects research, 134
medical research. *See under* smoking–cancer link
Meikle, Jeffrey, 26
menthol cigarettes, 40–1, 267n182
Millbank brand cigarettes, 36
Miller, Daniel, 5, 10
Miller, Gray, 18, 19

Monteith, Waldo, 168, 169
Montreal, 31–2, 98, *107*, 239
Morlidge, Arthur (soldier), 60
Morton, Desmond, 52
Morton, Suzanne, 218
motivated reasoning theory, 119, 141–2
motivation research, 211–12
Mulder, Stephen, 67–8
Munro, John, 14, 219, 227, *228*, 233–5, 237, 239
My Fortune brand cigarettes, 37

National Association of Tobacco and Confectionary Distributors, 230
National Cancer Institute (NCI), 160–3, 176, 204, 324n46
National Conference on Smoking and Health (1963), 147, 174–9
National Health and Welfare, Department of (NHW), 160, 163, 168, 169, 171, 218, 220–3, 239
National Research Council, 161
Nelson, Alfred (soldier), 66
Netherlands, the, 66–71
New England Journal of Medicine, 27
New York Times, 154
nicotine addiction, 44, 94–5
nicotine compensation, 193–5
Northwest Rebellion, 51

Ochsner, Alton, 126, 128
Offer, Avner, 68
Ogden's brand cigarettes, 106
Old Chum brand cigarettes, 52
Omstead, Gordon (soldier), 73–4
O'Neil-Dunne, Patrick, 13, 146, 152–7
Ontario Flue-Cured Tobacco Marketing Board, 120, 122, 230
Ontario tobacco growers, 18–19, 26, 30–2, 120, 121, 226. *See also* tobacco farming
Oreskes, Naomi, 248
Orval, Wilson (soldier), 64
Oxford brand cigarettes, 39

Pall Mall brand cigarettes, 93, *94*, 151
Paré, Paul, 186, 190, 219, 228, *229*, 230–3, 242–4, 246, 328n91, 329–30nn3–4
Patterson, James T., 141
Pearson, Lester, *115*, 173, 238
Pelletier, Gérard, 235
Penfold, Steve, 7, 84, 114

Peter Jackson, 15
Philip Morris, 39, 84, 145, 152, 207–9, 223
pipe smoking, 16, 32, 35, 82, 90, 124, 129–30
plain-end cigarettes, 135, 155
Player's brand cigarettes, 83–4, 86, 102, 105, 106, 262n81; Player's Filter, 197; Player's Filter Kings, 186; Player's Light, 183, 192–3, 198; Player's Navy Cut, 32, 39, 53, 67, 68, 105
Pogue, Forrest, 70–1
Pollay, Richard W., 199
Pope, Daniel, 199
premium promotions, 36–7, 38, 183–6, 189, 223, 233–6, 265n155, 266n157, 327n77
Proctor, Robert N., 9, 248
provincial cigarette taxes, 32, 120
psychology, 93–4
Public & Industrial Relations (PR firm), 175, 224, 229
public opinion surveys, 82, 140, 209. See also Gallup polls on smoking
public relations advertising, 23–7, 28, 29–30, 111, 152, 260n56

Quebec, smoking in, 120, 211

radio and television program sponsorship, 106
Ransom brand cigarettes, 190
Reader's Digest, 129
Red Cross, 54, 55, 72
Richmond brand cigarettes, 190, 313n39
Robertson, R.G., 235
Rock City Tobacco, 83, 151
Roffo, Angel H., 29
Roland, Charles, 74, 75
Rothmans (company), 145, 146, 151–7, 160, 186, 187, 189, 196
Rothmans brand cigarettes: Rothmans King Size, 152–3, 200; Rothmans Number 7, 185, 186
Roxy brand cigarettes, 39–40
Royal Canadian Legion, 53
Royal College of Physicians of London report (1962), 162–4
Royal Commission on Price Spreads and Mass Buying, 17, 22, 25
Ruby Queen brand cigarettes, 52
Rudy, Jarrett, 9, 33, 52
Rynard, Philip, 225

Saturday Night (magazine), 112, 130, 131, 134, 205, 235
Scandiffio, Francis (soldier), 56–7, 59
Scandiffio, Peter (soldier), 66
Second World War: POW camps, 72–6; rationing, 49, 50; smoking rates during, 47. See also soldiers; war brides
Selye, Hans, 162, 214, 224, 230, 232
Sim, David, 175, 239–40
Simcoe, Ontario, 30–1
Simonds, Guy (soldier), 69
Simpson, David (soldier), 60
Smallwood, Joey, 113–14
smokers, typologies of, 212–13
smoking. See cigarette smoking; cigar smoking; pipe smoking
smoking–cancer link: industry denial of, 29, 127, 148–51, 163–71, 176–7, 201–8, 232–3; media coverage of, 118, 127–34, 137, 149, 151, 205–6; medical research on, 27, 29, 118, 126–8, 162–3, 170; public awareness of, 138, 140, 209–10; skepticism of, 118–19, 130–3, 140–1, 162. See also US Surgeon General's report
smuggling of American cigarettes into Canada, 50, 117, 121–2
soldiers, 89; cigarette sharing, 46, 60, 64, 67–8; gift cigarettes, 47–9, 57, 58, 60; and scarcity of Canadian cigarettes, 56–7, 64–5. See also Great War; Second World War
Spafford, Earle, 19, 29
sponsorship promotion, 109, 184, 188–90, 236
Sportsman brand cigarettes, 151, 186, 193, 200
Spuds brand cigarettes, 40–1, 60
Squires, Ray (soldier), 75
Standing Committee on Health, Welfare and Social Affairs. See Isabelle Committee
Stevens, H.H., 18, 19, 21–3. See also Committee on Price Spreads and Mass Buying; Royal Commission on Price Spreads and Mass Buying
Stewart, David, 227
Stewart, May, 171
Stewart, Walter M., 19
St Laurent, Louis, 189
Stole, Inger L., 24
Stuyvesant brand cigarettes, 186, 189

Sweet Caporals ("Sweet Caps") brand cigarettes, 34, 52, 54, 72, 83–5, *85*, 86, 93, 106, *107*, 185–7, 262n81

Tabacofina, 151, 152
"tar advertising," 165–8
tar and cancer, 29, 127, 129, 153–4, 161. *See also* low-tar cigarettes
taxes on tobacco and cigarettes, 31, 50, 53, 112, 117, 119–22, 186, 261n68, 263n107
Taylor, John McGuire (soldier), 75–6
teen smoking. *See* cigarette consumption and sales: by age; cigarette smoking: by youth
Tennyson, Wilmat, 186, 189, 201–3, 223–4
Terry, Luther, 200
Terry report. *See* US Surgeon General's report
Thompson, Carl, 174, 225, 227, 229, 230
Tillsonburg, Ontario, 30, 121
Tim Hortons, 65
Tobacco and Health (industry booklet), 164–5
tobacco farming, 16, 30, 31, 112. *See also* Ontario tobacco growers
Tobacco Industry Research Committee (TIRC), 148, 156, 164–5, 174
Tobacco Restraint Act, 178
tobacco retailers, 19, 20, 22, 25, 102–5, *103*, 211, 287n110
tobacco tar. *See* "tar advertising"; tar and cancer
Toledo, Antonio, 188, 190, 224
Toronto Daily Star, 18, 71, 118, 127–8, 132, 134, 149
Trudeau, Pierre, 217–18, 235, 239
Trump, Donald, 248, 331n14
Tuckett Tobacco, 18, 20, 39, 83
Turpin, Bill (soldier), 65
Turpin, Geoffrey (soldier), 58
Turret brand cigarettes, 36, 37, 39, 262n81

United Cigar Stores, 18, 20
US Surgeon General's Advisory Committee on Smoking and Health, 170
US Surgeon General's report (Terry report), 142, 200–3, 205–6, 208, 240, 317n88

Vallieres, Stuart (soldier), 58–9
Vantage brand cigarettes, 245
Verdun, Quebec, 55–6
Viceroy brand cigarettes, 41, 135
Viscount brand cigarettes, 190, 200, 313n39

Wakeham, D.H., 207–9
Walden, Keith, 116
war brides, 93, 98
warning labels. *See* health warnings on cigarette packages
Warsh, Cheryl Krasnick, 47
Watkinson, E.A., 221
Watson, William (soldier), 64, 65
Williams, Raymond, 88
Wilmshurst, Sara, 133
Winchester brand cigarettes, 36, 54, 67, 83, 262n81
Winfield, Stanley H. (soldier), 46, 69–70
Wings brand cigarettes, 53
Woman's Christian Temperance Union, 15
women: in cigarette ads, 33, 99; as smokers, 32–4, 42, 96, 97–100; as workers, 25, 26, 93
Wood, Edward, 120, 149–50, 161, 163–8, 174, 175, 307n78
Wood, Gregory, 90
Woodbine brand cigarettes, 52
World War I. *See* Great War
World War II. *See* Second World War
Wright, William Henry, 15
Wynder, Ernest L., 126–9

Young, James Webb, 24